Advancing Nonviolence and Social Transformation

ADVANCING NONVIOLENCE AND SOCIAL TRANSFORMATION

New Perspectives on Nonviolent Theories

Edited by Heather Eaton and Lauren Michelle Levesque

equinox

SHEFFIELD uk   BRISTOL ct

Published by Equinox Publishing Ltd.

UK: Office 415, The Workstation, 15 Paternoster Row, Sheffield S1 2BX
USA: ISD, 70 Enterprise Drive, Bristol, CT 06010

www.equinoxpub.com

First published 2016

ISBN 978 1 78179 471 5   (hardback)
         978 1 78179 472 2   (paperback)

British Library Cataloguing-in-Publication Data

A catalogue record for this book is available from the British Library.

Library of Congress Cataloging-in-Publication Data

Names: Eaton, Heather, 1956- editor.
Title: Advancing nonviolence and social transformation : new perspectives on nonviolent theories / edited by Heather Eaton and Lauren Michelle Levesque.
Description: Bristol, CT : Equinox Pub. Ltd, 2016. | Includes bibliographical references and index.
Identifiers: LCCN 2016010542 (print) | LCCN 2016038749 (ebook) | ISBN 9781781794715 (hbk) | ISBN 9781781794722 (pbk) | ISBN 9781781794821 (e-PDF) | ISBN 9781781794838 (e-epub)
Subjects: LCSH: Nonviolence. | Social change.
Classification: LCC HM1281 .A335 2016 (print) | LCC HM1281 (ebook) | DDC 303.6/1--dc23
LC record available at https://lccn.loc.gov/2016010542

Typeset by CA Typesetting Ltd, Sheffield, UK

Printed and bound in the UK by Lightning Source UK Ltd, Milton Keynes and Lightning Source Inc, La Vergne, TN

If intellect plays a large part on the field of violence,
it plays a larger part on the field of nonviolence.

Mohandas Gandhi

Dedicated to Ursula Maria Franklin (1921 - 2016)

Contents

Part III
Nonviolence and Social Resistance

Foreword

Violence permeates human experience in many ways. We do violence to each other. We do violence to the Earth. We named ourselves—in our arrogance—the 'wise' ones: *Homo sapiens*. But we are also thinking animals and are capable of evolving. We have the ability to choose.

We can choose the path of nonviolence. Great social leaders—Jesus Christ, Mohandas K. Gandhi, Martin Luther King Jr., Coretta Scott King, Henry David Thoreau, Dorothy Day, the Dalai Lama, Rigoberta Menchu, Wangari Maathai, Aung San Suu Kyi—have all called us to this path, to the rejection of violence. The world's great religions also tell us to love each other, to love even our enemies. And as a number of contributors to this important collection attest, religions call on us to be gentle with the Earth. Stewardship, not subjugation, is our mandate.

As thinking animals, we can choose this mandate; yet, violence persists. Our cultural assumptions are entrenched with notions of hierarchy and patriarchy, in particular those stemming from the Judeo-Christian ethic underpinning Western civilization. Our economic system adds further layers of exploitation. We exploit the Earth for its riches. We exploit each other for power and advantage. Our overwhelming subservience to economic concerns leads to additional patterns of violence and exploitation—against the labour force and the natural resources that are, in another context, a sacred creation.

As a feminist, an ecologist, politician, and occasional student of theology, I am drawn to the thinking of Hannah Arendt, Thomas Berry, and Brian Swimme in understanding humanity and how we have become disconnected from our best selves—thinking animals who are capable of evolving and choosing paths other than domination, exploitation, power, and violence. But it was in Rosemary Radford Ruether's writing (1983) that I found a key to understanding the fundamental link between male-domination and violence. Ruether (1992) is one of the few social critics to link the violence of men against women, and humanity against Nature in the same analysis of power dynamics, linking the impacts of exploitation, dominance, and patriarchy.

Until we break the cycle of violence at all levels of human activity —nation against nation, religion against religion, man against woman, humans against Nature—we are bound to sabotage any effort to enhance the human condition, to build a more equitable society, and to ensure the biosphere is protected from the most reckless of our activities. We need to do this before we trigger an irreversible loss of those biological, biochemical, and physical forces that make life flourish on Earth. The ecological imperative is thus also a social imperative.

The stakes are very high. It is easy to turn our eyes to the most sadistically violent of human organizations, whether Boko Haram or ISIL, and postulate that we are on the verge of a new era of barbarism and chaos. It is essential that we counter such apocalyptic nihilism with a strong and compelling view of a better world. That utopian view is essential for bolstering us in the urgent task of saving life on earth. Unfortunately, cynicism is in fashion. Hope and idealism are not.

Somehow we must engage all the tools of social transformation in the work of rebuilding belief in a better world. As David Orr, teacher and social advocate of ecological literacy, wrote: 'Hope is a verb with its shirtsleeves rolled up' (2010: xix). Believing in the possibility of a better world and persuading others of that possibility is very hard work in a cynical society.

Advancing Nonviolence and Social Transformation: New Perspectives on Nonviolent Theories provides an invaluable contribution in making the case for a better world and a nonviolent future. The content is a blend of nonviolent theory and practice from India, South Africa, Europe, and Canada. The challenges of ecological and social crises have been examined through the lens of the ethic of nonviolence. This volume brings this ethic to a range of social issues, including democracy, religion, Indigenous rights, gender, ecology, music, education, and relations with other animals. It offers pathways for a possible nonviolent future in each of these areas. By drawing together thinkers and doers across a wide range of disciplines, Heather Eaton and Lauren Michelle Levesque have created a solid analysis of the requirements for social change.

Advancing Nonviolence and Social Transformation: New Perspectives on Nonviolent Theories is a welcomed, needed, and unique contribution from Canada to the expanding global interest in nonviolence theory and action. The call to end violence cannot be merely empty rhetoric. Ending violence is an urgent challenge. This book shows clearly that a viable social and ecological future depends on actions being rooted in a culture of nonviolence and peace.

About the Author

Elizabeth May is the Leader of the Green Party of Canada and its first elected Member of Parliament, representing Saanich-Gulf Islands in southern Vancouver Island, British Colombia. She is a longtime advocate for social justice, the environment, economic issues, and human rights. She is also a lawyer, author, and an Officer of the Order of Canada.

Acknowledgements

Many people are involved in a book project. The authors, editors, and publishers worked hard to bring this book, and the importance of nonviolence, to print. Thank you all very much. Thank you to Saint Paul University for hosting the conference Nonviolence: A Weapon of the Strong, and to all who presented and participated. The quality of your contributions became the incentive for this publication.

The completion of this volume on nonviolence and social transformation was a collaborative process, one that could not have occurred without the help of particular individuals, such as Eva Levesque. A standing ovation goes to Amy Dillon, whose careful work from the beginning of the conference to the end of the book is tremendous. Neither could have happened without her.

We hope this book, *Advancing Nonviolence and Social Transformation: New Perspectives on Nonviolent Theories,* contributes to a less violent future and assists in fostering cultures of peace.

Heather Eaton and Lauren Michelle Levesque

Introduction

Current Trends and New Perspectives on Nonviolent Theories

Heather Eaton

Violence and Nonviolence

How can we talk about nonviolence in the current geopolitical context? The protracted and violent conflicts in Syria, the Middle East, and various African nations; the activities of the Islamic State, Boko Haram, and the 'war on terror'; and the manoeuvrings of Western-allied nations to protect their interests around the world are evidence that violence seems endemic to human societies. Such entrenched inter- or intra-state violence gives rise to the displacement and death of hundreds of thousands of people. It creates vast numbers of refugees needing refugee camps. Dadaab in Kenya holds over 300,000 people and continues to expand. The transitions of democracies into intensified-security states confirm the belief that increased armed fortifications are necessary. Bombings, murders, shootings, and assaults are daily events throughout the world. In the US alone, there were 372 mass shootings in which more than four people were shot in 2015.[1]

Human histories attest to the fact that violence is woven into the fabric of social habits and structures. It is both pervasive and persistent. In attempting to define violence, some consider three interrelated forms: overt or physical, structural or indirect, and ideological or cultural. Others think that violence is on a continuum from personal to political, and ideological and cultural facets are substrata to overt expressions of violence. For example, the military/war ideology and industries constantly broadcast the necessity – indeed obligation – of war and overt violence to resolve conflicts. Structural and indirect violence is seen in systemic patterns of racism and ethnic oppression, violence against women, and economic deprivation. Cultural or ideological violence is manifest in entertainment industries that offer a constant diet of violence to feed the human imagination. Violence in all forms becomes interconnected and normalized.

The nature of human violence is a critical topic to consider. The question of whether violence is inherent in humans as a species is debated frequently with little actual clarity. The history of human violence would suggest that *Homo sapiens* is a particularly violent animal. Yet, within these same historical accounts, as well as in contemporary observations, it is readily seen that many humans and, indeed, communities shun or abhor violence, do not engage in overt violence, and deliberately choose nonviolent modes of conflict resolution. Nevertheless, violence is overall assumed to be part of human nature, not only as a capacity or defensive action, but also as a tendency or orientation. However, this perception cannot be accurate, because human violence is an uneven phenomenon. Not every human is violent. Why is this?

Interpretations differ. One is that humans, while having the capacity to be violent, are by nature co-operative. Violence is a not a *tendency*. It is *choice* and a last resort. Others suggest that while all humans are violent, as a social animal we can live it cathartically. For example, there are defensive (i.e., protective, aggressive) players in every society who carry out violence on behalf of others. Militaries, police, and security forces are allowed to use violence. Outside of war, the state is usually the only social player sanctioned to use overt violence. Other individuals or groups are not to engage in violence, and could be punished if they do.

Yet this observation is also not clear-cut. Most societies are tolerant of, if not directly sanctioning, several forms of violence. For example, violence against women, which although is often against the law, is rarely reported, effectively prosecuted or punished. Hence, it is tolerated. Similar examples regarding racism or other systemic discrimination could readily be considered to be violent. It is, therefore, reasonable to claim that most humans live within 'cultures of violence'.[2] Yet even so, only certain expressions of violence exercised by specific social players are allowed. Some forms of violence—such as random murders—are not acceptable, excluding specific circumstances. Ideas about who gets to do what, and in which culture, are socially 'understood', yet are amorphous. This is also too simplistic, because there are ideological shifts that take place in cultures, which influence the rates and types of violence. Thus, whatever human violence is, it is ambiguous. Little is straightforward or transparent when examining the manifestations as well as the ideological support for and communal acceptance of sanctioned or unsanctioned forms of personal or social violence. The study of the roots, expressions, and toleration of violence is an important field of investigation.

Given the prevalence of human violence, and the various anthropological and sociological theories used to justify it, one could surmise that there is no focused and developed genuine interest in diminishing human violence. For those who assume that violence—in any form—is inevitable, that it resolves political or cultural conflicts, or is intrinsic to human nature, this book is not for you. This book is about advancing and promoting theories and practices of nonviolence. The optic here is that while conflicts are inevitable: violence is a choice. We take the position that the roots of violence, while complex, are saturated with ideologies that support, sustain, and allow for many forms of violence, including war. This stance is influenced by the ongoing and growing work in nonviolence.

The goals of this book, *Advancing Nonviolence and Social Transformation: New Perspectives on Nonviolent Theories*, are to affirm and expand the thinking on nonviolence. The viewpoint is that nonviolence is both a theoretical and practical option for resisting violence and for constructive social change. These goals are rooted in two claims. First, it is obvious to some, if not many, that in general, violence begets violence. Violence and war do not work: they do not result in greater peace, social welfare, or justice. At the very least, it is obvious that violence, while at times effective in controlling people through fear, does not in the long term resolve conflicts. Second, if there is a genuine interest in reducing violence, then considerable and innovative intellectual effort needs to be put into thinking differently about violence and cultivating nonviolence. These will lead to alternative modes of conflict resolution. Mohandas Gandhi articulates the point well: 'If intellect plays a large part on the field of violence, it plays a larger part on the field of nonviolence'.[3]

Nonviolence has multifaceted meanings: a worldview, an intense intellectual inquiry, a moral orientation, a spiritual foundation, a political agenda, a strategy for social change, and an educational and training program. While there are distinctions among these terms – nonviolence, pacifism, civil disobedience or resistance, and peace activism – here they are assumed to be comparable. Although challenging to define precisely, the attention to and awareness of nonviolence is increasing all over the world and with astounding speed.

Public Interest in Nonviolence: New Developments

Until very recently, only a few, albeit prominent, historical players have taken nonviolence seriously. While some nonviolent social movements have been successful, these are eclipsed by the ideologies of violence. The contemporary world is saturated with violence: global actualities, wars, conflicts and terrorism, media obsession with violence, and entertainment industries fixated on violence. Our attention is always pushed towards violence, sustaining a sense of reality defined by violence. Most humans live within a fusion of fantasy, fiction, and nonfiction permeated with violence. How can there be any cultural space for the idea of nonviolence? Yet, it is occurring.

It seems that nonviolence is suddenly of social and global interest. Peace efforts and studies have a long and venerable history. However, until recently the term nonviolence has been avoided, even in peace research. This is shifting, and swiftly. There are new developments coming forth, affirming and expanding the meaning of and thinking about nonviolence. Yet, nonviolence is not a new historical phenomenon. There have been, and are, many kinds of nonviolent actions, perspectives, and people who have promoted nonviolence, from poets to politicians, academics, and activists. They come from several countries and contexts, address distinct problems, use different strategies, and embrace or oppose religion/spirituality. Some advocates for nonviolence are well known, such as Henry David Thoreau, Cesar Chavez, Betty Williams, Dom Hélder Câmara, Abraham Joshua Heschel, Wangari Maathai, Rigoberta Menchu, Coretta Scott King, Daniel Berrigan, Aung San Suu Kyi, Satish Kumar, Arundhati Roy, Thích Nhất Hạnh, Desmond Tutu, Ursula Franklin, Starhawk, John Dear, and John Paul Lederach. Many others are not publically known. Nonviolence is often associated with individuals, their specific views, and their courageous actions, and who frequently are denounced for their nonviolent stance.

Nobel Peace Prizes have been given to nonviolent activists. In recent years, Liu Xiaobo was awarded the 2010 Nobel Peace Prize for his nonviolent efforts for fundamental human rights in China. In 2011, leaders of nonviolent movements, Leymah Roberta Gbowee and Ellen Johnson Sirleaf in Liberia and Tawakkul Karmanfor in Yemen, received the Prize together for their nonviolent struggles for women's rights to security and full participation in peacebuilding work. The National Dialogue Quartet of Tunisia won the Nobel Peace Prize in 2015. This group of trade unions, employers, lawyers, and human rights activists is working for peace and a pluralistic democracy in the ongoing Jasmine Revolution, using nonviolent means. Tunisia is the only country where the Arab Spring was somewhat successful, in spite of harsh repressions.

The past ten years have seen an awakening of public interest in nonviolence, as well as an expansion of the meaning(s) of nonviolence. This emergence has included understanding with renewed depth the historical roots, definitions and explanations, theoretical bases, and social power of nonviolence. In turn, this has spawned myriad projects on nonviolence. A few examples will illustrate what is occurring and why it is astonishing, significant, and timely.

When people think of nonviolence, they general associate this with Mohandas Karamchand Gandhi. It is certainly accurate to claim that any discussion of nonviolent thought and action must consider the legacy, teachings, practices, and influence of Mahatma Gandhi. The Mahatma (meaning great soul) is one of the leading figures who experimented with nonviolence on a personal, social, and political scale.[4] Yet, in fact, few people know the extent of Gandhi's journey into nonviolence: the meaning, spiritual foundation, and intense training to use nonviolence as a social force. Also generally unknown are his vast publications and his view that nonviolence is more than a mechanism of civil resistance: it is also a constructive social program that is the basis of establishing a culture of nonviolence and peace.

Until recently, the collected works of Mahatma Gandhi were only available in select libraries around the world. Now his writings and teachings are readily obtainable, including in several new collections, republications, and Internet sites. They are online in Hindi, French, German, and English and free of charge. For example, the GandhiServe Foundation of Germany (2008), Gandhi Research Foundation of India (2012), and Gandhi Heritage Portal of India (2013) are a few of the places to access Gandhi's writings.[5] The amount of ashrams, institutes, research centres, educational programs, and websites, both online and physical, dedicated to Gandhi that have been established around the world in the past ten years is remarkable. The proliferation of material on and about Gandhi is more than noteworthy.

The popularizing of Mahatma Gandhi has also led to an intense awareness of nonviolence. There is substantial interest in making material available and learning about nonviolence. Endeavours such as Waging Nonviolence (US), The Nonviolence Project Foundation (Switzerland), Nonviolence International (Palestine and Washington DC), Nonviolent Peaceforce (Belgium and US), Campaign Nonviolence (US, Canada, England, Australia), and the Centre for Nonviolence and Social Justice (US) are but a few of the educational and activist organizations promoting nonviolence.[6] Many peace associations are doing something similar. Institutions and organizations are becoming hubs of free information and learning for those interested in nonviolent social change. They are forming global networks that are increasing the knowledge of and respect for nonviolence. They advance notions of and foundations for nonviolent cultures. They scrutinize political actions and events, provide in-depth conflict and cultural analyses, and connect issues of violence with economics, environment, governance, and so forth. They link groups, share stories, generate newsletters, and offer resources, with frequent, even daily, updates. Furthermore, several of these groups are engaging in nonviolent training, nonviolent action and civil resistance, and social-change campaigns. Collectively, these activities are about creating conditions for nonviolent revolutions. It is impossible to track the expansion of such efforts, as they are spreading and strengthening so rapidly.

In addition, within this trend to gain expertise in nonviolence, there is a growing number of courses and training programs in community spaces across the globe. For example, the nondenominational faith-based organization, Pace e Bene, utilizes their website as an information and learning hub while providing opportunities to work directly with staff through workshops and in-person teachings with experts.[7] The Metta Center for Nonviolence and the Karuna Centre for Peace-building offer a range of programs and services, including capacity building in conflict transformation for organizations, and seminars and guidance for nonviolence and peacebuilding. Articles, videos, lectures, books, and training manuals are also available.[8] Thus, whether through education, training for nonviolent resistance, nonviolence is becoming a recognized means of addressing violence and myriad social issues.

Another form of the developing interest in nonviolence is 'think tanks': well-developed and intellectually sophisticated organizations that deal with theoretical aspects of nonviolence. Some of these are the Centre for Applied Nonviolent Action and Strategies, The Albert Einstein Institution, The International Center on Nonviolent Conflict, The International Peace Research Association Foundation, The Palestinian Centre for the Study of Nonviolence (now part of Nonviolence International), The Syrian Nonviolence Movement, and A Force More Powerful.[9] There is an extensive array of other groups addressing peace, human rights, legal frameworks, democracy, social justice, military studies, disarmament, economics, and governance that have an aspect of their work focused directly on nonviolence. As a final example, nonviolence is entering university-level education around the world. Universities are creating centres and academic curricula on nonviolence and peace studies. There is a growing number of courses, multidisciplinary programs, and degrees with a concentration on nonviolence, predominantly in the US, and also in Canada, England, South Africa, India, and several European countries.

Scanning these initiatives reveals a widespread interest in nonviolence. It is a dynamic and creative realm, global in scope, and multifaceted in nature. At an accessible level, nonviolence is becoming recognized and valued. This popular interest in nonviolence is a recent global phenomenon, worthy of our attention.

Theoretical Interest in Nonviolence: Contributions and New Trends

In addition to a growing public awareness of nonviolence, there is an upsurge in theoretical research. There are specific innovations and advances occurring that are also contributing to a nonviolent revolution. To truly grapple with nonviolence an intellectual focus is essential. Nonviolence cannot be reduced to either specific actions or to passiveness. It is not a caprice, a utopian goal, a naïve belief in peace, or a dreamy notion from idealists who are unable, unlike the realists, to face the harshness of violence. Nonviolence is an alternative to violence, requiring the same, and indeed more, thought, comprehension, investment, training, and organizing as do violence and warfare. Hence, if clever minds have developed warfare, then even more astute minds are needed to develop nonviolence. Innovative thinking is needed for nonviolence to gain traction as a viable theoretical and practical option and as a feasible and reasonable political decision. Such inventive thought—that is, an intense intellectual investment in understanding and developing nonviolence—is beginning to occur.

There are new intellectual trends occurring regarding nonviolence that are both fascinating and politically powerful. Nonviolence is extending, escalating, and entering the world political stage. A few book publications that focus purposely on nonviolence will be mentioned for each trend, noting that there are many others and hundreds of academic articles. This is followed by a presentation of where our book, *Advancing Nonviolence and Social Transformation: New Perspectives on Nonviolent Theories*, fits within these recent developments.

The idea of nonviolence can be traced back to founding principles or peripheral themes within many of the world's major religious and cultural traditions. Despite this longer historical trajectory, the life and work of Mohandas Gandhi remain an important starting point for understanding the power and complexity of nonviolence; the spiritual, intellectual, and moral elements; the training; and the relationships to social transformation. Those familiar with nonviolence are equally aware of the legacy and influence of Martin Luther King Jr. For King, Gandhi was the leading proponent of nonviolence. Deeply inspired, King grappled with nonviolence as an anthropological orientation, a spiritual insight, a moral imperative, a social principle, and a strategic, effective means of beneficial social change. What is occurring now is a re-entering into the worlds and works of Gandhi and King, seeking their intellectual, spiritual, and moral foundations, studying their theoretical components and principles, and discerning the comprehensiveness of their understanding of nonviolence. In addition to republishing the works of Gandhi and King, their thoughts and actions are being probed, dissected, and made available in workshops, on websites, and in new publications.

Other scholars and social-change agents have studied and advanced nonviolence during their lifetimes, and their work is increasingly recognized. For example, Gene Sharp, founder and senior scholar of the Albert Einstein Institution in Boston, has spent over 40 years promoting research, policy studies, and education on the strategic uses of nonviolent struggle in the face of contemporary issues such as dictatorship, war, genocide, and oppression.[10] The Institution and Sharp's life work are about fostering freedom through nonviolent action and encouraging the strategic use of nonviolent action in conflict situations. Sharp has written many books on nonviolence and is a contemporary world expert. His contributions have spawned many deliberations about differentiations between principled and strategic understandings of nonviolence. Books by Sharp and others (see, e.g., Sharp and Paulson 2005), as well as videos and films on non-violence, are available online free or for a minimal fee in 36 languages through the Albert Einstein Institution.[11]

Mention must be made of the work of Michael Nagler, also a scholar and educator on nonviolence. Founder of the Peace and Conflict Studies Program at the University of California, Berkeley, as well as of the Metta Centre for Nonviolence, Nagler is a potent adherent and educator of nonviolence who produces, books, films, and a vast array of instructive materials on nonviolence.[12]

This trend of widely disseminating the works of Gandhi, King, Sharp, and Nagler has led to further developments that have expanded the field of nonviolence. While these people are considered to be founders or leaders of twentieth-century nonviolence, current research is going beyond their work and influence into new areas. As scholarly interest in nonviolence rises, so does the research into excavating historical movements and activities, and enlarging nonviolent theories. Three research trends will be mentioned, along with a few publications for each to indicate the timely nature of these discussions.

The first trend is the recognition that nonviolence has been more prevalent in human history than previously acknowledged. The book *A Force More Powerful: A Century of Nonviolent Conflict* (Ackerman and Duvall 2000) provides examples from a dozen countries of organized nonviolent achievements.[13] Similar publications are *Waging Nonviolent Struggle: 20th Century Practice and 21st Century Potential* (Sharp and Paulson 2005), *Nonviolent Revolutions: Civil Resistance in the Late 20th Century* (Erickson 2011), *Recovering Nonviolent History: Civil Resistance in Liberation Struggles* (Bartkowski 2013), and *Worth Fighting For: Canada's Tradition of War Resistance from 1812 to the War on Terror* (Campbell and Dawson 2015). These books retrace history and cite numerous examples of nonviolent efforts.

A second research trend involves theories and practices of nonviolence that are developing conjointly. Several innovative approaches are discerning nonviolent theories from practices, while others are bringing forth new ways of thinking about nonviolence and assessing the applicability in specific contexts. Some methods are predominantly theoretically focused, such as *Civil Resistance Today* (Schock 2015) and *Understanding Nonviolence* (Hallward and Norman 2015). Others are a blend of theory and case studies, such as *Why Civil Resistance Works: The Strategic Logic of Nonviolent Conflict* (Chenoweth and Stephan 2011), *Exploring the Power of Nonviolence: Peace, Politics and Practice* (Amster et al. 2013), and *Nonviolent Struggle: Theories, Strategies and Dynamics* (Nepstad 2015). Others are predominantly case studies, such as *Nonviolent Conflict and Civil Resistance* (Nepstad and Kurtz 2012) and *Civil Resistance: Comparative Perspectives on Nonviolent Struggle* (Schock, ed., 2015).

A final example of new research trends addresses the spectrum between global and local. Many collections have researchers and activists from around the world exchanging theories, practices, and stories. The global reach of interest in nonviolence is remarkable for its extensiveness. Some efforts address the local. For example, the publication *The Technology of Nonviolence: Social Media and Violence Prevention* (Bock 2012) focuses on thinking about, and addressing, violence prevention from and within local communities. These trends are spreading and strengthening the field of nonviolence. Several new publications are released each month.

In tandem with the emphasis on nonviolence is the rising criticism of war efforts. It is not possible to ignore the mounting evidence that violent interventions rarely succeed, always diminish life conditions and damage infrastructures, and often entrench conflicts. *The Dogs Are Eating Them Now: Our War in Afghanistan* (Smith 2013) is a scathing critique of Western efforts in Afghanistan and the dreadful failures of international engagement. The evidence is indisputable that war produces wreckage and does not offer a road to peace. For example, the book *Disarming Conflict: Why peace cannot be won on the battlefield* (Regehr 2015) shows unequivocally that recent wars have been tragedies. Those involved eventually relied on negotiation to settle the disputes, and most grievances remain unresolved.

From another angle, social critics concerned with justice and equality see the rise of global financial networks, the consolidation of political and economic powers, and the intensification of the security state directly related to increased inequality and injustices. Many foresee that the only way to confront this is with nonviolent global citizens' movements. Organizations such as Truthdig.org and the social commentaries of Chris Hedges suggest that revolt is required. In the 2015 book *Wages of Rebellion: The Moral Imperative of Revolt* (2015), Hedges claims that a global uprising is imminent, revolution is inevitable, and only nonviolent rebellions will succeed.

All these efforts within the past ten years are bringing the topic of nonviolence to the public arena. It is truly a new moment in human history. Together the accessibility of the topic of nonviolence, the media and Internet outreach, educational resources, intellectual studies and research, and the fatigue with war are paving the way for a global surge in nonviolent revolutions.

Advancing Nonviolence and Social Transformation: New Perspectives on Nonviolent Theories

This book adds fresh voices and novel perspectives to the burgeoning interest in and importance of nonviolence and has three distinct origins. The first is personal: I have a life-long commitment to peace with periodic studies of nonviolence, participation in many peace groups and organizations, and partaking in more protests than I can recall. Over time, the realization that protests are rarely affective became acute. The analysis of the issues may be outstanding, but the forms of political protests (campaigns, marches, petitions) are often unsuccessful, and some peace protestors have only anger to offer to the process of social change.

Protests, typically nonviolent, are not the same as nonviolent campaigns or movements. Nonviolence is far more comprehensive. This is obvious to any student of Gandhi or King. However, contemporary examples are harder to find. For years I was aware of Ekta Parishad (2015) in India and its efforts in nonviolent education, training, and social action. Since 1991, Ekta Parishad, a people's organization with the leadership of Rajagopal P.V., has been involved in grassroots training throughout India, and has engaged in countless nonviolent actions on land reform, governance. Under the leadership of Jill Carr-Harris, Ekta Parishad is also engaged in gender issues. Rajagopal has been a key leader for decades in nonviolence, and is arguably the most prominent nonviolent leader and activist in the world.[14]

In 2012 I went to India to study Gandhian nonviolence and Ekta Parishad, and to participate in the Jan Satyagraha, a *padyatra*: a long footmarch. This was the largest nonviolent action in human history, involving 100,000 people walking towards Delhi for several weeks for land reform. It was a colossal undertaking: years of preparation and nonviolent training, precise organization, ongoing government negotiations, and in the end, a constructive outcome. I understood something of the significance and implications of a nonviolent movement.[15]

The second origin of this book is the desire to bring an in-depth and renovated conversation on nonviolence to Canada. Several key people, such as Ursula Franklin and Douglas Roche, and organizations such as Project Ploughshares and Canadian Voice of Women for Peace have been longtime advocates for peace and nonviolence. However, only those already involved in peace organizations would be familiar with them. Also, I wanted to expand the notion of a commitment to peace by furthering a nuanced understanding of nonviolence as a movement and as a culture.

Rajagopal and the insights and experiences of Ekta Parishad are remarkable, and I wanted to bring them to Canada, to consider how to develop nonviolence pertaining to issues in the Canadian context. In 2014 I organized a conference using a phrase of Gandhi, 'Nonviolence: A Weapon of the Strong', with the purpose of Advancing Nonviolence, Spirituality, and Social Transformation.[16] The conference brought activists, academics, and popular educators to present, discuss, and promote nonviolence as a method and discipline. Rajagopal was one of ten experts in nonviolence from several countries including India, Iran, South Africa, France,

Belgium, the US, First Nations and Canada to examine various aspects of nonviolence. In addition, 30 panelists addressed nonviolence as it pertains to gender, ecology, governance, education, the arts, Indigenous concerns, children, and energy. Many conference participants are authors in this volume.

The third origin for this book comes from my work as a university professor in Conflict Studies and from being acutely aware of the extensiveness of violent social conflict. My areas of expertise are gender, ecological issues, and religion: how these are involved or implicated in conflict, and/or in movements of liberation and social transformation. Such areas are embroiled in many overt and violent conflicts. However, the roots—especially of gender and ecology—are typically found in systemic, structural, and ideological patterns of oppression that have countless cultural expressions. The theoretical work on nonviolence tends to deal more with overt violence and less with the systemic ideological roots and structural forms that are at play within a continuum of violence. These can be difficult to expose, let alone change.

There is a need to invest time, thought, and effort into developing nonviolent theories in relation to systemic, structural issues. While nonviolence theories are expanding their borders, several topics remain overlooked, such as gender oppression. The United Nations deems the gamut of violence against women to be the most serious and pervasive human rights violation throughout the world.[17] The World Health Organization (WHO) considers violence to be the most significant health risk to women—a global public health problem that affects between one- and two-thirds of women, depending on the culture.[18] To transform the ubiquitous domination of women requires in-depth analysis of how such oppression is sustained by cultural, structural, and symbolic systems. These patterns of oppression underlie the range of issues women face, from less pay for equal work to trafficking, physical and sexual assaults, and death. In all the work on nonviolence, the systematic violence against and structural oppression of women are rarely addressed.

The same analysis can be brought to ecological concerns. The decline of fresh and potable water, food insecurities, less arable land, and energy issues is accelerating. Climate change is occurring, but the consequences are unpredictable. Environmental insecurity is mounting around the world, and efforts are increasing to safeguard resources, often only for the affluent. Environmental scarcity of fresh water and arable soil is increasing, as will protection mechanisms. Ecological decline exacerbates existing social stresses, and when this occurs, violence can and does ensue (Homer-Dixon 1993). Environmental refugees have already surpassed the number of political refugees, according to the United Nations High Commissioner on Refugees. New thinking about ecological decline and nonviolence will be critical, if nonviolence is to be relevant to current global realities.

In addition, ecological decline is virtually always associated with human communities: resources, health, distribution, unequal access, corporate control, and so forth. Yet, these same factors affect the larger-than-human realm of other animals. Climate change, droughts, biodiversity deterioration, habitat loss, over-exploitation, poaching, hunting, and other factors are causing an era of animal extinction unparalleled for 65 million years. We are now in the sixth great extinction. Conflicts over human versus other animals' survival are taking place on every continent. These conflicts are another topic to be brought into conversation with nonviolence.

Advancing Nonviolence and Social Transformation is about addressing nonviolence and systemic social issues. It is also about expanding dialogue partners by adding *New Perspectives on Nonviolent Theories*. In short, the book is about this assertion by Gandhi: 'If intellect plays a large part on the field of violence, it plays a larger part on the field of nonviolence'. It is about furthering and promoting nonviolence as the most pertinent method of social transformation with new thinking about nonviolence—and religion, philosophy, politics, democracy, children, education, the arts, ecology, animal rights, and gender. In many ways, this book is an effort to advance a contemporary version of Gandhi's constructive program.

Each of the five sections examines a particular dimension of nonviolence and its diverse contributions to constructive social change. The first, a historical section, begins with a broad overview of various religions and nonviolence by Christopher Key Chapple, a scholar of Jainism and nonviolence. Gandhian expert, Ramin Jahanbegloo from Iran, presents a Gandhian vision of democracy. Alain Tschudin, scholar and human rights advocate from South Africa, offers rich insights into Gandhi, *ahimsa*, and nonviolence. Tamara Lorincz presents a historical overview of the importance of nonviolence in Canada. This section ends with some personal thoughts from Rajagopal P.V. and Jill Carr-Harris, entitled 'Gandhi in Action', as well has his reflections from the initial conference.

The next section considers specific philosophical and theoretical questions on nonviolence. Philosopher Sophie Cloutier examines Hannah Arendt's distinction between violence and power, asking if violence is an essential component of politics today. Richard Feist, philosophical ethicist, looks at the just-war theory and ponders if war can be fought in an ethical manner. Noel Salmond, a Gandhi and Hindu expert, examines idealistic elements of nonviolence and explores Gandhi's understandings of nonviolence as both practicable and practical. This section ends with Christopher Hrynkow, scholar of Christian ethics, ecology, and nonviolence, who considers principled nonviolence and positive peace through Pope Francis' 2015 ecological encyclical, *Laudato Si'*.

The third section examines nonviolence and systemic social issues. The conference included Indigenous leaders Heather Milton Lightening and Clayton Thomas-Muller who discussed the nonviolent Indigenous movement, Idle No More. Algonquin Elder Michel Thusky reflected on the painful realities in Barriere Lake, Quebec, where the longest non-violent protest in Canada continues, as well as the violent practice and legacy of residential schools. In order to include Indigenous views, we incorporated excerpts from *The Winter We Danced*, which describes the diversity and dynamism of the Idle No More Movement. Following this are two contributions on the importance of feminist analyses. Catherine Holtmann, an expert in intimate partner violence, shows that nonviolent responses are incomplete without attention to the dynamics of gender and violence in specific contexts. Eileen Kerwin Jones, gender expert and founder of PACT (Persons Against the Crime of Trafficking in Humans) addresses nonviolence and its relationship to human trafficking for sexual exploitation. Martin Samson and Marie Boglari assess the social and political dynamics of nonviolence in the 2012 student protests in Quebec, Canada.

The fourth section explores the intersections between nonviolence and ecological concerns. Nathan Townend examines the relationship between animal rights and nonviolence, including how to think about, and our responsibility towards, other animals. Religion and nature scholar, Todd LeVasseur, takes a stance for radical environmentalism and activism, such as that of Deep Green Resistance, including tactics that may involve strategic property damage. Animal rights lawyer and scholar Paul Waldau argues that humans' capabilities to care for others must extend beyond human-centeredness and include the greater than human world.

In the fifth and final section, each chapter suggests a future direction for the study of nonviolence. Simon Appolloni, religion and ecology scholar, explores the potential of wonder to act as a correction to violence by cultivating a deep sense of interdependence with all life. Lauren Michelle Levesque's brings her academic and personal expertise in spirituality, music, nonviolence, and social change to consider how nonviolence together with music can be seen as insightful and creative energies than can influence the social imagination. Renowned and celebrated singer, songwriter, and child advocate Raffi Cavoukian underscores the needs and rights of children. From his co-edited book, *Child Honouring: How to Turn this World Around*, Cavoukian identifies nonviolence as a key tenet of a child-honouring society. In the last chapter, environmental educator and academic Richard Kool argues that environmental educators must deliberate nonviolence, anti-violence, and contra-violence in order to confront a dominant culture in which environmental violence is accepted as normal and necessary.

Advancing Nonviolence and Social Transformation: New Perspectives on Nonviolent Theories is a contribution to the growing field and relevance of nonviolence. Hopefully it will assist in the development and political potential of nonviolence for social transformation, and in future nonviolent revolutions.

About the Author

Heather Eaton, PhD, is a full professor in Conflict Studies at Saint Paul University in Ottawa. Her recent work has focused on religious imagination; evolution; Earth dynamics; peace and conflict studies; gender, ecology, and religion; animal rights; and nonviolence. She has published numerous academic articles and several books, such as: *The Intellectual Journey of Thomas Berry* (2014) and *Ecological Awareness: Exploring Religion, Ethics and Aesthetics* with Sigurd Bergmann (2011).

Notes

1.   See http://www.pbs.org/newshour/rundown/2015-the-year-of-mass-shootings/.

2.   Many have used the term 'culture of violence'. Here the reference refers to a joint appeal made by several Nobel Peace laureates to the heads of state of all member countries of the general assembly of the United Nations in a letter entitled 'For the Children of the World'. They asked the United Nations to declare 2000–2010 be the Decade for a Culture of Nonviolence. They requested: 'That at the start of the decade the year 2000 be declared the Year of Education for Nonviolence; That nonviolence be taught at every level in our societies during this decade, to make the children of the world aware of the real, practical meaning and benefits of nonviolence in their daily lives, in order to reduce the violence, and consequent suffering, perpetrated against them and humanity in general. Together, we can build a new culture of nonviolence for humankind' (see http://www.peaceappeal.org/the-appeal-of-the-nobel-peace-laureates-for-peace-and-non-violence.html).

3.   Gandhi said this phrase near the end of a speech he gave in Wardha, India, 22 June 1940. It was published in Harijan on July 21, 1940 (Gandhi 1999: 350).

4.   Although Gandhi did not consider himself to be a great soul and avoided the term Mahatma, others recognize his personal, political, and spiritual maturity, and use the term as a sign of respect, which is also the case here.

5.   See GandhiServe Foundation: Mahatma Gandhi Research and Media Service, at http://www.gandhiserve.org/e/; Gandhi Research Foundation, at http://www.gandhifoundation.net/about%20grf.htm; Gandhi Heritage Portal, at https://www.gandhiheritageportal.org/; GandhiMedia: Bringing Mahatma Gandhi to Life!, at http://www.gandhimedia.org/.

6.   See Waging Nonviolence: People Powered News and Analysis, at http://waging-nonviolence.org/; The Nonviolence Project, at http://www.nonviolence.com/; Nonviolence International, at http://nonviolenceinternational.net/; Nonviolent Peaceforce, at http://www.nonviolentpeaceforce.org/. Campaign Nonviolence, available at http://www.paceebene.org/programs/campaign-nonviolence/; Centre for Nonviolence and Social Justice, at http://www.nonviolenceandsocialjustice.org/.

7. See Pace Bene, at http://www.paceebene.org/about/, http://www.paceebene.org/programs/.

8. See The Metta Centre for Nonviolence, at http://mettacenter.org/; Karuna Centre for Peace-building, at http://www.karunacenter.org/our-services.html.

9. See Centre for Applied Nonviolent Action and Strategies, at http://canvasopedia.org/; Albert Einstein Institution, at http://www.aeinstein.org/; The International Center on Nonviolent Conflict, at https://www.nonviolent-conflict.org/; The International Peace Research Association Foundation, at http://iprafoundation.org/; The Palestinian Centre for the Study of Nonviolence (Nonviolence International), at http://nonviolenceinternational.net/; The Syrian Nonviolence Movement, at http://www.alharak.org/; A Force More Powerful, at http://www.aforcemorepowerful.org/.

10. See Albert Einstein Institution, at http://www.aeinstein.org/about/mission-statement.

11. See Albert Einstein Institution, at http://www.aeinstein.org/about/mission-statement.

12. See, for example, Peace and Conflict Studies, at http://iastp.berkeley.edu/pacs; The Metta Centre for Nonviolence, at http://mettacenter.org/; Amster, Ndura-Ouédraogo, and Michael N. Nagler (2013).

13. This group also maintains an informative website, produces films, and founded the International Center on Nonviolent Conflict.

14. Rajagopal P. V. is renowned in peace and nonviolent activities. Books, films, and documentaries have been made about him, usually in relation to the work of Ekta Parishad (see https://en.wikipedia.org/wiki/Rajagopal_P._V).

15. Ekta Parishad is preparing for another mass action in 2020: *Jai Jagat*, which means 'victory of the world'. The underlying principle is similar to the Gandhian concept of *sarvodaya*, the wellbeing of all: if there is a victory then it should be the victory of our common humanity not the victory of one nation over another. It should also be based on the victory of living commodiously together, and of people coexisting with nature (http://www.ektaparishad.com/en-us/campaigns/jaijagat2020.aspx).

16. See http://ustpaul.ca/en/conference-nonviolence-a-weapon-of-the-strong-mahatma-gandhi-advancing-nonviolence-spirituality-and-social-transformation_1601_17.htm.

17. See United Nations Humans Rights: Office of the High Commission for Human Rights, at http://www.ohchr.org/EN/NewsEvents/Pages/ViolenceAgainstWomen.aspx.

18. See WHO, 'Global and regional estimates of violence against women: prevalence and health effects of intimate partner violence and non-partner sexual violence' (2013), at www.who.int/iris/.../9789241564625_eng.pd.

Part I

Historical Perspectives

Chapter 1

Religion and Nonviolence

Christopher Key Chapple

Prophetic Monotheisms and Violence

The prophetic monotheisms include Judaism, Christianity, and Islam, which further subdivide into hundreds of denominations. These traditions rely upon an origin story that places a creator deity at the heart of the narrative, a deity who rendered the world in seven days, created the first man and woman, blessing them with dominion over the created realm, then cursing them due to their impudence, impertinence, and imprudence. Each tradition seeks to restore and recover the state of original blessing, following guidance from prophets who stand in a place of privileged communication with the deity.

Descendants of Adam and Eve came to populate many areas of the earth and lived to tell stories of the great flood, a worldwide occurrence of high water events. Abraham, the earliest known prophet of these traditions, was asked to spare his son from an act of ritual violence. According to Jews and Christians, he spared his son Isaac, born of Sarah, and sent Ishmael, born of Hagar, into exile (OUP 1970, Gen. 22:1-18). According to Islam, Abraham rescued Ishmael from the sacrificial altar, visiting mother and child in Mecca after they moved south from the Euphrates Valley (Khanam, ed. 2014, 2:124, 37:99-111). Some have speculated that ritual child slaughter was an adaptive strategy employed to control population growth in a land of little rain. For instance, *The Interpreter's Bible* states that this was a 'custom which already existed' (Buttrick *et al.*, eds. 1952, Gen. 1:1009) and *Encyclopedia Judaica* suggests that the Abraham story is a 'protest against human sacrifice' (Keter 1971, Gen. 2:481). Abraham changed this pattern, substituting circumcision for all new born sons for an earlier violent ritual action.

The sons of Isaac were eventually taken into captivity by the Egyptians and enslaved for hundreds of years. The prophet Moses descended from the ruling class once he discovered his pre-adoption identity and brought the Jewish people out of Egypt to the Sinai Peninsula. God, who had spoken to him in the form of a burning bush, commanded Moses to teach ten rules of protection, creating a covenant of protection for those who adhered to this new code. Most of the rules were affirmations of earlier ethical codes, such as do not murder, do not commit adultery, do not steal, and honour one's parents. Others rules were overtly theological, such as do not worship graven images. This latter commandment put the Jews at odds with the peoples dwelling in Palestine, the erstwhile home of Isaac, to which they returned. After some decades of struggle and violence, they established sovereignty in the region, eventually anointing David as King, succeeded by Solomon, who built the ritual center in Jerusalem, the first Jewish temple. After nearly five centuries, invaders from the east destroyed the temple and took the Jews as slaves to Babylon. During this nearly eight-decade period, the Jews survived by continual study of their sacred literature, the Torah, and adherence to the legal code found therein. When allowed by a benevolent Zoroastrian ruler to return to Jerusalem, they rebuilt the original temple, prospered, and entered a period of diaspora, establishing Jewish communities in Egypt, North Africa, throughout the Mediterranean region, the east coast of Africa, and the west coast of India. The central kingdom was destroyed by the Romans in 72 CE, and for nearly two millennia the Jewish people ruled no land, sustaining their religious identity through adherence to Jewish law and study of the Torah.

Christianity arose as a resistance movement during the second collapse of Jerusalem. Jesus of Nazareth stood in opposition to Roman religion, which sought to displace Judaism in Jerusalem, and he challenged the ritual requirements of the Jewish faith. His life ended chaotically in crucifixion, an act of ritual violence that subsequently provided a central symbol of self-sacrifice for Christians. Disciples of Jesus gathered in remembrance of his life, performing Eucharist weekly and forming home churches to elude persecution by Roman authorities. A Jewish scholar named Saul underwent a conversion to the Christian faith and spread the religion throughout the eastern Mediterranean region under the name of Paul. Christians endured fierce persecutions and martyrdoms under Roman rule until its legalization under Constantine in 325 CE.

Islam arose in the Arabian Peninsula city of Mecca, taking shape when the prophet Muhammad moved his followers to the city of Medina in September, 622 CE. Like Abraham, Moses, and Jesus, Muhammad worked against the status quo, in this case speaking out against social injustice, offering a critique, as did Jesus, of corrupt religious practices. Like Moses, Muhammad required the abandonment of graven images, which had been under active worship until his time. Like Jesus, Muhammad required adherence to a new ethics as revealed in the Quran, the word of God as spoken through the prophet. The new faith contained five pillars: belief in one God, a yearly month-long fast, tithing of one's wealth to support the poor, prayer five times each day in direction of the holy city of Mecca, and, if possible, pilgrimage to Mecca at least once in one's lifetime for participation in commemorative rituals. This new faith expanded significantly in its first four centuries, spreading westward throughout northern Africa, northward into Iraq and Turkey, and eastward into Central Asia and the Indian peninsula.

Each of these religions sought to bring peace to its adherents, establishing pathways through which its adherents could return to a state of grace experienced by all humanity before the fall and the expulsion from the Garden of Eden. For Jews, this takes place through adherence to the Levitican and Mosaic Law. For Christians, it takes place through the recitation of the Lord's Prayer and participation in the Eucharist. For Muslims, reconciliation can be found in the observance of the Five Pillars.

Along with bringing peace to its adherents, each of these traditions arose through struggle and violent encounters. The early Jews endured slavery at the hands of the Pharaohs and the Babylonians, persecutions and expulsion by the Romans, and centuries of pogroms culminating with the Holocaust during the Second World War. Christians, whose founding leader was publicly flogged and slain by the Romans, endured stadium slaughter by gladiators. Even after Christianity became legal and eventually became the official faith of the Roman Empire, repeated violence erupted, primarily through attempts to establish and maintain orthodoxy.

In the 1140s a movement emerged in Italy known as the Cathar Church, the church of the 'pure', the founding of which has been linked to cloth merchants who introduced Bogomil ideas from the Balkan Peninsula (Russell 1965: 192; Runciman 1982: 118, 169). By the end of the twelfth century it had spread also to France, Germany, and England. The Cathars, also known as Albigensians, taught a complex, docetist theology that denounced the material world as the work of the devil and disavowed most of the Old Testament. According to the Cathars, the purpose of human life was to purify the soul through chastity and vegetarianism, thereby avoiding reincarnation and attaining release. The killing of animals was forbidden because animals were said to possess a soul; meat, eggs, and milk were all forbidden because they arose from the sinful act of sexual intercourse (Russell 1965: 204-6, 209-10). They divided their followers into the Believers and the Perfect. The Perfect, who could be male or female, essentially had achieved a divinized state, and were worshipped by the Believers. The Cathars fasted frequently and occasionally encouraged sick members to embark on a fast unto death, known as the Endura. In the thirteenth century, many French nobilities embraced the Cathar sect, most notably Count Raymond of Toulouse. The Inquisition, however, set out to destroy the renegade church. Two hundred Perfects were burned without trial at Montsegur in 1238 and 1243. Many nobilities similarly perished in 1244. In 1326, the 'last Cathar in France, Limosus Niget, was burned' (Leff 1967: 450). In 1412, 15 Cathars were burned to death in Chieri, Italy (Leff 1967: 451).

Attempts to reclaim the Holy Land resulted in the Crusades, a bloody tradition that lasted hundreds of years. Martin Luther's Protestant movement, established in 1452, brought violent conflict between Catholics and Protestants, with some disputes lasting a hundred years. Even the Good Friday Agreement negotiated by George Mitchell in 1998 has brought only a tenuous peace to a divided Ireland (McEvoy 2008).

The Muslim world has endured conflict since its time of origin. Armed conflict allowed Muhammad's followers to survive raids against Meccan traders. Following his death, disputes arose over succession, eventually opening a split between Sunnis, who follow the lineage established by Muhammad's uncle, and the Shi'ias who follow the lineage established by the descendants of Muhammad's daughter. This conflict persists into the present day, with rifts between Sunnis and Shi'ias responsible for hundreds and sometimes thousands of deaths each year in such places as Iraq, Iran, and Pakistan.

When each of these traditions gained ascendancy into power, each approved the use of violence for the sake of not only protection but also expansion. The Crusades, the conflict between Mary Queen of Scots and Queen Elizabeth I of England, the Salem witch trials, the horrific Iran-Iraq War of the 1980s, and so many more such tragedies attest to the power of religious belief to stir deep emotions. Throughout the history of the prophetic monotheisms, humans have clung to a dualistic outlook, pitting one side against the other, whether Jew against Philistine, Protestant against Catholic, Shi'ia against Sunni, Greek against Ottoman Turk, Nazi against Jew. Firmly held beliefs morph into hardened views. As a result, an 'othering' takes place that strips the human being of compassion or empathy for those perceived as different, opening a chasm that holds only anger and hatred. Violence results.

In the history of the West, a form of dualistic thinking arose that strengthened the division between subject and object. René Descartes' *Discourse on the Method of Rightly Conducting One's Reason and of Seeking Truth in the Sciences* (2006) accorded supremacy to human perception, making the human person the measure of all things. This method gave way to the ability to observe, predict, and manipulate the material world in ways not imaginable in prior centuries. Francis Bacon (1561–1626), who was both a politician and a foremost philosopher in the area of empiricist natural philosophy and scientific methodology, viewed the material world as a resource to be exploited for human benefit (Merchant 1983: 182-83). In the decades that followed, science became married first to the development of increasingly effective technology, and eventually to the marketplace. In terms of warfare, the new technology allowed for the repeating artillery of the American Civil War, the mustard gas of the First World War, the atom bomb of the Second World War, and the drones that now allow remote mayhem from thousands of miles away. The psychological sciences have empowered marketers to conceive and mass market items unimaginable in prior decades. Luxuries such as hot water, central heat, and electricity are now regarded by many in the world as necessities, not to mention automobiles and telephones.

Asian Religions:
Hinduism, Buddhism, Jainism, Sikhism, Confucianism, Daoism

The Asian religions, perhaps with the exception of Shinto, do not include an underlying cosmogonic narrative that depends on the unfolding of a chronological history. The earliest surviving account of world origins for South Asia can be found in the *Ṛg Veda* (ca. 5000 to 2500 BCE), a collection of ancient hymns and verses from which the Indian philosophical traditions draw their origins. A main narrative in the text recounts a recurrent process through which the deity Indra returns each year, from time without beginning, to slay the dragon, Vṛtra, releasing life-giving waters with the advent of the annual monsoon. The creation cycle can be seen in a rhythm that begins in unformed chaos (*asat*), moves into structure (*sat*), invites collaborative creativity through sacrificial and intentional action (*yajña*), and results in a culminating moment of order (*ṛta*). After this culminating experience, chaos returns, requiring the re-enactment of the process in order to foster the reconstitution of the world, or perhaps more accurately, another world (*loka*) (de Nicolás 1978). The process may be understood as a description of a human life, beginning in a childhood filled with potential, moving through the stages of education into a state of adulthood, taking up a profession and creating a family, and, after reflection that all things have been achieved, a return to the state of chaos through old age and death. It also can be interpreted by thinking about the life-giving processes of each meal, each breath, each day cycling through sunrise, the brightness of noontime, sunset, and the return of the night. As Hindu thinkers began to enumerate myriad possibilities based on these interpretations of the *Ṛg Veda*, they specified huge cycles of epochal time into the trillions, generating speculative numbers that exceed even those generated by contemporary scientists equipped with Hubble telescopes.

The philosophies and theologies arising from this expansive creation narrative articulate multiple points of view (Mahoney 1998). For Hindus, the numbers of gods and goddesses are infinite; the *Ṛg Veda* counts 330 million gods at minimum. For Buddhists, this narrative makes it impossible to know when it began, or even *if* it began, and when it will end.

The Buddha turned the narrative inward, stating that the most important question must arise from oneself and lead to self-discovery, emphasizing that suffering (*duḥkha*) must be traced to its cause in clinging (*tṛṣṇā*) and brought to a state of disclosure and resolution (*nirodha*). He refused to engage in speculative conversation about the origins or ending of the material world, always taking a psychological approach. Jainas adhere to a philosophy of infinitude, stating that the world has always been here, will always be here, and that countless souls (*jīva*) advance toward a state of undying freedom (*kaivalyam*) through purification of karma. Each of these traditions requires staunch adherence to a strict ethical code to honour the goal of advancing the human person toward a state of spiritual freedom (*mokṣa nirvāṇa, kevala*).

The ancient thought systems of China, Confucianism, and Daoism arose in the middle of the first millennium BCE and build upon earlier literature such as the *Yi Jing / I Ching*. Just as the early Vedic system describes a movement from chaos into order that can be redeemed, Chinese thought emerges from a governing metaphor: the need to balance *yin* and *yang*, passive and active cosmic and personal forces. Like India, Chinese thought gravitates around a process of movement and flow. The Daoists state that a person must recede into a state of observation, of non-action and non-resistance, allowing the Way of Heaven to emerge. The Confucianists require active formation and control of human impulse through the cultivation of virtues instilled and followed from infancy through old age. Duty to family and community requires strict principles of self-control that ensure harmony within the larger group.

The social history of Asia reflects adherence to these underlying structures in many different ways. The sphere of Indian cultural influence has extended from Afghanistan through the subcontinent to Southeast Asia and Indonesia. The great temple complex of Angkor Wat honours Hindu deities, and the magnificent *stūpa* in Borobudur narrates the life of the Buddha. Throughout this cultural area, hundreds of kings (*rājās*) and great kings (*mahārājas*) ruled over contiguous lands distinguished by local languages and cultural variants, but grounded in a common agreement about social structure and the centrality of the ritual process. This ritual process included the enactment of a Horse Sacrifice every twelve years, during which a Hindu king would wander for one year, following a consecrated horse into frontier lands that would be annexed, marked with the bloody ritual killing of the horse. Conflict between kingdoms would be seasonal, arising during lulls between planting and harvesting, a time when farm workers could take up arms to defend or expand the king's realm. Occasionally, kingdoms would be amalgamated into empires, as under Asoka (ca. 300 BCE) and Chandragupta (ca. 300 CE). But these arrangements were more instances of strategic alliance with local rule than a model of direct governance. Even during the period of British rule in India, more than a third of the kingdoms remained independent, numbering more than 200.

China produced the earliest large-scale governmental system in human history. Through universal education in the pictographic writing system, communication was made possible over vast distances in regions where the local languages bore no phonic or even grammatical similarity to Mandarin Chinese. The Confucian emphasis on conformity gave rise to a governmental system that required its workers to memorize and internalize the *Analects*, a collection of sayings by Confucius that relates his teachings and are considered to be the best pathway to personal and societal harmony (Chan 1963: 18-48). Great armies were amassed to enforce the peace and expand the empire, linking peoples of north and south and encouraging cultural and governmental expansion from the coast inland. The Maoist annexation of Tibetan and Uighur cultural areas in the middle of the twentieth century marked the culmination of the Chinese version of Manifest Destiny. Today the Chinese government, which had once forbidden the practice of religion, now allows and supports the Christian and Islamic faiths, with recognition given to the importance of civil order as taught in Confucian propriety, the insights of Buddhist meditation, and the Daoist way of acceptance.

Just as conflicts have plagued the worlds of Europe and the Middle East, so also warfare and strife has been found in Asia, but to varying degrees. The expansion and maintenance of the central Chinese governmental authority required periodic wars of expansion and the building of the Great Wall to delineate the Middle Kingdom. In times of governmental collapse, warring factions would emerge until the ascent of new imperial rule. Successive dynasties were governed by the Shang, Zhou, Han, Tang, Song, Yuan (Mongol), Ming, and Manchu families. Korea and Japan followed parallel tracks, with periods of stability interrupted by times of strife. India, as noted earlier, tended more toward decentralized rule, but was subjected periodically by Greek, Mughal, and British invaders, who held sway over parts of India in the third century CE, from 1500 to 1750, and from 1750 to 1947, respectively. Sikhism, founded by Guru Nanak in the fifteenth century, originally advocated a peaceful lifestyle, but was driven to militarize under Mughal persecution. Militaristic advocacy to separate a Sikh homeland known as Khalistan from central Indian rule in the 1980s resulted in a violent suppression and spurred the assassination of Prime Minister Indira Gandhi.

Buddhism, though ostensibly a monastic and nonviolent religion, also engaged in the creation of empire. Just as with Christianity, Buddhist leaders came into alignment with state power, particularly in Southeast Asia. The great Mongolian conqueror, Genghis Khan, renowned for his acts of violence, embraced Tibetan Vajrayāna Buddhism. Zen Buddhism, combined with a Samurai ethic, helped gird Japanese warriors for acts of war during the Second World War. In contemporary times, Buddhist leadership has taken an active role in the support of the military suppression of Tamil Hindus in Sri Lanka as well as the killing of Muslims in Thailand and Myanmar. Yet, Thich Nhat Hanh, a Buddhist monk and nonviolent activist, helped negotiate the end of the Vietnam War, and the Dalai Lama, the spiritual leader of the Tibetan people, has won the Nobel Peace Prize.

Peace, Nonviolence, and Religion

This brings us to a discussion of ways in which the religions of the world have supported and advanced the cause of peace. Examples will be given of what may be termed 'peace themes' in each of the faiths mentioned above. This will be followed by descriptions of historical and contemporary figures who have stood up for peace through the invocation of faith.

The prophetic monotheisms have set forth rules of personal comportment that help foster circumstances that lead to peace. The adherence to the Levitican code and Mosaic Law helped reduce conflict within the Jewish community. Clear guidelines for human behaviour allowed for the ministrations of culturally accepted justice. Early Christians were nonviolent. Jesus advocated turning swords into plowshares and turning the other cheek. Muhammad sought to bring peace between warring factions in Medina, the city that invited him to be a peacemaker between different Arab tribes and to establish harmonious relations with Jews and Christians. However, as noted above, when a counter-cultural movement assumes the responsibilities of governance, practicalities such as the defence of borders emerge. Augustine developed justifiable war theory as Christianity became state-sanctioned and in turn sanctified the state to engage in acts of war. When the Hebrews returned to the Promised Land as exiles and refugees, they eventually established governmental structures, including armies. The expansion of Islam, particularly between 750 and 1250 CE, required arms to bring the message of peace. In each instance, even the goal of maintaining military strength has been to establish a state of civic stability and peace, albeit with undeniable self-interest. In all these instances, observance of religious practices serves to generate a feeling of good will, whether through adherence to the Mosaic code and attendance at synagogue, or participation in weekly church services, or prayer toward Mecca five times each day plus visitation to the mosque.

Asian traditions tend to be less congregational with more emphasis on family and on personal practice. India developed a social structure that emphasizes endogamy among like groups. China developed a tradition of ancestor veneration with importance placed on honouring one's parents for granting the gift of life. Both cultural regions developed extended patrilocal family households, maximizing economic advantage and providing for needier family members. According to Confucian traditions, harmony begins in the home and extends to the village; clusters of harmonious villages naturally accord into districts and regions, making the job of the Emperor easy. When harmony extends from person to family to village and then to the province, the Emperor need only face south, the direction of warmth and ease.

Peace for the individual can be established through the observance of home rituals and periodic visits to sacred sites such as temples or pilgrimage destinations. Home shrines near the hearth may honour an array of gods and goddesses, illuminated with the ever-present flame of the cooking fire. Simple home rituals known as *Pūjās* permit auspicious forces such as wealth, knowledge, and culture to suffuse the household. Placing a dab of colour on the forehead, touching the feet of one's parents and elders, bowing to sacred images, and adorning sacred trees create a rhythm of daily worship throughout Asia, establishing a general atmosphere of calm and peace.

The specifics of this cultural grammar vary from location to location, from family to family, and from faith to faith. Some families in India revere Kṛṣṇa with Rādhā and Rāma with Sītā; others revere Śiva, and Pārvatī; many will include homage to multiple sacred persons on the home altar, including Jesus. Buddhist homes throughout Southeast Asia, China, Korea, and Japan often include various images alongside Confucian-inspired ancestral shrines. In Japan, rocks and mountains take on religious significance to practitioners of Shinto, resulting in loving protection of many natural sites.

Jaina Nonviolence

The Jaina religion, until recently found only in India, developed a theology that emphasizes peace and respect for all living forms starting more than 2500 years ago. Jaina philosophy advances the view that all entities, including ones that would be declared inert by Aristotelian categories, hold life and merit protection. These include elemental life forms such as rocks, bacteria, plants, and all manner of reptiles, birds, and mammals. Jainism teaches a pervasive biocentrism, in contrast to a narrow anthropocentrism. It also proclaims that all life entities have never been created nor can they be destroyed. At the end of one embodiment, each life form enters a new embodiment, depending on the karmic action committed. For instance, according to Jaina theory, a loyal dog could be born as a human due to its good deeds; an evil human being most likely would be born as a cruel animal or in a hell realm to atone for wrong deeds. The universe becomes the testing ground for moral behaviour. Jainas developed vows to shape and guide its adherents to live in such a way as to minimize all harm.

The vows and philosophical speculations of both Jaina laypersons and monastics provide the world's most thorough-going foundation for cultivating a lifestyle grounded in peace. The key term for this practice, *ahiṃsā*, finds support with two additional words: *aparigraha*—minimization of possessions, and *anekānta*—non-adherence to a singular point of view, sometimes translated as tolerance. However, this third term does not signify relativism, as Jainas would not assent to any form of violence except in extreme conditions requiring self-defence.

The Jaina theory of *karma* states that particles of colourful matter adhere to the soul with each act of violence, obscuring its purity. Through careful observance of vows, an individual slowly removes *karma*, revealing incrementally one's inherent luminosity. Jainas developed a lacto-vegetarian diet, thereby avoiding harm to animals. In recent years, many Jainas, because of concern with the abuses of the industrialized dairy process, are becoming vegan.[1] The more conservative Jainas also avoid foods with an abundance of seeds such as tomatoes and eggplants, and eschew root vegetables such as carrots, potatoes, onions, and garlic. Jainas generally engage in professions that do not entail the taking of animal life or the production or distribution of weaponry. Many engage in textiles, trade, publishing, finance, education, and law. In India, the Jaina faith is particularly associated with merchant families, and adherents are well known for their success in this realm. Jainas would generally not serve in the military, although it is not uncommon for Jainas to hold leadership positions in law enforcement.

Three twentieth-century Jainas advanced the practice of *ahiṃsā* on a global scale. Acarya Tulsi (1914–1997) promulgated Anuvrat, a new interpretation of Jaina ethics with emphasis on such topics as non-use of atomic weaponry and pollution reduction (Chapple 1993: 61-63). L. M. Singhvi (1941–2007), a lawyer who served in India's Parliament and regularly argued cases in front of India's Supreme Court, wrote and circulated, 'The Jain Declaration on Nature', a treatise through which Jaina philosophy engaged environmental issues (Chapple 2002). Satish Kumar (1936–) joined a Jaina monastic order at the age of nine, but left to join ranks with the land distribution movement inspired by Gandhian thought. After working on social justice issues with the Gandhian activist Vinoba Bhave (1895–1982), Kumar took up anti-nuclear advocacy before settling in England, where he directs Schumacher College, focused on issues of ecology and peace (Kumar 1992, 1999).

Quaker Nonviolence

As noted earlier, Jesus urged his followers to turn swords into plowshares. The early Christians, because of their non-approved, non-governmental status, did not participate in conventional power structures. They met clandestinely in home-church movements hosted by women. For the first three hundred years, to be Christian meant to be under suspicion, counter-cultural, and without power. Once Christianity gained public acceptance and thinkers such as St Augustine provided rationale for full participation of the Christian community in matters of state, Christianity no longer stood at the edges but itself became a tool for the perpetuation of imperial interests. Violent measures were taken within the church to ensure fidelity to approved dogmas. Non-conformists were persecuted. Many were burned at the stake. In the seventeenth century, while Europe underwent a huge cultural shift because of the discovery of the New World and the ongoing after-effects of the Protestant Reformation, a peace movement arose in England that altered the course of human history: the Religious Society of Friends.

George Fox

William James (1842–1910) wrote extensively of George Fox (1624–1691), the founder of the Religious Society of Friends in his classic work, *Varieties of Religious Experience* (1961). He considered the Quaker tradition to provide the template for self-transformative spirituality. James writes: 'Religious rapture, moral enthusiasm, ontological wonder, cosmic emotion, are all unifying states of mind, in which the sand and grit of the selfhood incline to disappear, and tenderness to rule' (1961: 225). The word tenderness borrows heavily from the journal of George Fox, wherein Fox coins several new usages of English words. Tenderness denotes a state of empathy and concern, which in turn can lead to conviction and resolve. Combined with Quaker discernment, the resultant actions taken have altered the course of history.

As a young man, George Fox underwent a prolonged spiritual quest, wandering from village to village, questioning and challenging the authorities of the day. His disruption of Church of England services resulted in years of imprisonment. He described his apotheosis as follows: 'I knew nothing but pureness, and innocence, and righteousness; being renewed into the image of God by Christ Jesus, to the state of Adam, which he was in before he fell. The creation was opened to me; and it was showed to me how all things had their names given them according to their nature and virtue' (in Jones [1694] 1963: 97). Fox conferred with Oliver Cromwell during the times of upheaval in England and even traveled to the

Caribbean and the colonies, where many Quakers had settled during times of persecution. He consistently taught the observance of nonviolence and non-capitulation to unjust authority.

The voice of the Quakers was instrumental in the liberation of women and slaves. Women convened silent meetings for worship in the early years of the movement, among them the widow Margaret Fell who eventually took Fox as her husband. Sarah Grimke (1792–1873) composed the first feminist reading of the Bible. Elizabeth Cady Stanton, a devout Quaker, worked closely with Susan B. Anthony on two significant campaigns: abolition of slavery and women's rights (Gordon 2009; Stanton 1895). Following World War One, Quakers were instrumental in gaining conscientious objector status for individuals whose conscience forbade participation in warfare. Quakers were also instrumental in ending the Vietnam War. Sadly, Tom Fox, killed in Baghdad during the American invasion of Iraq which began in 2003, was part of a Quaker peace initiative (*LA Times* 2006).

The Religious Society of Friends sought successfully to upend patterns in social organization that had endured for thousands of years. Archaeology has revealed that, for at least three thousand years, human societies have been organized around principles based on hierarchies. Ancient Indo-European stratification delineated four major groupings based on role: Priests, Landowners, Merchants, and Workers. These correlate to the Brahmins, Kṣatriyas, Vaiśyas, and Śūdras as delineated in the Dharmaśāstra literature of India. Similar social organization can be found in the feudal society of medieval Europe that continued in the system of *casta* in Portugal, *caste* in France, the peasants-serfs of Russia, and the rigid British system of lords and labourers (Dumézil 1973).

With the conquests of the new world, enslavement of non-white peoples robbed millions of once-free people of their dignity. Fox witnessed this emergence first hand by visiting the American colonies in 1671 and 1672. He urged that, 'after certain years of servitude, they would make them free' (in Jones [1694] 1963: 491). He was hosted by Native Americans in what is now southern New Jersey, before any white settlement was built there. Persecuted Quakers later founded Pennsylvania and, although they undoubtedly played a role in the displacement of native peoples, Quaker educators were instrumental in the survival of the Seneca Nation on the Allegheny River near the current city of Salamanca in New York State's Southern Tier following their devastating defeat during the Revolutionary War.

The seventeenth century brought about the settlement of the New World. The Jesuits, who followed early trappers and traders from France, sought to first learn the ways of native peoples and then convince them of the benefits of conversion to Christianity. In the world's first extensive ethnography since the Greek geographers Megasthenes (350-290 BCE) and

Strabo (64 BCE–24 CE), the Jesuit missionaries created a massive document providing details and analysis of the life-ways observed by hundreds of First Nation peoples. Starting in 1610 and ending in 1791 (a period when the Society of Jesus was banned because of their advocacy for the rights of South American native peoples), the Jesuits crafted not only a magnificent narrative of their own struggles in adapting to the new continents but also a robust account of the rich spiritual and psychological life of New World peoples. These writings inspired Montesquieu (1689–1755), Jean-Jacques Rousseau (1712–1778), and others to laud the 'noble savage' and decry the despoiling of the Americas by predatory European colonizers.

The seeds for the end of feudalism and the birth of democratic societies were also sown during this time. John Locke (1632–1704), a contemporary of George Fox, advocated for all farmers to be able to own their own land, wresting the hegemony of property from the domain of the aristocracy. Lockean ideals of ownership no doubt contributed to the migration of farmers from Holland, England, Ireland, Scotland, France, and Germany to the New World in search of economic autonomy. Martin Luther (1483–1546) had sown the seeds of the Protestant Reformation that set the stage for Quakerism and other movements of radical reform. During the consequent European Enlightenment, Descartes gave voice to the integrity of the human self ('I think therefore I am'), Montesquieu advocated a move toward democracy ('government should be set up so that no man need be afraid of another'), Rousseau romanticized the Noble Savage, and Locke saw land ownership as key to human dignity (Bristow 2011).

These new ideas created change, unsettling to many, for decades across Europe. Martin Luther's quest to undo hierarchies unleashed a split between northern and southern Europe. Menno Simons (1496–1561) promoted the Anabaptist movement and established a 'peace church' that even now requires simple living among its followers, the Mennonites. Ignatius of Loyola (1591–1556) brought about the Counter Reformation within the Catholic Church. He established the Society of Jesus, an order that for centuries has taken education as its central mission. George Fox's theology of the inner light promoted equality of men and women and eschewal of outer authority.

The American Revolution ushered in new ideas of how to establish a nation that emphasized the 'pursuit of liberty and happiness', albeit for landholding white men. In France, Montesquieu's philosophy eventually inspired the overthrow of monarchy, aristocracy, and church authority with the slogan: *Liberté, Egalité, Fraternité*. Thomas Jefferson declared universal public education to be an essential facet of any successful democracy, proclaiming to the effect that an unlettered electorate would subject themselves to tyranny.

With the success of the great American experiment, Transcendental-ism and what might be loosely referred to as the movement for civil rights based on the notion of human dignity began. Henry David Thoreau (1817–1862) and Ralph Waldo Emerson (1803–1882) provided intellectual and spiritual support for the Abolitionist movement taken up by the Quak-ers some years earlier. Thoreau and Emerson eagerly studied the newly translated literature from Asia and took great inspiration from the *Bhaga-vad Gītā*, the *Upaniṣads,* and the texts of Confucianism and Daoism. Thore-au's book and essay, *Walden* and 'Civil Disobedience', published in 1849 and 1854 respectively, have been required reading for generations of Ameri-can students and convey powerful messages in regard to individual con-science and self-reliance.

Sarah Grimke (1792–1873) converted to Quakerism in 1821 and became an outspoken advocate for both Abolition and Women's Rights. Her early essays on the important role of women in the early church became widely influential. African-American women abolitionists such as Sojourner Truth (1797–1883) and Harriet Tubman (1822–1913) wrote about the depra-vation and human suffering inflicted by slavery. Elizabeth Cady Stanton (1815–1902), another Quaker woman, joined forces with Susan B. Anthony (1820–1906) in Rochester, New York, to campaign for women's suffrage, the next major cause to arise following Abolition. Jane Addams (1860–1935), a proponent of progressivism and pragmatism, established Hull House in 1889, which provided open education to all.

In the latter part of the nineteenth century, two thinkers emerged who took up the cause of human dignity. John Ruskin (1819–1900) wrote movingly of the plight of the working person in his book *Unto This Last* (1860). Leo Tolstoy (1821–1910), who had been in correspondence with Quakers, published *The Kingdom of God Is Within You* in 1894 and supported Gandhi's employment of civil disobedience as a strategy to achieve change. Mahatma Gandhi (1869–1948), influenced deeply by Ruskin and Tolstoy, took on the next major progressive cause: the reversal of colo-nialism. Gandhi's life and work have been widely documented through his own extensive autobiography, newsreels, and the Richard Attenbor-ough movie, *Gandhi* (1982). Gandhi's most well-known successor, Vinoba Bhave, worked tirelessly to achieve land redistribution (*bhū-dāna*), having calculated that if each landowner surrendered just one-sixth of owned property, all farmers could become stakeholders in the newly indepen-dent India.

Emerson, Thoreau, Ruskin, Tolstoy, Addams, Gandhi, and Bhave hold in common a commitment to enact social change. The work of Jane Addams and other Christian reformers has been referred to as the Social Gospel Movement, a movement based on a religiously inspired desire to extend peace through the enactment of justice. For Gandhi, this motivation transcended faith boundaries. One of his most staunch supporters, Khan Abdul Ghaffar Khan (1890–1988), known as the Frontier Gandhi, worked against the partition of India despite his own allegiance to the Muslim faith. Gandhi drew liberally from his natal Vaiṣṇava faith, drawing inspiration daily from the last nineteen verses of the second chapter of the *Bhagavad Gītā*. He considered Rajchand Bhai, a Jaina layman, to be one of his great teachers. He took Kriyā Yoga initiation from Paramahamsa Yogananda and learned Yoga postures from Kuvalyananda. He also took inspiration from Christian teachers and activists such as Tolstoy (Howard 2013).

Gandhi's commitment to nonviolent passive resistance continues to inspire generations of activists. After the horrors of the Second World War and the toll to human life caused by the rise of totalitarianism in Russia and China and the Cold War, something of an agreement arose from the ashes of destruction. Eleanor Roosevelt (1886–1962), moved deeply by the sufferings she witnessed in her childhood and through both World Wars, chaired a drafting committee that issued the Declaration of Human Rights in 1948. The document relied heavily on the wisdom of an international team of philosophers and legal experts, including representatives from Lebanon, China, and India. Its preamble states that, 'recognition of the inherent dignity and of the equal and inalienable rights of all members of the human family is the foundation of freedom, justice, and peace in the world'. Many nonviolent activists and political leaders have drawn inspiration from this document, including Martin Luther King Jr, Cesar Chavez, and Jimmy Carter. Roosevelt, King, Chavez, and Carter all drew deeply from their respective religious faiths, working toward the earthly realization of a heavenly kingdom. It must be noted that Roosevelt's advisors included a contemporary Confucian, P. C. Chang, who employed the term 'dignity' as a rough translation of the Confucian term *ren* or 'human-heartedness'. Hansa Mehta, a social activist and reformist from India, insisted that Roosevelt strengthen the advocacy for women in the document (Glendon 2001).

Reverend James Lawson, a confidant of Martin Luther King Jr, who currently teaches at California State University in Northridge, traveled to India to learn techniques of nonviolent passive resistance from Gandhian organizers. The stretch of Gandhi's influence cannot be over-estimated. At the Parliament of the World's Religions convened in Capetown, South Africa in 1999, Nobel Prize winner Nelson Mandela, in a public address to the entire assembly, stated that faith gave him the courage and inspiration to endure more than two decades in his Robben Island prison. He cited his studies of Gandhi's beloved *Bhagavad Gītā* at the Hindu temple on the island, his studies of the Quran at the island's mosque, and the study of the Bible as being his lifeline to hope. Religion played a central role in his lifelong struggle against Apartheid. Hinduism, Islam, and Christianity taught Mandela how to abandon hatred and nonetheless speak truth to power.

Nonviolent Resistance Movements in the Twenty-first Century

The latter part of the twentieth century saw the rise of Liberation Theology in Latin America and a dawning awareness of looming threats posed to human wellbeing by climate change and species decimation. A new critique arose in the early twenty-first century known as the Occupy Movement, a largely anarchistic expression of outrage against the power of corporations to colonize the minds and bodies of human beings through advertising, un-needed goods and services. Amartya Sen (1933-) has written eloquently regarding the need for universal education not only in India but worldwide in order to counter ignorance and poverty. He writes: 'The smart boy or clever girl who is deprived of the opportunity of schooling...not only loses the opportunities he or she could have had, but also adds to [a] massive waste of talent' (Sen 2005: 344). In addition, Vandana Shiva (1952-) has worked tirelessly for wide-scale adoption of organic farming methods. She has written that:

> We have two choices: we can make a nature-centered, people-centered transition to a fossil fuel free future, with meaningful work and decent and dignified living for all; or we can continue on our current path toward a market-centered future, which will make the crisis deeper for the poor and the marginalized and provide a *temporary* escape for the privileged (Shiva 2008: 4).

Many issues coalesce in these various movements: concern for human suffering, for the suffering of animals, and for the suffering of the planetary climate system.

As individuals grow in conscious awareness of these complex issues, a sense of conscience arises. At the Parliament of the World's Religions in Cape Town, South Africa in 1999, Dada Vaswani (1918-) made the following observation: the eighteenth century brought the liberation of men. The nineteenth century saw the liberation of slaves. In the twentieth century many women gained liberation. The task of the twenty-first century will be liberation of animals and the earth.

Conclusion

In summary, the world's religions have been deeply implicated in both the creation and amelioration of violence. Throughout various periods of history in cultures around the globe, contention over religious beliefs has spawned conflict and war. Yet, a message of peace can be found at the core of many religions. Generally, strife cannot be separated from a complex array of historical, sociological, economic, and political factors; religion in isolation does not foment war. Remarkable leaders in religious communities, such as Martin Luther King Jr, cleaving to the precept of peace found in nearly all faiths, have advocated successfully for the development, enactment, and realization of a blessed community in which the higher values of harmony may prevail.

About the Author

Christopher Key Chapple, PhD, is the Doshi Professor of Indic and Comparative Theology and Director of the Master of Arts in Yoga Studies at Loyola Marymount University. A specialist in the Religions of India, he has published more than fifteen books on Yoga, Jainism, and Buddhism as well as on Asian religions and ecology. He edits the journal *Worldviews: Global Religions, Culture, and Ecology*.

Notes

1. Jain Vegans (n.d.), at http://www.jainvegans.org/why-vegan.

Chapter 2

The Gandhian Vision of Democracy*

Ramin Jahanbegloo

Gandhian nonviolence has captured the attention of many civic actors and democratic theorists around the world for more than half a century. Yet, the Gandhian vision of democracy is still missing tragically in most of the world's debates on democratic theory. But it is time for comparative and inter-cultural democratic theory to open up to the Gandhian legacy of democratic thought and ask questions about its relevance for our political world that is suffering from a crisis of democratic passion and democratic leadership. How does Gandhi understand democracy? In which way does his alternative model of democracy differ from the well-known liberal view of representative democracy? Could he provide us today with an original response to the shortcomings of neo-liberalism in our world? All these questions need to be discussed in relation to Gandhi's admiration for what can be called the integral democracy and his critique of its liberal weaknesses in the West. In Gandhi's integral democracy, there would be no representative government, no capitalist greed, and certainly no social or political hierarchy. In many ways, Gandhi's advocacy of citizenship duty and his insistence on ethical renewal of democracy in terms of character building (people leadership) and enlightened citizenship (democratic passion) are first and foremost responses to what he took to be certain enduring tensions between spirituality and politics, and individual and state in Western liberal political life.

Jawaharlal Nehru, India's first prime minister and a companion of Gandhi in India's movement for independence, reminds us that Gandhi was vague in his theory of state and government (Nehru 1941: 76). However, some recent scholars on Mahatma Gandhi's political thought place him firmly within the liberal camp (Chandrasekaran 2011). There are good reasons for this: Gandhi's nonviolence embodies more famously than any other political theory the spirit of freedom and democratic individualism that seems to underpin modern liberalism. However, Gandhi's insistence on ethical commitment in citizen politics, his critique of representative democracy, and his practice of civil disobedience against unjust laws do not portray him as a typical liberal thinker.

Modern liberal thought has been primarily considered as an economic sphere based on the play of *laissez-faire* and a political sphere founded on the idea of individual freedom and the separation of the private and the public. However, for Gandhi, an individual is not considered as a rational economic agent with particular wants and rights. Quite the contrary, Gandhi insists on the duties of individuals as *moral* agents rather than *free* agents pursuing their self-interests. Thus, the Gandhian conception of social and political life is directly opposed to the social, political, and economic structures of the liberal thought. Consequently, Gandhi maintains democracy as a form of shared sovereignty rather than a political institution in which people play a minimum role through representation and election. As such, Gandhi advocates democracy as a form of self-instituted society in which ethics is a crucial yardstick for management. As a supporter of the Indian civilization and a critic of modern Western society, Gandhi offers us a model of ethical politics that is relatively rare in both Western and Eastern traditions of thought. Unlike Tagore, Coomaraswamy, and Aurobindo, who schooled in the speculative metaphysics of the Indian gnostic tradition, Gandhi finds a balance between ethics, politics, and spirituality and applies his moral standards of nonviolence and truth to all spheres of life. Therefore, the transformative dynamic of Gandhi's philosophy of nonviolence provides a way for him to develop the idea of democracy from being a solely political problem to being essentially a potential ethical solution to the problems of injustice and inequality.

Democracy as an Ethical Solution

Cherishing the dual role of a political thinker and a civic activist, Gandhi believes that it is indeed possible to reconcile his philosophy of nonviolence with the effective pursuit of what he called an enlightened democracy. Moreover, he develops his vision of a nonviolent democracy that represents the necessary condition of a responsible and truthful society. In other words, Gandhi argues that the path of democratic governance can be achieved without putting aside the ethical imperatives of nonviolence. The task before Gandhi is therefore clear. According to him, Indian democracy, if it has to have moral authority, cannot be based on violence and exclusivism. 'Democracy and violence can ill go together', says Gandhi (1960a: 188). Furthermore,

> The states that are today nominally democratic have either to become frankly totalitarian or if they are to become truly democratic, they must become courageously nonviolent. It is a blasphemy to say that nonviolence can only be practiced by individuals and never by nations which are composed of individuals. (Gandhi 1960a: 188)

This key statement contains Gandhi's own standards for the successful resolution of his synthesis between the inclusive principles of nonviolence and the practical realization of an integral democracy. The spirit behind Gandhi's integral democracy and its translatability into pluralistic and pragmatic politics is the individualistic, deceptive, and self-destructive tendencies of modernity and liberal thought. This is well reflected in his first written book, *Hind Swaraj*, published in 1909, while he was still active as a lawyer and a civil activist in South Africa. We can consider *Hind Swaraj* as the philosophical foundation of Gandhi's thinking and doing, but also a severe critique of the exclusive and unethical nature of modern civilization. To quote Gandhi, 'This civilization takes note neither of morality, nor of religion... Civilization seeks to increase bodily comforts' (1997: 37). Gandhi goes on to point out that true civilization should be defined in terms of good conduct and path of duty. He writes: 'Civilization is that mode of conduct which points out to man the path of duty' (1997: 67).

As we can see, Gandhi does not criticize modern civilization because it is Western or liberal, but because it is exploitative and exclusionary. Therefore, for Gandhi, in contradistinction to modern liberal civilization, true civilization goes hand in hand with true self-rule (*swaraj*). Feeding on spiritual and cultural elements of India's ancient civilization, Gandhi develops in *Hind Swaraj* his model of Indian nationhood and what later becomes his conception of an inclusive and participative democracy by referring to the idea of self-sufficient village communities and principles of solidaristic citizenship. As such, while Gandhi agrees with liberals in the appreciation of civil liberties, he differs from their acceptance of the Western superiority of modern liberalism. Therefore, Gandhi condemns the dark side of English liberal rule (i.e., colonialism) as the reverse of his conception of democratic rule. In other words, Gandhi's conception of democratic rule does not correspond necessarily with the overthrowing of the British rule. For Gandhi, the problem is not only British rule, but also the liberal spirit in the name of which Western civilization pretends to dominate Indian culture and society. Lord Bhikhu Parekh is a scholar who has gone into a detailed investigation of Gandhi's critique of the liberal state. His basic argument is:

> Gandhi was convinced that the 'rule' of British *civilisation* could continue even if the British government were to stop ruling over India and British *capital* to cease exploiting it. British imperialism was unacceptable not only because of its political and even economic but moral and cultural consequences. (Parekh 1989: 18)

Gandhi's critique of modern liberalism includes not only the lack of moral legitimacy of economic and political domination of India, but also integrates a critique of a culture of passivity and conformity among

Indians who submit to the materialist and body-centred view of the West. In general terms, we can say that Gandhi focuses his attention on the spiritual content of civilization motivated by an operative method to conceive ethical and legal obligations as universal for all human beings. It is true that Gandhi's spiritual vision of human civilization alienates him from liberal society—a society whose complexity he is incapable of grasping. He nevertheless appropriates the theoretical achievements of modern liberalism but rejects as incomplete the very political institutions that generate and sustain it. That is why Gandhi tries to persuade his fellow Indians to concentrate their energies on the resurgence of traditional Indian values. In this relation, one needs to point out that Gandhi rarely uses nationalist language to talk about Indianness. His support of Indianness has 'nothing in common with the ethnic or even cultural nationalism of Tilak and Aurobindo, let alone such Hindu fundamentalists as Savarkar' (Parekh 1989: 194).

Moreover, the debate between Gandhi and Western liberal civilization is completed by his disavowing of the views of those Indians who, in the words of Sunil Khilnani, either 'chose to devise an ostentatiously "traditional" self, [or] declared for a more stridently Western or modern one' (1997: 8). Gandhi's entire democratic theory can therefore be understood as formulated around his commitment to an authentic expression of ethical politics and spiritual Indianness. However, 'Gandhi always rejected the extremism of Hindu orthodoxy, but he too, was tremendously attracted to the notion that timeless truth resided in an ancient Indian civilization and its spiritual wisdom' (Steger 2000: 95). When one reads *Hind Swaraj*, one is explicitly and permanently referred to the idea of India's moral superiority exemplified by the two concepts of *kama* (avoidance of pain) and *artha* (power) as 'the proper objects of the active life' (Gandhi 1960a: xlix). It is in the context of the Indian mode of life and the traditional wisdom of his ancestors that Gandhi takes a critical view of representative democracy. More importantly, he opposes the idea of the uniqueness and centrality of village governance (the Panchayat Raj) to that of a representative government and a centralized state. That is why the Gandhian view of democracy goes hand in hand with the idea of a minimal state. At the same time, he is aware of the fact that the democratic spirit can be restored in the shadow of a centralized power.

Critiquing Governmentality

This discussion of Gandhi's conception of democracy brings forth the need to reinterpret Gandhi's critique of governmentality in the shadow of his reform of modern political theory in general. Gandhi is highly critical of Western thinkers such as Hobbes and Rousseau who see a close relationship between violence and social order. Unlike Hobbes, for whom authority is a modern means of political legitimation, Gandhi criticizes the entire liberal approach to human governance by replacing the basic Hobbesian impulse of self-preservation with the idea of self-sacrifice. This makes Gandhi reject the principle of modern statehood and search for moral foundations of power. Gandhi's concept of governance is, therefore, that which governs the least. Gandhi liked to quote from Henry David Thoreau's famous essay on *Civil Disobedience*, that 'government is best that governs least, or not at all' (in Owen 1966: 224). Like Thoreau, Gandhi believes that the spirit of democracy is at odds with liberal governance because liberal institutions can produce laws that violate democratic principles. Thus, Gandhi does not recognize the moral authority of liberal unjust laws, although he accepts the fact that they are liberal. He therefore rejects the Hobbesian idea of commonwealth and the Rousseauist concept of general will that both tend to create an indivisible political community to which all are equally subject. Under the terms of Gandhian politics, authority and sovereignty are not derived from the law of preservation or that which involves a loss of liberty, because the state has no instrumental value in the making of the collective political entity. For Gandhi the only way to attain the ideal of democracy is through a self-sufficient and self-reliant community that he enunciates as village *swaraj*. As he says:

> My idea of village *swaraj* is that it is a complete republic, independent of its neighbors for its own vital wants, and yet interdependent for many others in which dependence is a necessity. Thus every village's first concern will be to grow its own food crops and cotton for its cloth... As far as possible every activity will be conducted on the co-operative basis. There will be no castes such as we have today with their graded untouchability. Nonviolence with its technique of satyagraha and non-co-operation will be the sanction of the village community... The government of the village will be conducted by the *Panchayat* of five persons annually elected by the adult villagers, male and female, possessing minimum prescribed qualifications... Since there will be no system of punishment in the accepted sense, this *Panchayat* will be the legislature, judiciary and executive combined to operate for its year of office... Here is the perfect democracy based upon individual freedom. The individual is the architect of his own government. The law of nonviolence rules him and his government. (Gandhi 1963: 31-32)

Thus we can see, on the basis of his decentralized approach to the question of politics and power, Gandhi's democratic theory tries to bring the old system of village life in tune with the democratic value of self-government. Gandhi sees the necessity to cultivate *internal* self-government in order to reduce the *external* form of sovereignty and governmentality. This brings him to reverse the pyramid of authority and power in a way that the pursuit of individual rights follows transformative self-rule. For Gandhi, then, democracy is primarily *swaraj*, the rule over oneself. As we can see, unlike many of his contemporary political and spiritual thinkers in India, such as Tagore, Aurobindo, and Nehru, Gandhi sets forth a theory of democracy that is related to a theory of the self. The recurrent theme in his theory of democracy is self-realization, self-restraint, and self-discipline. In other words, for Gandhi, democracy cannot exist without an enlightened and self-conscious citizenship. Gandhi views 'democracy disciplined and enlightened (as) the finest thing in the world', but he adds: 'A democracy prejudiced, ignorant, superstitious will land itself in chaos and be self-destroyed' ([1931] 2009: 106, vol. 75). If this is the case, then we can say that from Gandhi's point of view, democracy is *autonomy* as opposed to *heteronomy*. As Gandhi affirms: 'It is *swaraj* when we learn to rule ourselves' (1997: 73). But for Gandhi, this self-rule is also a *shared* sovereignty (i.e., a capacity of self-governing with others). According to him, only such a self-governing community can protect individual freedom and regulate economic life and social relations based on justice. Thus for Gandhi, democracy constitutes the interplay between multiple liberties and multiple interests based on shared ethical values. This becomes all the more obvious in Gandhi's effort to transcend the dichotomy between private interests and public common good. This he does by enunciating a very novel idea of what he calls 'spiritualization of politics'.[1]

It would be wrong to think, as some might say, that the introduction by Gandhi of spirituality into politics could violate the true nature of politics. This is so perhaps because for Gandhi, politics does not arise from competition among political parties, but it is, on the contrary, the outcome of collaboration among citizens. In other words, politics is the pursuit of freedom through a conscious self-transforming act. This self-transforming act must be executed for the benefit of others and not in the sense of enclosing the self within ramparts of self-interest. As Gandhi says, 'Action leads to bondage unless it is performed in a spirit of sacrifice. Sacrifice (*yajna*) means exerting oneself for the benefit of others, in a word, service. And when service is rendered for service's sake, there is no room for attachment, likes and dislikes' (1960b: 13). For Gandhi, therefore, politics is based on the internalization of the otherness of the Other, which finds expression in and is supported by the self-institution of democracy. The vitality of this self-institution depends on a meaningful relationship between individuals and institutions. According to Gandhi:

> A dynamic democracy can grow only out of meaningful relationships and spontaneous organization that spring among people, when they come together at the local level to solve their basic problems by cooperation among themselves. In such a community achievement of self-sufficiency

and security by neighbourly cooperation engenders a strong sense of local strength and solidarity, and the individual's sense of responsibility to community and concern for its welfare are at their highest. (in Nayyar 1958: 581, vol. 2)

We should note the emphasis that Gandhi puts on the two concepts of solidarity and responsibility. This is important because Gandhi challenges the idea of an externally imposed law. His conception of democracy is, thus, based on a process of self-government followed by a plea against centralization and the pyramidal principle of politics. Gandhi opts instead for a political principle that highlights the moulding of structures that put an end to the split between civil society and political order. In this perspective, the Gandhian vision of democracy is also characterized by the inseparability of the private and the public and the self-transformation of the former in favour of the latter. In the Gandhian perspective of democratic governance, there is a close correlation between the private and the public. As stated earlier, Mahatma Gandhi's vision of democratic rule of the people is possible only if it is ensured by the way of *gram swarajya* (the management of the affairs by the people themselves). That is why Gandhi suggests, 'The spirit of democracy requires the inculcation of the spirit of brotherhood' (2009: 84, vol.19). And he adds, 'democracy has to be built up inch by inch in economic, social and political life' (2009: 77, vol. 89). Furthermore, Gandhi insists on the moral purpose of democracy as an art of developing the sense of mobilization and disobedience to unjust laws among the people. Gandhi's original contribution is his addition of the ethical conception of nonviolent disobedience of the law, which has been overlooked in liberalism.

Moral Obligation and Civic Duty

From a Gandhian perspective, one of the shortcomings of liberal theory of democracy is its inability to incorporate the two dimensions of civil disobedience and nonviolent action within a comprehensive model of shared sovereignty that will not be completely subordinated to formal requirements of an idealized concept of right. As such, the axiomatic idea that informs Gandhi's conception of civil disobedience is that of a radical response to the liberal separation of political and moral obligation. By pointing out that such a separation undermines disastrously the concept of individual duty and responsibility, Gandhi rejects rights-oriented liberalism as an insufficient theory of democracy and refuses to give individual rights a central role in our understanding of moral and political life. Gandhi's principal problem with liberal democracy is its separation of rights and duties. According to him, by separating the 'ought' from the 'is,' politics loses its moral focus. In other words, from Gandhi's point of view, rights are dependent on duties. Therefore, in order to claim their rights, citizens need to fulfill their duties to themselves and others. For Gandhi, the notion of duty comes before that of rights, which is subordinate to the former. That is to say, a right is not effective by itself, but only in relation to the duty to which it corresponds. The effective exercise of a right springs not from the individual who possesses it, but from her or his responsibility toward others. According to Gandhi, a right is recognized through the sense of duty toward others. As such, a right that is separate from a duty is not worth very much. The *performance* appears, therefore, in Gandhi's eyes as a requirement for a comprehensive conception of rights. 'Every man has an equal right to the necessaries of life even as birds and beasts have', writes Gandhi in *Young India* on March 26, 1931 (2009: 106, vol. 75). Moreover,

> [S]ince every right carries with it a corresponding duty and a corresponding remedy for resisting any attack upon it, it is merely a matter of finding out the corresponding duties and remedies to vindicate the elementary fundamental equality. The corresponding duty is to labour with my limbs and the corresponding remedy is to non-cooperate with him who deprives me of the fruit of my labour. (Mark Lindley in Darshan 2006: 2)

Predictably, the application of the principle of duty by Gandhi to the social, economic, and political spheres brings him into sharp conflict with the traditional defenders of the liberal notion of rights and the notion that we are free and independent selves, undetermined by prior moral ties. Gandhi tries to secure rights in relation with the concept of *dharma* as social duty. As Anthony Parel suggests:

> There is a strong element of realism in Gandhi's philosophy of dharma as duty... It recognizes the fact that history in significant part involves a struggle between duty and interest. The chances of duty gaining ascendancy over interest depend on virtue. Modern society, by contrast, has placed its bets on rights rather than on virtue, which to Gandhi was a matter of deep concern. He wanted modern society to place equal emphasis on rights, duties and virtue. (Parel 2006: 98)

Therefore, Gandhi's severe critique of the modern state brings him to notify us of the imperative relationship between the individual and the community in the sharing of moral and political responsibilities. It is in this sense that the Gandhian vision of democracy secures individual rights within the limits of practice of soul-force and not brute force. In other words, for Gandhi, to be democratic is to be truthful to nonviolence but at the same time assuming one's duty to protect rights in relation to an original moral experience. Gandhi's insight is that good governance is the right balance between a minimum democratic state and a vibrant society of citizens. He affirms:

> I admit that there are certain things which cannot be done without political power, but there are numerous other things which do not at all depend upon political power... This means that when people come into possession of political power, the interference with the freedom of the people is reduced to a minimum. In other words, a nation that runs its affairs smoothly and effectively without much State interference is truly democratic. Where such condition is absent, the form of government is democratic in name. (Gandhi 2009: 92, vol. 62)

Certainly, this might bring to mind the arguments of some of the European anarchists like Bakunin, Proudhon, and Tolstoy. However, Gandhi gave little value to the violent thoughts of Bakunin and Proudhon, and although he was directly influenced by the spiritual thoughts of Tolstoy, he was more of a political theorist than was Tolstoy and thought pragmatically in terms of decentralized local polities in India. His use of the word 'anarchy' is directly related to his understanding of Thoreau's argument on minimal government. Writing in 1939, Gandhi calls this approach 'enlightened anarchy'. He says:

> Political power, in my opinion, cannot be our ultimate aim. It is one of the means used by men for their all-round advancement. The power to control national life through national representatives is called political power. Representatives will become unnecessary if the national life becomes so perfect as to be self-controlled. It will then be a state of enlightened anarchy in which each person will become his own ruler. He will conduct himself in such a way that his behavior will not hamper the well-being of his neighbours. In an ideal State there will be no political institution and therefore no political power. That is why Thoreau has said in his classic statement that that government is the best which governs the least. (Gandhi [1939] 2009: 340, vol. 48)

This exposition suggests that in Gandhi's ideal of democracy many of his core beliefs and arguments came together, such as moral growth of the individual, the primacy of the spiritual in nonviolent action, and the interdependence of all departments of life. But how did Gandhi expect these principles to work in everyday life? Gandhi had come to the conclusion that democracy, like any other aspect of social and political life, would not function in the framework of a meaningless civilization with no sense of ethics and spirituality. By 'spirituality', Gandhi understands freedom from illusion, possessiveness, and prejudice. But he also approaches the spiritual in life as the unity of all being. Spirituality, therefore, is a necessary condition for *swaraj*, self-discipline, and social responsibility. This is the point at which the personal and the political join each other in Gandhi's theory of democracy. '*Swaraj* of a people', says Gandhi, 'means the sum total of the *swaraj* (self-rule) of individuals. And such *swaraj* comes only from performance by individuals of their duty as citizens. In it no one thinks of his rights. They come, when they are needed, for better performance of duty' ([1939] 2009: 340, vol. 48). Thus, for Gandhi, democracy is the best expression of self-government as a form of civic awareness. He argues his case in these terms:

> Self-government depends entirely upon our internal strength, upon our ability to fight against the heaviest odds. Indeed, self-government which does not require that continuous striving to attain it and to sustain it is not worth the name. I have therefore endeavoured to show both in word and in deed, that, political self-government, that is, self-government for a large number of men and women, is no better than individual self-government, and therefore it is to be attained by precisely the same means that are required for individual self-government or self-rule. (Gandhi [1927] 2009)

As we can see, for Gandhi, the only way to sustain and reform the democratic order is through civic practices. However, in order to enlarge the work of the public sphere while narrowing down the individualistic and hedonistic inclinations of the individual in the private realm, Gandhi suggests redefining the concept of citizenship by the virtue of the duty of the citizens and their participation in the political community. For him, this experience of redefinition of the citizen as a duty-oriented citizen is a better way to defend the rights of the individual, while rectifying the unequal balance of power in a democracy between the political elite and the weaker social groups and minorities. In other words, Gandhi's idea of democracy is understood as a means to fulfil one's civic duty as an individual participating in a community, and as an end to be attained through nonviolent resistance to all forms of centralization of power.

Gandhi and Western Democratic Theory

It is with regard to Gandhi's suggested redefinition of citizenship that his conception of democracy becomes relevant and significant to contemporary democratic theory. However, many Western democratic theorists still see no need to read Gandhi. Despite the increasing concern with the study of non-Western traditions of contemporary democratic theory, the political philosophy of Mahatma Gandhi remains largely unknown in the Anglo-American world. Needless to say, Gandhi's approach to politics in terms of resistance and protest beyond a conception of domination over others provides a potential antidote to the contemporary crisis of democracy. With this in mind, Gandhi can be said to be oriented towards reinventing politics as a capacity for self-realization and self-transformation of the society. The democratic process of society is in this sense conceived as a process of self-rule in which community is a result of an ethical effort to limit and to surpass violence. The tension between the liberal concept of private liberties—in the manner of a thinker such as Benjamin Constant, who formulates it as the sphere of private life—and the public sphere of civic citizenship within the concept of self-rule has significant implications for contemporary democratic practice, but has been neglected in democratic theory.[2] Democratic theorists have yet to explore thoroughly the distinction between the rule of the private over the self, and the rule of the citizen as a member of the collective over itself. Here the Gandhian matrix of civic nonviolence exemplified by the idea of *swaraj* allows us to probe more deeply into an understanding and practice of democracy as self-rule. The concept of self-rule as presented in the works of Mahatma Gandhi offers the possibility of expressing the core aims of an integral democratic politics in a manner divorced from neo-Marxist or liberal theories of democracy. For Gandhi, democracy is an unfinished project by its very nature, and remains an unfinished project whatever the degree of its realization. This is because, from his point of view, no realization of democratic rule will be perfect. In addition, he sees democracy as essentially a process: to be democratic is to be engaged in a process of democratization. Might one nevertheless say that a Gandhian vision of democracy requires the instauration of a civic culture that recognizes the importance and value of self-discipline and responsibility? Yes, certainly. And must this dimension of self-discipline and responsibility be paramount? Must it in the last instance take precedence over the private sphere of the individual? The answer to this question is not so certain, yet from Gandhi's point of view such questions are the very ones that an integral and constructive democracy must grapple with. As Gandhi puts it, 'Democracy disciplined and enlightened is the finest thing in the world. A democracy prejudiced, ignorant, superstitious will land itself in chaos and may be self-destroyed' (1960a: 188).

About the Author

Ramin Jahanbegloo, PhD, is Professor and Vice-Dean at the School of Law and Director at the Mahatma Gandhi Centre for Peace Studies, Jindal Global University, India. He is an Iranian-Canadian philosopher who has taught at the University of Toronto and York University, and has been a Noor-York Visiting Chair in Islamic Studies at York University, Toronto. He is the author of more than 24 books in Persian, English, and French on philosophy, comparative politics, and nonviolence. His most recent works are *Introduction to Nonviolence* (2014) and his autobiography, *Time Will Say Nothing* (2014).

Notes

* This chapter was originally published as an article entitled 'Can Politics Be Spiritualized' in the *Journal of Democratic Theory* (1963): 325-32. Online (2014), at http://www.unipune.ac.in/snc/cssh/ipq/english/IPQ/6-10%20volumes/06%2002/PDF/6-2-14.pdf.

1. Jahanbegloo (2014), at http://www.unipune.ac.in/snc/cssh/ipq/english/IPQ/ 6-10%20volumes/06%2002/PDF/6-2-14.pdf.

2. Constant (2015), at http://www.earlymoderntexts.com/assets/pdfs/constant18 19.pdf.

Chapter 3

Power Perfected in Weakness:
The Paradox of Fighting for Peace*

Alain Tschudin

> [I]n order to keep me from becoming conceited, I was given a thorn in my flesh...to torment me... I pleaded with the Lord to take it away from me. But he said to me, 'My grace is sufficient for you, for my power is made perfect in weakness'. Therefore, I will boast all the more gladly about my weaknesses... That is why, for Christ's sake, I delight in weaknesses, in insults, in hardships, in persecutions, in difficulties. For when I am weak, then I am strong. (Cor. 12:7-10)

Introduction**

I feel it only appropriate to issue some disclaimers at the outset of this chapter. Although we shall be engaging some of the most famous involved in the nonviolence movement, they are all men; the absence of women is deplorable given that women actively form the backbone of the struggle for nonviolence, peace, and liberation in South Africa and around the world. Albert Luthuli, winner of the Nobel Peace Prize in 1961, recognized this when he dedicated his autobiography to his mother and to his wife, as follows:

> To Mother Africa, so long in fetters;
> To all who love her and strive to set her free;
> And to two noble women of Africa;
> Mtonya, my late mother, and Nokukhanya, my wife,
> To whom, under God, I am most deeply indebted. (Luthuli 1962: 5)

The recognition that needs to be afforded to women is crucial. The gender imbalance of the patriarchal, official leadership of the nonviolence movement is an undeniable historical fact but is, thankfully, currently in transformation.

The second disclaimer is that because the topics of nonviolence, spirituality, and social transformation are monumental, it is simply not possible to cover all the bases when discussing them. Mindful of my own limitations, I shall claim no specific expertise as an authority, either on Mahatma Gandhi or on nonviolence. I coordinate a conflict transformation and peace studies programme; my own areas of academic specialization are psychology and anthropology on the one hand, and moral philosophy and theology on the other; my research is on self-other relations with street traders, refugees, and marginalized peoples. Cognisant of the current complexity, my focus is on particular intersections between nonviolence, spirituality, and social transformation in the South African context.

I take my cue from Luthuli:

> If I have anything to say, it is not because of any particular distinction, but because I am identified with those who love South Africa, and will resist with them the attempt to smash a noble land with base and ignoble doctrines, and sub-human practices. (Luthuli 1962:15)

I am South African, and if what Luthuli said of the South Africa of the 1960s was true then, as it most certainly was, it is all the more applicable to those of us who identify with and love humanity in our contemporary world: we who identify with the poor, marginalized, and oppressed and who wish to resist and overcome the ideologies and practices of the manifold violence that debase our shared human dignity. Within our global humanity, however, there is something unique about South Africa: our fledgling democracy. In the following, reference is made to Mahatma Gandhi, Albert Luthuli, and Nelson Mandela: all icons of peace who cut their nonviolence teeth in the 'rainbow' nation.

South Africa:
Where 'African' Particularism and Global Nonviolence Meet

Max du Preez, acclaimed political analyst and journalist, writes in the foreword to Wendy Orr's memoir of the Truth and Reconciliation Commission (TRC):

> I regard myself as very fortunate to have lived as a South African in the second half of the twentieth century. Where else could one have experienced all the basic human frailties and strengths on such a grand-scale? Our despair was as dark as a moonless Karoo night, our hatred as fierce as a runaway veld fire, our evil like staring directly into the eyes of a hissing cobra. But that made our hope so much sweeter, our love so much more intense, our good so much more pure. For every Verwoerd, we had a Luthuli. For every Vorster we had a Sisulu. For every Botha we had a Tambo. And as a bonus the Creator gave us a Tutu and a Mandela. (du Preez in Orr 2000: i)

Three of the above protagonists, Albert Luthuli, Desmond Tutu, and Nelson Mandela, were Nobel Prize winners for their pursuit of peace.

South Africa truly represents a context in which the very best and the very worst of humanity come into contact with each other. Given its historical timeline of both black and white conquest, South Africa represents a site of struggle and a locus of violence, colonization, and imperialism that implicates anyone and everyone from local tribes, to the Portuguese and Dutch precursors, to the later land expansion and dominance of the British and Boer settlers. This inescapable reality leads Alfred Wierzbicki to comment, 'Already at the time of *satyagraha* [soul force] in South Africa (1906–1914), we find manifest all the spiritual elements of Gandhian nonviolence: truth, love and what Gandhi termed self-suffering' (1992: 211).

One might ask what it is about 'African particularism', as Mahmood Mamdani (1996) terms it, that distinguishes our context from the rest of the world. Despite our gains in South Africa, we remain painfully aware of our unresolved issues: abuse of power, corruption and mismanagement, lack of service delivery, police brutality, poverty, and unemployment. In one time zone to our east, one of my close friends and humanitarian colleagues accompanied a convoy of 1,300 Muslims fleeing the violence of Anti-Balaka rebels in the Central African Republic where Christians have been implicated in atrocities. The convoy was attacked three times, several people were injured, and two died. Amidst this violence, five births were recorded. The miracle of life continues to enter the world amidst a culture of death. One time zone to our west, Boko Haram continues to terrorise the Christian and moderate Muslim populations of Nigeria.

Despite the immense suffering and death that our continent has witnessed, or perhaps precisely because of the resilience that is required to survive, Africa continues to offer something to the world. Achille Mbembe recalls the words of Stephen Biko, the leader of the Black Consciousness Movement in South Africa, slain by apartheid police, who prophesied that a 'great gift' would come from Africa: 'The great powers of the world may have done wonders in giving the world an industrial and military look, but the great gift still has to come from Africa—giving the world a more human face' (Mbembe 2007: 148).

Notwithstanding the euphoria experienced regarding this 'rainbow' nation and the iconic stature of our first democratically elected president, Mandela, we South Africans have our issues. The Long Walk to Freedom is far from being over. South Africa, albeit having passed through the window of a *transitional* democracy, is not yet a *consolidated* democracy. This actuality arises on account of an elite and popular divide, within which the vast majority of citizens have yet to benefit meaningfully from the social and economic emancipation intended to follow from political liberation. In this regard, Xolela Mangcu reiterates Frantz Fanon's caution over the 'post-colonial elite', stating that, 'in place of a public philosophy of community building, South Africans live under a cult of leadership that exemplifies and inspires self-interest' (Mangcu 2014: 287).

I shall argue that the struggle, as we popularly termed the movement for liberation during the apartheid era, is not yet over. Yet, how do we reconcile the justice- and peace-related challenges confronting us in the face of ongoing violence at a multiplicity of levels and in a plethora of diverse forms? Is the notion of fighting for peace truly a paradox? Let us dive in and see.

Historical Roots: Mahatma Gandhi and *Satyagraha*

Archbishop Desmond Tutu, Nobel Peace Prize winner, comments as follows:

> We South Africans boast that we have a rather substantial share in the great soul—the Mahatma, whose philosophy, life and actions have inspired us greatly... [W]ithin 10 days of his arriving in our beautiful South Africa... he suffered the humiliation of being ejected from a first class compartment of the train in which he was travelling, despite possessing a valid ticket... [H]e later himself described that particular event as the most creative experience of his life for it opened his eyes to the plight of Indians in South Africa and led him to evolve his *Satyagraha*—adherence to truth through non-violent action. (Tutu 2007: 44)

Given the profound effect that his time in South Africa exercised on Gandhi, we need some elaboration. In his autobiography, Gandhi signals his first encounter with violence in South Africa and his being ejected on account of his being of 'colour'. His response was to refuse to leave voluntarily (2001: 114). The harassment did not end there. Gandhi was again victimized on the coach from Charlestown to Johannesburg and assaulted. He recalls, 'He was strong and I was weak. Some of the passengers were moved to pity and exclaimed: "Man, let him alone. Don't beat him. He is not to blame. He is right. If he can't stay there, let him come and sit with us"' (Gandhi 2001: 116). It is here that the tension between physical weakness and moral strength is first articulated.

Suffice it to suggest that in his own words, Gandhi believed the racial prejudice to be 'only temporary and local' (2001: 166). His subsequent life experience was to prove otherwise. It is thus necessary for us to explore his *satyagraha* in greater detail. Gandhi notes that passive resistance is too limited to explain and as being 'too narrowly construed [and] supposed to be a weapon of the weak', but one that 'could be characterized by hatred... and could finally manifest itself as violence' (2001: 291). Rather, *satyagraha* may be defined as *satya* (or 'truth', which implies love) and *agraha* ('firmness', which implies force); hence it is 'the force which is born of truth and love or non-violence' (Wierzbicki 1992: 208).

Wierzbicki suggests that underpinning *sat* as 'being, reality' is the foundation of truth (1992: 237), and within this conception, 'Love is the process of becoming one with all men, with all being unto total identification with Truth or God' (1992: 245). Read this way, *ahimsa* is synonymous with love. Anthony De Luca identifies the 'close alignment' to self-discipline and self-denial of:

> the practice of *ahimsa*, which stressed nonviolence and the force of love in human relations. As the architect of a new political message, Gandhi was the first to extend the doctrine of nonviolence to the level of human and social relations. For Gandhi, *ahimsa* and truth were inextricably intertwined, with nonviolence serving as the means and truth as the end. (de Luca 2000: 16-17)

Ahimsa, for Gandhi, has multiple sources: the Hindu scriptures, the *Baghavad-Gita* and the *Upanishads*; the New Testament—Sermon on the Mount; and Western writers such as Thoreau, Ruskin, and Tolstoy. Three key figures embody the 'most perfect realization of nonviolence' for Gandhi: Buddha (reform of Hinduism), Socrates (one of the first *satyagrahi*), and Jesus (who lived a life of perfectly embodied *satyagraha*) (Wierzbicki 1992: 224).

The Importance of *Ahimsa*

Monier Monier-Williams provides a cursory definition of *ahimsa* in his Sanskrit-English Dictionary as 'not injuring anything, harmlessness, security, safeness, devoted to harmlessness or gentleness' (1899: 125). However, this does not convey the richness of the term and neglects its etymological significance.

Sadly, in contemporary times, *ahimsa* has been further detached from its roots and misappropriated by so-called 'New Age' proponents. Consider Nathaniel Altman, whose book, *The Nonviolent Revolution: A Comprehensive Guide to Ahimsa—the Philosophy of Dynamic Harmlessness* (1988), was inspired by 'seeing a magnificent sunset' in Bolivia. Whilst on a drive through Canada, he 'turned off the radio and began to day-dream', writing that, 'I soon found myself thinking what philosophers call "deep thoughts" and asked myself what I would do if I had one or two years to live' (Altman 1988: ix). And then the epiphany, 'the *ahimsa* book', had to be addressed as a '"top priority", even if incomplete' (Altman 1988: x).

To avoid doing further violence to the notion of *ahimsa* and in order to grasp this central concept in Gandhi's practice appropriately, it is necessary to turn to its ancient roots to unpack its evolutionary trajectory. Unto Taehtinen, in his comprehensive study on *ahimsa*, identifies six 'comprehensive philosophies' of nonviolence in Indian thought—Jainism, Buddhism, Vedic in the Vedas, the Dharmasastras and the Puranas in ancient literature, and Gandhi's philosophy of nonviolence (1976: xii). He points out early on that it is 'wrongly assumed *ahimsa* means non-killing; rather *hims* refers to physical injury which in extreme cases might result in death' (Taehtinen 1976: 1-2).

Taehtinen recognizes that in its popular meaning, *himsa* referred to the killing of a living being, *ahimsa* to the non-killing a living being. In Jainism *ahimsa* referred to not killing mobile beings, whilst the Vedic conception of *himsa* connoted cutting down trees or destroying properties of another (Taehtinen 1976: 3). It was an action requiring compensation, an injury to other harmless beings for the sake of one's own pleasure, or simply hurting innocent beings. Importantly, it also means 'to speak ill', as demonstrated by the proverb 'he killed her by his words'. *Himsa* can also mean 'doing against' the wishes of parents and teachers; unjust levying of taxes does injury; and physically, mentally, or vocally going against Vedic injunctions (Taehtinen 1976: 4). The Vedic reading of *ahimsa*, as per the *Chhandogya Upanisad*, suggests that 'he who practises *ahimsa* towards all creatures, except at holy places, does not return to the world again' (Taehtinen 1976: 4). In Sanskrit, *ahimsa* connotes, 'abstention from causing pain to others by speech, mind, body; relieving living beings from pain and refraining from causing pain to a living being' (Taehtinen 1976: 6). For the ascetics, *himsa* was regarded as 'hurting of life-principles due to passionate activity, any injury to material or conscious vitalities of life through passionate activity' unless it dispassionately 'follows code of right conduct' (Taehtinen 1976: 6). Critically, as Taehtinen observes, 'Ascetic *ahimsa* differs from Vedic by not including any form of justified violence; nor does it imply that any type of *himsa* is morally good' (Taehtinen 1976: 8). Given the above, the ascetics part company from the Vedics insofar as 'they hold to non-violence even in the face of violence[;] there are no exceptions to the rule' (Taehtinen 1976: 51).

It should be noted that *ahimsa* is not merely a 'negative' ethical norm but also a 'positive' ethical norm given its 'good motive' and holistic conception of action, as reflected in the maxim '*ahimsa paramo dharmah*', which regards *ahimsa* as the highest duty (Taehtinen 1976: 62). As a 'moral good', *ahimsa* emphasizes compassion (Taehtinen 1976: 64) and is included in a substantial number of virtues (Taehtinen 1976: 70-73). Taehtinen notes that concerning perfect *ahimsa*, 'In practice the ideal can never be reached, because the goal ever recedes from us. Victory lies in full effort' (1976: 121-22). Hence, 'A genuinely non-violent man must transform his society. He cannot tolerate inequality, exploitation or tyranny in his environment' (Taehtinen 1976: 123). On this reading, 'Peace is an outcome of the application of social and economic non-violence, when they materialise sufficiently. Mankind can avoid military violence only through nonviolence' (Taehtinen 1976: 123).

Picking up on the ancient divergence of the ascetic and Vedic traditions of *ahimsa*, I would now like to advance our argument on nonviolence
as inviolable moral principle versus nonviolence as pragmatic expediency
within the experimental laboratory of South Africa. Gandhi himself, like
any other human being, a proponent of violence—albeit non-intentional
and largely non-physical in his case—consciously strove to minimize this
and pursue nonviolence as his life progressed. He typifies what I refer to
as the 'ascetic' or 'absolute' school.

The Ascetic or Absolute School of Nonviolence: Albert Luthuli

Within the South African context, I shall argue that Chief Albert Luthuli,
a Zulu tribal leader and the seventh president of the African National Congress (ANC) (1952–1967), was deeply influenced both by his witness to
the Gospel as a Christian minister and as a follower of Gandhi. He was a
close friend of Gandhi's son, Manilal Gandhi. I argue that Luthuli's absolute commitment to nonviolent struggle represents a continuation of the
ascetic tradition.

Scott Couper recognizes that Luthuli was strongly set in the tradition of
John Dube, the founder of the ANC, who was

> an educator, a political leader and a Christian ambassador seeking racial
> reconciliation though peaceful means... For Dube and Luthuli, education
> and hard work were the tools by which to achieve liberation. Violence and
> revolution were not a part of the recipe. (Couper 2010: 27)

Quite paradoxically, therefore, Luthuli starts off his autobiography
with a discussion of Waterloo, the demise of Napoleon, and a comparison
to Shaka Zulu, 'the greatest of the Zulu kings' (1962: 17). However, whilst
praising Zulu's 'strength to withstand the power exerted over his people'
and Zulu's army as 'the mightiest military force in Africa', Luthuli points
to Zulu's demise 'allowing his soldiers little time for the pursuit of peace'
and bemoans his dictatorship. Appalled by the increasing violence against
black people by the state, Luthuli writes:

> We Africans are depersonalized by the whites, our humanity and dignity
> is reduced in their imaginations to a minimum... We are not, to them,
> really quite people, scarcely more than units in a labour force and parts of
> a 'native problem'. (Luthuli 1962: 155)

In his response to such atrocities, Luthuli reveals his truly ascetic and
principled stance of nonviolence: 'The strength to combat and rectify
their false doctrines...does not lie in my depersonalizing them and going
apart into an antisomebody camp. It lies rather in the things I believe in...
within me' (Luthuli 1962: 155). Statements such as these are significant,
given that the South Africa of the 1960s was a ticking time-bomb, waiting

to explode. The black majority had been progressively depersonalized and had responded with peaceful protest and nonviolent resistance. However, in 1959, no longer content with nonviolence and racial inclusivity, some 'radical Africanists' broke away as 'exclusivists' to form the Pan-Africanist Congress (PAC) (de Luca 2000: 73).

At Sharpeville, on 21 March 1960, a massacre ensued when protesters encircled a police station to protest pass laws and were shot, with 69 dead and 189 injured. This catastrophe served as a pivot that encouraged younger, more radical black political leaders to go underground and adopt violent guerilla tactics (de Luca 2000: 74). AB Xuma's words to lobby the UN on behalf of starving Africans were, 'When we ask for bread, we get lead' (in de Luca 2000: 77). However, it would be an error to assume that the turn to violence as a means of resistance only arose after Sharpeville. Tim Juckes suggests that 'Mandela had anticipated this turn to violence years earlier, although he had resisted it as long as he thought negotiation was possible' (1995: 101).

De Luca suggests that, already in 1952, Mandela made it known 'that his willingness to embrace nonviolent protest based on Gandhi's model of 'passive resistance' was not absolute but conditional, since the government's overwhelming military and police superiority dictated the choice to be one of nonviolence as a "practical necessity"' (de Luca 2000: 69). Given the increasingly hostile situation of the 1950s, some ANC members argued to 'alter the nature of the struggle', leading to the development of the M-Plan, 'which would see the ANC initiate underground cell structures in anticipation of [this] necessity' (de Luca 2000: 70).

Suffice it to say that given the times, it was not easy for Luthuli to adhere to nonviolent means espoused by Gandhi. Couper refers to:

> Luthuli's tortuous hesitancy to compromise on the use of violence. In July 1961, Luthuli wrestled with two voices: one of Gandhi's espousals of *satyagraha*...and Mandela's persuasive arguments in favour of violence... The ANC and Mandela referenced Gandhi when introducing ethical qualifications to legitimize the use of violence. (Couper 2010: 50)

Gandhi had indeed suggested that 'where there is only a choice between cowardice and violence, I would advise violence', going so afar as to 'advocate training in arms for those who believe in the method of violence' (1948: 1). This utterance was, however, severely qualified by his belief that 'non-violence is infinitely superior to violence, forgiveness is more manly than punishment' (Gandhi 1948: 1).

Couper proposes that, 'The ANC and Mandela were both disingenuous when utilizing the...statement by Gandhi to justify their own stance on violence. Likewise, the ANC and Mandela are disingenuous when they claimed Luthuli supported the turn to violent methods' (2010: 121).

Couper notes the sheer paradox of naming an armed guerilla unit after Luthuli as a 'means by which to justify the armed struggle in the name of a man whose political, social and physical death rendered him unable to continue to speak for the values for which he received the Nobel Peace Prize' (2010: 3).

For Gandhi, 'dynamic' nonviolence equates with 'conscious suffering'; 'it does not mean meek submission to the will of the evildoer but it means putting of one's whole soul against the will of the tyrant' (1948: 3). Gandhi is cautious to distinguish this peaceful non-cooperation from *Sinn Feinism* because *satyagraha* cannot co-exist with violence. Prophetically he recognizes, 'It [*satyagraha*] will not fail through its inherent weakness. It may fail because of poverty of response. Then will be the time for real danger. The high-souled men...will want to vent their wrath. They will take to violence' (1948: 3).

As if to echo this, Luthuli writes:

> We do not struggle with guns and violence, and the Supremacist's array of weapons is powerless against the spirit...and every time cruel men injure or kill defenceless ones, they lose ground. The Supremacist illusion is that this is a battle of numbers, a battle of race, a battle of modern armaments against primitives. It is not. It is right against wrong, good against evil. (Luthuli 1962: 229)

Luthuli explicitly used strategies inspired by Gandhian nonviolence in both the 1952 and 1954 Defiance Campaign marches. Luthuli's call for 50,000 Freedom Volunteers recalled 'Gandhi's call for *satyagrahis* (those committed to non-violence and soldiers of truth)'; Luthuli echoes Gandhi in his own words: 'Non-violent resistance in any provocative situation is our best instrument. Our strongest weapon is to acquaint our people and the world with the facts of our situation' (in Couper 2010: 67).

As a sign of his lifelong commitment to the way of nonviolence, Luthuli confirms:

> In practice...from Malaya to Scandinavia, from Tanganyika to the British Isles, there are people in earnest about being their brother's keeper. I make it clear that we mean to cling to methods such as this, to nonviolence, and we mean increasingly to use these weapons even against such tyrants as South Africa's present government. This is not only a question of morality. As long as our patience can be made to hold out, we shall not jeopardize the South Africa of tomorrow by precipitating violence today. (Luthuli 1962: 219-20)

Of the younger generation, Juckes writes, 'Mandela and his colleagues [had] only two forms of action possible: "submit or fight". They differed from the old-guard leaders like Matthews and Luthuli' (1995: 102). Upon learning of the emergence of uMkhonto weSizwe (MK) as the ANC's military wing, Luthuli threatened to resign, and to prevent this, MK was separated from the ANC. Despite the emergence of an armed wing, Luthuli was awarded the Nobel Peace Prize of 1961 for championing change through nonviolence, a cause that he continued to support until his suspicious death after being hit by a train near his home in July 1967. There have been calls for an investigation into the dubious nature of his death several times.

The Expedient School: Nelson Mandela

By comparison with the above proponents of the ascetic or absolute school of nonviolence, Gandhi and Luthuli, I argue that Mandela represents an interesting departure, demonstrating an expedient use of nonviolence. Initially content to use peaceful protest, Mandela soon realized that nonviolence was getting nowhere and turned to armed struggle.

Born on 18 July 1918 and groomed in the home of his uncle, the regent of the Thembu people, Chief Jongintaba, some commentators suggest that Mandela embraced both a 'militant African nationalism' and Gandhi's more global view that 'no people in one part of the world could really be free while their brothers in other parts were still under foreign rule' (de Luca 2000: 67-68). He embraced Gandhi's message, despite the fact that Gandhi did not seem to be concerned with African rights. Only subsequently, in 1950, did the ANC, the Indians, and communists join forces to protest for South Africa's liberation.

In late 1956, Mandela and other ANC stalwarts were arrested and charged with high treason. It is common knowledge that the government tried to prove that the ANC had 'plotted violence' but they could not; hence a verdict of not guilty was returned. Again on trial for treason in what became known as the Rivonia trial (1963–1964), after the state uncovered guerilla warfare plans for 'Operation *Mayibuye*', Mandela emphasized that 'once the government had denied the black community 'an avenue of peaceful protest', the movement decided to undertake 'violent forms of political struggle and...form uMkhonto weSizwe (the Spear of the Nation—the military wing of the ANC)' (in de Luca 2000: 79). Although the judge declared the defendants guilty on all counts, he sentenced them to life imprisonment instead of death because it was not 'high treason' (de Luca 2000: 79).

Significantly, Couper's assertion, 'The ANC's own published narratives demonstrate that the initiation of violence was ill-conceived, inept, haphazard and ultimately a fast-track strategy to derailing the liberation movement in the short and medium term' (2010: 144) can be contested. In a personal communication, a highly regarded statesman, now retired and formerly with MK recalled:

> When Oliver Tambo was training the first MK cadres, he was explicit[:] 'You are not murderers; we are not training you to be murderers'. If you have a gun you need to know how to use it—but for the right reasons. You will not shoot at a white man because he is white. How do you know he is not an ANC member? You are being trained as political cadres in the fight for peace. (Anonymous 2014)

After a pause, the statesman added, 'It takes a thief to catch a thief' (Anonymous 2014).

Mandela remained in prison for 27 years until he walked free on 11 February 1990. Although Mandela's 'fighting talk' continued, his address to the US Congress on 26 June 1990 confirmed the message of peace: 'Let us keep our arms locked together so that we form a solid phalanx against racism to ensure that that day comes now...then we shall all be entitled to acknowledge the salute when others say of us, "Blessed are the peacemakers"' (1993: 42). Hence, the one who turned from nonviolence to violence appears to have returned to the fold of nonviolence. Perhaps the greatest example of this was illustrated upon the assassination on 10 April 1993 of Chris Hani, whom Mandela greatly favoured and who was an icon amongst the youth and the people at large. On the brink of civil war and disaster, 'Mandela maintained his composure: "the solution *is* peace; it *is* reconciliation; it *is* political tolerance"' (in de Luca 2000: 87).

Biko and Black Consciousness

Whereas Luthuli and his generation of absolute proponents of peace were viewed as 'old school' to the young firebrands of the time, such as Mandela, it is helpful to note that Mandela and his ilk (whilst imprisoned on Robben Island) likewise were similarly viewed by the next generation. The leadership vacuum created by their imprisonment was filled by yet another generation of young struggle icons, who were more zealous in their approach, albeit using the language of nonviolence (Moore 1973). Their spearhead was the founder of the Black Consciousness Movement (BCM or BC)—Biko—who coined the phrase, 'At the heart of this kind of thinking is the realization by blacks that the most potent weapon in the hands of the oppressor is the mind of the oppressed' (2009: 74).

De Luca notes that BCM disturbed Mandela because it created a generation gap, and he 'remained uncomfortable with the attitudes, tactics, and style of this new breed of black revolutionary' (2000: 82). In Mandela's words: '[T]hese angry and audacious young people were [the] progeny' of Bantu Education, who 'had come back to haunt its creators' (in de Luca 2000: 82). Biko's understanding of the situation was:

The last step in BC is to broaden the base of our operation. One of the basic tenets of BC is totality of involvement... We are oppressed because we are black. We must use that very concept to unite ourselves and to respond as a cohesive group. We must cling to each other with a tenacity that will shock the perpetrators of evil. Our preparedness to take upon ourselves the cudgels of the struggle will see us through. We must remove from our vocabulary completely the concept of fear. Truth must ultimately triumph over evil, and the white man has always nourished his greed on this basic fear that shows itself in the black community... [A] struggle without casualties is no struggle. (Biko 2007: 162)

Whilst a detailed engagement with Biko, a central figure in the history of South Africa's liberation struggle, lies beyond the constraints of this chapter, it ought to be noted that in the case of Biko, another form of expedient nonviolence appears to manifest itself. He seemingly uses the narrative of nonviolence as a rhetorical device, although, as is observed above, the ambivalence and underlying militancy (e.g., the reference to casualties) is undeniable.

Juckes, for one, argues that Biko's personality—namely, 'his ability to express the ideas of Black Consciousness without degenerating into racist attacks'—'made his activity contribute to the defining of the developing society', whereas, 'an aggressive individual might have precipitated violence and insurrection leading to civil war' (1995: 166). However, Mangcu observes the subtler strategising at play: 'He [Biko] eschewed armed struggle without counting it out' and thus was able to 'stay on this side of the law' (2014: 196).

In an apparent confirmation of this position, Lindy Wilson suggests that as the conduit for BC, the Black People's Congress (BPC) 'line' was to explore the nonviolent road within the country, but there was also the view 'that the present Nationalist government can only be unseated by people operating a military wing' (in Pityana et al. 1991: 66). She recalls Biko's own opinion that 'in the end there is going to be a totality of effect of a number of change agencies operating in South Africa' (in Pityana et al. 1991: 66). Biko wanted to see the PAC, ANC, and BCM forming one liberation group to 'effect the greatest result' (Wilson in Pityana et al. 1991: 67). Tragically and with bitter irony, Biko himself, as the head of Black Consciousness, died a violent death from head wounds sustained in detention at the hands of the notorious apartheid security police (Orr 2000). His premature departure precludes us from a definitive analysis of what future direction his path would have taken in terms of nonviolence or its alternative.

Now, having considered representatives of both ascetic or absolute and expedient traditions of nonviolence, it is time to flip the coin and consider one who espoused radical violence as a matter of principle and in practice: Saul of Tarsus, also known as St Paul the Apostle.

Paul: Weakness and the Power of Transformation

Paul was most likely born in the middle of the first decade CE, because circa 62 CE he describes himself as an old man near 55 years of age. He hailed from Tarsus, an important economic and political centre and capital of the Roman province of Cilicia. Paul most likely belonged to a Jewish family of the Diaspora, holding Roman citizenship from an earlier generation and was a member of the urban middle class. Within the community of Pharisees, he lived according to the Torah, and his zeal for preserving the Torah made him a persecutor of Christians (Schnelle 2003).

Paul testifies to having 'persecuted the churches of God' in 1 Corinthians 15:9, Galatians 1:13, and Philippians 3:6. The Acts of the Apostles record how Paul conducts house-to-house searches to have men and women thrown into prison, advocating the death penalty against them, forcing them to recant their faith, having them whipped and lashed, whilst having himself deputized to persecute Christians as far away as Damascus (Schnelle 2003). It is ironic that at Damascus in 33 CE, as Udo Schnelle points out, Paul became a disciple at the very place where he was persecuting Christians (2003: 84-85). The 'new knowledge' that arises out of the Damascan experience emphasizes its importance as an 'external experience of transcendence that lays the foundation for a new identity', allowing Paul to develop 'a network of meaning that relates one's individual existence to its social obligations' (Schnelle 2003: 100-102).

The passage at the start of this chapter was drawn from Paul's 'Fool's Speech' in 2 Corinthians (11:22–12:10). The speech is considered by some to be highly polemical and relies largely on ruthless irony and parody of the self-accomplishment and signs of being an apostle (Murphy-O'Connor 1991; see also Sumney 1990). Timothy Savage, for example, claims that 'no student of the New Testament can neglect the second epistle of St Paul to the Corinthians since Paul's autobiography reaches its peak in 12:10… "When I am weak, then I am strong"' (1996: 1). Whilst this appears to be a 'meaningless contradiction', 'at the core of Paul's teaching in 2 Corinthians lies an important paradox' (Savage 1996: 1).

From another angle, during the first century CE, *soteria* (salvation/deliverance) was concerned with 'matters of this life', such as 'health, wealth, protection and sustenance', salvation was understood in the present, as the benefits that the gods rendered to the people (Savage 1996: 28). Hence, people yearned to see magical 'divine power' at work; the more powerful one's gods, the more strength one was expected to display. 'The Corinthians wanted Paul to conform to the "self-exalting standards of their secular environment"; they were 'dismayed by Paul's humility [and] his "weakness" and questioned his status as a minister of Christ' (Savage 1996: 187). His opponents further inflamed issues.

Jerry Sumney gives us some insight into Paul's opponents. They claim to be 'apostles, missionaries, and servants of God... [T]hey claim support from the congregation, probably on the basis of their claims to these offices' (1990: 162). They 'contend that true apostles should be impressive individuals. They should be dynamic and persuasive speakers and have a commanding demeanor... Paul's rivals have taken up this way of life at Corinth and act as superiors towards the Corinthian church' (Sumney 1990: 162). Moreover, they present their qualifications and market themselves as being Jewish, leveraging off this to claim 'special authority and rights' and to justify their receipt of payment. For Paul, this self-exaltation is an 'aberrant understanding of the Christian message' (Sumney 1990: 172). He therefore turns their logic on its head and renounces the self-exalting tendencies of his world (Savage 1996). Chastising them for being so 'wise' that they allow 'fools' to walk all over them, allowing the false apostles to lord it over them and abuse them, Paul admonishes them for having been 'duped' by the false apostles on the 'social' level, which he sees as dangerous to the 'theological level' (Murphy-O'Connor 1991: 114)).

Jerome Murphy-O'Connor suggests that 'Paul's description of himself as "weak" is the inevitable outcome of the reality of the human condition... [H]e was without power, status or security. His converts were...marginalized... [and] victimized by the false value system of society which imposed on them an egocentric mode of existence' (1991: 116). Thus, Paul's 'weakness' is the condition of being subject to 'insults, hardships, persecution, difficulties' (2 Corinthians 12:10). In worldly terms he is powerless, and the chance of success is negligible; his 'weakness', rather than being interpreted psychologically as inadequacy or 'self-abasement', is social: 'the condition of being without anything that in the eyes of the world would make his mission feasible, together with the concomitant mental and physical suffering' (Murphy-O'Connor 1991: 116).

Thus, at Corinth, whilst weak, in fear, and trembling, Paul is paradoxically empowered with the Spirit, and the result is the Corinthian Christians (Murphy-O'Connor 1991: 120). It is now that the paradox reaches its fullest power, as Savage recognises: '[P]recisely in the radical self-abnegation of the crucified Messiah...the power of God had come to its mightiest expression. It was in human weakness that God had chosen to manifest his illimitable power' (Savage 1996: 189). As Johannes Munck recognises, Paul, an apostle of peace, comes to stand before the mighty emperor of Rome, facing certain death: '[He] could therefore express in his usual matter-of-fact way... "I have fought the good fight, I have finished the race, I have kept the faith"' (1959: 334). Having transcended human weakness with spiritual power, the paradox of fighting for peace impedes Paul no longer.

Deliverance and Ultimate Destiny

If there is a continuity in the process of salvation in the present, here-and-now (Fiddles: 1989), which links us with the past and with our ultimate destiny, then, as Juan-Luis Segundo recognizes, 'becoming visible' is eschatological, and it has to do directly with meta-history. But it has to do equally with the hidden dimension of history here and now...it means that we are going to see how supra-historical life is ultimately injected into what has been accomplished in history (Segundo 1986: 157).

Thus, we arrive at forgiveness, which Paul Fiddles regards as

> a 'shattering experience' for the one who forgives as well as for the one who is forgiven...because forgiveness...seeks to win the offender back into relationship... Reconciliation is a costly process because there are resistances to it in the attitude of the person who has offended; the one who sets out to forgive must aim to remove these blockages and restore the relationship. (Fiddles 1989: 16)

As ascetics, Gandhi and Luthuli wish to keep the door open to nonviolence and the inclusion and conversion of the enemy. To Gandhi, 'Man as animal is violent, but as Spirit is non-violent. The moment he awakes to the spirit within he cannot remain violent. Either he progresses towards *ahimsa* or rushes to his doom' (1948: 311). He reiterates this by suggesting,

> Strength does not come from physical capacity. It comes from an indomitable will... Non-violence is the law of our species as violence is the law of the brute... The dignity of man requires obedience to a higher law... [T]he strength of the spirit...*satyagraha* and its offshoots, non-cooperation and civil resistance, are...new names for the law of suffering. (Gandhi 1948: 1, 2)

Mandela flags the importance of Gandhi's realisation by saying,

> In a world driven by violence and strife, Gandhi's message of peace and non-violence holds the key to human survival in the twenty-first century. He rightly believed in the efficacy of pitching the soul force called the *Satyagraha* against the brute force of the oppressor, and in effect converting the oppressor to the right and moral point. (Mandela 2007: 20)

Soul Force and *Satyagraha* as the Moral Equivalent of War, but Against What?

As soul force, *satyagraha* is therefore more than political technique and serves as 'moral soteriology', but it is salvific? (Wierzbicki 1992: 235). We are cautioned against dismissing the spiritual or theological motivations and foundations that are apparent in both Gandhi and Luthuli, which could serve to distort the entire agenda of their political and philosophical motivation. Couper writes that

> Luthuli did not subscribe to the ANC as his god... [I]nterpreters of Luthuli's life erroneously understand Luthuli to have been political before being spiritual. For Luthuli, the opposite held true. In his autobiography...he professed, 'I am in Congress precisely because I am a Christian'. (Couper 2010: 121)

Vis-à-vis the Mahatma, Luthuli's musings were 'often similarly overlooked' (Couper 2010: 121):

> Luthuli admired and emulated Gandhi's use of strictly non-violent methods of resistance. His speeches contain hundreds of quotations advocating a 'strategic pacifism'... Luthuli and Gandhi did not consider those who fought utilizing non-violent means to be cowards... [T]o fight not using violence—to sacrifice and die while fighting non-violently—was in fact the bravest of options. (Couper 2010: 335-36)

Picking up on the notion of fighting nonviolently, Sonia Gandhi suggests that for Gandhi, '*Satyagraha* was the end of a quest for a moral equivalent of war' (2007: 23). H. J. N. Horsburgh, in his analysis of *satyagraha*, suggests that its method of resistance must differ from war: it must not suffer the moral deficiencies of war (or at least reduce these), it must be universally applicable, and it must have some prospect of being effective. He concludes that *satyagraha* fulfils all these conditions, in principle (Horsburgh 1968).

Gandhi himself writes,

> Arms are surely unnecessary for a training in *ahimsa*. Just as one must learn the art of killing in the training of violence, one must learn the art of dying in the training of non-violence... [H]e who has not overcome all fear cannot practise *ahimsa* to its highest perfection. The votary of *ahimsa* has only one fear, that is of God... Training in nonviolence is thus diametrically opposed to training in violence'. (Gandhi 1948: 335)

But where, one might ask, might we apply *ahimsa* in the face of violence today? It is not only direct violence that confronts us, but indirect violence in the forms of cultural and structural violence. In addition to the obvious context of direct suffering as is manifested in international wars, internal armed conflicts, or physical violence of any form, we run headlong into gender-based violence, social and economic class-based conflict, ethno-religious and ecological disputes. In this way, Hélder Câmara famous 'spiral of violence' (1971) is more like a *funnel-web* of violence.

A small but meaningful clue for how to apply *ahimsa* today may arise from Gandhi's own writing on the demobilization of soldiers, fitting perhaps as Canada marks its military withdrawal from Afghanistan. He suggests that 'the weaver...can truly become the liberator of his country and hence a true soldier' (Gandhi 1948: 16). There is a consistent emphasis on local autonomy and subsidiarity in the Gandhian tradition. In contexts such as South Africa, at local, provincial, and national levels, we have a sharp surge in the support of populist movements, such as the Economic Freedom Fighters (mark the name), who promise emancipation to desperate measures, despite their questionable 'nonviolent' leadership.

Mandela prudently notes that 'Gandhi's insistence on self-sufficiency is the basic economic principle that if followed today could contribute significantly to alleviating Third World poverty and stimulating development' (2007: 19). Whilst Gandhi encourages those 'with means' to 'learn to fight, either with arms or with the weapon of non-violence', they are not his priority (1948: 372). He rather suggests: 'Enjoy your crores [monetary denomination of India] by all means. But understand that your wealth is not yours; it belongs to the people. Take what you require for your legitimate needs, and use the remainder for society' (Gandhi 1948: 372. Consistent with preaching and practising the true Gospel of love and solidarity of various spiritual traditions, he embodies, unequivocally, a 'preferential option for the Poor' and prophesies:

> I have visions that the end of this war will mean also the end of the rule of capital. I see coming the day of the rule of the poor...through force of arms or of non-violence. Let it be remembered that physical force is transitory even as the body is transitory. But the power of the spirit is permanent, even as the spirit is everlasting. (Gandhi 1948: 372-73)

Aluta continua! 'The struggle continues', was the cry of the liberation movement in South Africa and it has only just begun. In the fight for justice and peace, as proponents of nonviolence, let us not be deterred by physical or material weakness, for this merely breeds spiritual strength and resilience as our protagonists confirm. As demonstrated above, power truly is paradoxically perfected in weakness, and transformation remains possible for all beings in the most unlikely of places and at the most difficult of times.

About the Author

Alain Tschudin, PhD, has broad research and community engagement interests and has worked for various Universities in Africa and Europe, the European Commission, iNGOs, and as CEO of a leadership development agency. He has an adjunct association with the International Centre of Non-violence (ICON) and the Peacebuilding Programme at the Durban University of Technology. He is the Executive Director of the SADC office of Good Governance Africa, an NGO dedicated to enhancing governance throughout Africa.

Notes

* This chapter is based on a keynote address given at the Nonviolence: A Weapon of the Strong Conference, held on May 8-11, 2014, at Saint Paul University, Ottawa, Canada. In my introductory remarks, I acknowledged the presence of the conference 'on this revered Anishinaabeg—Algonquin land' and thanked the Rector of Saint Paul University, Heather Eaton, my fellow invitees, as well as the audience for organizing and participating in an event that restored 'the intersecting themes of nonviolence, spirituality, and social transformation to their rightful place on the radar screen of our critical attention'. My opening comments were:

> Just one year ago, Dr Heather Eaton and her group of '14' students were 13,567 kilometers and seven time zones away, in Durban, South Africa, with us at the University of KwaZulu-Natal. There, we shared guest lectures, seminars, and a colloquium for our students. Mindful that the experience should not be a 'talk-shop', we ventured out into our surroundings, exploring the Phoenix Settlement, home to Mahatma Gandhi, the nearby Ohlange High School established by John Dube, founder of the African National Congress (ANC) and predecessor to leaders such as Chief Albert Luthuli and Nelson Mandela. We also visited the Denis Hurley Centre, named after the late Oblate Archbishop of Durban, human rights champion, justice, and peace activist, who received his last honorary doctorate from Saint Paul University in 1996. Travelling inland, we visited sites of active research in the southern Ukhahlamba-Drakensberg Mountains, shared by South Africa and Lesotho. I would like to believe that the shared experience was transformational for us all. In that same spirit, I hope to make a meaningful contribution with this chapter.

** This chapter is dedicated to Ela Gandhi, Billy Modise, Andrew Mlangeni, Ahmed Kathrada, Denis Hurley and justice and peace-loving friends everywhere, for your life-long commitment to the 'good fight'. Take heart that your legacy will endure. *Aluta continua!.*

Chapter 4

A Brief History of the Power of Nonviolence in Canada

Tamara Lorincz

Introduction

Nonviolence has a long, rich, and important history in Canada. It is a history that is not well-known and not well-researched, but it has had a profound impact on Canadian society and politics. From pacifists who refused to participate in early British colonial wars to peace activists who used nonviolent direct action to ban the bomb during the Cold War, nonviolence has been a persistent and powerful force. Nonviolence may be simply and broadly understood as the rejection of all forms of violence and war. However, in his book, *Non-violence: The History of a Dangerous Idea*, Mark Kurlansky adds that it is also a form of persuasion, a source of strength, an expression of love, and a tactic for political activism that requires more imagination than the use of force (Kurlansky 2007: 6-8).

Nonviolence as a conviction is central to religious and radical pacifism and animates peace activists and organizations. It inspired courageous Canadian politicians such as Agnes Macphail, who was the first woman elected to the House of Commons, and James Shaver Woodsworth, who was first leader of the Co-operative Commonwealth Federation. It informed the work of activists, such as James Endicott, who led the Canadian Peace Congress, and organizations such as the Voice of Women—*La Voix des Femmes*. The many adherents to nonviolence understood its interconnectedness with democracy, feminism, socialism, and internationalism. They linked the pursuit of peace with the struggle for women's and Indigenous rights and social and economic justice at home and abroad. Their success in changing public opinion and government policy affirm the power of nonviolence.

In this chapter, I briefly scan the power of nonviolence in five periods of Canadian history. First, I look at religious pacifism and conscientious objection during the colonial wars of the nineteenth century to World War I. Second, I examine the shift to radical pacifism and the influence of peace in politics during the interwar period to World War II. Third, I survey the influence of the nuclear disarmament campaigns and the inception of the Voice of Women—*La Voix des Femmes* during the Cold War. Fourth, I investigate the anti-war resistance to the Vietnam War and the transnational nature of nonviolence. Fifth, I canvass the nonviolent activism of the Refuse the Cruise campaign in the 1980s and the post-Cold War active nonviolent resistance by groups such as the Christian Peacemaker Teams. Throughout this chapter, I assess the varied and unique expression of nonviolence in the words and actions of courageous Canadians and the social and political change that they created.

Religious Pacifism and Conscientious Objection from the Eighteenth Century to World War I

Since the eighteenth century, nonviolence has been seen in the pacifist traditions of several European Christian communities that immigrated to British North America. The pacifism of the Anabaptists, Mennonites, Quakers (Society of Friends), Hutterites, and Tunkers (Brethren in Christ) derived from their strict observance of biblical doctrine, particularly Jesus's Sermon on the Mount (Socknat 1987: 13, 2007: 236-39; Franklin 2006: 36). The Quakers, for example, published their commitment to peace and opposition to violence and war in their peace testimony in 1660 (Franklin 2006: 36). During times of armed conflict and war, the Quakers and the other religious pacifists declared their neutrality and refused serving in the militia or paying taxes for warfare. They petitioned the Upper Canada government to recognize their faith and dissent in The Militia Bill of 1793, which exempted them from bearing arms (Socknat 1987: 13). However, in the war of 1812–1814, these communities had their property confiscated and they were fined for their resistance (Socknat 1987: 14). After the war, they mobilized and pressured the government to end the practice of fining in a new Militia Act of 1849 and to exempt them from military service in a special Confederation order of 1873 (Socknat 1987: 14-15).

In the late nineteenth century, the Doukhobors, a Russian Christian pacifist sect, came to Canada to escape persecution by the Tsar. The Doukhobors espoused the tenets of love and brotherhood and openly resisted militarism and materialism (Socknat 1987: 14-15). They engaged in mass parades, nude demonstrations, and the burning of their property to ensure their exemptions from conscription and taxation for war (Bennett 1997: 157). During the British colonial wars overseas, such as the Boer Wars in South Africa, Canadian religious pacifists declared their opposition and refused to serve. Many of them provided overseas relief and assisted refugees (Frost 1997: 422; Socknat 1987: 10).

In 1909, it was the influence of the Protestant pacifist churches that led to the formation of the Canadian Peace and Arbitration Society (Socknat 1987: 54). This national society was part of an international effort that called on states to disarm and resolve conflict nonviolently through negotiations. Although the Society was not successful in preventing the First World War, it offered a nonviolent alternative to war. As Thomas Socknat explains, these early peace churches laid the foundation for a tradition of nonviolence in Canada (1987: 41).

In the nineteenth century, the power of nonviolence for social change is well-portrayed in the relationship between the Children of Peace and politicians Louis LaFontaine and Robert Baldwin. The Children of Peace was a divergent Quaker group formed in 1812 and led by David Willison (Socknat 1987: 14).[1] Willison and his members wanted their church to have a more active role in society promoting their values of peace, equality, and social justice. They established a unique society, a cooperative economy, and a distinct temple in their village of Sharon, also known as Hope, in Upper Canada.[2] The temple was used for charity, shelter for the homeless, and public and political gatherings. Reformers LaFontaine, a politician from Canada East, and Baldwin, a politician from Canada West, met and spoke at the temple many times and sought the support of the Children of Peace. The pacifist community fervently campaigned for LaFontaine and Baldwin, ensuring their election to the first Legislative Assembly of the Province of Canada.

During the violent riots of the Orange Order militias in the 1840s, LaFontaine and Baldwin resisted calling on the army but instead peacefully quelled the civil strife through conciliation and ensured the passage of democratic reforms (Saul 2010: 193-94). The founders of responsible government in Canada also facilitated a closer alliance between French and English Canada and achieved more autonomy from Great Britain. As John Ralston Saul describes:

> These two men took on the core beliefs of the most powerful empire of the day... They outmanoeuvred it with ideas and language. And the essence of what they accomplished was Responsible Government. It was the value of moderation when faced with persistent crisis and violence. What's more, unlike most men in politics, they were willing to suffer personal humiliation in order to avoid the use of violence. (Saul 2010: 14)

Although the Children of Peace community ended in 1889, their pacifist influence endures in the democratic legacy of LaFontaine and Baldwin.

Overcoming the patriotic fervour and propaganda of World War I made conscientious objection and peace advocacy acts of great courage. The major churches, labour organizations, and farm communities initially supported the war effort in 1914 and mandatory conscription that was introduced in 1916 (Tough 2015: 66). Although most of the religious pacifist sects were exempted from military service, other Canadians who objected to the war struggled to stay out of it. Frederick John Dixon, an elected Member of the Manitoba Legislature and a committed pacifist, urged Canadians to resist national registration and conscription (Sock-nat 1987: 65-66). He believed that war was immoral and barbaric and led to private profiteering and public debt. For his anti-war views, Dixon was called a traitor, assaulted, and faced a recall campaign (Gutkin and Gutkin 1997: 26-28). Yet he persisted in his outspoken and brave opposition to the war. David Tough argues that the resistance to conscription during the First World War paved the way to political agitation for greater social reforms during the interwar period (Tough 2015: 73).

Radical Pacifism and the Politics of Peace from the Interwar Years to World War II

The public outrage to the devastation and debt from the First World War led to a broader and stronger social critique against war, inequality, and economic injustice (Socknat 1987: 90-91). In this milieu, a more radical pacifism formed with links to socialism and feminism. Women in Canada, having finally achieved federal suffrage in 1918, started new peace initiatives that challenged the capitalist and patriarchal order that had led to the war. The Canadian Women's Peace Party was founded to promote the International Congress of Women's agenda for international arbitration, universal disarmament, and a league of democratic nations (Socknat 1987: 56). In 1919, the first official Canadian chapter of the Women's International League for Peace and Freedom (WILPF) was established in Ontario (Boutilier 1988: 3). By 1929, WILPF had branches in British Columbia and Manitoba and official support of women's farm organizations in Alberta and Saskatchewan (Boutilier 1988: 51, 96).

One prominent member of the Canadian chapter of WILPF was Agnes Macphail, who was the first female Member of Parliament elected to the House of Commons and a member of the disarmament committee of the League of Nations (Boutilier 1988: 77-79). She was an outspoken political advocate of peace and nonviolence and supported the No More War movement (Socknat 1987: 108). Macphail and WILPF led successful national campaigns against militaristic curriculum in textbooks and compulsory cadet training in schools.[3] In 1924, Macphail organized a train called the Pax Special that brought to Toronto 25 women leaders from various European peace organizations, who had been attending an international WILPF conference in Washington, DC (Boutilier 1988: 92). Frequently in the House of Commons, Macphail derided government spending on military defence, munitions, the Royal Military College, and cadet programs, and instead demanded that the revenues be allocated to social programs to help the elderly, unemployed, and disabled Canadians (Pennington 1989: 173, 215). During the interwar period in Canada, WILPF and Macphail were especially effective at stimulating public support for peace and building bridges of solidarity with like-minded groups around the world.

The first leader of the Co-operative Commonwealth Federation, a political party formed on the prairies in 1932, was staunch pacifist and social welfare reformer Woodsworth. His wife, Lucy, was the co-founder of the Vancouver chapter of WILPF (Mills 1991: 192). In 1935, Woodsworth was elected to the Canadian Parliament, and he maintained that the threat or use of force was wrong and pushed for disarmament and a nonviolent civil defence force (Mills 1991: 212-14). Four years later, Woodsworth was the only Member of Parliament who voted against Canada's participation in World War II. On the floor of the House of Commons, he gave a famous and stirring appeal for neutrality and nonviolence. Woodsworth would later receive thousands of letters from across the country expressing admiration for his moral and political courage (Socknat 1987: 195, 197). He also advocated for conscientious objection and by the end of World War II over 12,000 Canadian men were classified as conscientious objectors and allowed to participate in alternative service, such as working in hospitals, schools, and national parks (Socknat 2007: 66). As Socknat elucidates, 'The importance of the Canadian government's acceptance of alternative service as a legitimate exemption from military service cannot be over emphasized for it set an important legal precedent for the continued recognition of a pacifist alternative in the future' (2007: 72). Macphail's and Woodsworth's radical pacifism, which challenged militarism and promoted social welfare, opened the doors to the politics of peace in Canada.

Nuclear Disarmament and 'Refuse the Cruise' Campaigns during the Cold War

The US atomic bombings of the Japanese cities of Hiroshima and Nagasaki at the end of World War II and the proliferation of nuclear weapons during the Cold War re-ignited the peace movement in Canada. In 1949, James Endicott, a charismatic Christian missionary who served in China, was asked to lead the Canadian Peace Congress, an umbrella organization that brought together peace councils, ecumenical groups, and student activists in the country to work on nuclear disarmament (Socknat 1987: 290-91). Although he was not an absolute pacifist, Endicott was an anti-war activist who opposed Western imperialism and protested the US and Canadian involvement in the Korean War. Employing creative nonviolent actions for political and social change, the Congress attracted thousands of Canadians to its rallies, conferences, and campaigns. On May 7, 1950, twelve thousand people came to hear Endicott speak at a peace rally in Toronto (Endicott 1980: 157, 277-302). The Congress initiated a Ban the Bomb national petition drive, which collected approximately 300,000 signatures of Canadians who wanted an unconditional ban on nuclear weapons. With growing public support, Endicott called on the federal government to have an independent foreign policy from the US to pursue peace and not to prepare for war. In an attempt to dampen Endicott's message and to derail the Canadian Peace Congress, the Lester B. Pearson government pilloried the leader as a treasonous communist and the police brutally assaulted members (McKay and Swift 2012: 127, 131). The media also scorned Endicott as public enemy number one and vituperatively covered the Congress's activities (Endicott 1980: 277).

In his book on nonviolence (2007), Mark Kurlansky describes how proponents of nonviolence are often considered dangerous by the state. Throughout Canadian history, pacifists and peace activists, such as Endicott, have been arrested, imprisoned, harassed, and spied on by federal and provincial police. They have also been red-baited as Communists and smeared as traitors by the government and the media in an attempt to discredit and silence them (Hammond-Callahan 2015: 135-45). By courageously challenging the state's use of force or its decision to go to war, nonviolence must be seen as a subversive concept. Kurlansky asserts that nonviolence has been 'marginalized because it is one of the rare, truly revolutionary ideas, an idea that seeks to completely change the nature of society, a threat to the established order. And it has always been treated as something profoundly dangerous' (Kurlansky 2007: 5). Overcoming a reactionary government and an antagonistic media, Endicott and the Canadian Peace Congress helped to unite religious and radical pacifism with student and secular activism into a powerful national peace movement.

The landscape of the Canadian peace movement shifted dramatically with the emergence of the Voice of Women—*La Voix des Femmes* (VOW) in 1960.[4] In May of that year, women across the country responded to an impassioned column written by journalist Lotta Dempsey in the *Toronto Daily Star* urging women to help end the Cold War tension and the threat of nuclear war. In July, 100 women came to the founding meeting of VOW in Toronto and by the end of its first year, the organization had over 5000 members in ten provinces and one northern territory. VOW attracted women from all walks of life appealing to their maternal instincts and their feminist desires for peace (Ball 1994: 136; Hammond-Callahan 2015: 135). Most importantly, the organization created a safe and supportive space for women to bring their gendered perspectives to the debates on domestic and foreign affairs and to plan collective action. Peggy Hope-Simpson, co-founder of the Nova Scotia chapter, confirms that nonviolence as a way of life is central to the Voice of Women (Ball 1994: 361). In her book, *Pacifism as a Map*, Ursula Franklin, renowned scientist and VOW member, explains that peace is not just the absence of violence or war, but 'is the absence of fear. Peace is the presence of justice' (2006: 106). VOW members understood and articulated the links among gender inequality, violence against women, economic injustice, militarism, and war.

With its savvy use of the media, VOW organized 24-hour silent vigils, Mothers' Day demonstrations, and war-toy campaigns to raise public awareness and political pressure (Socknat 2007: 68; Hutchinson 2015: 150-51). The organization engaged in mass letter-writing, lobbying, and ministerial meetings to influence government policy. Kay Macpherson explains that VOW pushed for a 'new, nonviolent, cooperative process of negotiation' in Canadian domestic and foreign affairs (1989: 210). The women prepared and circulated briefings on a variety of peace and disarmament topics, including the dangers of radioactive fallout and chemical and biological weapons (Kerans 1996: 111). One of VOW's most ambitious and well-known projects was its collection and testing of baby teeth for Strontium-90 to show that children were at risk from their exposure to atmospheric nuclear weapons testing. This national campaign was part of the global civil society effort that paved the way for the Partial Nuclear Test Ban Treaty. VOW also arranged international women's delegations to other countries, such as the Soviet Union and Vietnam, and a global conference on 'Women for Peace' bringing together women from 30 different countries. It also fundraised in 1961 for the establishment of the Canadian Peace Research Institute, which was one of the first and most prestigious institutes of its kind at the time (Macpherson and Good 1987: 2).[5] The innovative nonviolent campaigning of the Voice of Women and the Canadian Peace Congress helped to keep Canada out of the nuclear arms race, expand the national peace movement, advance peace research, and promote international solidarity (Langille 2008: 27-32).

Anti-War Resistance during the Vietnam War

The Canadian nonviolent nuclear disarmament movement evolved into an emboldened anti-war resistance during the Vietnam War. Across Canada, there were demonstrations held outside the US consulate offices, and teach-ins convened on university campuses to stir opposition to the US war in Southeast Asia. Peace activists in Vancouver, Winnipeg, Ottawa, Montreal, and Toronto coordinated a national network to support US draft-dodgers and deserters who were coming into the country (Squires 2015: 175). Jessica Squires characterizes this network as 'a multigenerational movement with influences from multiple sources—peace churches, pacifist traditions, and the crucible of radical ideas of the sixties' (2015: 177). The two leading *ad hoc* organizations, the Toronto Anti-Draft Programme and the Vancouver Committee to Aid American War Objectors, disseminated resources and strategies for anti-draft resistance (Squires 2015: 175). In less than a decade, an estimated 80,000 US war resisters arrived in Canada, and many subsequently became involved in the Canadian peace movement (Socknat 2007: 69). To increase support for US war resisters, a pan-Canadian conference was held in Montreal in 1970 and many activists from the United States attended (Squires 2015: 177). The transnational flow of ideas and people shaped the discourse and practice of nonviolence in Canada.

Cross-border solidarity between the Canadian and US anti-war movements was strengthened through the shared struggle against the US's war in Vietnam. In 1967, Martin Luther King Jr, the US civil rights leader and Nobel Peace Prize winner, was invited to deliver the seventh annual Massey Lectures for the Canadian Broadcasting Corporation (CBC). In a five-part series, King explained the theory and tactic of nonviolent resistance to a Canadian audience. He stated on air:

> I would like to suggest that modern man really go all out to study the meaning of nonviolence, its philosophy and its strategy. We have experimented with the meaning of nonviolence in our struggle for racial justice in the United States, but now the time has come for man to experiment with nonviolence in all areas of human conflict, and that means nonviolence on an international scale. (King 1967a)

King connected the racism and police violence in black neighbourhoods in the US to its war in Vietnam. He decried domestic poverty and unemployment while the Lyndon B. Johnson administration spent so much money on warfare. On the CBC, King spoke about the need to broaden the civil rights movement into a peace and anti-poverty campaign. King emphasized that nonviolence is interrelated and interdependent with economic and social justice and expounded its revolutionary potential and power. Four months after his Massey Lecture, King was assassinated in Memphis, Tennessee. King's Canadian radio broadcast, which was later transcribed as a book entitled *Conscience for Change*, is an example of the international exchange of knowledge of nonviolence.

Under the leadership of Macpherson and Muriel Duckworth, the Voice of Women organized many anti-war rallies and public meetings to raise public opposition to the Vietnam War, and many members welcomed US war resisters into their homes (Kerans 1996: 89; Squires 2013: 54-55). VOW also funded and organized a major delegation of Vietnamese women to share their tragic experiences across Canada and the US (Macpherson and Good 1987: 2). Most critically, VOW helped to expose Canada's complicity in the US's war. Claire Culhane, a Canadian woman with a nursing background, served for two years as a hospital administrative assistant in a Canadian-funded health clinic in South Vietnam and witnessed the terrible suffering of civilians (Brookfield 2015: 187). After her return, Culhane published a shocking exposé entitled, *Why is Canada in Vietnam? The Truth About Our Foreign Aid* (1972), which revealed that Canada's presence in Vietnam was not truly independent and not strictly humanitarian but in many ways abetted the war waged by the US. She demanded that the federal government investigate the clinic and withdraw from Vietnam but was rebuffed. Culhane, a grandmother, joined VOW and was supported by the peace organization in her cross-country speaking tour and activism. Unable to shift the federal government's position on Vietnam through letter-writing and lobbying, Culhane began to engage bravely in nonviolent civil disobedience with the support of VOW. She went on two hunger strikes on Parliament Hill in the late 1960s and disrupted the House of Commons, an action for which she was arrested (Culhane 1972: 9-10). Culhane's nonviolent direct action was emblematic of the greater risks activists and organizations were willing to take for peace.

Nonviolent Activism from the 'Refuse the Cruise' to the Christian Peacemaker Teams

After the Vietnam War, the peace movement diversified and new groups were formed specializing in different issues. Yet, nonviolence was still evident in the ideology these groups espoused and the methods they used. For example, in 1976, Project Ploughshares was formed as an ecumenical effort to challenge militarism and promote disarmament for development (Langille 2008: 28). A few years later, Conscience Canada was established to encourage the withholding of taxes for military activities, which built on the legacy of conscientious objection (Socknat 2007: 70). Professional peace networks were also developed, including Physicians for the Prevention of Nuclear War, Science for Peace, and Lawyers for Social Responsibility. In 1983, the Women's Action for Peace and the Cruise Missile Conversion Project organized nonviolent direct action training in preparation for a week of resistance against Litton Systems of Canada, a company in Ontario that was manufacturing the guidance systems for US nuclear cruise missiles. Over three days in November of that year, 127 women and men were arrested for trespassing onto the company's property and peacefully protesting. In a protracted and high-profile court case, the defendants expounded their use of nonviolent direct action and their commitment to nuclear disarmament. Although the judge found them guilty, he gave them suspended sentences (Williamson 1989: 175-76, 182).

In 1985, the Canadian Peace Alliance (CPA) brought together over 100 organizations to coordinate national actions and collectively lobby the government (Socknat 2007: 70; Langille 2008: 27-32). The Alliance worked together under the Refuse the Cruise banner to stop the United States from testing cruise missiles in Canada. The CPA also collaborated with the Assembly of First Nations on a major peace campaign that linked militarism, Indigenous rights, and the environment (Williamson and Gorham 1989: 20). Together they supported the Innu community that was struggling to stop NATO from testing low-level fighter jets over their Nitassinan territory, which traverses the Provinces of Quebec and Newfoundland-Labrador.[6] The Innu people complained that the Canadian government disrespected their traditional hunting grounds by allowing military activity and the subsonic jet noise and high-level radio frequencies from the fighter jets. In peaceful protest, the Innu recurrently trespassed on the base and held prayer ceremonies on the tarmac; many elders and Indigenous women were arrested (Williamson and Gorham 1989: 21). Maggie Helwig explains how the Canadian government militarized First Nations' territories by permitting the Department of National Defence to establish bases, engage in weapons testing, and mine for uranium, but that it has been the Indigenous peoples who led the nonviolent resistance, from blockading runways to occupying military sites (1993: 52-53).

Across Canada, peace groups have often assisted Indigenous communities in their struggle to prevent the dispossession, damage, and militarization of their land and resources. For example, Canadian Christian Peacemaker Teams (CPT) were dispatched to support the Mohawk people during the Oka crisis in Kanesatake, Quebec in 1990 and to assist the Mik'maq people during the fisheries conflict in Esgenoopetitj (Burnt Church), New Brunswick in 2000 (Hrynkow 2009: 117; Loney 2011: 9). As Christopher Hrynkow describes, CPT uses 'the spirit of embedded engagement' by physically putting their bodies in the way of violence (2009: 117, 119). The Mennonite and the Brethren in Christ churches launched the CPT in 1986 to intensify their commitment to pacifism and to use nonviolent direct action to end armed conflict and war (Hrynkow 2009: 112). They employ violence-reduction and conflict-prevention techniques, such as monitoring and accompaniment, to help at risk communities. Canadian CPT members have travelled to international conflict zones including Haiti, Hebron, the Congo, and Iraq.

In his book, *Captivity: 118 Days in Iraq and the Struggle for a World Without War* (2011), Canadian CPT member James Loney explains:

> We [CPT] see ourselves as allies working to confront, expose and transform the systematic injustices that we so often find at the root of a violent conflict. We are trained in non-violent direct action and are ready to perform non-violent civil disobedience (i.e., break unjust laws) in order to expose injustice and mobilize positive social change. (Loney 2011: 8)

In the lead up to the US-led war in Iraq in 2003, CPT members joined hundreds of thousands of Canadians in pressuring the federal government to stay out of the US military coalition (Loney 2011: 8, 85). In 2004,

Loney and another Canadian CPT member, Harmeet Singh Sooden, went to Iraq to bear witness against the war but were kidnapped by the Swords of Righteousness Brigade and held hostage in Baghdad. Upon their rescue and release, Loney and Sooden issued a statement of unconditional forgiveness to their captors and added 'in our view, the catastrophic level of violence and the lack of effective protection of human rights in Iraq is inextricably linked to the US-led invasion and occupation' (Loney 2011: 395). Loney and Sooden's ordeal brought worldwide attention to the CPT and their practice of nonviolent resistance. In Canada, other organizations such as Peace Brigades International and Nonviolent Peaceforce do similar protective accompaniment and nonviolent civil disobedience as the CPT (Hrynkow 2009: 113). These groups reflect the deepening commitment to nonviolence and the transnational solidarity in the Canadian peace movement.

Conclusion

This chapter has broadly and briefly traced some of the history of nonviolence in Canada. Five historical periods were explored to locate the significant ideas, individuals, and organizations that exemplified the power of nonviolence. From religious pacifism in the nineteenth century to anti-war resistance in the twenty-first century, nonviolence has been a common conviction. Yet, this study shows that the understanding of nonviolence has evolved over time and has been expanded by socialism, feminism, and internationalism. In Canada, the expression of nonviolence has been shaped and reshaped by the transnational exchange of knowledge and experience with other peace activists and organizations from around the world, such as the Women's International League for Peace and Freedom and the Christian Peacemaker Teams. The study also reveals that the subversiveness and solidarism of nonviolence were direct challenges to the state and the status quo that maintained the strictures of militarism, patriarchy, and capitalism.

Canadian pacifists and peace activists, such as Endicott and Culhane, overcame the hostility of the government and media to carry forward the philosophy and practice of nonviolence. Pacifist politicians, such as MacPhail and Woodsworth, opened the doors more widely to the politics of peace. Through their creative campaigns and educational programs, the Canadian Peace Congress and the Voice of Women offered alternatives to violent conflict and war and have shown how peace can be a possibility. Yet, it has been the historical peace churches, women's organizations, and Indigenous communities that have especially and courageously harnessed the power of nonviolence to effect lasting positive social and political change in Canada.

About the Author

Tamara Lorincz's research interests include peace history and activism, militarism, defence policies and procurement, nonviolence and nuclear disarmament. In 2014, Lorincz was a senior researcher for the International Peace Bureau in Geneva, Switzerland. She authored the report, 'Demilitarization for Deep Decarbonization'. Lorincz is on the national board of the Canadian Voice of Women for Peace and on the international advisory committee of the Global Network Against Weapons and Nuclear Power in Space. She is also a member of the Women's International League for Peace & Freedom.

Notes

1. The Temple, also known as Sharon Temple, is located in Sharon, Ontario, and is now a National Peace Site.

2. See Sharon Temple National Historic Site, at http://www.sharontemple.ca/index.php?option=com_content&view=section&id=6&Itemid=.

3. See Comacchio (2015: 79-91); Wyatt (2000: 80); and Pennington (1989: 48-49).

4. Now known as the Canadian Voice of Women for Peace—*La Voix des Femmes Canadiennes pour La Paix*, at http://vowpeace.org/.

5. The Canadian Peace Research Institute no longer exists.

6. See MacDonald and Sarson (2008), at http://www.nsvow.org/wp-content/uploads/2015/04/A-Walk-Down-Memory-Lane.pdf.

Chapter 5

Gandhi in Action:
Nonviolent Movements, Gandhi, and Contemporary Challenges

Rajagopal P. V. and Jill Carr-Harris

This chapter is a collection of personal reflections based on the authors' experiences and extensive work as an advocate for nonviolent social change across India. The reflections are illustrative of the challenges and issues faced by grassroots, nonviolent activists in India, a country characterized by a vast and complex array of historical, cultural, religious and political realities. Each section provides a snapshot of how nonviolent, grassroots activities in India are engaging with current challenges. The chapter concludes with Rajagopal's reflections from the Conference *Nonviolence: A Weapon of the Strong: Advancing Nonviolence, Spirituality, and Social Transformation.*

Gandhi in Action Among the Adivasi

When I am travelling across the globe, people often ask me about how and where they can find Gandhi in India. I am sorry to say that in a globalizing world, Gandhi is totally marginalized, even in his country of birth. Looking at Delhi and Bombay, or any other city in India, it is difficult for a visitor to find traces of Gandhi in the kind of supermarkets and malls that are being built. Many of the institutions that take on Gandhi's name are more like museums: places that do not generate actions for constructive social change. Political parties in India are competing to deify Gandhi. In the southern part of India, many social movements now reject Gandhi, as they do not see their liberation being brought about in his name. They have identified their own leaders whose philosophies can be the bases for their liberation.

I know the picture I am painting may sound unsatisfying, but frustration is not my intention. I want to underscore that, even in a complex and diverse context such as India where Gandhi is for the most part marginalized, there are a few examples of communities that have kept his spirit and philosophy alive. Two impressive examples are to be found in Jharkhand.

Jharkhand is a new state born out of Bihar in 2001. The struggle for a separate Jharkhand was long and drawn out. The reason given for the establishment of Jharkhand was to respect and promote the aspirations of the Adivasis, who are the majority people in the new state. It is unfortunate that even after this new state was born, the Adivasis' objectives were not respected. In fact, their experience was not dissimilar from what happened to the poor after India's Independence in the late 1940s. Even though there was transfer of political power from the colonial rulers to Indian leaders, this transfer did not lead to justice for all. This is because many Indian leaders were deeply colonized in their thinking and hence behaved exactly like the colonizers.

Similarly in the case of Jharkhand, power was transferred from non-Adivasis to the Adivasis, but the ruling class of Adivasis did not respect the aspirations of the ordinary people. History, therefore, has been repeating itself. As a result, in this state, many people are simply left to continue to struggle to protect their life and dignity. In this conflict, however, people have many options. They can opt for violent or nonviolent struggle. They can opt for democratic or undemocratic struggle.

The Adivasis of Jharkhand are proving again and again that they respect democracy and that they respect nonviolence. They are also proud to relate their struggle to Gandhi. The Adivasis, who are ridiculed by the Indian mainstream as uneducated and primitive, have shown a deeper understanding of Gandhi by putting his philosophy into practice in their day-to-day lives. For example, the Adivasis have no interest in accumulating wealth. They find richness in living with nature and in living simply. Their interest in Gandhi is not limited to day-to-day life, however. They are also using the methods of nonviolence effectively. Let me give two examples of such struggles in Jharkhand.

The first struggle was against a dam that was to be constructed by bringing two rivers together, the Koel and the Karo, to generate electricity: the Koel-Karo project. The dam would displace several villages. According to a rough estimate, 240 villages would be submerged and some 150,000 people would be displaced. The local people used their wisdom and declared a non-cooperation movement. While they did not completely object to the project, they decided not to cooperate in any way to promote it. They also used their traditional system of decision-making to condemn the government system behind the project. They used a method of non-cooperation called 'Janata curfew' to prevent the government officials and outsiders from entering into the region. They did not allow the Prime Minister or the Chief Minister to inaugurate the project. Their mobilization was so strong that the government finally decided to stop the work and withdraw its army and police.

People interested in learning about this struggle should spend a week in one of these villages, or travel through the area with Rajan and Vijay, the young leaders of the movement. They should also meet the old and young Rajas who have held the community together in a very humble way. If other activists would travel to this region and spend time with these leaders, they would find Gandhi—his spirit and philosophy—alive in the struggle in which people are trying to protect their lands, livelihoods, and resources as well as their freedom and dignity through nonviolent means. These nonviolent activities have taught the activists in Jharkhand that they have to refuse the divisions caused by politics, religions, castes, and so forth, and work together for their collective future.

The second example can be drawn from Netarath, where women played a leading role in the nonviolent struggle. In 1993, the government decided to establish an army base in Netarath. This decision displaced 245 villages and 262,853 people in a 206-square kilometer area. The lives of these people were suddenly and totally disrupted. The local people commented that by introducing such a huge displacement project, they would lose their community, families, relation with nature, and their culture. For an Adivasi, those are all important, so they decided to fight back and tell the government that they would not support their own destruction.

When the military vehicles moved in, the women sat on the road. They were abused and beaten by military personnel, but they did not retaliate. They wanted to conduct a nonviolent struggle against the army. Violence and nonviolence came face to face in this context. The fight went on for many months: unarmed nonviolent people on one side and heavily armed military personnel on the other. Without describing the story in great detail, let me acknowledge that the people's nonviolent movement resulted in their victory for the time being.

Although repeated efforts were made by the army to confiscate the land and establish a military base, the Adivasis who were determined to use nonviolence as a force for resistance and change defeated them. In a public hearing session held in Netarath in the aftermath of this struggle, people stood up one after the other to speak about Gandhi and nonviolence. They were proud of their victory, especially a victory that was achieved through nonviolent methods.

The larger question that the Adivasis are now facing is whether the government will reintroduce the project or whether it will be shelved. The indications are that the project will be reintroduced with the idea of building an army base. Rather than coming in large numbers, however, the army is now taking over small areas in the region for use as police camps. People are frightened but still alert and organized to resist any expansion and takeover of their land and resources. However, they need national and international support if they are to resist the design of the government for many years to come.

People in France can understand this struggle, as there is a similar attempt by the French army to take over a large area in the eastern part of the country. Lanza del Vasto, a renowned leader of nonviolence, lived in India with Gandhi and later became an influential nonviolent campaigner and activist in Italy, Algeria, Palestine, India and then in France. My friend José Bové, farmer, anti-military activist and now a member of the European Parliament and a leader of the farmers' movement, showed me how they are now able to organize the land in the interest of the farmers. Another friend, Louis Campana, was the first one to take me to this area. He is now heading an organization called Gandhi International that attempts to connect nonviolent movements in India with those happening across the globe. Other friends, such as Stéphane Hessel, who is supporting nonviolent struggles in Palestine, and Majid Rahanama in Iran are looking for innovative methods that people can use to fight oppressive regimes. The innovative nonviolent methods used by people in Netarath and Koel-Karo described above are just two examples of communities standing up to oppression.

As noted, these are but a few examples of the nonviolent movements taking root today. I was recently in a place called Betala in the district of Palamu, India. Here, the organized effort of local Adivasis was able to stop a large dam that was going to displace many villages and thousands of villagers. This was an interesting story because of how they organized people at the local level as well as networked with many individuals and organizations at the national level to stop the Uranga dam. Across the tribal belt of India, I witnessed similar situations. People's resources are taken and if they oppose, they are classified as supporters of armed rebel groups. In the face of such violence and oppression, it is amazing to see how the Adivasis of India have kept their faith in Gandhi and continue to fight against all odds by using nonviolence. I hope the world at large will take note of it and express their solidarity, because nonviolence is dear to all of us and we should not allow the spirit of nonviolent actors to wither and die.

Crying for Peace While Feeding the Crocodile of Violence

We keep hearing about violence in India. When you read the morning paper, there are many reports about violence. Sometimes we are given the impression that the newspapers and television channels have become popular because of the sensational news and crime that they report. I always wonder why nonviolent actions are not so prominently reported.

An article in *Time Magazine* described how a country like Norway brought down their crime rate. There were two interesting steps that the Norwegian government took. One step was to convert jails into reform centers. The idea was to help people to reform rather than to punish them. The second step was to reduce crime reporting in the media. According to this article, both these steps had a tremendous impact on the Norwegian population and the crime rate came down significantly. Unfortunately, in the country of Buddha and Gandhi, we continue to enjoy reading about violence and crime. As a result, the media are feeding this need for sensationalism. Some time back, I did a random survey to find out how many items associated with criminal activities were reported in an English newspaper on a particular day. I was surprised to see 17 reports on that single day.

To prepare for the largest *yatra* in human history, I began the Samwad Yatra, a year-long program starting on 2 October 2011. This was a national mobilization in India leading up to the Jan Satyagraha or March for Justice in October 2012. Along with 20 other Ekta Parishad workers, I travelled 80,000 km in a caravan of jeeps to 350 districts from the south to the north of India over the course of the year (October 2011 to September 2012). The goal of the Samwad Yatra and the Jan Satyagraha 2012 were to increase access and ownership of land, improve livelihoods, and contribute to sustainable development. We wanted to champion the rights of the poor and strove to change land laws and policies for the benefit of agricultural laborers, peasants and small-scale farmers, and disenfranchised tribal people. Promoting rights to land, forest, and water and building a nonviolent economy is needed to strengthen people's control over vital resources, to promote economic and social development locally, and to contribute to food security globally.

My intention in the Samwad Yatra was to see the levels of violence and nonviolence being used by various groups to address their problems. After being four months on the road and covering a distance of about 25,000 km, I came to understand with certainty and confidence that nonviolent actions outnumber violent actions in India. Unfortunately, however, only violent actions continue to be reported in the media. This is truly an obsession, for if they have crime reporters in their magazines and newspapers, could they not also have peace reporters? If there can be journalism based on crime reporting, why not promote peace journalism as well? Why are we so fascinated with violence and not with nonviolence? This is not only a question of what journalists are reporting and what the readers are consuming. It is also related to the financial resources allocated for dealing with violence. The India government is using crime reporting to justify spending more money on counter-terrorism. Therefore, an impression is created that the main problem in India today is terrorism—from both external and internal sources.

The idea of external terrorism gives an opportunity for the Defense Ministry to increase their budget and sign new contracts to buy arms and strengthen the military. The idea of internal terrorism gives an opportunity for the Home Ministry to increase police stations in the name of internal security. This situation has been going on for many years now in India. In most cases, proposals submitted to the government to rethink their approach or to spend some money on the promotion of peace get a negative response. The government is not interested in spending anything on peace education or on the promotion of peace. There is no ministry for peace and not even a secretary with whom you can discuss the issue. It looks as if violence has become a well-paid business and as a result, there is no interest in talking about peace processes. Rather than being interested in peace processes, the government is trying to stop all those groups that are trying to find a solution to violence by using nonviolent methods. Indirectly, this system is feeding into the desire for violence in many contexts by blocking all possibilities for nonviolent alternatives.

Despite these circumstances, I have seen indications from Koodankulam to Jharkhand of people's faith in nonviolence. I have not encountered a single group that believes in democratic processes through the promotion of violence. The movements in Koodankulam and Jaitapur are good examples of nonviolent struggles against nuclear plants. Furthermore, there is no reason why the police should have used violence against the nonviolent actors in Jaitapur. Similarly, the nonviolent agitation in Chengara by Adivasis and Dalits for land has been going on for years. Many struggles against dams, mining, and industries across the country are pursued nonviolently. It was through strong nonviolent struggles that people were able to protect Gandhamardhn in Orissa.[1] Again, it was nonviolent struggle by Adivasis in Jharkhand that blocked the possibility of displacing large numbers of people through the Koel-Karo dam project.

Unfortunately, it has become fashionable for the police or paramilitary forces to open fire on innocent people. I wish the state would realize the conditions in which these people are living.

On the one hand, the Indian state is trying to destroy nonviolent movements by using violence. On the other hand, it is trying to build its capacity to use violence by propagating the view that the country is facing tremendous internal and external violence. Fortunately, people are slowly realizing this contradiction. They have started questioning the state and the excessive use of violence against its own citizens. While poor people are often the victims on the ground, Indian intellectuals are often indifferent and look the other way. This leaves the country in a profoundly difficult situation.

In Front of a Vast Graveyard of Words and Values

I am more and more concerned about the lack of respect for words. There was a time when people used to say 'a word is a word and you cannot break it'. This was the basis for marriages in India. Two families would exchange 'a word' and they would keep to it. Much of the transactions in society took place on the basis of one's words. It is only recently that we have moved from an oral tradition to a legal one. Unfortunately, in this process, we have lost our respect for words. The acts of announcement and pronouncement are no longer valued. During election periods, for example, politicians can say and promise anything. These words and promises are promptly forgotten after the elections are over. My concern is that people are getting used to this lack of respect for words and for the power of naming and speaking. Even in villages, oral transactions are no longer respected. Today, you can get away with not keeping your word.

I find that it is only among some Adivasis and poor people that words are still meaningful. You will often find that a poor person will give away his/her land merely on the basis of a word from a senior government official. The official promises they will be given jobs in exchange for giving up their land. They take the word of an educated person so seriously that they do not think twice about getting the word-commitment in writing. I remember when working at a bonded labour Inquiry Commission for the Supreme Court in India. I was trying to convince a very poor person that he did not have to return the loan taken from a farmer as he was now released from the bondage. This individual had a strong look on his face and he said, 'Sir, I want to keep my promise and I will return the money'. For this individual, legal provisions were not important. What was important was his oral commitment that he would return the loaned money.

In my travels and during nonviolent campaigns, I encounter many people standing in front of government offices with petitions. They are told that the *mem/saheb* will only understand written language. The government officials will not entertain any oral discussion. What are the poor people trying to tell the official? Their main grievances are a lack of drinking water in their village, dealers selling rice and oil on the black market, or that they want the liquor shop to be removed from the village. Is this something that the officer cannot understand if villagers state it orally? Why make things so complicated for these people? Why waste so much time and resources for people to write an application and stand in a queue to meet the official for such a small thing? Perhaps one of the reasons is that this process is big business. There is a person drafting letters who charges ten rupees per letter. There is also a typist who charges another ten rupees per page and a person who makes a living making photocopies of the same applications. So grows these individuals' businesses as well as the Gross Domestic Product of the country.

We have found new methods to take the resources from the pockets of poor people and put it into the market in the name of a 'legal' culture. One person in a village told me:

> Government officials rarely come to the village and if they come at all, they only come to punish us, not to solve our problems. The policeman comes to take our people to the *thana*, the forest officials come with a search warrant or other officials are into the village when they need to make some extra money or collect some good vegetables.

Why should so many people be kept on the government payroll to punish innocent people? The poor were never trained to deal with this system. They were not even told that this kind of a system was being created and what services would be provided. How can we morally accept this exploitation of people by a highly corrupt system? Many of the stories I have listened to on this matter have given me a profound sense that there is a large gap between the lives of the poor and the governments meant to serve and protect them.

Democracy was once a word that was highly cherished in India. Now it has become a joke. People use this word for all kinds of purposes. Democratic action is not longer something dear to our society. People think democracy can simply be equated with elections. So while we are highly undemocratic and authoritarian in day-to-day life, we still claim that we are part of the biggest democracy in the world.

The word 'democracy' is losing its meaning very fast because even in democratic elections, people are now using money and power to win. Those who do not practice democratic values in elections are supposed to promote democratic values in society. This is becoming a deep-rooted problem in India. The idea that the other person also has a view, and that view also needs to be respected, is more of a drama than a reality. In the last ten to twenty years, words like 'participation' or 'inclusion' have been so loosely used that they are dying a slow death.

There was also a time when teachers in the classroom used to speak about the phrase *manasa, vacha, karmana*, which means there should be harmony between what you think, what you say, and what you do. We were told that this is how civilized people should behave. The lesser the contradiction between thinking, speaking, and doing, the more civilized you became in your interactions with others. Today, we see the opposite in our day-to-day lives. In our democracy, people are proud when they can make a speech and do the opposite of that they said. They are proud when they were able to fool others. More than economic poverty, this poverty of values is becoming more and more frightening.

Out of these realities, a series of questions arise: What do you do in a country where words and terminologies are no longer important? How can you trust anybody when you know that you are cheated again and again through the use of similar words and similar promises? What will happen to a society where people finally conclude that whether it is oral or legal, words are not important? Is it one's capacity to undermine the value of words and bully one's way to 'success' that is important? What do we achieve by creating this vast graveyard of words and values?

Two Streams—Where Do You Want to Be?

India is going through a very challenging period. One can clearly see that there are two streams of people influencing (or trying to influence) the country. I identify these as a stream of violence and a stream of nonviolence. Only the future will tell us which stream will succeed.

As things stand today, the stream of violence is spreading fast. This stream is led by corporate forces, which are violent toward both nature and people. For profit, they are willing to surrender all values. Some of them do it knowingly while others follow them unwittingly. Political parties support this stream. You can see these parties parading just behind the corporations facilitating their violence, promoting them, and sharing the corporate messages in all ways possible. This is then used to contest elections. In these circumstances, election victories become the means by which the natural resources of the country are sold to 'friends' in various industries with politicians increasing their own bank balances.

Some of these corporate leaders are also part of political parties. Thus, they are able to advocate for policies that benefit their particular industry. Behind them, the entire administration can be seen ruthlessly following the orders of their political bosses and corporate houses. The same corporation employs many of these officials' children. And so, once again there is conflict of interest. There is another group parading just out of sight; that is the police and paramilitary forces. They are supposed to shoot down all opposition to the theft of extraction of resources for profit, violent or nonviolent. They suppress the voices of people who are trying to protect their resources and dignity in a very disciplined way.

And just behind them, you can see armed groups. They are part of private armies and security forces. Though they are behind in this game of politics, strategy, and suppression, they would like to march ahead and also take control of the country's resources. Each one of these groups uses violence as a method. They abuse human rights, and together they have an interest in defeating nonviolence. Each one of them will claim that ultimately, through their ruthless processes, they will bring peace and justice to the world. Their audience is sitting at a distance, however, not able to see their behaviour but listening to their claims that violence will bring about peace, justice, and 'development.'

In the name of peace, justice, and development, the audience is clapping and supporting them in whatever they do. And even when the audience is able to see the violence and injustice, they turn a blind eye because they feel they can do nothing to change the game in which the leading players have enormous power. This sense of helplessness is compounded by the fact that their own incomes, their food, the education of their children, the interest payments on the many loans they have taken out, all depend on the huge salaries these corporations pay them. Many even think that just because they are now able to go to beautiful malls and buy international brands that the country has finally 'developed'. After several decades of such growth, this rising and affluent middle class takes pride in becoming 'developed'. Not only to they fear going back to those dreaded times of the past, they also see a younger generation besieged with unemployment, which reinforces their positions that such 'development' is good.

But there is another stream in which you can find women, Adivasis, Dalits, nomads, fisher folk, farmers, small shopkeepers and urban poor parading in the front. There are also small groups of HIV affected people, Devadasis, and transgendered people among them. They are struggling nonviolently to resist this takeover, even though they are often very isolated. Behind them are many voluntary organizations and people's movements parading with an interest in supporting these groups. However, these groups can be divided.

They are divided in terms of Gandhians, Lohities, Ambedkarites, and Marxists. Their intentions are very good. They want to protect and support marginalized communities to survive against the onslaught of corporations. Behind these social movements, you can also see some intellectuals and media parading as a small team. Compared to the number of intellectuals and media supporting the violent stream, this group of people is small. In this stream of nonviolence, you can see people with determination and good intentions but they have not yet come together around a common purpose and goal.

By looking at this portrait, you can see for yourself that the nonviolent stream, though pious and good, is weak. It will find it extremely difficult to contain or challenge the violent stream in which people have identified mutual interest and a common goal. I have provided the above description to help my readers to understand what a gigantic task Jan Satyagraha is trying to achieve. By travelling through the country, we are trying to link thousands of voluntary organizations and social movements across ideological barriers, articulating a common agenda of protecting the land and livelihood resources of the people in order to protect their lives and culture.

This is the time when we need all likeminded people to join us. This is a historically important and decisive action for nonviolent social change in India. It is not every day that such a decisive struggle for justice takes place. This struggle is a result of many years of painstaking efforts to use nonviolence for the benefit of marginalized people. Please join us today and throw your weight and might behind this movement for social transformation in India.

Concluding Conference Reflections:
Nonviolence, the Weapon of the Strong:
Advancing Nonviolence, Spirituality, and Social Transformation

One important issue that has come up frequently is that we live in a world in which literally trillions of dollars are being spent annually to promote war and violence. As responsible citizens, we have to use every available opportunity to preempt violence and promote the agenda of nonviolence. Every day, people who are benefitting from violence are sharpening the weapons in their arsenal. It is time to break this myth and to sharpen the arguments and tools for nonviolent social change.

Recently, I came across an article about the various marketing surveys that are being conducted in different parts of the world, such as those of soft drink companies and mobile phone manufacturers. It was found that the soft drink companies have tapped about sixty percent of the world's population in the purchase of soft drinks whereas forty percent of the global population has cell phones. Yet the shocking part of this article was the marketing of small arms. The author of the article assessed that about two percent of people in the world have already purchased small arms. This means that in many countries where there are large un-captured markets, aggressive advertising and sales are being carried out that endorse the sale of these arms and ammunitions! People in the business of selling arms are outpacing those who believe in nonviolence.

There are three important aspects in the promotion of nonviolence. First, we need to begin where people are located. We need to understand their problems, and see how nonviolence can be applied in their daily lives as a way to solve their problems. Bringing theory and practice together is relevant for people because it gives them a sense of confidence that nonviolence actually works. Having faith in people's capacity to use nonviolence as a way of dealing with conflicts further vitalizes nonviolence.

Second, people practice nonviolence without always seeing that what they are doing is nonviolent. Rather than telling people that *they must use* nonviolence, we can begin by appreciating the work that is already being carried out and identify the component parts that are nonviolent.

A third aspect is to respect people's propensities for nonviolence. Some people take time to develop nonviolent approaches, and this does not always fit with those whose response time is fast. It is important to realize that people have their own knowledge systems, their own capacities and skills, and that there is no one way to practice nonviolence. Thus, these three aspects lay out some of the difficulties of bringing nonviolent action into practice.

Experiencing the daily life of ordinary people has been the way that I have gained deeper insights into the application of nonviolence in people's lives. I began my work with young people in a region of India that was famous for violence. The guiding principle for us was the talisman of Mahatma Gandhi: 'Focus on the weakest and poorest when you have to make a decision'. It was young people's sustained effort with the poorest and weakest bandits in the region that led to their laying down of their arms.

Through this process, we were able to understand the various methods that deal with direct and indirect forms of violence. This also gave us a deeper understanding of how indirect violence is breeding direct violence. There are many examples of how I acquired experiential knowledge of indirect violence. People at the grassroots kept challenging my notion of 'development' and my values because they found them unacceptable. Let me give a small example from when I was appointed as Supreme Court Commissioner for bonded labourers in 1990.

As Commissioner, I had the authority to release people who were in economic bondage. One day, I went to a poor bonded laborer and I used my authority to waive his debt. I told him that he did not have to repay the money he took from the landlord. This poor man looked at me with surprise and said:

> Mr. Rajagopal, do not teach us your value of 'not repaying what you have borrowed'. In our culture, we pay back what we have borrowed. Maybe there is no written document to prove that I have taken the money but for us oral agreement is good enough and I would like to repay the principle whenever I can.

It was difficult for me to understand the reason why this person, who had already repaid the equivalent to the principal in interest, would insist to repay the full amount. At first I was unable to accept this argument that was seemingly unjust, but with more thought, I realized I had a lot to learn from the so-called common ordinary people who cherish ethical over material values.

For many years, I have worked with young people to facilitate training processes that help people to understand their anger and divert it into positive action. I see anger as a form of energy, such as solar or wind energy. If it can be diverted into other forms of energy for the benefit of humanity, then large problems can be solved in order to create a better world. I have used this theory in all my actions during the past 20 years. I now have the confidence to propose this as a possibility, not only in India, but in other parts of the world as well.

Young people are angry for various reasons. In some parts of the world, this anger can stem from injustice and poverty. In other parts of the world, it can be unemployment and overconsumption; yet given an opportunity, every young person can use this anger positively. If we fail to direct young people's anger, conflict and violence are inevitable. This is the anger that is felt in a market dominated by those who produce and sell armaments and incite wars. Or it is the anger that is felt over genetically modified species that are disrupting local crop production and dispossessing small farmers. Or this anger arises from the spending of funds on world football matches at the cost of people not having basic services.

One way that nonviolent advocates lose out is by inaction. In our training in India, we facilitate processes in which young people understand a three-fold approach to social change: struggle, dialogue, and constructive programs. One has to struggle for change, but things do not change just because of struggle. One must also be willing to dialogue with those who have more power in negotiating power-sharing arrangements. When there is no opportunity for struggle or dialogue, then it is important to engage in constructive work or investing time and energy into community building. Each of these provides activists with actions necessary for transforming society nonviolently.

During the conference discussions, participants have looked in detail at various issues related to nonviolence. There has been so much to learn from each session that having parallel sessions made it difficult for participants to engage in all the interactions. In my opinion, some of the key insights were these:

1. to connect the macro- and the micro-levels. People seemed to agree that larger change is based on the cumulative actions of people at the grassroots level;
2. to connect to the ideas of Gandhi, Martin Luther King, Nelson Mandela, and many other international peace promoters in order to have models in leadership development; and
3. to have repeated references to ideas like *ahimsa*, *sarvodaya* and *satyagraha*—nonviolent direct action, truth, and reconciliation.

This understanding helped me to reflect back on my own situation in India and to realize how marginalized Gandhi has become, whether in the fields of politics or economics. There seems to be a systematic rejection of Gandhi and Gandhian values. This is best exemplified in the educational system that is driving young people to believe that material gain is more important than all other ethical values. India is missing a great opportunity to help the world to think differently and act differently. By using Gandhian philosophy, India could uniquely demonstrate that there is a different way to approach education, politics, and economics, but to date this is not the case.

There was a wide range of nonviolent concepts and responses that were presented during this conference related to several aspects: animals and non-human life, energy, environment, gender, children, religion, theatre, and the state police forces, to name a few. This conference created a learning environment that enabled participants to expand and deepen concepts of nonviolence. The application of nonviolence as a lens from which to recognize the scope of different conflicts in society was introduced. This is a lens that states could use to measure the results of their policy plans and programs. By using a nonviolent lens, policy makers could pre-empt violence that is injected into society in the name of expanding economic development at the cost of social and environmental relations. To take the learning of the conference into practice may mean introducing this kind of lens to various state governments for their planning and implementation of development schemes. The introduction of such a lens could result in a dramatic change in the culture of governance and would be salutary for society.

The conference also introduced many challenges. The first challenge is the notion of ethics and justice. Can progress and development be measured just by materialistic gains without the component of ethics and justice? Gandhi has repeatedly written about accumulating wealth without the ethic of thinking of the other. I am reminded of an aphorism that everything economically correct need not be ethically correct. You may recollect that when Gandhi was asked whether he would like to follow a British model of development, his answer was that it took half of the world's resources to make England prosper. It would take more than one universe for India to imitate that development model.

A second challenge was that young people participating in this conference questioned whether education was part of the solution or part of the problem. As the venue for the conference was a University with large student participation, they were interrogating whether higher education was liberating them or preparing them for a kind of slavery. This is a serious issue that was addressed in different speakers' remarks. Personally, I kept hearing about the disconnect that has been created between the educational system and the functioning of the brain and the heart. While people are becoming more intelligent with the kind of information and knowledge available, there is less affective learning, which develops the heart and the capacity to feel (intuit) the problems along the way.

For instance, people are looking at distribution of goods and services but not questioning from where commodities are originating. From where is our food coming? How is food produced? What is happening to the producer of that food? The materiality of food is obvious because we eat it every day. Do we think about the producer of the food and the problems they encounter in today's world in that production process? Do we think of whether food is poisonous and how that is affecting the food chain? Do we use nonviolence as a way of determining consumer choice? Do we link this consumerism with the way we are treating the planet? Do we realize that while discussing issues of climate change and global warming, we actually continue to pollute and poison the planet's scarce resources? These disconnects need to be addressed, and young people at this conference were asking these questions.

A third challenge was the connection between what is happening internally in people and what is occurring externally. While some people are developing externally with material wealth and new computer gadgets, others are becoming hollow inside. In spite of all the material wealth and achievements, there is still a craving for understanding of oneself. This desire needs to be addressed to realize that this competition for external achievements is not sustainable without spiritual development. It is time to remember what Gandhi said: 'There is enough for everyone's need but not for anyone's greed'. This will be an important area for follow-up after this conference.

A fourth challenge is educating and training people in nonviolence and sensitizing state agencies to use and promote nonviolence in places where institutions are carrying out indirect and direct violence. This is a time to recognize the efforts being made by some states in terms of promoting a culture of nonviolence. What is being done by Norway is worth noticing: they have transformed their prisons into reform centers. Journalists have decided to stop crime reporting. A small country like Georgia has introduced a Ministry for Reconciliation and Civil Equality. Bhutan has introduced the Gross National Happiness index. These are examples that showcase the efforts being made by people and state actors.

A last challenge to which I would like to draw attention is the speed at which we are transforming society through nonviolent methods. If we understand that the problems we face are acute and these problems are affecting the lives of millions of people and the planet itself, then we need to redesign our approach to solving these problems. When a house is on fire, people take it as an emergency and behave differently than they would in normal times. This metaphor invites nonviolent activists and thinkers to see how they can speed up the process of nonviolent practice. It is not good enough to have ten places where water is heating at ten degrees centigrade. What is important is to have water boiling at 100 degrees in one place.

This is a very serious matter, but I want to tell you a humorous story. There was a friend who used to run five kilometers a day. One day he ran ten kilometers. When asked why he doubled his distance, he explained that there was a dog chasing him. The realization was that when there is something urgent, people would find out how to increase the speed and augment the commitment needed to remedy the situation. In my meeting with young people, I have shared two quotations to help them recognize the importance of acting: 'If you are not indifferent, the world will be different' and 'between silence and violence, there is active nonviolence'. Getting these messages to the younger generation is one way of creating a sense of urgency.

As far as civil society-action in India, Ekta Parishad and International Initiatives are developing an action plan from 2015 to 2020. In 2015, there were events addressing Gandhi's historic return to India from South Africa. In 2016, there will be women leaders from different parts of the world coming together to look at women's transformative power and nonviolent action. In 2017, there will be centenary celebrations of Gandhi's struggle with farmers and landless labourers that he carried out a hundred years earlier in Champaran in the state of Bihar. In 2018, there will be an international gathering to look at nonviolent economy in its theory. In 2019, there is a proposed long march from Delhi to Geneva covering a distance of 8000 km over 15 months by an international team of 100 nonviolent actors. In 2020, there will be a march of one million people in India and different parts of the world, demanding a paradigm shift in the development process worldwide based on the Gandhian concept of *sarvodaya* (wellbeing of all). This is a historic time for all of us to join hands and create new international nonviolent policies and processes based on ethics and justice.

About the Authors

Rajagopal P. V. has been a Gandhian activist for decades. He is the former Vice Chairman of the Gandhi Peace Foundation, New Delhi, and is the president and founding member of Ekta Parishad. In 2007, Ekta Parishad under the leadership of Rajagopal used the Gandhian method of *Padayatra* or foot-marches. After extensive mobilization and organization, 25,000 people walked for a month from Gwalior to Delhi, insisting on land reform and forest rights. A similar march was held in 2012, Jan Satyagraha, with 100,000 people. These and other activities utilize a range of Gandhian approaches: teaching, training, mobilization, discussions with governing bodies, fasting, nonviolent resistance, and constrictive social programs. Several documentaries and publications have been made of Rajagopal's work and the effort to promote and demonstrate nonviolence, and establish and international solidarity of the poor regarding land reform issues.

Rajagopal, along with the work of Ekta Parishad, provide world leadership for nonviolent struggles, training, and actions.

Jill Carr-Harris has worked with Ekta Parishad and Rajagopal for over 20 years. During this time she has been a part of the women's movement building, training and empowerment, and gender policy research in India, Bangladesh, and the Philippines. She was one of the prominent women leaders of the most significant land-rights marches for landless poor women in post-independence India. She has worked on many international solidarity projects. She has founded and led civil-society organizations in India on agrarian reform as well as gender equality. She has spent the last 30 years in India, much of the time assisting poor women and marginalized communities in the Hindi belt. She is currently the Director of the International Gandhi Institute for Nonviolence and Peace (IGINP) in South India, an organization designed to train people in nonviolent leadership and social action.

Notes

1. Gandhamaradhn is a hill in Western Orissa famous for its medicinal plants. Legend says that Hanuman, a Hindu deity, carried it there from the Himalayas.

Part II

Philosophical and Theoretical Considerations

Chapter 6

Violence and Politics: A Reading of Hannah Arendt's Distinction between Violence and Power

Sophie Cloutier

Introduction

Since December 2010, with the events of the Arab Spring, the question of revolution has quickly risen to the forefront of geopolitical concerns. Today our political landscape is marked by protests, riots, terrorist attacks, and civil wars in many countries around the globe. Images in the media are very often violent, depicting scenes of war or police use of violence to pacify protesters. Given these changes, the question of the relation between violence and politics seems altogether relevant and timely, especially when considering the matter of revolution. We might ask: is violence an essential component of politics today? Does revolution have to be violent as such? An easy answer would be to say 'no' and to give the example of the Indian Revolution led by Mahatma Gandhi and his followers. But is the Indian Revolution the exception to the norm?

Indeed, Karl Marx justified the use of violence as a means of attaining the greater good, of attaining a new political and economic system. Marx's conception of violence for political means raises the question of the justification of violence in politics. In order to shed light on these questions, the political contributions of Hannah Arendt can be helpful. Arendt wrote on totalitarianism, revolution, and student protests, among many other topics relevant to political philosophy. She was interested in the question of violence in politics, both on theoretical and practical grounds. She is one of the rare philosophers who have distinguished between power and violence, a distinction aimed at getting to the root of political action, which is any action that is not subjected to some form of domination. She was critical of the role of violence in politics and was not in agreement with Jean Paul Sartre's idea of violence as the creator of humanity,[1] advanced in his Preface to Frantz Fanon's Les Damnés de la Terre (The Wretched of the Earth).

In this chapter, I propose to begin with what seems like a curious paradox—that violence is powerless—in order to present the functional limits of violent action in the political sphere. I will argue that violence is regarded as a substitute for power by the excluded and that violence is not a valid political category *per se*. Arendt understood that violence may have an impact on liberation from oppression; however, she also argued that violence must be surpassed. From her distinction between violence and power, we can reinterpret violence as a response to powerlessness and thereby better understand the violence of decolonization movements. My aim is to disentangle two political experiences too often amalgamated in the literature on violence in political philosophy. My argument will be developed in three parts. I will begin with a conceptual distinction between power and violence. I will then summarize Arendt's distinction between the activities of the *vita activa*. Following from these conceptual distinctions, I will finally address the limits of violent action.

A Conceptual Distinction between Power and Violence

In *The Human Condition* (1961) Arendt first distinguished between violence and power. This book was Arendt's response to totalitarianism, in which she established the foundation of her political thought. If totalitarianism is the flipside of politics, a regime trying to undermine the essential conditions of a political life—that is, freedom and plurality manifested in political action—an important task left to political philosophers is to rethink politics. For her, plurality is the condition of all political life: it is because we are many that we are political beings in the first place. She defines plurality as the twofold character of equality and distinction. She writes:

> Action would be an unnecessary luxury, a capricious interference with general laws of behaviour, if men were endlessly reproducible repetitions of the same model, whose nature or essence was the same for all and as predictable as the nature or essence of any other thing. Plurality is the condition of human action because we are all the same, that is, human, in such a way that nobody is ever the same as anyone else who ever lived, lives, or will live. (Arendt 1998: 8)

Arendt finds in the Athenian *polis* a model of public space grounded in plurality and thus, allowing for a disclosure of power. Going back to the etymology of the word 'power' in the Greek *dynamis*, she explains that power is always a potentiality, a *potential power*. This potential character of power prevents us from considering it as something measurable or quantifiable, as we can do with 'energy' or 'force'. According to Arendt, it is impossible to store up power and keep it in reserve as we can do with the instruments of violence. Power exists only within its actualization. Wherever people gather together, power is potentially active, but not necessarily so, and not forever. It 'is actualized', writes Arendt, 'only where word and deeds have not parted company, where words are not empty and deeds not brutal, where words are not used to veil intentions but to disclose realities, and deeds are not used to violate and destroy but to establish relations and create new realities' (1998: 200). Arendt is following the Roman political legacy, which Cicero gave expression to: '*Cum potestas in populo auctoritas in senatu sit*: While power resides in the people, authority rests with the Senate' (in Arendt 2006: 122).

Arendt opposes power to strength. While strength is the natural quality of an individual in isolation, power only springs up between humans when they act together and vanishes when they disperse. In a battle between two persons, it is strength that will dominate, whether physical or intellectual. However, politics is not an activity of singular and isolated individuals; it is grounded in plurality. If a person would rather isolate oneself than participate in a common action, he or she will lose his or her power, and thus becomes impotent, whatever his or her strength may otherwise be. The way Arendt describes popular revolt exemplifies how she understands power. She writes:

> Popular revolt against materially strong rulers...may engender an almost irresistible power even if it foregoes the use of violence in the face of materially vastly superior forces. To call this 'passive resistance' is certainly an ironic idea; it is one of the most active and efficient ways of action ever devised, because it cannot be countered by fighting, where there may be defeat or victory, but only by mass slaughter in which the victor is defeated, cheated of his prize, since nobody can rule over dead men. (Arendt 1998: 200-01)

Arendt understands that the great potential of pacific resistance rests in the disclosure of power. All participants equally share in this action, and fundamentally the action lies in togetherness, meaning that individuals are freely joining together in a concerted action.

Contrary to violence, power is not based on constraint but on consent and shared speech. Power comes from the association of persons in political communities; it comes from the original political pact that is reaffirmed every time individuals act together. Violence, on the other hand, does not need this solidarity because it has instruments with which to compensate for its lack. Therefore, one of the more characteristic differences between power and violence is that power rests on the people and requires plurality, whereas violence can go without plurality because of the compensation provided by its instruments. One single individual could appropriate for him or herself all the instruments of violence, but could never do the same with power. An armed individual could dominate a group of people but could never use his or her weapons to generate power. The strength of one individual cannot overcome the power of a group of people. Only violence could separate the group and make its power vanish. However, violence can never replace power. It is impossible to force power violently to spring up or to import it, as we sometimes think we do when we 'import' democracy.

In her argument, Arendt relies on Montesquieu, who saw that tyranny rests on isolation: the tyrant is isolated from his or her subjects. Because of this lack of plurality, tyranny prevents the development of power and produces a sort of impotence. As Arendt remarks:

> This, in Montesquieu's interpretation, makes it necessary to assign it a special position in the theory of political bodies: it alone is unable to develop enough power to remain at all in the space of appearance, the public realm; on the contrary, it develops the germs of its own destruction the moment it comes into existence. (Arendt 1998: 203)

Tyranny tries to substitute violence for power, but this substitution causes its own doom. In order to preserve the potentiality of power, we have to preserve the common world, understood as the public space where people can freely talk and act together. It is also important not to exclude anybody or any group from this public space, because exclusion would be experienced as a form of impotence. The excluded then risk turning to violence as a substitute for power. Our contemporary world is full of examples of the excluded turning to violence. Before discussing the limits of violent action, however, we must first understand Arendt's conceptualization of human activities, of the *vita activa*, because it is at the basis of her distinction between power and violence.

Our Human Condition

Arendt analyzes the modern use of violence in politics as a loss of the genuine meaning of political action. She believes that the original spirit of public life has evaporated because we have regarded the state or government as a work of art, as if we could build a state like a house. A totalitarian regime can be seen as the paradigm of this use of violence in politics, a regime trying to undermine the human capacity for freedom and spontaneity by eradicating plurality, while trying to build a nation and transform human nature. *The Human Condition* can thus be read as Arendt's response to totalitarianism. In order to recover the original meaning of politics, she analyzes the basic conditions under which life on earth has been given to human beings. She distinguishes three conditions: life, worldliness, and plurality. Each of these conditions corresponds to a specific activity: labor, work, and action. The problem is that the distinctions between these activities have been blurred over time, and the result is that we now understand politics through the model of the activity of work. I will not go into detail here, but a schematization of the different conditions and activities of active life will help to clarify and demonstrate how certain means of violence were introduced to and legitimated in politics.

The first activity is labor, which corresponds to the condition of life itself. Arendt first explains that the difference between labor and work is difficult to grasp because the modern conditions of work have contributed to obscuring this distinction. However, Arendt points out, 'every European language, ancient and modern, contains two etymologically unrelated words for what we have come to think of as the same activity, and retains them in the face of their persistent synonymous usage' (1998: 80). One way to distinguish between labor and work is to underline the dimension of pain and effort characteristic of labor. More specifically, what characterizes labor is its relation to the entire body. In fact, labor meets the condition of life, and life is given to us through the body. We must labor to keep our body alive. The activity of labor means precisely this relationship between nature and the body. That is to say, we fill the needs of our body with our body. Therefore, labor is not an activity done freely, rather, it points to necessity. We must accommodate, feed, and clothe ourselves. The Greeks thought of labor in terms of *a-skholia*, non-rest. It is in this sense that they opposed the necessity to satisfy needs in life with the ability to participate freely in public life. The Greeks soon realized that they had to reduce their burden of work in order to attend to public affairs. Affluent Greek citizens thus forced slaves to accomplish tasks the citizens would not do themselves. Through violence, citizens unburdened themselves of the cares of everyday life in order to be free for political life. They also recognized that labor is not a specifically human activity, as it leaves no trace behind, and carries no possibility for immortal fame. Indeed, the products of labor are intended for immediate consumption, another aspect distinguishing labor from work, the product of which has permanence. Life requires human effort that relates to the animal, which is why we call the individual who labours *animal laborans*.

Labor also has a very paradoxical position because it entails both effort and joy. It combines the joy of living and the fear of dying. Labor brings joy because reward immediately follows effort. Labor is thus caught in a time loop that resembles the cycle of nature, which continually regenerates itself. The cyclical movement of labor repeats the endless cycle of nature. The cycle of labor also refers to the fact that it is constantly producing goods that should immediately be consumed before they spoil. Each need repeats itself and whenever it is met, the pleasure is renewed. Short-term pain and happiness are always repeated and constantly multiplying.

In her chapter on labor, Arendt provides a critique of Marx. According to Arendt, Marx brought an activity that had always remained in the shadows to the light of the public sphere. Labor, as the maintenance of biological life, is a private activity. According to Arendt, we can bring labor into the public sphere, reduce working hours, organize labor more effectively, or even automate it; doing so would not change the fundamental nature of labor, which is to meet our essential biological needs. Making labor more productive will only increase the speed of the consumer cycle and wear down the durability of the world. It is no surprise that our labor society is also a consumer society. The problem is that consumer society threatens the sustainability of the world. Arendt writes:

> The rather uncomfortable truth of the matter is that the triumph the modern world has achieved over necessity is due to the emancipation of labor, that is, to the fact that the *animal laborans* was permitted to occupy the public realm; and yet, as long as the *animal laborans* remains in possession of it, there can be no true public realm, but only private activities displayed in the open. (Arendt 1998: 133-34)

The activity of work enables human beings to leave the ever-recurrent cycle of labor because it produces a permanent human world. Indeed, work—the Greek *poiesis*—produces objects and artefacts that are not destined to be consumed. Consumer goods will necessarily be doomed to destruction, while the use of objects will only wear them out over time. The products of work are not made to be consumed and their destruction is only incidental to their use. Thus, work responds to the human condition of worldliness. Facing their own mortality and finitude, it seems that human beings feel the impulsion to create a world that would outlast them, as if they had a natural impulsion to create an artificial world—that is, a world of objects, very different from any natural environment. Indeed, our homes have a longer service life than an individual's, and some monuments—pyramids, for instance—have survived for centuries. Hence, there is a function of permanence in the activity of work: in work, humans aim to create a permanent habitat for themselves.

With *homo faber*—the human being who works—we leave the cycle of life in which the *animal laborans* is trapped. The characteristic of *homo faber* is precisely to transcend, to go beyond the natural process of life, to create a human artifice. This transcendence is related to the fact that the human artifice exceeds biological necessity. For instance, the construction of cathedrals is not related to a biological need *per se*; we could very well survive without them. The sole purpose of *homo faber* is to build a genuinely human world that will ensure the stability of human existence. However, *homo faber* is not a creator-like god. He or she cannot create *ex nihilo*, but needs to take from nature the materials to create his or her object. It is for this reason that there is an intrinsic element of violence in the activity of work. For example, the artisan who wants to build a table must first kill a tree. Arendt adds that the 'experience of this violence is the most elemental experience of human strength and, therefore, the very opposite of the painful, exhausting effort experienced in sheer labor' (1998: 140). Arendt suggests that the 'work of our hands' is like a Promethean revolt because the human world can be erected only after destroying part of the

God-created world. This violence done to nature is justified by the very production of the object, of the human-created world. Arendt writes:

> The process of making is itself entirely determined by the categories of means and ends. The fabricated thing is an end product in the twofold sense that the production process comes to an end in it ('the process disappears in the product', as Marx said), and that it is only a means to produce this end. (Arendt 1998: 143)

The idea that the end justifies the means is very characteristic of fabrication; instrumentality is the typical mentality of *homo faber*. The mark of fabrication is having both a definite beginning and a predictable end, which contrasts with the cyclical movement of the body's life process, or the openness of action, which has a beginning but no predictable end. Arendt concludes:

> *Homo faber* is indeed a lord and master, not only because he is the master or has set himself up as the master of all nature but because he is master of himself and his doings. This is true neither of the *animal laborans*, which is subject to the necessity of his own life, nor of the man of action, who remains in dependence upon his fellow men. Alone with his image of the future product, *homo faber* is free to produce, and again facing alone the work of his hands, he is free to destroy. (Arendt 1998: 144)

Attention must be given to the characteristics of work Arendt describes, because these are the key to understanding her analysis of the political situation of our times. She explains that political life and action were modeled on fabrication by the Western tradition of political philosophy. Philosophers unhappy with the contingency of action and the unpredictability of human affairs have tried to create the perfect city, legitimating, in so doing, the means of violence to achieve their end; they introduced instrumentality into politics. The underlying problem with this circumstance is that the process of instrumentality has no end in itself because every end can become a new means for some other end: the glass is the end of the fabrication process but becomes the means to drink. Arendt worries that the generalization of the mentality of *homo faber* will degrade all things into means and make them lose their intrinsic and independent value, and more fundamentally, cause the meaning of free action to be lost.

Human beings need material objects to live, but we also need to regulate our relations with intangible things, such as institutions, laws, or customs. Thus, to make the material world a common world and a homeland for humans, the dimension of action is essential. For Arendt, the world becomes human only when it becomes an object of dialogue. All things become truly human when we debate about them with fellow beings. Our humanity becomes evident in our ability to share the world with others.

Action will come to play a vital role in creating a common reality; it corresponds to the condition of plurality—that is, the fact that we are a plurality of unique beings. Human beings are not only distinct from each other; we also have the capacity to express this very distinction, to distinguish ourselves, and to reveal our unique distinctness through speech and action. We insert ourselves into the human world with words and deeds. And this insertion is not conditioned by necessity but by the fact that we were born as newcomers into a world that precedes us. We respond to this novelty by beginning something new, on our own initiative, or as Arendt puts it, 'because they are *initium*, newcomers and beginners by virtue of their birth, men take initiative, are prompted into action' (1998: 177). In this sense, action always appears in the guise of a miracle, as something that could not have been predicted. Arendt links plurality to her concept of natality:

> And this again is possible only because each man is unique, so that with each birth something entirely new comes into the world. With respect to this somebody who is unique it can be truly said that nobody was there before. If action as beginning corresponds to the fact of birth, if it is the actualization of the human condition of natality, then speech corresponds to the fact of distinctness and is the actualization of the human condition of plurality, that is, of living as a distinct and unique being among equals. (Arendt 1998: 178)

Action is the only activity that connects human beings without the intermediary of objects. Arendt describes action as something unpredictable, unexpected, boundless, and ambiguous. These characteristics clearly show that action cannot be imposed by necessity; we cannot impose action in the form of an imperative of productivity. The only function that we will be able to assign to action is to appear in the world or to reveal the singularity of an individual. To gain a clearer understanding of these aspects, we will summarize the four characteristics of the action: boundlessness, unpredictability, irreversibility, and ambiguity.

The boundlessness of action refers to the fact that we always act with others so that others will react to our actions, thus creating a web of interactions. As Arendt puts it, 'Since action acts upon beings who are capable of their own actions, reaction, apart from being a response, is always a new action that strikes out on its own and affects others' (1998: 190). In this sense, there are no boundaries to action, no limitations. The Greeks knew very well this characteristic of action as they established moderation—keeping within bounds—as the political virtue *par excellence*. They also knew very well that the major political temptation was *hubris*.

The second characteristic of action is its unpredictability. The fact that we cannot predict all the consequences of an action is not only because of our inability to calculate all the logical consequences of an action (otherwise a very strong computer would be able to foretell the future) but also a result of the nature of action itself. Human beings act spontaneously and freely; thus, it is impossible to deduce how free individuals will react to a given action. As actors, we also never know how people will react to our deeds, how they will interpret our speech, and which kinds of chains of reactions our deeds will produce. Action is also irreversible because it does not create a tangible product that can be destroyed. Once the action is done, it is too late. We cannot change anything. We cannot erase acts done or words spoken; these events automatically enter an infinite network of human relationships. Therefore, while the artisan can still destroy his or her product, this is not the case with his or her actions, which are irreversible. The infinite network of human relationships also reflects the fact that action is ambiguous. The meaning of an action is never really clear for the actor as it is always subject to the interpretations of the people around him or her. Arendt goes so far as to say, 'action reveals itself fully only to the storyteller, that is, to the backward glance of the historian, who indeed always knows better what it was all about than the participants' (1998: 192). To really understand an act, it must be viewed within its context; it has to be put back into the network of events. As such, we need a certain distance to achieve the overarching view required. The ambiguity of action is also because of the fact that the actor is an enigmatic being who reveals his or her own identity in the course of his or her action. Therefore, even the actor, who does not control his or her own manifestation, does not know exactly what he or she is revealing.

Therefore, Arendt develops a particular conceptualization of human identity, similar in some respects to the narrative identity of Paul Ricoeur.[2] She says that the actor never controls his or her appearance because the action is spontaneous. To illustrate this idea, she gives the example of the Greek *daimōn* 'who accompanies each man throughout his life, who is his distinct identity, but appears and is visible only to others' (1998: 193). This *daimōn* cannot be grasped by the self and ultimately is revealed only in the death of the actor. As long as the person is alive, his or her *daimōn* can change. So it is only death that will complete someone's identity. It is only after death that we can tell someone's life story; death comes to seal the person's identity. But it is only in the action that individuals can prove their uniqueness, that they can be singular beings. Spontaneous action says a lot more about someone than a calculated move. It is in situations of crisis that we can see who someone is, what his or her moral character is, and whether he or she is brave or a coward.

Ultimately these four characteristics, boundlessness, unpredictability, irreversibility, and ambiguity, reveal the frailty of human affairs. Deeds and speech need to be heard and seen to acquire a certain reality. The fragility of action lies precisely in this intangibility, which is to say that it produces nothing except its own appearance. The action loses its effectiveness if it is not heard or seen, for it needs others to acquire its meaning. The actor is the instigator of the initiative, but he or she is never the absolute master. Indeed, the plurality is always implicit in the action, and the action will always insert itself in the network of human relationships. The actor is always at the same time patient. He or she will undergo the unpredictable consequences of her or his action. The action goes beyond the content of the intention of the actor, and thereby becomes elusive because it fits into the network of human relationships. In this sense, action always incorporates a mixture of singularity and plurality. The singularity refers to the initiative of the agent, and the plurality refers to the fact that the action is essentially an activity whose power is effective in achieving a concerted action. Action always involves others. Unlike the activity of work, which has a predictable process and a definitive end, the activity of action is unpredictable, and unlike the activity of labor, it is not subjected to necessity. Action is the only activity in which we can reveal our uniqueness and in which the meaning of our shared world can appear. Of course, some might be tempted to overcome the frailty of human affairs by understanding action as the activity of work and, thus, reject the genuine meaning of action. However, in so doing, they prevent the potentiality for power, and, thus, create impotence. In return, impotence will likely create the favourable conditions for the emergence of violence.

Limits of Violent Action

In 1970 Arendt returned to her original distinction between violence and power in her essay, 'On Violence', published in *Crises of the Republic* (1972). She had witnessed the student protests in New York in 1967 and at Columbia University in 1968. During this time, she became particularly concerned with the Marxist phraseology of the New Left. She remarked that the humanism of the left is grounded in the idea that human beings can create themselves. She writes:

> [T]he idea of man creating himself is strictly in the tradition of Hegelian and Marxian thinking; it is the very basis of all leftist humanism. But according to Hegel man 'produces himself through thought, whereas for Marx, who turned Hegel's 'idealism' upside down, it was labor, the human form of metabolism with nature, that fulfilled this function. (Arendt 1972: 114-115)

Sartre, who radicalized Marx's thought, especially in his preface to Fanon's *The Wretched of the Earth*, states that 'irrepressible violence...is man recreating himself' (in Arendt 1972: 114; see Fanon 2002: 29-30). Thus, with Sartre, we face this idea of violence as generating an identity: the wretched of the earth could regain their humanity and dignity through violence.

Arendt does not agree with this philosophical position. Instead, she tackles the question from a different perspective, insisting that violence springs from impotence. She maintains that violence carries the hope of finding a substitute for impotence, but this hope must be in vain, for violence cannot generate power. As she writes: 'Violence appears where power is in jeopardy, but left to its own course it ends in power's disappearance... Violence can destroy power; it is utterly incapable of creating it' (Arendt 1972: 155). Violence, therefore, is unable to create the conditions of equality necessary for the actualization of power. Furthermore, the instruments of violence produce an imbalance of forces that render mutuality impossible. Power springs from the encounter of equals, and not from a military threat (Arendt 1972: 152).

We find in modern political philosophy many attempts to justify the use of violence in politics. Historically, violence is legitimated by two metaphors. The first illustrates the fact that only violence can respond to violence. We have to become like a dragon to fight the dragon. The modern formulation of this logic borrows from the Hegelian dialectic between the master and the slave. In Hegel, the slave finishes the dialectical journey by becoming the master of nature and by reaching self-consciousness[3]. Analogically, the persecuted, through the use of violence, should finish the dialectical path by becoming the persecutor. It is in this sense that Fanon (2002) argues that oppressed people should exchange their role with the oppressor. The dream of the persecuted is to play the role of the persecutor.

The second metaphor—labor pains—illustrates the idea relied upon by Marx, that violence is necessary for any new beginning. Marx writes, 'Violence is the midwife of every old society pregnant with a new one' (Marx in Arendt 2006: 21).[4] This Marxist model legitimizes the use of violence, because violence and pain are seen as necessary for the birth of a new society. Revolutionaries are permitted to use the means of violence because they are working to bring to life a new society. This instrumentalist logic is typical of violence for which the end justifies the means. Arendt explains that for Marx, the possession of the means of violence is constituent of government wherein the entire political sphere is characterized by the use of violence (Arendt 2006: 22). However, this logic of instrumentality does not belong in the political sphere. Greek and Latin Antiquity did not consider politics in these instrumental terms; rather, this is a modern understanding of politics—one that corresponds to an oblivion of the meaning of freedom and praxis.[5] Arendt understands Marx's glorification of violence; she regards it as an anti-traditional hostility held towards speech and a fundamental challenge to tradition. Arendt insists on the Aristotelian definition of human as *zoon logon echon*, 'a being attaining his highest possibility in the faculty of speech' (2006: 24). Arendt adds, 'Greeks, living together in a *polis*, conducted their affairs by means of speech, through persuasion, and not by means of violence, through mute coercion' (2006: 24).

According to Arendt, we can make sense of the justifications of violence by understanding its great attractiveness. Impotence provokes an intense rage that will seek to find relief in violence. When this rage is combined with incitement to take up arms, a feeling of vitality in the face of death is produced. Arendt explains that when 'faced collectively and in action, death changes its countenance; now nothing seems more likely to intensify our vitality than its proximity' (1972: 165). As Fanon argues in *The Wretched of the Earth*, violence liberates the oppressed and colonized from their inferiority complex. Violent action unites the oppressed and generates a form of ecstasy that is unique. The oppressed are not afraid of death anymore because their personal existence is devoted to the liberation of their group and to a greater good. The liberation from oppression, as the end to their actions, justifies all means. However, even if this feeling of ecstasy is real, it is not essentially political. In *The Wretched of the Earth*, Fanon, who is less extreme than Sartre in certain regards, tries to escape the mirage of violence. He is aware that brutality is counter-revolutionary. If violence and brutality are not overcome, they will lead the movement to its defeat and create an escalation of violence.[6] Violent action can never be a long-term solution. Violence has to cease in order to restore an authentic political space whence power can appear.

Arendt directs our attention to the limit of violent action. Her analysis of violence in politics shows that while violence can play a role in liberation from oppression and in the creation of solidarity among the oppressed, it can also lead the revolutionary movement to its defeat if it is not surpassed. The escalation of violence will destroy the potentiality of political power. According to Arendt, we have to distinguish between rebellion and revolution, a distinction that overlaps the distinction between liberation and freedom.[7] Liberation might involve an element of violence, that is, the persecuted might use the means of violence to free themselves from oppression. As Arendt states in 'On Violence': 'Violence does not promote causes, neither history nor revolution, neither progress nor reaction; but it can serve to dramatize grievances and bring them to public attention' and she adds 'indeed, violence, contrary to what its prophets try to tell us, is more the weapon of reform than of revolution' (1972: 176). For Arendt, revolution cannot be confined to a limited interpretation of liberation from oppression or rebellion. In *On Revolution* (1963), she explains that revolution must combine two elements: 1) the inaugural rupture, that is, the liberation from oppression and 2) the *constitutio libertatis,* that is, the institution of a public space for liberties and freedom. In a nutshell, liberation is a condition for freedom but revolution implies much more than liberation; it must guarantee a public space whence power will spring. Violence plays no role in the *constitutio libertatis*; the institution of a public space must take place between equals, and it must guarantee that everyone will be able to appear as singular individuals. Hence, revolution is not only about the exchange of roles, in which the persecuted become persecutors, but also about opening a space wherein citizens are equals and can co-participate in public affairs, reveal their uniqueness, and be initiators. If there is only an exchange of roles, and the persecuted become the persecutors, the logic of persecution and of violence remains.[8] In this context, there can be no space for freedom. To be free does not mean to be a persecutor but to live among equals.

In a way, we can understand why some people might be tempted to use violent means to liberate themselves from oppression. Violence can be attractive because it often seems effective or because it is seen as necessary in order to create a new state, such as the violence of the craftsman who will have to destroy nature to erect his man-created world. If we follow Arendt's argument carefully, we can see the error in this understanding of politics. We can recover a more authentic meaning of politics in which power is distinguished from violence, and violence is not regarded as an intrinsic characteristic of politics.

Conclusion

As a young German Jew in the 1920s, Hannah Arendt faced the violence of a new form of political regime. From then on, the question of politics and how to live together became the main focus of her research. She did not turn away from politics or from the common world, as philosophers often do when confronted with the desolate contingency of human affairs. Rather, as expressed in her texts, she thought that our greatest task was to rethink politics and the human condition. Her work can thus be read as an act of resistance against political oblivion—that is, against our loss of the memory of what it is to engage in a concerted action or to have freedom. She uncovered political experiences that demonstrate the authentic meaning of political action and power.

Arendt's distinction between power and violence helps us understand the violence of colonized and oppressed people as an unfulfilled desire for political freedom. Or, as she puts it, 'I am inclined to think that much of the present glorification of violence is caused by severe frustration of the faculty of action in the modern world' (1972: 180). The marginalized and oppressed—that is, those who cannot participate as equals in public affairs—may turn to violence as a substitute for power. Thus, violent polit-ical movements may be understood as responses to impotence. Therefore, we can analyze these movements as proof of a latent but authentic desire for power and political action. We can see violent political movements as cries for freedom that have not yet found their fullest and best expres-sions. Arendt's analysis demonstrates that the more people can partici-pate actively in public affairs, the more they become involved in decision making, and the less they will be attracted to violence. Hence, it seems to me that a way to fight violence is to fight political exclusion.

About the Author

Sophie Cloutier, PhD, is a professor at the School in Public Ethics at Saint Paul University in Ottawa. Her research interests include the political thought of Hannah Arendt, multiculturalism, political judgment, ethics of hospitality and ethics of care. She has published several articles and book chapters and co-edited *Le temps de l'hospitalité. Réception de l'oeuvre de Daniel Innerarity* (2015), with Luc Vigneault, Navarro Pardinas Blanca, and Domi-nic Desroches.

Notes

1.   Sartre writes, for instance: '[C]ette violence irrépressible, il [Fanon] le montre parfaitement, n'est pas une absurde tempête ni la résurrection d'instincts sauvages ni même un effet du ressentiment: c'est l'homme lui-même se recomposant' (in Fanon 2002: 29-30).

2.   For a fuller account of Ricoeur's concept of 'narrative identity', refer to *Temps et Récit* (1983).

3.   See Hegel, Section A of Chapter IV in *The Phenomenology of Spirit* (1977). I am fol-lowing the reading of Kojève (1947).

4.   Arendt explains that this statement occurs in both the writings of Marx and of Engels in many different variations.

5.   Villa develops this idea at length in his book (1996), especially in chapter 2, 'Thinking Action against the Tradition'.

6.   In an end note in her essay 'On Violence', Arendt writes, paraphrasing Fanon: 'Fanon himself, however, is much more doubtful about violence than his admirers. It seems that only the book's first chapter, 'Concerning Violence', has been widely read. Fanon knows of the 'unmixed and total brutality [which], if not immediately combat-ted, invariably leads to the defeat of the movement within a few weeks' (1972: 116, *en* 19).

7.   For a fuller account of this distinction between liberation and freedom and the role violence might play in liberation as well as its limits, refer to Arendt (1990), espe-cially chapter 4, 'Foundation I: Constitutio Libertatis' and chapter 5, 'Foundation II: Novus Ordo Saeclorum'.

8.   Arendt writes: 'Who has ever doubted that the violated dream of violence, that the oppressed "dream at least once a day of setting" themselves up in the oppressor's place, that the poor dream of the possessions of the rich, the persecuted of exchanging "the role of the quarry for that of the hunter", and the last of the kingdom where "the

last shall be first, and the first last"? The point, as Marx saw it, is that dreams never come true... To identify the national liberation movements with such outbursts is to prophesy their doom—quite apart from the fact that the unlikely victory would not result in changing the world (or the system), but only its personnel' (Marx in Arendt 1972: 123).

Chapter 7

Victory: A Vacuous Concept?

Richard Feist

Introduction

It has been pointed out by several scholars that war is as old as civilization, perhaps even older. The cave paintings at Lascaux, some twenty thousand years old, contain images of human beings arranged in ways that strongly suggest some kind of organized fighting; the participants are arranged in groups, seemingly armed, facing each other, and the artistic style appears to represent the figures as though they are in motion (O'Connell 1989: 27). Admittedly, it is impossible to be certain that these arrangements are military in nature. It remains possible to interpret these paintings in non-military ways, such as religious rites or as symbolic dancing. However, as many historians have noted, once a group of humans achieves the level of organization deemed 'civilization'—that is, a semi-organized society capable of recording in literary and mathematical ways its own activities—war is present (Gat 2006: 67). The first works of Western literature, the *Epic of Gilgamesh* and Homer's *Iliad*, clearly attest to war's presence in early human civilization. Moreover, archaeological evidence, such as that from architecture, abounds with representations of war (O'Connell 1989: 56). It is sad to think that it is likely a dream that there could be a civilization that emerges and develops yet manages to escape the scourge of war (Porter 1994: 58).

Whether or not it is possible for a civilization to emerge without the experience of war is not, however, my concern here. Even if it were a historical law that every civilization must experience war as part of its development, it certainly does not follow that war is forever a part of all human civilizations. A necessary developmental stage is not a permanent end state. War has been, without a doubt, an important part of human history. It has played its role, for better and for worse, in the development of all nation-states and nearly all groups of people (Porter 1994: 60). Attesting to this is the simple fact that nearly all writings that deal with reflections on society, whether these writings are from South America, Europe, Asia—and today North America as well—illustrate numerous attempts to come to grips with war. These attempts I will simply group under the notion of the 'just-war tradition'. This tradition represents a long conversation in which two questions are posed, discussed, and to a certain degree answered: when is it justified to go to war and how can war be fought in an ethical manner?

To make my discussion more manageable, I will concentrate on the West's history of the just-war tradition (see, e.g., Christopher 1994; Walzer 2006). This tradition has its roots in the thought of Plato and Aristotle. It was later refined by the Romans—especially Cicero—before being taken up and developed in much more detail by St Augustine in the fourth century. The just-war tradition continued long after early and late antiquity. The medieval monks in Bologna, who rediscovered Roman law, took it and the new techniques arising from medieval logic and political theology to develop further the just-war tradition. St Thomas Aquinas pushed just-war thinking further, introducing perhaps the key notion that, in some ways, is a foundational aspect of just-war thinking today: the doctrine of double effect (1964: 7). This doctrine, which stresses the distinction between foreseen but unintended effects and foreseen and intended effects, is perhaps the only way that one can justify any sensible notion of collateral damage. Without such a distinction, all foreseen effects would be in the same category, either all intended or unintended. In the first case, collateral damage would be intended, hence unjustifiable. In the second case the whole notion of a mission, which is to create an intended effect, would be rendered senseless. Aquinas did not invent the notion of 'double effect', but was one of the first to apply it to military scenarios.

There was an explosion in the number of thinkers concerning themselves with war after the middle ages. Given the developments in armaments and the age of colonialism, nearly all major thinkers during this time period had something to say about war and conflict among different peoples. Many of these thinkers were developing the just-war tradition along the lines laid down by their medieval predecessors. Without a doubt, the major thinker of the time was the great Dutch philosopher, Hugo Grotius (2007), a renaissance Humanist who systematized the principles of just-war thinking into a format that we largely use today. In fact, it could be said that Grotius is the just-war tradition's greatest thinker. Moreover, it is Grotius's work that allows us to speak of an actual just-war theory. Today's cutting edge debates in the philosophical community regarding the ethics of just-war theory, interestingly enough, more or less use the same concepts as Grotius did. Indeed, one of the main writers on just-war theory today, Jeff McMahan (2009: 43), notes that the best part of what is currently understood about this theory can be found in the writings of Grotius. Contemporary arguments, however, are over just how we are to interpret the concepts in just-war theory and, perhaps more importantly, how those concepts are supposed to relate to each other.

Talk of concepts and their interrelations may seem like some removed, academic exercise in conceptual analysis. In many ways, it is. However, the ramifications of the analyses of concepts can, in some cases, be enormous and extremely concrete. Consider the following example. Philosophers often debate the issue of characterizing the nature of the self and the concept of personhood. How can one say for sure what constitutes the nature of a person? What makes a given person today the same person as he or she was two weeks ago? These kinds of questions are rather abstract, but the answers to them will eventually lead to very concrete—and often controversial—positions taken on when personhood begins, a discussion that can ultimately plunge one into the intricacies of the abortion debate.

As mentioned, much of the debate about whether or not to go to war and how to use just-war theory turns on the understanding of the theory's concepts. My central concern in this chapter is that of understanding the notion of victory. The concept of victory plays a key role in the foundations of just-war theory. That is, without the notion of victory, just-war theory is unworkable. Despite this importance, the concept of victory is not entirely clear. Consequently, lurking at the very heart of the attempt to impose an ethical framework upon war is a fundamental vagary. If this is so, then what sense can we really make of an ethics of war? This is an important question—one to which I will return throughout this chapter.

Of course, one could simply stipulate what victory is—for example, 'the meeting of an objective'. However, this does not mean that such a stipulation will be accepted. Indeed, many times in the history of warfare, once a particular war has gone awry or at least departed from the original intentions of its perpetrators, victory has simply been *declared*. Perhaps the most famous recent example of this is the 1 May 2003 speech by President George W. Bush, given on the deck of the battleship *USS Abraham Lincoln*, in the background of which hung a huge banner declaring, 'Mission Accomplished'. There was much debate as to whether or not the banner meant that the entire mission in Iraq was accomplished or simply that the *USS Lincoln*'s mission was completed. My point here is that the notion of victory is easily pushed into the area of debate. Put another way, the notion of victory is certainly not self-evident.

Another example of the question of victory in warfare is that in March of 2014, when Canada ended its twelve-year engagement in Afghanistan. During Canada's time in this country, Prime Minister Stephen Harper repeatedly stated that Canada would not 'cut and run', but would stay until the job was done. Again, this understanding has a notion of victory built into it. A 'job done' in war is just another example of victory talk. The stress upon the necessity of victory is further enhanced by claims that to leave before the 'job is done' is to declare somehow that those who gave their lives in pursuit of the objective did so in vain. As the logic goes, unless there is victory, the lives lost have no meaning. Simply put, victory gives us meaning. Nonetheless, the fact that the feeling of victory, its celebration, glorification, and declaration, all give us meaning does not entail that the very notion of victory itself is meaningful.

A vacuous concept can, in principle, be a source of meaning. Think, for example, about the debates regarding the existence of God. There is plenty of debate as to whether or not such a concept has any content. A key issue in the positivist movement of the early twentieth century was that religious concepts were void of meaning and all propositions in religious context were neither true nor false, but senseless.[1] Nonetheless, for many people, religious concepts, such as 'God', provide much meaning and even serve to organize their lives. More generally put, myths can easily have no serious basis in reality and yet provide much meaning for their adherents. This brief discussion is reminiscent of Augustine's reflections on time. He says that he uses the term 'time' without hesitation. He is perfectly comfortable with it and suggests that everyone else is, too. However, do not ask him to define it.

In the end, the possible meaningfulness of vacuous concepts is part of a larger debate concerning war. The noted war correspondent and author, Christopher Hedges (2003), argues that war is a particular kind of myth to which we have an addiction. This addiction is one that cultures can have a hard time breaking. The reason for such addiction is precisely because war provides us with meaning. It offers opportunities to do things that could not be done in everyday life. One often hears this when potential soldiers talk about joining the military in order to make a serious difference in the world. One of the twentieth century's greatest philosophers, Ludwig Wittgenstein, came from an extremely wealthy family but abandoned his inheritance for the pursuit of philosophy. When philosophy proved unsatisfactory, Wittgenstein enlisted in the Austrian Army during World War I. He volunteered for some of the most dangerous duties, such as a machine-gun nest officer, which put him in harm's way constantly. He had no interest, he says, in the experience of killing. Rather, it was the experience of war that was going to lead him into a true experience of what it is to be human (Monk 1990: 110-66). This thinking about war, that it somehow reveals human essence to us, can be traced back to antiquity. One finds it stated quite clearly in Thucydides, the Athenian general, who wrote what is the West's first history book: *The Peloponnesian War* (year). In chapter 82 Thucydides stresses that war lays bare the souls of men and is a most violent teacher.

The Role of Victory in Just-war Theory

In this chapter I will illustrate the importance of the concept of victory in just-war theory. After discussing the importance of the concept of victory, I will then consider some of the main problems with this concept, drawing on the work of Michael Howard and Robert Mandel. These thinkers essentially agree that the notion of victory is critically important and—at least to this day—extremely problematic. Although I would not go so far as to say that military action is completely useless, I would argue that the main price to be paid for it far outweighs any of its benefits. In this sense, I have many sympathies with William James's (1910) view, which argued that we must find a moral alternative to war. As I do not reject war purely on idealistic, anti-violence grounds, but more on pragmatic grounds, my thinking on anti-violence aligns less with Gandhi than with the likes of Gene Sharp. Sharp stresses that one does not have to be a strict pacifist to embrace an anti-war position. War, Sharp argues, is really a poor and ineffective way to settle differences—again, its costs far outweigh any of its benefits (2005: 45).

To begin, just-war theory is not a single theory, written down and accepted in one format by all those who refer to themselves as 'just-war theorists'. Rather, as we have seen, just-war theory is the result of the various reflections of many people over a long period of time on the nature of war and on seeking those conditions under which war may be justifiable. Needless to say, the just-war tradition presupposes that war can be justified, concentrating on the conditions of justification (Frowe 2011: 56). This logic is reminiscent of the old adage in theology of 'faith seeking understanding'. In this view, God's existence is assumed, and the task for theologians is to prove that God exists and to understand Divine Nature. The similarity between the structures of just-war thinking and Christian theology is not surprising: in many ways, the just-war tradition has been a branch of the church's thinking for centuries.

Although the conditions under which war was thought justifiable changed over the centuries, these changes arguably centre on the developments of a few key themes. The first is that for a war to be just, it must have a just cause. The problem now is to ascertain what constitutes a just cause. The second key theme is twofold: proportionality and necessity. If one has a just cause, then the amount of force used in the name of that cause must be proportionate to the cause. If your cause is just and the force you use brings about that good, the force you use cannot also bring about considerable amounts of destruction. Simply put, you cannot cause more misery to exist than before you started. Even if you do manage via war to create more good than misery, there remains the requirement that it was necessary to achieve that good via war. In other words, it must be that only the resort to war would bring about the good that was sought. If that good could have been brought about by other (non-war) means, then it is not justified to resort to war.

Note that these issues—just cause, proportionality, and necessity—do not constitute all the criteria to consider before one launches into a war. These criteria and others are typically grouped under the term *jus ad bellum,* which translates roughly as 'justice for war'. But the issue of the ethics of war does not end when war starts. Rather, when fighting begins, one has to continue the analysis and ask, 'Is there an ethical way to fight a war?' Many argue that this question is analogous to the age-old concept of a 'clean' fight. This is, in some sense, like the rules for boxing. Others, however, argue that this notion of the ethics of fighting a war is an oxymoron since it involves the notion of saying that under certain circumstances it is ethically permissible to kill.

These are deep and thorny questions that we cannot concern ourselves with here because of space constraints. Suffice it to say that just-war theory makes a fairly strong presupposition about killing. A weak presupposition would be that it is possible to excuse killing in certain cases. That is, we might say that it was wrong to kill, to condemn the killing, but not the killer. A simple example might be a person facing an extremely frightening attacker. Gripped by fear, the person kills the attacker. It could very well be the case that killing, in this instance, was an over-reaction. Hence, it was not morally permissible to kill the attacker. As a counterargument, we might agree that nearly anyone else faced with such an attacker would have killed the attacker. It is not a contradiction to excuse the killer while morally condemning the killing. In this case, it may be simple to separate ethics and psychology.

As mentioned, however, just-war theory makes a stronger presupposition than excusing killers. In fact, just-war theory holds that it is possible that killing itself can be morally justified. In this sense, the killing could be a praiseworthy action—that is, morally permissible. However, just-war theory does not stop with morally permissible killing. It also presupposes that it is possible to be morally *obligated* to kill. This notion of a moral obligation to kill arises in discussions of what has come to be known as 'humanitarian military intervention'. The main point, however, is that just-war theory presupposes that it is possible to fight ethically, and the debate is about what those ethical conditions of fighting are. The conditions governing the ethical conduct of war are referred to as *jus in bello,* which translates as 'justice in war'.

So far we have seen two sets of conditions, *jus ad bellum* and *jus in bello.* For much of the just-war tradition and certainly for much of the last 40 years, these two sets were regarded as independent of each other.[2] This independence represented the separation of power and its execution, or the political and the military. The ascertaining of whether or not it is ethical to go to war was the domain of the political. Once that decision is made, the actual fighting of the war in an ethical manner was the domain of the military. It is true that in some cases, such as dictatorships, the military and the political are fused. That does not mean that the separation collapses; rather, it moves. That is, the decision makers may be politicians and military personnel and thus they would hold responsibility for the decision to go to war, but those actually fighting in it, such as the soldiers, are only responsible for their conduct in the war. In such a case, the separation of *jus ad bellum* and *jus in bello* does not lie between the political and the military but would cut right through the military itself (Table 1).

The last few years have seen many attacks on this distinction, stating that it cannot be maintained. These attacks have been conceptual in nature. However, the underpinning of these attacks can easily come from a historical perspective as well. The different ethical conditions imposed on war were all, during early periods, developments from larger collections of concepts. As the tradition developed, certain concepts were broken up and analyzed as different parts. Over time, people began to think of these parts as independent. This separation of concepts often happens in the history of the development of knowledge. In fact, separating concepts is a natural part of any human attempt to understand the surrounding world. Consider a simple example from science: an ecologist, when trying to understand the environment, is faced with a unity, namely the entire universe. No scientist tries to take on the whole universe at once. Even physicists who use terms like 'grand unified theory' do not claim that such a theory will explain why you prefer tea over coffee. The ecologist does not even take on a much smaller unity—the earth—as a single ecosystem. That still would be too much. Thus, the ecologist splits it, considers just a single pond, for instance. Even in this case, the ecologist has to isolate the pond from the surrounding environment. This example is a necessary simplification but certainly not a perfectly accurate representation of the real situation, that is, of reality itself. The point here is that all the concepts of just-war theory are intimately linked. One cannot truly understand one of them without involving the others.

Table 1: Concepts Involved in a Modern Representation of Just-war Theory[3]

Jus ad bellum	Jus in bello
Just cause	Fought only by legitimate combatants
Proportionality	Only legitimate targets are attacked
Reasonable chance of success	Only legitimate tactics are employed
Legitimate authority	Prisoners of war are legitimately treated
Right intention	
Last resort	
Public declaration of war	

Globally speaking, the moral constraints on war serve to distinguish it immediately from a mere game. That is, despite the fact that historically speaking, war was referred to as the 'sport of kings', the moral conditions of *jus ad bellum* prohibit entering into war merely for amusement. War is entered into only for the sake of winning, for the sake of victory. Moreover, the notion of victory plays a role in particular in *jus ad bellum* as the condition of reasonable chance of success. One does not enter into a war unless one can make the case that it is distinctly possible to achieve victory. But what is victory? Is it the total annihilation of the enemy? This question will immediately raise further questions regarding proportionality and necessity. In order to ascertain proportionality and necessity, questions concerning justice will also need to be raised.

When declaring war publically, a government would also be duty bound and pragmatically wise to explain what the final state is to look like. Governments that declare war without specifying the conditions of victory are severely criticized and risk losing support during a campaign. The main point is, in addition to the interconnectedness of all these concepts, that the very notion of a reasonable chance of success makes no clear sense unless one has managed to articulate the notion of victory. Consequently, without an understanding of victory, the whole conceptual apparatus of just-war theory is left with a gaping hole.

Further Thoughts on Victory:
Reflections on the Concepts of Michael Howard and Robert Mandel

In addition to the key role that victory plays in the just-war tradition, Robert Mandel points out that victory has a long-standing and broad-ranging capacity for influencing grand ideas such as the destiny of nations, and the pettiest ideas such as the thirst for revenge. Without a doubt, victory shapes the notions of post-war expectations (Mandel 2007: 461). Now, in addition to the ethical and the strategic importance of victory, Mandel points out that victory is an extremely difficult concept to ascribe any kind of metric. There are two standard approaches to trying to measure the notion of victory: a fixed end-state identification and a fluid cost-benefit ratio.

The fixed end-state is simply to ask whether or not the objectives set out, that is, the desired end-state projected at the onset of the war, were in fact actually met. Mandel points out several problems here, but they can be grouped under two headings. First, the declarations of the desired end-state are typically framed in a political context. These are notoriously vague, such as a state of peace, of reconciliation, prosperity, and so on. They are admittedly admirable and serve to exert a pull on the emotions that is not counterbalanced by clarity. In addition to this vagueness, this approach is susceptible to the vicissitudes of war. Mandel writes:

> Victory is not always a product of premeditated strategic choice: war ter-
> mination often lacks order and coherence, with the possibility of differ-
> ent parties ending their participation at different times; and wars rarely
> follow a course anticipated by the participants. (Mandel 2007: 462)

The second approach to operationalizing victory avoids trying to fix the end-state and instead examines the situation from a fluid cost-benefit perspective. This approach leads to questions such as: was the war worth the effort and did it justify the money and lives spent? This approach, Mandel points out, contains contradictory elements. That is, there are many ways that one could ascribe a metric to victory; however, these ways are not consistent with each other and there is no objective way to rank them. Mandel provides a number of examples, but perhaps the clearest one is the following: if one goes to war for some kind of gain, then what is the basis for measuring that gain? To what is the gain relative, the enemy or oneself? Is it more important that one gains in war more than the enemy does or that one gains a better predicament than one had prior to the war? Would it be a victory if one gained a number of spoils at the enemy's expense, but that the ensuing situation is not much different? Would it be a victory if the ensuing situation was better, but not much was gained? Arguments could be made for both.

Causing all of these problems at a deeper level, Mandel suggests, is that in the end, the notion of victory is extremely subjective. The deeper cause of the subjectivity is that there are problems of time and perspective. With regards to time, it is the standard problem that consequentialist analyses face. If one wishes to assess the results of action X, how far into the future should one go? If I go to the dentist and look for immediate effects, I may easily conclude that dentists only cause pain and therefore should be avoided. Of course, we look at the long-term effects: the immediate pain caused is for long-term gain. In a complex, dynamic, and semi-archaic world of international relations, how long into the future should we allow when assessing the results of war? Again, this is highly susceptible to varying interpretations. In addition to the problematic of the temporal duration, there is the perspectival problem. For instance, if countries A and B go to war, is the notion of victory interpreted only via the perspectives of the leaders of A and B? What if the leaders disagree on the terms of victory or whether or not any kind of victory has been achieved? Moreover, do the populations of A and B count?

Mandel points out quite correctly that these problems are difficult enough within the context of symmetric warfare, that is, the classical confrontation of states. In today's world, with the emergence of non-state actors and asymmetric warfare, the notion of victory is further problematized, because:

Disruptive non-state forces in the international system can as easily label military defeat as political victory—with credibility in the eyes of regional onlookers—as they can label terrorists as freedom fighters. Similarly, when comparing perspectives on victory across culture, more powerful and dominant cultures may see victory as a way of offensively establishing hegemony and control, while weaker and more peripheral cultures may see victory as a way of defensively maintaining sovereignty and warding off external interference. (Mandel 2007: 465)

Mandel goes on to argue that the solution to this problem lies ultimately in splitting up the concept of victory into two key phases: military and strategic victory. Military victory is exactly as it sounds: victory on the battlefield. Strategic victory is the ensuing aspect of winning peace, the hearts, and the minds of the militarily defeated side. Confusing these two aspects of victory has been deeply embedded in the history of military thought.[4] The historian Don Howard argues that the allies after WWI confused these aspects of victory and ultimately helped pave the way to WWII (1999: 126-35).

In sum, if the concept of victory is necessary to just-war theory but at the same time problematic unless it is split into the notions of military and strategic victory, then it is natural to ask: can we do without the notion of military victory altogether and just concentrate on strategic victory? After all, the analyses of military victory seem to show that, at best, military victories create, as Howard argues, 'political opportunities for the victors—and even those opportunities are likely to be limited by circumstances beyond their control' (1999: 132). In essence, the violence preceding the strategic road to victory may have helped create those conditions for strategic victory, but these are certainly not optimal conditions.

The world is messy indeed—one may argue—and thus, there are no ways to create optimal conditions for strategic victories. That is quite true; however, there are many proposals that have made headway in the argument for circumventing violence. In other words, it is time to consider seriously the possibility for creating the conditions for strategic victory without having to pass through a military victory. This brings me to consider, briefly, the arguments of Gene Sharp.

Victory without the Military: Some Reflections on the Concepts of Gene Sharp

Perhaps the most striking aspect of Sharp's work on nonviolence is its explicitly pragmatic tone. He declares and argues the point that it is not necessary to be against violence as a matter of principle; being against violence is rather a sensible position based solely on the fact that violence is a poor methodology in problem solving, and that humans are stubborn creatures. We do not naturally obey each other, but that does not mean that we use violence as a result. Sharp's point is that humans often get their way simply by refusing to play another's oppressive game (2005: 23). All of this is related to the fact, as we have seen, that the notion of victory via violence is intrinsically subjective, and as the split within the concept of victory shows, it is always the situation after the violence in which the real solutions are worked out.

But if this is the case, and given that violence-bred conditions are difficult ones in which to sort out a lasting solution, why not just bypass violence? This question, however, presupposes an affirmative answer to a more fundamental one: namely, is it possible to bypass violence? To answer this more fundamental question in all its dimensions is beyond the scope of this chapter, thus, I will only consider it from a framing perspective. That is, I will consider it from a broad perspective, namely, dealing with a potentially violent aggressor (or the conditions in which an aggressor can in fact be produced) and from a narrow one, namely, dealing with an actual, violent aggressor. For this, I bring in the work of Sharp. In other words, I am considering the question from the broad perspective of preventing the growth of violent aggressors and the narrow one of what to do when confronted by a violent aggressor. Of course, both perspectives are major investigations in themselves; consequently, I will have to put further limits on them as well, but this will be evident as I go along.

Just-war theorists often claim that while they vehemently oppose war, it is nonetheless the case that in some circumstances, war is inevitable. This statement has to be carefully unpacked as it can be quite misleading. The key idea here is that calling an event E inevitable is dependent on the temporal perspective that one takes. For instance, if a car is speeding towards a barrier, then one may say at the last second prior to impact that the impact is inevitable. No doubt this is true. However, the statement is true in a *limited* sense, namely, right before the impact. This limited inevitability cannot be immediately generalized. Perhaps the driver had fallen asleep at the wheel and awoke just prior to impact. But had the driver awakened several seconds *prior* to the impact, there may have been time to avoid a collision. In sum, short-term inevitability of an event E does not imply the inevitability of E simpliciter. The inevitability of E is always temporally bounded—unless one takes a rigidly deterministic view of the world.

Just-war theorists then, presuppose that war, at least in some cases, is radically inevitable: it is going to happen; it is unstoppable, and thus to limit the damage, one should have it ethically bounded. History does not seem to bear this out. As increasing numbers of trade deals, international agreements, and so on point out, the disagreements and wars that were previously fought lose any kind of justification. As the number of alternatives to war rise, not only does the justification for going to war lose its strength, but the very appeal of going to war, the mass-psychological dimension of war, withers. Of course, a number of qualifications and caveats must be inserted in such a complex discussion, but overall, the evidence indicates that war is increasingly seen as a useless and ineffective means of interstate relations.

This discussion is within the context of major war, that is, war between symmetric state powers. This type of war has declined dramatically over the last few centuries.[5] Most of the conflicts today are intrastate conflicts, low-level wars, and terrorism (non-state, asymmetric conflicts), all of which appear to be on the rise. Even lower than these low-level conflicts between non-state groups are conflicts that are on the personal and societal level. In other words, it would appear that the levels of violence on these lower levels in general has been dropping throughout the last few centuries.[6] The point here is that large-scale violence—interstate war—is dropping and that small-scale (i.e., interpersonal) violence shows evidence of dropping as well. Thus, it could very well be the case that middle-range violence, such as low-level conflicts and the like, will see their time but eventually drop as well.

Even if the above scenario—that war overall is declining and will continue to decline—comes to pass, what about the situation of being faced with an actual aggressor? Here it is best to take an example, one that those who favour war often take, namely, what about dealing nonviolently with someone like Hitler? Here I draw upon two examples: the resistance of Norwegian teachers in 1942 and the rescue of Jewish workers in 1943.

Germany rapidly overran Norway in 1940. Within the span of roughly two months, the military occupation was complete; however, there soon followed civilian resistance to the Nazi occupiers. The teachers' unions were abolished and replaced with a new fascist teachers' union, one that teachers were expected to join and to which they would declare their allegiance. The result would eventually be that Nazi ideology would be brought into the schools. The Norwegian teachers *en masse* refused to declare their allegiance to the new union. The regime's reaction was predictable: threats were issued and all schools were closed for a month. Teachers responded by holding secret classes in parents' homes, while still refusing to join the union. As word spread in the Norwegian population concerning school closures and the pressures on teachers, citizens poured protest letters into government departments. In March of 1941, about 1,000 male teachers were sent to a concentration camp. The schools were reopened and the teachers who resumed classroom instruction were informed that their colleagues would be killed unless they were to sign and pledge allegiance to the fascist union. They continued to refuse. Some of the teachers were killed by the Nazis, but the growing public outrage caused much concern in the pro-Nazi Norwegian government. Eventually the entire project for the fascist union was scuttled—as ultimately ordered by Hitler himself (Sharp 2005: 135-41).

Sharp's second example (2005: 143-48) involves an incident in the heart of Nazi Germany—Berlin—concerning the resistance of a group of women to the arrests of their Jewish husbands. In 1943, the Gestapo, furious over a number of recent German battlefront defeats, decided to take revenge by rounding up (male) Jewish workers in order to rid Berlin of its remaining Jewish population. The wives began immediately to protest this action, staging several peaceful but vocal protests outside the jail where the men were kept. News of these protests grew and eventually reached the office of the Minster of Propaganda himself, Josef Goebbels. Such a widespread opposition to the incarceration was threatening Goebbels's plan for implementing the concept of total war; he therefore decided, along with the support of Hitler, to release the Jewish men to their wives. The interesting point is that, while this protest occurred and resulted in the husbands' release, other incarcerated Jewish men were in fact shipped off to concentration camps. For these unfortunate Jewish men, there were no protestors raising public awareness of their particular situation. This lends great support to the view that the nonviolent actions of the women protesters were indeed the cause of their husbands' release. In other words, nonviolence works.

Conclusions

In sum, I have argued that the notion of victory is an intrinsically contestable concept. It is susceptible to charges of subjectivity and historical volatility. Even efforts to make it more precise by splitting it into military and strategic victory serve mainly to show that one may make sense of defeat and victory on a battlefield, but true, strategic victory only occurs after the physical fight. The physical fight may lay the conditions for strategic victory, but conditions constructed by violence are ultimately tainted. However, the just-war theory has built victory into its foundations and thus remains with a highly contestable term at its very heart.

I also argued that, in the end, the whole project of war—the means of solving problems via violence—is on the decline and that it is not a necessary means in any case. Nonviolence is by no means a perfect solution, but the reality of the world is never a choice in which one of the options is perfect. Nonviolence is messy, too. People are killed when using nonviolence. Some of the Norwegian teachers died as a result of nonviolent action as did some of the German wives and their Jewish husbands. The point, however, is that nonviolence is possible, it does have positive effects, it can work—and it can work in some of the darkest and most difficult places.

But the main goal of this chapter was to provide the argument that would lead to a deeper conclusion, or at least provide a strong motivation to consider seriously the following conclusion: that war is and has been overrated. War has been, in simple terms, mythologized. Many regard it as an effective way for dealing with problems. By looking at some of the thinking about war, I wished to show that we have regarded violence as ineffective in many other contexts, as an obsolete way of resolving differences, and thus we should extend this kind of thinking in order to see war—and violence—as obsolete as well.

About the Author

Richard Feist, PhD, is an associate professor of philosophy in the Faculty of Human Sciences and Philosophy at Saint Paul University in Ottawa. He has published articles in the philosophy of science, metaphysics, ethics and war. Feist is currently working on a study of victory and just-war theory as well as several articles in metaphysics and ethics.

Notes

1. One of the many classic texts of the positivist movement is Ayer's *Language, Truth and Logic* (1936). This work established the 'verificationist' principle as the main semantic test for meaning, a test that become canonical for the positivist movement.

2. However, this is not an iron-clad generalization. One can find instances in Grotius that question this separation, and Thoreau (2008) rejects it. Perhaps because of the overwhelming influence of Walzer (2006), who insists on the separation, it has been largely (but falsely) assumed as historically entrenched.

3. These are all taken from Frowe (2011), chapters 3 and 5. Frowe's text is a well-recognized, standard, introductory text to just-war theory and thus can be taken as an orthodox representation of the tenets of just-war theory.

4. For some historical details, see Bond (1996). For a current and extremely detailed historical and analytic examination of the concept of victory, see Martel (2011). Finally, for Mandel's full study of the inherent problems of victory, see his *The Meaning of Military Victory* (2006).

5. For discussions of the decline of the 'major war thesis'—and the numerous controversies surrounding this thesis—see Levy and Thompson (2010). For a solid collection of a variety of papers on this topic, see Varyrynen (2006).

6. Pinker's (2011) large-scale study of violence argues this very point. Admittedly, this study is not perfect, but its overall thesis, that violence in many ways was thought of as necessary for running a society—capital punishment for instance—has been slowly eradicated from humans' thinking about their interrelations.

Chapter 8

Reflecting on Gandhian Nonviolence:
Is it a Counsel of Perfection for Religious Virtuosi?

Noel A. Salmond

Introduction

Not by enmity are enmities quelled,
Whatever the occasion here.
By the absence of enmity they are quelled.
This is an ancient truth. (2000: 1:5)[1]

Religious teachings across many traditions frequently contain admonitions against violence or make claims that a better alternative to violence is nonviolence or love. For example, the verse from the Buddhist *Dhamma-pada* in the epigraph above illustrates these two contentions. The first we might call the negative formulation: that enmity is not quelled by enmity or violence by violence. The second we can call the positive formulation: that enmity is (only) quelled by non-enmity or violence by nonviolence or love. Regarding these two contentions, many of us would find it relatively easy to concur with the first. It does appear in our everyday experience that retaliation against wrongdoing often leads to counter retaliation in an escalating spiral of recrimination or violence. That violence begets violence and revenge begets more vengeance is easy to see. This seems empirically true; it is common experience, even common sense.

But does the opposite hold that returning violence with love always results in the ending or overcoming of violence? This is more difficult to endorse. Does it not seem like wishful thinking not supported by empirical realities on the ground? Is it really true that only love conquers hatred?

Mahatma Gandhi is renowned as the great twentieth-century teacher and exemplar of nonviolence. The question is frequently asked if the efficacy of Gandhi's nonviolence is understandable only in the singular circumstances of British colonial rule in South Africa and India or if it is generalizable. But beyond the question of the universality or particularity of Gandhian nonviolence as a technique, I am concerned with the matter of nonviolence as a religious ideal and as an ideal perhaps beyond mundane actualization. Is Gandhi's nonviolence so far outside the capacities of more ordinary mortals that it is to be located in the realm of piety, not praxis? And if so, is it to be relegated to the status of a pious ideal: an ideal that is simply way beyond the pale of realpolitik?

While a Hindu, Gandhi drew on many sources for his commitment to nonviolence. I begin by examining how some of the religious traditions that inform Gandhi's nonviolence manage the gap between nonviolence as a religious ideal on the one hand and the exigencies of ordinary life for ordinary followers on the other. Various religious traditions have developed conceptual strategies to manage this divide between precept and practice, religious ideal and real-world limitations. I argue that Gandhi sought to close that gap by modeling nonviolent behavior that was not to be regarded as an impossible religious ideal nor relegated to the domain of religious professionals, or in Max Weber's formulation, the religious virtuosi.[2]

Gandhi is not only the best known advocate of nonviolence close to our own times, he is also the most famous Hindu of the twentieth century. But Gandhi was a cosmopolitan figure and it is well known that he drew on multiple sources beyond his own Hindu tradition in articulating his position on nonviolence. He was friends with Jews and Muslims and influenced by exposure to Jains in his native Gujarat—Jainism is of course most famous for championing non-harming (*ahimsa*), a value also found in Hinduism. Gandhi recounts the impact of his encounter with Christians including Quakers during his time in London and South Africa. As a young law student in England, Gandhi read the New Testament Sermon on the Mount and was greatly impressed by its ethic. This was reinforced for him later through his reading of, and then correspondence with, Leo Tolstoy, who in the last years of his life had come to adopt a total pacifist standpoint. I turn to a brief discussion of Gandhi's religious influences in relation to the question of how religions cope with the seemingly impossible demands of religious ideals.

Indian Traditions

Indian religions display a variety of strategies for coping with religious ideals (including nonviolence) given the exigencies of the real world. In Buddhism, all Buddhists are supposed to follow the Five Precepts of abstaining from killing, theft, lying, sexual misconduct, and intoxicants, but monastics must adhere to additional precepts and a far lengthier behavioural code. It is recognized that the moral and contemplative lifestyle expected of the monk is not realistic for the householder, the layperson in the world, and hence the notion arises that the layperson, while incapable of emulating the monk now in this lifetime, can hope for rebirth as a monk in a future existence. Such an eventuality can be generated by the merit accrued by supporting the monastic community. Jainism also has this divide between monastics on one tier and laypersons on another.

Classical Hindu thought has addressed the apparent impossibility of perfect nonviolence for all through a number of conceptualizations of a variety of individual human goals, a variety of stages in the life of the individual, and collectively a variety of divisions within human society.[3] Each category has four components. A person is said to have as legitimate goals in life pleasure, prosperity, duty, and liberation. Pursuit of each of these goals is determined by their suitability to the different stages in one's life. These stages are given as four: student, householder, forest dweller, and renouncer. Clearly, perfect non-possession and nonviolence is easier in the last stages of withdrawal and renunciation. But some in society might choose to embark on a life of renunciation of worldly ties early in their lifetime and not wait for the final stage of life. These individuals constitute the huge number of ascetics, *sadhus*, and itinerant holy men (and some women) in India even to this day.

Lastly, society was classically conceived as being constituted by four classes: servants, merchants, rulers, and priests. Nonviolence was more expected of priests than servants, and rulers were expected to exercise the legitimate use of force and violence. As a result, approximations of perfect nonviolence were deemed to be the province of priests, renouncers, or those in the final stages of life.[4]

Christianity and 'Counsels of Perfection'

> You have heard that it was said, 'An eye for an eye and a tooth for a tooth'. But I say to you, Do not resist an evildoer. But if anyone strikes you on the right cheek, turn the other also; and if anyone wants to sue you and take your coat, give your cloak as well... You have heard that it was said, 'You shall love your neighbour and hate your enemy.' But I say, Love your enemies and pray for those who persecute you, so that you may be children of your Father in heaven; for he makes his sun rise on the evil and on the good, and sends rain on the righteous and the unrighteous... Be perfect, therefore, as your heavenly father is perfect. (Matthew 5:38-43)

Tolstoy, who as noted above was a major influence on Gandhi, read these cited verses from the Sermon on the Mount in a literalist way and focused on Matthew 5:39 and nonresistance to evil. How is such a text to be interpreted, let alone actualized, in daily life? Keith Ward discusses several types of Christian response to the seemingly unattainable directives of Jesus in the Sermon on the Mount (2008, ch. 12). Ward suggests that one response is to see them as hyperbole given to drive home a memorable point, not as a rule to be followed literally (2008: 124). Another response has been to see these as directives realizable but only by small groups of heroic disciples committed to pacifism and poverty. Total nonviolence may be unrealistic for all, but a small number of heroic individuals who practice it may influence society like leaven in a dough. Given that such heroism is impossible for all, a third response has been to regard the exhortation to total nonviolence and non-possession as counsels of perfection[5] directed at those afforded a special charism or grace to pursue moral perfection in the professed life, in other words, for religious professionals or virtuosi. All Christians are expected to abide by basic moral precepts such as not lying, killing, or stealing, but some rare individuals may be gifted with a calling to seek to actualize through poverty, chastity, and obedience a life in which non-retribution for evil, in other words perfect nonviolence, may be possible.[6]

Tolstoy rejected the view that these statements by Jesus found in Matthew were either hyperbole or acts of supererogation beyond what was expected of ordinary practitioners and thus applicable only to virtuosi. This view aligned with that of Gandhi who had already practiced heroic nonviolence before corresponding with Tolstoy.

Gandhi and Nonviolence

Having noted both the Indian and the Christian influences on Gandhi, what is interesting about Gandhi is that he is not prepared to let absolute nonviolence languish in the realm of a 'counsel of perfection' applicable only to a religious elite (as in the traditional Catholic view) nor for it to be relegated to the preserve of professional religious virtuosi like monks, *sannyasins*, or *sadhus* (as characteristic of Indian traditions). Gandhi modeled an asceticism and avoidance of all violence for everyone, not just renouncers or *sannyasins*. He carried the ascetic willingness to suffer into the political arena as the method of voluntarily submitting to suffering through nonviolent resistance. This was largely unprecedented in the history of India. His charisma was partly derived from the long-standing admiration in India for the renouncer. But he was a renouncer *in* society—in Weberian terms, an inner-worldly ascetic engaged in a political process.[7]

It is important to note, however, that Gandhi qualified the practice of nonviolence: violence is preferable to cowardice, hence his vehement assertion that it is not simply 'passivity' but 'a weapon of the strong' (1958: 384).[8] He states in 1920:

> I do believe that where there is only a choice between cowardice and violence I would advise violence. Thus when my eldest son asked me what he should have done, had he been present when I was almost fatally assaulted in 1908, whether he should have run away and seen me killed or whether he should have used his physical force which he could and wanted to use, and defended me, I told him that it was his duty to defend me even by using violence. (Gandhi 1920)

The practice of nonviolence requires tremendous courage.[9] And those who practice it need to be fully trained, like elite warriors. They are disciplined holders of truth (see below) who are trained in nonviolent method. Gandhi said in 1931: 'It takes a fairly strenuous course of training to attain to a mental state of nonviolence. In daily life it has to be a course of discipline though one may not like it, like, for instance, the life of a soldier'. When Gandhi felt that his highly effective nation-wide protests were straying from nonviolence he would call them off, often to the consternation of even his close followers.

Nonviolent resistance for Gandhi is *satyagraha*: holding to the power or force of truth. And Gandhi is convinced that truth ultimately wins.[10] He states: 'For truth and non-violence are, to me, faces of the same coin' (Gandhi 1958: 384). Remember that Gandhi preached and modeled nonviolence, yes, but he also preached and modeled civil disobedience. And civil disobedience means breaking the law in answer to the call of a higher moral law. But for Gandhi, breaking the law did not include doing violence to living beings, and for him the ends never justify the means. Gandhi taught and above all modeled nonviolence, but it is also important to emphasize that refusing to perpetrate violence is not the same thing as avoiding violent situations. Quite the contrary, it may mean heroically wading into violent situations or willingly accepting violence directed at oneself.

Gandhi was not a utopian anarchist. He did believe firmly in the rule of law but equally that it is a moral duty to protest against and not obey unjust laws. Also, it is important to note that from a Gandhian perspective, those who engage in civil disobedience should not be surprised or outraged that the consequence is arrest or imprisonment—this goes with the territory; it is the price that has to be paid.

Does the rule of law presuppose the state with its monopoly, as Weber put it, on the legitimate means of violence? Gandhi did not envisage a free India post-Independence with no police or military. Given that he had actively recruited for the British war effort in World War I, it is perhaps less surprising that he did agree, perhaps reluctantly, to independent India's military intervention in Kashmir in 1947. He did envisage an India primarily made up of multiple small-scale communities of largely self-sustaining villages. Some local force might be employed, including the killing of rabid dogs or poisonous snakes, but there would be minimal need for the means of state violence. This was perhaps utopian, and his chosen successor, Jawaharlal Nehru as first Prime Minister of independent India, moved quickly in the direction of promoting the industrial development of the country.[11]

Critics or skeptics regarding Gandhi's nonviolence often bring up the relatively benign opponent he was facing in the British Raj. Nonviolence may have worked against the British in India, they say, but would it work against a Pol Pot, Hitler, or Stalin? Does it work in the jungles of Assam or Chattisgarh where there are no media to record heroic acts of nonviolent resistance?[12] Or, they ask, is it applicable even to the struggle of Indigenous peoples in various countries where they may represent only three or four percent of the population today as against Gandhi's India, where the occupier was a few hundred thousand against the non-cooperation of 250 million?

Discussion: Gandhi and King

We have seen that religious traditions may seek to manage the gulf between ideal and actuality, between precept and praxis through various strategies: Christians in the past by invoking the notion of counsels of perfection; Hindus by delineating different capacities and aims appropriate for different classes and stages of life; Buddhists and Jains by deeming monastics as religious virtuosi capable of following a code unrealistic and unattainable for laypersons. Gandhi, like Tolstoy, rejects much of this compartmentalization. Further, Gandhi seeks to demonstrate that pursuit of truth and total nonviolence is applicable to all and applicable in the world.

Martin Luther King Jr is perhaps the best demonstration of Gandhi's nonviolence transcending the particularities of late colonial British India. King reintroduced the method to America.[13] He tells us that Gandhi demonstrated for him that an ethos of nonviolence could not only be actualized in dealing with immediate personal relationships but also could be a potent force in dealing with large groups, even nations:

> As I delved deeper into the philosophy of Gandhi my skepticism concerning the power of love gradually diminished, and I came to see for the first time its potency in the area of social reform. Prior to reading Gandhi, I had about concluded that the ethics of Jesus were only effective in individual relationships. The 'turn the other cheek' philosophy and the 'love your enemies' philosophy were only valid, I felt, when individuals were in conflict with other individuals; when racial groups and nations were in conflict a more realistic approach seemed necessary. But after reading Gandhi, I saw how utterly mistaken I was. Gandhi was probably the first person in history to lift the love ethic of Jesus above mere interaction between individuals to a powerful and effective social force on a large scale.[14] (King Jr 1958: 96-97)

Conclusion

As I said in the introduction, I think most of us could agree with the negative formulation that reliance on reprisal, retribution, and vengeance tends to increase violence in a spiraling chain reaction of escalating animosity. This is obviously to be avoided, for 'an eye for an eye can only make the whole world blind'.[15] But how many of us trust in the positive formulation that love conquers all? This seems like a stretch, or a wish-fulfilment fantasy, or some sort of precious piety, which appears utterly unrealistic on the interpersonal level when dealing, for instance, with a sociopath, and on the collective or international level utterly divorced from on-the-ground realpolitik.

Is total nonviolence possible? Total nonviolence is perhaps impossible, or rather *is* impossible. We live by eating, which means we live by virtue of the death of other organisms, be they cows or cabbages. Of course, we can seek to minimize our violence by eating low on the food chain, for instance. Compromises with biological reality and how to minimize violence have, of course, been minutely worked out in the Jain tradition, a religious tradition that has held *ahimsa* or non-harming as a central focus. Like the Jains, we can hold the image of nonviolence as an ideal, as a horizon—one that perhaps ever recedes, is never totally realizable, but is nevertheless important as an orientation and aspiration.

Maintaining nonviolence as an ideal does not mean banishing it to the domain of a naïve idealism. Nonviolence really is important as an ideal even when it cannot always and in every situation be actualized. I also would argue that to maintain nonviolence as an ideal is not identical with saying there is no such thing as the legitimate use of violence or no such thing as a just war. Holding nonviolence as an ideal while also allowing for legitimate violence and war is not contradictory. Honouring nonviolence as an ideal can mean placing violence at the end of the queue as a means of last resort. I suggest that honouring nonviolence as an ideal also means respecting those who *do* hold that there is no legitimate use of violence and that just war is an oxymoron. They, like the nonviolence ideal itself, can act as a deterrent to the quick reactive use of violence. And above all, exemplars of the nonviolence ideal like Gandhi and King keep nonviolence from simply being dismissed as a religious platitude not applicable in the real world. Gandhi showed that it could be a peaceful weapon of the masses, not just a counsel of perfection only for the saints. He was himself a religious virtuoso who demonstrated that nonviolence was not only for religious virtuosi.

About the Author
Noel Salmond, PhD, is an associate professor in the College of the Humanities at Carleton University in Ottawa. His research interests include religion and visual culture, modernist movements in Hinduism and Buddhism, religion and discourses on the environment, and theories of religion.

Notes

1. This has been more loosely rendered as 'For hate is not conquered by hate: hate is conquered by love. This is a law eternal' (1973: 1:5).

2. 'All intensive religiosity has a tendency toward a sort of *status stratification*, in accordance with differences in the charismatic qualifications. "Heroic" or "virtuoso" religiosity is opposed to mass religiosity' (Weber 1958: 267). The passage is from Weber's essay 'The Social Psychology of the World Religions'.

3. For a fuller discussion see Sharma (2000).

4. The schematization given here was a Brahminical construct rather than a sociological reality on the ground but nonetheless it speaks to the need to situate religious ideals in the context of day to day realities. An ideal like nonviolence was hypothetically located in very particular circumstances of class and stage of life.

5. In Matthew 19:21, Jesus tells the rich young man who has already told him that he keeps the ten commandments: 'If you wish to be perfect, go sell your possessions, and give the money to the poor, and you will have treasure in heaven; then come, follow me' (*Bible, New Revised Standard Version*). Hence, the notion of counsels of perfection. Acknowledging that not all will follow through with giving away all to the poor and embracing poverty, the church came to teach, however, that some would be gifted to do so. Monastics or consecrated religious were those who took on poverty and the other two Evangelical Counsels of chastity and obedience.

6. Ward reminds us that Protestantism is suspicious of this two-tiered notion and that Luther's response to the demands of the Sermon was to say that they really are applicable to all but that their very unattainability leads to the Christian relying on grace instead.

7. He relied on the *Bhagavad Gita*'s notion of *karma yoga* (the discipline of action), which teaches that renunciation is not necessarily the renunciation of action but is rather the renunciation of the fruit of action. Gandhi's assassin ironically was also a Hindu inspired by the *Bhagavad Gita*. But Godse (2014) saw in this text a legitimation of political violence and in his last speech at his trial in 1949 construed the assassination as an act of piety and national duty.

8. The expression occurs in an address he gave titled 'My Faith in Non-violence' in 1931 on board ship bound for the Round Table Conference in London.

9. The most heart-rending description of the sort of heroism involved is found in Miller (1936: 195). Webb Miller, an American journalist, was an eye witness to the savage beating of nonviolent resisters at the Dharasana Salt Works *satyagraha*, Gujarat, May 21, 1930: 'Not one of the marchers even raised an arm to fend off the blows. They went down like ten-pins. From where I stood I heard the sickening whacks of the clubs on unprotected skulls. The waiting crowd of watchers groaned and sucked in their breaths in sympathetic pain at every blow. Those struck down fell sprawling, unconscious or writhing in pain with fractured skulls or broken shoulders. In two or three minutes the ground was quilted with bodies. Great patches of blood widened on their white clothes. The survivors without breaking ranks silently and doggedly marched on until struck down. When every one of the first column was knocked down stretcher bearers rushed up unmolested by the police and carried off the injured to a thatched hut which had been arranged as a temporary hospital.'

10. This becomes ensconced as India's motto, '*satyam eva jayate*': truth alone triumphs (*Mundaka Upanishad* 3.1.6).

11. Eventually, India tested its first nuclear weapon (ironically code-named Smiling

Buddha and detonated on the Buddha's birthday) in 1974. India is currently testing its first nuclear-powered and nuclear-armed submarine.

12. Indian author and activist Arundhati Roy has argued that Gandhian nonviolence requires an audience afforded by press and media. See her interview by Sagarika Ghosh of CNN-IBN (2013), at http://www.firstpost.com/india/maoist-attacks-are-a-counter-violence-of-resistance-against-the-state-arundhati-roy-820173.html.

13. 'I had come to see early that the Christian doctrine of love operating through the Gandhian method of nonviolence was one of the most potent weapons available to the Negro in his struggle for freedom... Nonviolent resistance had emerged as the technique of the movement, while love stood as the regulating ideal. In other words, Christ furnished the spirit and motivation, while Gandhi furnished the method' (King Jr 1958: 85). Of course, nonviolent civil disobedience had been articulated a century earlier in America by Henry David Thoreau (1966), whom Gandhi credits as one of his inspirations.

14. If King stayed with Gandhi's nonviolence to his end, Mandela, while enormously indebted to Gandhi, ultimately abandoned total nonviolence in his South African campaign: 'Gandhi remained committed to nonviolence; I followed the Gandhian strategy for as long as I could, but then there came a point in our struggle when the brute force of the oppressor could no longer be countered through passive resistance alone' (1999: 124-25).

15. A saying often attributed to Gandhi but perhaps apocryphal.

Chapter 9

No to War and Yes to So Much More:
Pope Francis, Principled Nonviolence, and Positive Peace

Christopher Hrynkow

Introduction

> Nonviolence is a power which can be wielded equally by all—provided
> they have a living faith in the God of Love and have therefore equal love
> for all mankind. When nonviolence is accepted as the law of life it must
> pervade the whole being and not only applied to isolated acts. (Gandhi in
> Fahley and Armstrong 1992: 174)

Peace Studies scholars and conflict transformation practitioners have
made a distinction between principled and pragmatic nonviolence.[1] This
distinction is made so that principled nonviolence comes to both suggest
and support an integral approach to peacebuilding, which is relational
rather than utilitarian in character. As a result, the distinction implies a
preference for moving beyond tactical use of nonviolence (Sharp 1995).
Accordingly, a definitive feature of principled nonviolence is that it seeks
consistency between means and ends in projects actively fostering positive social change.[2] There is also a realm of confluence here between
principled nonviolence's relational underpinnings and peace theorists'
reflections on positive peace. To cite the prime example, peace researcher
Johan Galtung originally framed positive peace as the absence of structural violence, and he shaded negative peace as the absence of direct or
interpersonal violence.[3]

In slight opposition to Galtung's view, Trudy Govier suggests that 'we
might charitably amend the concept so that positive peace amounts to
the absence of *both* interpersonal *and* structural violence' (2008: 64). Considering principled nonviolence and positive peace in tandem can cast a
very wide net for transformative nonviolence and peacebuilding. Applying Govier's charitable amendment to principled nonviolent efforts to
build positive peace would imply a need for violence intervention and
prevention in instances of both personal and structural violence. In this
light, it must be conceded that Pope Francis (Jorge Mario Bergoglio, b.
1936) does not currently practice violence intervention and prevention

in the same manner that, to cite one prime example, members of Christian Peacemaker Teams do when reading the 'signs of the times' and putting themselves in the way of direct violence.[4] However, Francis has also displayed the aptitude of a peacebuilder who addresses local and global challenges in accord with frameworks of principled nonviolence and positive peace.

Pope Francis's Peace Witness, Principled Nonviolence, and Positive Peace

In terms of geopolitics, the assertion that closes the last section can be supported by referencing Pope Francis's peacebuilding discussions with Vladimir Putin over Syria[5] and Ukraine.[6] In both cases, Francis encouraged resolution of the conflict in a manner that respected principles of social justice and the common good. In addition, the pontiff publicly offered 'his house' at the Vatican to Palestinian and Israeli leaders as a place of mutual prayer for peace during his May 2014 visit to the Holy Land. Despite rising tensions, which at the time of writing have boiled over into increased levels of direct violence,[7] this invitation was virtually impossible to decline. As a result, June 2014 brought images of the presidents of Palestine and Israel, Mahmoud Abbas and Shimon Peres, embracing in the Vatican gardens with Pope Francis looking on. That occasion also included the participation of the Eastern Orthodox ecumenical patriarch Bartholomew I, who joined with Francis, Abbas, and Peres in jointly employing shovels to contribute to the planting of an olive tree in the Vatican gardens.[8] Later the pope and ecumenical patriarch, along with other Christian, Jewish, and Muslim leaders, all joined together in reciting multilinguistic prayers representing their faith traditions' intentions for 'peace in the Holy Land, in the Middle East and in the entire world'.[9] On that remarkable day, Francis spoke of peacemaking in a way that resonates well with the conceptual underpinnings of principled nonviolence and positive peace:

> Peacemaking calls for courage, much more so than warfare. It calls for the courage to say yes to encounter and no to conflict: yes to dialogue and no to violence; yes to negotiations and no to hostilities; yes to respect for agreements and no to acts of provocation; yes to sincerity and no to duplicity. All of this takes courage, it takes strength and tenacity.[10]

Further integrating these moral sentiments at the close of 2014, Francis also helped foster a somewhat unexpected détente in US-Cuban relations. This thawing of a conflict with roots in Cold War ideologies took place even as the pope principally focused on another issue of peace and justice: closing the Guantanamo Bay prison.[11] The détente earned him praise from both Cuban and American leaders. In the former case, President Raul Castro was given a rare Sunday audience to thank Pope Francis personally for his role in warming the long-hostile relations across the Straits of Florida. After that audience and looking forward to the pontiff's September 2015 visit to Cuba, Castro spoke, invoking Francis's wisdom, modesty, and concern for the poor:

> When the Pope comes to Cuba in September, I promise to go to all his masses and I will be happy to do so... I told the prime minister if the Pope continues to talk as he does, sooner or later I will start praying again and return to the Catholic Church, and I am not kidding.[12]

Castro kept this promise, attending all three public masses said by Francis during his reconciliation-themed visit to Cuba.[13] This noteworthy statement by Castro also points to how, on a more micro-level, Pope Francis's success in undertaking the hard work of being a peacemaker is perhaps more effective than, but certainly related to, his contributions to geopolitical peacemaking. That claim is evidenced poignantly by the fact that many who previously disagreed on a whole host of issues remain highly supportive of the direction taken by the present papacy. One factor operative here is that Francis has thus far been largely able to avoid entrenching himself in left- and right-wing ideologies that have caused division within and among local Roman Catholic churches. Indeed, on his trip to Cuba in September 2015, he explicitly extolled the value of love and service over ideology by asserting during his homily at Sunday Mass in Havana's Revolution Square that 'service is never ideological, for we do not serve ideas, we serve people'.[14]

Perhaps Francis, like the best of green politics, is offering an alternative to dominant ideologies. Although in this regard, it is interesting to consider how even rumours concerning the content of his first social encyclical generated a certain pushback from what might be described as more right-wing elements within the Catholic Church. That demographic may be identified by opposition to environmentalism or reform or both.[15] For example, speaking just before the release of *Laudato Si'*, Republican presidential candidate Rick Santorum, who is known for his devotional Catholicism,[16] tried to detract from Pope Francis's authority to speak on climate change. Santorum did so by making problematic claims about media misrepresentation of the present papacy, the Galileo affair,[17] and Catholic bishops' tendency to overstep their bounds:

> The perception that the media would like to give of Pope Francis and the reality are two different things... I'm a huge fan of his, and his focus on making sure that we have a healthier society... I support completely the Pope's call for us to do more to create opportunities for people to be able to rise in society and to care for the poor. That's our obligation as a

society. The question is how we do it... The Church has gotten it wrong a few times on science, and I think we're probably [here speaking for the Roman Catholic Church!] better off leaving science to the scientists and focus on what we're really good on, which is theology and morality. When we get involved with political and controversial scientific theories, then I think the Church is probably not as forceful and credible... I've said this to Catholic bishops many times: when they get involved with agriculture policy or things like that that are really outside the scope of what the Church's main message is, that we're better off sticking to things that are really the core teachings of the Church as opposed to getting involved, you know, with every other kind of issue that happens to be popular at the time.[18]

Perhaps more prominently in the mainstream media, fellow Catholic Jeb Bush weighed in on these matters. Bush, on a campaign stop seeking the Republican nomination to run for President of the United States, also found it expedient to share his thoughts in the run up to the release of Francis's first social encyclical. After praising the pope for his very cool, accessible style that was bringing people back to the faith, Bush asserted his independence from the Catholic hierarchy by emphasizing that he did not take economic and policy advice from priests, bishops, or popes.[19] Bush further implied that the pope was stepping over his bounds with the subject matter of *Laudato Si'*.[20] In what may be taken as a response to such sentiments, Francis employed an invitational tone after the Angelus on 14 June 2015 to provide his own shading of the content of the papal letter that was to be released four days later:

As it was announced, an Encyclical Letter on the care of creation will be published. I invite you to accompany this event with a renewed attention to the situation of environmental degradation, but also of recovery, in its territories. This Encyclical is addressed to all: let us pray so that all may receive its message and grow in the responsibility towards the common home that God has entrusted to all.[21]

As this invitational tone demonstrates and as the opening of Santorum's and Bush's above-cited comments indicate (or, perhaps, necessarily concede), Francis is operating out of the papal office in a manner that revitalizes its function as a symbol of unity for the vast majority of Catholics. In this regard, it is informative to consider the premise that lasting and substantive witness for peace transforms a culture by moving relationships from fear and destruction toward love and mutuality.[22] If, through such dynamic processes, Pope Francis can tactfully reorient the Roman Catholic Church to the point that it more fully incarnates some or all of the constitutive values of principled nonviolence, we will undoubtedly be able not only to see a transformation toward incarnating positive peace in that Church but also in the wider world.

More simply put, the possibilities arising from Pope Francis's employ-ing his office to foster a growth in principled nonviolence hold the prom-ise of adding a significant measure of momentum to the project of more fully incarnating positive peace on this planet. Such a peace witness is needed in our time, when consequences of challenges like global cli-mate change for the world's most vulnerable make it increasingly unten-able to separate social, political, and ecological qualities of positive peace (Hrynkow and O'Hara 2014: 23-32). In this light, the implications of Fran-cis's laying the proper foundations that will allow for the nurturing of a Church for the poor with a global perspective come into focus in a cogent manner. Any movement toward such a green transformation, coupling social justice, ecological health, and substantive peace, has the potential to make a tangible global impact. One particular place for Francis to make such an impact is through his papal teaching office,[23] a possibility to which I now turn.

Pope Francis's Contributions to Catholic Social Teaching, Principled Nonviolence, and Substantive Peace

In fact, there are many resonances with principled nonviolence and pos-itive peace in Francis's first two major contributions to Catholic social teaching: the apostolic exhortation, *Evangelii Gaudium* (2013) and the encyc-lical, *Laudato Si'* (2015). Some of these resonances can be highlighted with reference to Peace Studies literature. For example, Walker Wink describes Jesus's peace witness as representing a third way, which leaves behind passivity and violence in favour of transformative nonviolence (1999: 97). Similarly, Francis proposes that a transformative 'third way...is the best way to deal with conflict. It is the willingness to face conflict head on, to resolve it and to make it a link in the chain of a new process'.[24] Reflecting on such processes, John Dear argues that the twentieth-century papal affirmations of scholarly approaches to biblical interpretation that are supported by the documents of the Second Vatican Council[25] can serve to downplay the natural law and just-war traditions, helping move Cath-olics toward an active (re)embrace of the Gospel of Peace. For Dear, the sometimes amorphous 'spirit of Vatican II' (O'Malley 2008: 310-11) recov-ers Jesus's much needed nonviolent peace witness.[26] In accord with Dear's characterization of the peace witness of the Second Vatican Council, Francis connects peacebuilding and the new evangelization:

> The Church proclaims 'the Gospel of peace' (*Eph* 6:15) and she wishes to cooperate with all national and international authorities in safeguarding this immense universal good. By preaching Jesus Christ, who is himself peace (cf. *Eph* 2:14), the new evangelization calls on every baptized person to be a peacemaker and a credible witness to a reconciled life.[27]

Also recalling Wink's concern for naming and countering systems of domination (2003: 28), Francis presents a vision of positive peace. Filling in his view of substantive peace as consisting of much more than the mere absence of war, Francis writes:

> Peace in society cannot be understood as pacification or the mere absence of violence resulting from the domination of one part of society over others. Nor does true peace act as a pretext for justifying a social structure which silences or appeases the poor, so that the more affluent can placidly support their lifestyle while others have to make do as they can. Demands involving the distribution of wealth, concern for the poor and human rights cannot be suppressed under the guise of creating a consensus on paper or a transient peace for a contented minority. The dignity of the human person and the common good rank higher than the comfort of those who refuse to renounce their privileges. When these values are threatened, a prophetic voice must be raised.[28]

Employing language that also has resonances with Wink's project (1997: 114), Francis further understands peace as connected to a responsible citizenship that does not conform to 'the powers that be'.[29] Thus, 'progress in building a people in peace' is fostered through 'an ongoing process in which every new generation must take part: a slow and arduous effort calling for a desire for integration and a willingness to achieve this through the growth of a peaceful and multifaceted culture of encounter'.[30] That process, in turn, is connected to an inclusive and justice-oriented participation.[31] Francis continues, 'In a culture which privileges dialogue as a form of encounter, it is time to devise a means for building consensus and agreement while seeking the goal of a just, responsive and inclusive society'.[32] Mitigating against the manifestations of conflict that serve to fracture relationships, Francis's culture of encounter actively seeks to foster unity. This ethical orientation informs his image of worldly existence as akin to a pilgrimage, presumably of craftspeople, wherein 'trusting others is an art and peace is an art' and 'ecumenism can be seen as a contribution to the unity of the human family'.[33]

Turning his attention to the common home of all families, the violence of people against 'our Sister, Mother Earth, who sustains and governs us'[34] is characterized in the opening of *Laudato Si'* as not only relational but also deeply personal. Further, Francis asserts that this ecological violence multiplies as a result of the sin in our hearts, and is tangibly 'reflected in the symptoms of sickness evident in the soil, in the water, in the air and in all forms of life'.[35] In this manner, the encyclical's social ethics explicitly couple human ecology and the common good, imaging them as joined through intimate bonds. Moreover, for Francis this intimacy is related to a deep image of nonviolence:

The common good calls for social peace, the stability and security provided by a certain order which cannot be achieved without particular
concern for distributive justice; whenever this is violated, violence
always ensues. Society as a whole, and the state in particular, are obliged
to defend and promote the common good.[36]

The pope also extends this sentiment toward a cosmic common good[37]
in a manner recalling both Thomas Berry's poignant assertion that the
universe cannot be considered a mere collection of objects[38] and Wink's
reflections on the character of the nonviolent third way of Jesus (2003: 88).
In this regard, Francis's exegesis offers support for a substantive vision of
peace that actively challenges the ethics of domination:

> The biblical accounts of creation invite us to see each human being as a
> subject who can never be reduced to the status of an object. Yet it would
> also be mistaken to view other living beings as mere objects subjected to
> arbitrary human domination. When nature is viewed solely as a source
> of profit and gain, this has serious consequences for society. This vision
> of 'might is right' has engendered immense inequality, injustice and acts
> of violence against the majority of humanity, since resources end up in
> the hands of the first comer or the most powerful: the winner takes all.
> Completely at odds with this model are the ideals of harmony, justice,
> fraternity and peace as proposed by Jesus.[39]

In accord with this full meaning of principled nonviolence oriented
toward establishing incarnations of positive peace, *Laudato Si'* is clear
that we have an inescapable duty to defend and promote actively a green
common good. For example, invoking the anthropogenic nature of ecological degradation in support of a Câmarian style of countering spirals
of violence with responsibility-taking based upon a dialogical approach
(Câmara 1971), Francis opens the fifth chapter of the encyclical in the following manner:

> So far I have attempted to take stock of our present situation, pointing to
> the cracks in the planet that we inhabit as well as to the profoundly human
> causes of environmental degradation. Although the contemplation of this
> reality in itself has already shown the need for a change of direction and
> other courses of action, now we shall try to outline the major paths of dia-
> logue which can help us escape the spiral of self-destruction which cur-
> rently engulfs us.[40]

Also in line with Câmara's example of nonviolent social change in terms
of the educational project (see, e.g., Ruether 1999: 26), particularly as it
is brought forward by Ivone Gebara (2009), Francis is clear that Christian
formation ought to foster socio-ecological flourishing:

> All Christian communities have an important role to play in ecological
> education. It is my hope that our seminaries and houses of formation will

provide an education in responsible simplicity of life, in grateful contemplation of God's world, and in concern for the needs of the poor and the protection of the environment.[41]

As Elise Boulding (2000) highlights, such an integral approach to the educational project serves to promote cultures of nonviolence and peace.

Continuing his coupling of ecological concern with a preferential option for those living in poverty, and citing the lack of a robust human ecology as problematic, Francis solidifies the connection between (1) virulent proliferations of eco-alienation, and (2) violence in urban contexts:

> The extreme poverty experienced in areas lacking harmony, open spaces or potential for integration, can lead to incidents of brutality and to exploitation by criminal organizations. In the unstable neighbourhoods of mega-cities, the daily experience of overcrowding and social anonymity can create a sense of uprootedness which spawns antisocial behaviour and violence.[42]

Moreover, Francis emphasizes that dominant techno-economic cultural models encourage the adoption of unsustainable ways of being in the world. As a result of their hyper-consumerist character, they also reinforce what Francis names as 'an economy of exclusion and inequality'[43] because they are obtainable by only a small percentage of the world's population. For example, to cite a fact commonly named by ecological activists, if every person on the planet consumed at the same level as the US's national average, it would take the resources of five planets to maintain that standard of living.[44]

As such, for Francis, dominant techno-economic cultural models represent another seedbed of violence: 'Obsession with a consumerist lifestyle, above all when few people are capable of maintaining it, can only lead to violence and mutual destruction'.[45] In this sense, Francis remarkably identifies the *Earth Charter*[46] as a peacebuilding document that encourages 'us to leave behind a period of self-destruction and make a new start' by embracing a perspective of 'universal awareness' in joyful celebration of vital work for peace and justice.[47] In this regard, with a formulation that recalls a portion of Câmara's (1971) and Gandhi's prescriptions for breaking the hold of spirals of violence in this world,[48] *Laudato Si'* upholds nonviolent love with reference to a saint popularly known, through a grounded and ecologically themed handle, as the little flower of Jesus:[49]

> Saint Therese of Lisieux invites us to practise the little way of love, not to miss out on a kind word, a smile or any small gesture which sows peace and friendship. An integral ecology is also made up of simple daily gestures which break with the logic of violence, exploitation and selfishness.[50]

The treatment of such green joy in *Laudato Si'* is firmly connected to peace in a manner that can be read as perceiving simple living as violence intervention and prevention that, as per Wink's thought, necessarily eschews domination (1992: 314).[51] As Francis, describing the violent hubris of ecological harm, writes in a pastoral tone, 'Once we lose our humility, and become enthralled with the possibility of limitless mastery over everything, we inevitably end up harming society and the environment'.[52] This choice against both domination and consumerist orientation in favour of growth understood in terms of positive relationships is an integral part of the peace witness in *Laudato Si'*. This feature is further evidenced pastorally in Francis's profile of what may be understood as chosen green simplicity during his discussion of peace and joy in the encyclical:

> Such sobriety, when lived freely and consciously, is liberating. It is not a lesser life or one lived with less intensity. On the contrary, it is a way of living life to the full. In reality, those who enjoy more and live better each moment are those who have given up dipping here and there, always on the look-out for what they do not have. They experience what it means to appreciate each person and each thing, learning familiarity with the simplest things and how to enjoy them. So they are able to shed unsatisfied needs, reducing their obsessiveness and weariness. Even living on little, they can live a lot, above all when they cultivate other pleasures and find satisfaction in fraternal encounters, in service, in developing their gifts, in music and art, in contact with nature, in prayer. Happiness means knowing how to limit some needs which only diminish us, and being open to the many different possibilities which life can offer.[53]

Here we can begin to see how *Laudato Si'* offers a specific and effective antidote to a prosperity gospel that equates God's favour with 'spiritual, physical and financial mastery [and] that dominates not only much of the American religion scene but also some of the largest churches around the globe' (Bowler 2013: 3). Indeed, Francis firmly situates Christian spirituality as removing the basis for the dynamics of domination by supporting a lived ethic of substantive peace and joy in line with chosen green asceticism:

> Christian spirituality proposes a growth marked by moderation and the capacity to be happy with little. It is a return to that simplicity which allows us to stop and appreciate the small things, to be grateful for the opportunities which life affords us, to be spiritually detached from what we possess, and not to succumb to sadness for what we lack. This implies avoiding the dynamic of dominion and the mere accumulation of pleasures.[54]

In describing green ascetic practices, Jeffrey Jacob notes that practitioners of voluntary simplicity often seek to connect what may at first seem paradoxical states: the inner peace flowing from simple living with world peace (1997: 93). Francis embraces this proposition with his concept of positive peace being firmly linked to inner peace within a spiritual world-view, which can cultivate wonder at the magnificence of creation:

> An adequate understanding of spirituality consists in filling out what we mean by peace, which is much more than the absence of war. Inner peace is closely related to care for ecology and for the common good because, lived out authentically, it is reflected in a balanced lifestyle together with a capacity for wonder which takes us to a deeper understanding of life.[55]

Herein voluntary simple living becomes a more emancipatory path to positive peace, which in turn contributes to world peace in line with the Gandhian insight that simple living supports wider spaces for the realization of socio-ecological flourishing.[56] Significantly, this is a path accessible to a much wider swath of humanity than is represented in the segmented group of economic and political power brokers who currently control too many of the other factors, including instruments of mass violence, that mitigate against substantive world peace.[57] The delineation of that path, in concert with other insights mapped in this section and further connected in the conclusion that follows, combines to mark a significant measure of support for green understandings of principled nonviolence and positive peace within the pages of *Evangelii Gaudium* and *Laudato Si'*.

Conclusion

After John XXIII's untimely death, a key papal moment dealing with peace that was both important at a time of transition and set the tone for the Second Vatican Council's treatment of peace issues occurred when Paul VI addressed the United Nations General Assembly in New York City. For this address, he symbolically chose the feast of Saint Francis[58] on 4 October 1965. This date also meant his address was delivered at a time when the council was in session at St Peter's. In the speech Paul VI declared famously, 'No More War! War Never Again!'[59] As council father Remi De Roo (2012) notes, this speech had a significant impact in Rome during Vatican II, symbolized by Paul VI's being welcomed back from New York by those bishops gathered in St Peter's with rigorous applause.

A key result of the momentum[60] signified by such applause was *Gaudium et Spes* (arguably best understood as the pastoral constitution on the church in the contemporary world). *Gaudium et Spes* outlines the task of the church in the world to preach the gospel to all nations in a nonviolent manner by promoting justice, peace, and cultural development. Gregory Baum notes that the ethical horizon of *Gaudium et Spes*, embracing the fostering of freedom, equality, and participation within a framework of universal solidarity, marks an important new point in the life of the Roman Catholic Church (2005: 44).

Francis has moved to integrate this framework of universal solidarity and has repeated Paul VI's sentiment by affirming the value of negative peace[61] (in this case the absence of the direct violence of war). He, however, went further by embracing a conception of positive peace that emphasized 'both common and differentiated responsibilities' to foster equality and participation for all peoples within an Earth community understood to be God's good creation.[62] Indeed, lest there be any doubt concerning his commitment to principled nonviolence and positive peace, consider a statement Francis made in St Peter's Square early in his papacy:

> Today, dear brothers and sisters, I wish to add my voice to the cry which rises up with increasing anguish from every part of the world, from every people, from the heart of each person, from the one great family which is humanity: it is the cry for peace! It is a cry which declares with force: we want a peaceful world, we want to be men and women of peace, and we want in our society, torn apart by divisions and conflict, that peace break out! War never again! Never again war! Peace is a precious gift, which must be promoted and protected.[63]

Here, we see an unambiguous instance where Francis's expressed vision included not only an emphatic 'no' to the direct violence of war, recalling Paul VI's words, but 'yes' to so much more. Hence, we can conclude that although the present pontiff's writings and peacebuilding actions are certainly not without its flaws, notably in terms of a marked absence of an integral view of gender justice, Pope Francis nonetheless presents a substantive view of positive peace whose main threads provide multiple supports for potentially transformative principled nonviolence at this important juncture in planetary history, when 'our common home'[64] is marked by a reality of 'socio-ecological crisis' (Eaton 2013: 105).

Not only for the world's 1.2 billion Catholics, but also for those from outside of that faith who are inspired by the present pope, Francis's contributions on the levels of insight[65] and action open up particular spaces for 'creative energy' (Berry 1999: 67) to help incarnate principled nonviolent action and positive peace. This project of incarnating these important peace studies principles is buttressed by the pope's advocacy for a 'new and universal solidarity'[66] extending to both marginalized people and the larger Earth community. The wellspring of this particular space is remarkable, given its source in a papal office that would have been ill-equipped to foster such a realm of insight and action in a similar way before the spring of 2013, when Francis began to practice his distinct invitational and pastoral approach to being Bishop of Rome (Francis's preferred descriptive title for his current job).

Yet, we have now arrived at a 'historical moment' (Berry 1999: 7) wherein those who take papal teaching and action as a reflective model can bear witness to structural violence inherent in what Sallie McFague names as 'the intrinsic connection between all forms of oppression, and especially between that of poor people and degraded nature' (2000: 33). Boff (1997) adds that the liberation of the Earth community and marginalized people living in poverty are intimately connected. The Catholic tradition has a mixed record in this regard (see, e.g., White Jr. 1967; Gutierrez 2003). However, for Boff (2011) as for Câmara before him, what is essential is that liberation comes about through imaginative exercises of principled nonviolent action. Because they hold the potential to foster this type of creative spirit, despite his own myopic flaws in terms of gender,[67] the spaces Francis helps to open up for principled nonviolent action and positive peace can nonetheless be viewed as locations wherein the religious and human project, in accord with Ivone Gebara's formulation, are understood 'in light of making justice, of right relationships with women, men, and all living beings' (2003: 103).

When made fuller through the integration of such ecofeminist and liberationist insights as brought forward by Câmara (1971), McFague (2000), Boff (1997, 2011), and Gebara (2003), these spaces are well positioned to foster personal, spiritual, social, and political transformations in support of social justice, ecological health, and substantive peace. Indeed, when adequately integrated in this manner, the threads of the present pope's peace witness as presented above serve as a corrective both for gender myopia and the failure of the Catholic Church to apply fully its social teaching principles to itself. The implication here is that Francis's approach to caring for our common home, in so much as it supports positive peace and principled nonviolence, also cries out for much deeper equality than the dominant discourse that peppers Catholic social teaching with a view of gender complementarity.[68] This is an important point to emphasize because such dichotomous views of male and female roles limit the prospects for gender justice and autonomy within the institutional Catholic Church. As a result, for example, it becomes clear that principled nonviolence and positive peace combine to require much transformation of Catholicism in this world. This required transformation reaches far beyond narrowly understood personal spirituality to the way Catholics live out their lives as members of cultures, communities, and societies. In fact, the associated values and practices of principled nonviolence and positive peace as defined by Peace Studies theorists clearly call the institutional Roman Catholic Church toward deep transformation in terms of areas like its governance, wealth, and differential gender roles.

Nonetheless, as we have begun to see above, the relationship here need not be unidirectional in terms of activating the potential to foster an integral peace. In this regard, Francis's social teaching and peacebuilding actions may be said to help bring deeper socio-ecological consciousness to concepts of principled nonviolence and positive peace as they are normally articulated among peace theorists, social activists, and conflict resolution practitioners. The result may be both a fuller and more vital understanding of positive peace and a concomitant ecological expansion of a range of actions and concerns for principled nonviolent activism. In turn, at their best, Francis's peacebuilding efforts and his social teachings' treatment of contemporary ethical imperatives to address injustice in its many manifestations can open transformative spaces. When such spaces are made fuller by the integration of ecofeminist and liberationist insights, they are well positioned to give momentum to a much needed confluence. That confluence will be marked by a web of multidirectional and dynamic connections energizing a mutuality enhancing feedback loop between greener incarnations of both principled nonviolence and positive peace to the benefit of a growth in socio-ecological flourishing on this planet. This deep green outcome represents so much more than a negation of war. Rather, it is a strong affirmation of the intrinsic value of the whole Earth community in the face of the structural and direct violence that threatens our common home—a 'yes!' to vital and diverse life represented by cultures of dialogue, encounter, nonviolence, and peace.

About the Author

Christopher Hrynkow, PhD, is an associate professor in the Department of Religion and Culture at St Thomas More College, University of Saskatchewan, Canada. His research interests include cultural and social sustainability, religion and ecology, ecojustice, peace and social justice, and nonviolent activism. He also researches and publishes on Catholic social teaching, ecological ethics, transformative learning, cross-cultural education, religion and politics, and green living.

Notes

1. On the distinction between principled and pragmatic nonviolence from a Gandhian perspective, see Bharadwaj (1998: 79-81).

2. For a set of sources for principled nonviolence see King Jr (1967b, 1967c, 2010).

3. Peace Studies genealogy is often traced to Galtung's (1969) landmark article on peace research. Peace research, however, has a longer pedigree than Peace Studies proper. Other origins lie in the opposition to the Viet Nam War and the civil rights movement in places like the US and Northern Ireland. A longer genealogy would then mark a certain contemporariness with the work of people like Abraham Joshua Heschel and Martin Luther King Jr, who both employed language that would later be adopted by peace studies scholars and practitioners. For a taste of Heschel's and King's writings inclusive of their concern for green principles of nonviolence and social justice, see Heschel and Heschel (2011); King Jr (1967b, 1967c).

4. This methodology of reading the 'signs of the times' is not only associated with John XXIII's methodological inspiration for the Second Vatican Council but can presumably be considered a biblical imperative:

> The Pharisees and Sadducees came to Jesus and tested him by asking him to show them a sign from heaven. He replied, 'When evening comes, you say, "It will be fair weather, for the sky is red", and in the morning, "Today it will be stormy, for the sky is red and overcast". You know how to interpret the appearance of the sky, but you cannot interpret the signs of the times'. (Matthew 16: 1-3, NIV)

Interestingly for the subject matter of this chapter, *Sign of the Times* is also the title of Christian Peacemaker Teams' newsletter. For more on this group see Hrynkow (2009: 111-34). John XXIII introduces his 'signs of the times' phrase as a subject heading in an encyclical dealing with peace on this planet. Below the 'signs of the times' heading in *Pacem in Terris*, he asserts that people 'nowadays are becoming more and more convinced that any disputes which may arise between nations must be resolved by negotiation and agreement, and not by recourse to arms' (1963), at https://w2.vatican.va/content/john-xxiii/en/encyclicals/documents/hf_j-xxiii_enc_11041963_pacem.html.

5. RT News Staff (2013), at http://rt.com/news/putin-pope-christians-east-274/.

6. Kirchgaessner (2015), at http://www.theguardian.com/world/2015/jun/10/pope-francis-putin-sincere-peace-effort-ukraine-russia-vatican.

7. BBC News Staff (2015), at http://www.bbc.com/news/world-middle-east-3456 7988.

8. Pope Francis (2014b), at http://www.catholicherald.co.uk/news/2014/06/08/pope-francis-tells-presidents-only-god-can-bring-peace-to-holy-land/.

9. Pope Francis (2014a), at http://w2.vatican.va/content/francesco/en/speeches/2014/june/documents/papa-francesco_20140608_invocazione-pace.html#Distinguished_Presidents.

10. Pope Francis (2014a), at
http://w2.vatican.va/content/francesco/en/speeches/2014/june/documents/papa-francesco_20140608_invocazione-pace.html#Distinguished_Presidents.

11. Hooper (2015), at http://www.theguardian.com/world/2014/dec/17/us-cuba-pope-franicis-key-roles.

12. Raul Castro quoted in Pullella (2015), at http://uk.reuters.com/article/2015/05/10/uk-pope-cuba-castro-idUKKBN0NV0AP20150510.

13. Pullella and Hamre (2015), at http://www.reuters.com/article/2015/09/22/us-pope-cuba-idUSKCN0RK07X20150922.

14. Pope Francis (2015c), at http://w2.vatican.va/content/francesco/en/homilies/2015/documents/papa-francesco_20150920_cuba-omelia-la-habana.html.

15. For example, in May 2015, Cascioli wrote in reaction to anticipation surrounding then upcoming social encyclical that such anticipation was fervent because 'it looks as if finally a goal which until recently seemed unattainable is finally within reach, the Catholic church swept into the ecological chorus of religions in support of the official doctrine on the climate'. For Cascioli, the results erode the special status of human life espoused by Benedict XVI in favour of population control: 'It's the usual story, to eliminate poverty, all you have to do is to physically eliminate the poor' (2015, at http://www.thegwpf.com/riccardo-cascioli-climate-change-sustainbale-development-and-the-catholic-church/#sthash.DfNVluot.dpuf).

16. For example, just before conceding his Senate seat in 2006, it is well known that Santorum attended a private mass at the Omni William Penn Hotel in Pittsburgh. This service points to his particular take on Catholic identity, which, in turn informs his views on, for instance, homosexual acts. See Gilgoff and Marrapodi (2012), at http://religion.blogs.cnn.com/2012/01/07/seeking-to-reverse-jfk-santorum-marries-catholicism-and-politics/.

17. In opposition to the notion that the Galileo Affair represented an instance of conflict between Roman Catholicism and science invoked by Santorum here, during his impressive tracing of the genealogy of the conflict, Harrison argues that the Roman Catholic Church was both a firm supporter of science and had scientific consensus on its side. As such, he continues, the Galileo Affair 'might be better to characterize the episode as a conflict *within* science (or more strictly within astronomy and natural philosophy) rather than religion and science' (Harrison 2015: 173). Additionally, Gingerich notes that Galileo's proofs for a heliocentric system have now been falsified and that he fanned the flames of a personality clash with Pope Urban VIII by putting the pontiff's favoured view in the mouth of fool character Simplicius in *The Dialogue on the Two Chief World System* (1632) (Gingerich 2014: 47-49).

18. Santorum (2015), at https://embed.radio.com/clip/59060539/?ref_url=http%3A%2F%2Fphiladelphia.cbslocal.com%2F2015%2F06%2F01%2Frick-santorum-on-pope-francis-letter-on-climate-change-leave-the-science-to-the-scientist%2F&station_id=121&rollup_ga_id=UA-2438645-53&ads_ga_page_tracker=UA-17434257-35#.

19. Bush (2015), at https://www.youtube.com/watch?v=Zj7LcxQQX7k.

20. Pope Francis (2015a), at http://w2.vatican.va/content/dam/francesco/pdf/encyclicals/documents/papa-francesco_20150524_enciclica-laudato-si_en.pdf.

21. Pope Francis (2015b), at http://www.zenit.org/en/articles/angelus-on-the-parable-of-the-seed.

22. The language here recalls Mennonite peacebuilder Lederach's preference for the transformation of systems (moving towards more positive and substantively peaceful relationships), rather than their destruction (2001: 848).

23. Pope Francis (2015a), at http://w2.vatican.va/content/dam/francesco/pdf/en cyclicals/documents/ papa-francesco_20150524_enciclica-laudato-si_en.pdf.

24. Pope Francis (2013b), at http://w2.vatican.va/content/dam/francesco/pdf/apost_exhortations/documents/papa-francesco_esortazione-ap_20131124_evangelii-gaudium_en.pdf.

25. See, in particular, Second Vatican Council (1965), at http://www.vatican.va/archive/hist_councils/ii_vatican_council/documents/vat-ii_const_19651118_dei-verbum_en.html.

26. Dear argues that Vatican II's orientation toward *resourcement* and scripture allows for an important recovery of the Gospel of peace (2005: 115-25).

27. Pope Francis (2013b), at http://w2.vatican.va/content/dam/francesco/pdf/apost_exhortations/documents/papa-francesco_esortazione-ap_20131124_evangelii-gaud-ium_en.pdf.

28. Pope Francis (2013b), at http://w2.vatican.va/content/dam/francesco/pdf/apost_exhortations/documents/papa-francesco_esortazione-ap_20131124_evangelii-gaudium_en.pdf.

29. Pope Francis (2013b), at http://w2.vatican.va/content/dam/francesco/pdf/apost_exhortations/documents/papa-francesco_esortazione-ap_20131124_evangelii-gaud-ium_en.pdf.

30. Pope Francis (2013b), at http://w2.vatican.va/content/dam/francesco/pdf/

apost_exhortations/documents/papa-francesco_esortazione-ap_20131124_evangelii-gaudium_en.pdf.

31. It is in this light that one of Francis's well known phrases from *Evangelii Gaudium* is perhaps best read—a passage that we might also note reverses the assumed direction of evangelization, invoking a participatory image of community: 'I want a Church which is poor and for the poor. They have much to teach us. Not only do they share in the *sensus fidei*, but in their difficulties they know the suffering Christ. We need to let ourselves be evangelized by them. The new evangelization is an invitation to acknowledge the saving power at work in their lives and to put them at the centre of the church's pilgrim way. We are called to find Christ in them, to lend our voice to their causes, but also to be their friends, to listen to them, to speak for them and to embrace the mysterious wisdom which God wishes to share with us through them' (2013b, at http://w2.vatican.va/content/dam/francesco/pdf/apost_exhortations/documents/papa-francesco_esortazione-ap_20131124_evangelii-gaudium_en.pdf).

32. Pope Francis (2013b), at http://w2.vatican.va/content/dam/francesco/pdf/apost_exhortations/documents/papa-francesco_esortazione-ap_20131124_evangelii-gaudium_en.pdf.

33. Pope Francis (2013b), at http://w2.vatican.va/content/dam/francesco/pdf/apost_exhortations/documents/papa-francesco_esortazione-ap_20131124_evangelii-gaudium_en.pdf.

34. Pope Francis (2015a), at http://w2.vatican.va/content/dam/francesco/pdf/encyclicals/documents/papa-francesco_20150524_enciclica-laudato-si_en.pdf. See also McKay (2003: 521); Lyons (2007), at https://www.youtube.com/watch?v=HiA4_e4YwZE.

35. Pope Francis (2015a), at http://w2.vatican.va/content/dam/francesco/pdf/encyclicals/documents/papa-francesco_20150524_enciclica-laudato-si_en.pdf.

36. Pope Francis (2015a), at http://w2.vatican.va/content/dam/francesco/pdf/encyclicals/documents/papa-francesco_20150524_enciclica-laudato-si_en.pdf.

37. See, for example, Scheid (2011:125-44); Hart (2013): 223-24.

38. Berry sees this situation of interconnectedness in the universe as arising from its quality as the only self-referent mode of being. It follows that: 'Since all living beings, including humans, emerge out of this single community there must have been a biospiritual component of the universe from the beginning. Indeed we must say that the universe is a communion of subjects rather than a collection of objects' (Berry 1996, http://www.earthcommunity.org/images/Ethics%20and%20Ecology%201996-Edited.pdf).

39. Pope Francis (2015a), at http://w2.vatican.va/content/dam/francesco/pdf/encyclicals/documents/papa-francesco_20150524_enciclica-laudato-si_en.pdf.

40. Pope Francis (2015a), at http://w2.vatican.va/content/dam/francesco/pdf/encyclicals/documents/ papa-francesco_20150524_enciclica-laudato-si_en.pdf.

41. Pope Francis (2015a), at http://w2.vatican.va/content/dam/francesco/pdf/encyclicals/documents/ papa-francesco_20150524_enciclica-laudato-si_en.pdf.

42. Pope Francis (2015a), at http://w2.vatican.va/content/dam/francesco/pdf/encyclicals/documents/papa-francesco_20150524_enciclica-laudato-si_en.pdf.

43. Pope Francis (2013b), at http://w2.vatican.va/content/dam/francesco/pdf/apost_exhortations/documents/papa-francesco_esortazione-ap_20131124_evangelii-gaudium_en.pdf.

44. Natural News Staff, (2008), at http://www.naturalnews.com/022890.html.

45. Pope Francis (2015a), at http://w2.vatican.va/content/dam/francesco/pdf/encyclicals/documents/papa-francesco_20150524_enciclica-laudato-si_en.pdf.

46. Earth Charter Commission (2000), at http://www.earthcharterinaction.org/invent/images/uploads/echarter_english.pdf. Interestingly, Boff has cited a Spanish version of the *Earth Charter* as one of the documents, along with a selection of his books and a draft UN document on the common good of mother Earth and humanity, that he passed to Pope Francis through trusted intermediaries to provide 'bricks' that would help the pope build the foundations for *Laudato Si'* (Boff 2015: 7, 9). See also Cox (1988).

47. Pope Francis (2015a), at http://w2.vatican.va/content/dam/francesco/pdf/en cyclicals/documents/papa-francesco_20150524_enciclica-laudato-si_en.pdf.

48. See Gandhi quote at the beginning of this chapter. It is in this principled spirit that nonviolence contributes to integral and positive social change in the sense upheld in this chapter.

49. Capturing some of the creative energy associated with the wild in ecotheological discourse, this title properly refers to wild flowers, of fields and valleys, and explicitly not tended ones planted in gardens. See, for example, Therese of Lisieux (1912: 275).

50. Pope Francis (2015a), at http://w2.vatican.va/content/dam/francesco/pdf/en cyclicals/documents/papa-francesco_20150524_enciclica-laudato-si_en.pdf.

51. See also Latin American Bishops at Medellin, Colombia, 'Peace' (1968), at http://personal.stthomas.edu/gwschlabach/docs/medellin.htm#peace.

52. Pope Francis (2015a), at http://w2.vatican.va/content/dam/francesco/pdf/en cyclicals/documents/ papa-francesco_20150524_enciclica-laudato-si_en.pdf.

53. Pope Francis (2015a), at http://w2.vatican.va/content/dam/francesco/pdf/en cyclicals/documents/papa-francesco_20150524_enciclica-laudato-si_en.pdf.

54. Pope Francis (2015a), at http://w2.vatican.va/content/dam/francesco/pdf/en cyclicals/documents/papa-francesco_20150524_enciclica-laudato-si_en.pdf.

55. Pope Francis (2015a), at http://w2.vatican.va/content/dam/francesco/pdf/en cyclicals/documents/papa-francesco_20150524_enciclica-laudato-si_en.pdf.

56. The reference here is to the Gandhian concept of living simply so that others may simply live.

57. Pope Benedict XVI (2009), at http://www.vatican.va/holy_father/benedict_xvi/messages/peace/documents/hf_ben-xvi_mes_20091208_xliii-world-day-peace_en.html.

58. This choice rests, in part, on Francis of Assisi being associated with peace. On that association, see, for example, Boff (2001, 2006).

59. Pope Paul VI (1964), at http://unyearbook.un.org/1965YUN/1965_P1_SEC1_CH 16.pdf.

60. Part of this momentum was also provided by the famous Catholic principled nonviolent activists Dorothy Day and Dom Hélder Câmara campaigning in Rome during the fall sessions in an effort to assure that the council did not forget the Poor in its statements (Kaiser 2012, at http://www.thetablet.co.uk/page/lectureTablet2012).

61. To make the implied link here explicit, in Galtung's (1969) view, negative peace involves direct violence. To cite some examples: murder, physical harm, and war. See the introduction to this chapter.

62. Pope Francis (2015a), at http://w2.vatican.va/content/dam/francesco/pdf/en cyclicals/documents/papa-francesco_20150524_enciclica-laudato-si_en.pdf.

63. Pope Francis (2013b), at http://w2.vatican.va/content/francesco/en/angelus/2013/documents/papa-francesco_angelus_20130901.html.

64. Pope Francis names a 'growing conviction that our planet is a homeland and

that humanity is one people living in a common home' (Francis 2015a, at http://w2.
vatican.va/content/dam/francesco/pdf/encyclicals/documents/papa-francesco
_20150524_enciclica-laudato-si_en.pdf.

65. See Eaton's (2007) argument that the response to the current global climate
crisis needs to work more out of insight and less from a mere data-based perspective (at http://tyne.ca/ief2007/uploads/Heather_Eaton.doc). On the use of insight in
a transformative manner, see Melchin and Picard (2008).

66. Pope Francis (2015a), at http://w2.vatican.va/content/dam/francesco/pdf/en
cyclicals/documents/papa-francesco_20150524_enciclica-laudato-si_en.pdf.

67. See Francis's comments about problems flowing from the myopia in power politics (2015a, at http://w2.vatican.va/content/dam/francesco/pdf/encyclicals/docum
ents/papa-francesco_20150524_enciclica-laudato-si_en.pdf).

68. Pope Francis (2015a), at http://w2.vatican.va/content/dam/francesco/pdf/en
cyclicals/documents/papa-francesco_20150524_enciclica-laudato-si_en.pdf.

Part III

Nonviolence and Social Resistance

Chapter 10

Indigenous Voices

Tara Williamson, Glen Coulthard, Jessica Gordon, Nina Wilson, Sylvia McAdam (Saysewahum), Sheelah McLean, and Waneek Horn-Miller

Come My Way[1]

Tara Williamson

I've always been fighting, I've tried to be brave
But, while the others are marching, my mind wanders away
I wonder why we're hiding, there's no need to be ashamed
If it weren't for love we wouldn't have to protest anyway

So, come my way, love
Come my way

The women shut the cities down, the men they stopped the trains
A hundred fires, a fasting *kwe* whose hunger marks our days
A nation waits with baited breath, while another nation breathes
And, if you were here, I wouldn't have to say it you'd just see

You'd just see, love

I've never been idle, I've tried to be brave
But, while the others are marching, my mind wanders away
I wonder why we're hiding, there's no need to be ashamed
If it weren't for love we wouldn't have to protest anyway

So, come my way, love
Come my way

My heart's been on fire a hundred times before
My heart's been on fire a hundred times before
My heart's been on fire a hundred times before

My heart's been on fire
My heart, she's on fire

#IdleNoMore in Historical Context[2]

Glen Coulthard

Much has been said recently in the media about the relationship between the inspiring expression of Indigenous resurgent activity at the core of the #IdleNoMore movement and the heightened decade of Native activism that led Canada to establish the Royal Commission on Aboriginal Peoples (RCAP) in 1991. I offer this short analysis of the historical context that led to RCAP in an effort to get a better sense of the transformative political possibilities in our present moment of struggle.

The federal government was forced to launch RCAP in the wake of two national crises that erupted in the tumultuous 'Indian summer' of 1990. The first involved the legislative stonewalling of the Meech Lake Accord by Cree Manitoba MLA Elijah Harper. The Meech Lake Accord was a failed constitutional amendment package negotiated in 1987 by then Prime Minister of Canada, Brian Mulroney, and the ten provincial premiers. The process was the federal government's attempt to bring Quebec back into the constitutional fold in the wake of the province's refusal to accept the constitutional repatriation deal of 1981, which formed the basis of *The Constitution Act, 1982*. Indigenous opposition to the Meech Lake Accord was staunch and vocal, in large part due to the fact that the privileged white men negotiating the agreement once again refused to recognize the political concerns and aspirations of First Nations. In a disruptive act of legislative protest, Elijah Harper initiated a filibuster in the days immediately leading up to the accord's ratification deadline, which ultimately prevented the province from endorsing the package. The agreement subsequently tanked because it failed to gain the required ratification of all ten provinces within three years of reaching a deal.

The second crisis involved a 78-day armed standoff beginning 11 July 1990, between the Mohawk nation of Kanesatake, the Quebec provincial police (SQ), and the Canadian armed forces near the town of Oka in Quebec province. On 30 June 1990, the municipality of Oka was granted a court injunction to dismantle a peaceful barricade erected by the people of Kanesatake in an effort to defend their sacred lands from further encroachment by non-Native developers. The territory in question was slotted for development by a local golf course, which planned on extending nine holes onto land the Mohawks had been fighting to have recognized as their own for almost 300 years. Eleven days later, on 11 July 1990, 100 heavily armed members of the SQ stormed the community. The police invasion culminated in a 24-second exchange of gunfire that killed SQ Corporal Marcel Lemay. In a display of solidarity, the neighbouring Mohawk nation of Kahnawake set up their own barricades, including one that blocked the Mercier Bridge leading into the greater Montreal area. Galvanized by the Mohawk resistance, Indigenous peoples from across the continent followed suit, engaging in a diverse array of solidarity actions that ranged from leafleting, to the establishment of peace encampments, to the erection of blockades on several major Canadian transport corridors, both road and rail. Although polls conducted during the standoff showed some support by non-Native Canadians outside of Quebec for the Mohawk cause, most received their information about the so-called 'Oka Crisis' through the corporate media, which overwhelmingly represented the event as a 'law and order' issue fundamentally undermined by Indigenous peoples' anger and resentment-fuelled criminality.[3]

For many Indigenous people and their supporters, however, these two national crises were seen as the inevitable culmination of a near decade-long escalation of Native frustration with a colonial state that steadfastly refused to uphold the rights that had been recently 'recognized and affirmed' in section 35 (1) of *The Constitution Act, 1982*. By the late 1980s, this frustration was clearly boiling over, resulting in a marked rise in First Nations' militancy and land-based direct action. The following are some of the more well-documented examples from the time:

- The Innu occupation and blockade of the Canadian Air Force/NATO base at Goose Bay, Labrador. The occupation was led largely by Innu women to challenge the further dispossession of their territories and the destruction of their land-based way of life by the military industrial complex's encroachment onto the Innu peoples' homeland of *Nitassinan*;
- The Lubicon Cree struggle against oil and gas development on their traditional territories in present-day Alberta. The Lubicon Cree have been struggling to protect a way of life threatened by intensified capitalist development on their homelands since at least 1939. Over the years, the community has engaged in a number of very public protests to get their message across, including a well-publicized boycott of the 1988 Calgary Winter Olympics and the associated Glenbow Museum exhibit, *The Spirit Sings*;
- First Nations blockades in British Columbia. Throughout the 1980s, First Nations in British Columbia grew extremely frustrated with the painfully slow pace of the federal government's comprehensive land-claims process and the province's racist refusal to recognize Aboriginal title within its borders. The result was a decade's worth of very disruptive blockades, which at its height in 1990 were such a common occurrence that Vancouver newspapers felt the need to publish traffic advisories identifying delays caused

by First Nations roadblocks in the province's interior. Many of the blockades were able to halt resource extraction on Native land for protracted periods of time;

- The Algonquins of Barriere Lake. By 1989, the Algonquins of Barrier Lake were embroiled in a struggle to stop clear-cut logging within their traditional territories in present-day Quebec because these practices threatened their land and way of life. Under the leadership of customary chief Jean-Maurice Matchewan, the community used blockades to successfully impede clear-cutting activities affecting their community; and

- The Temagami First Nation blockades of 1988 and 1989 in present-day Ontario. The Temagami blockades were set up to protect their nation's homeland from further encroachment by non-Native development. The blockades of 1988–89 were the most recent assertions of Temagami sovereignty in over a century-long struggle to protect the community's right to land and freedom from colonial settlement and development.[4]

From the vantage point of the colonial state, by the time the 78-day stand-off at Kanesatake had begun, things were already out of control in Indian Country. If settler-state stability and authority are required to ensure 'certainty' over lands and resources to create a climate friendly for expanded capitalist accumulation, then the barrage of Indigenous practices of disruptive counter-sovereignty that emerged with increased frequency in the 1980s was an embarrassing demonstration that Canada no longer had its shit together with respect to managing the so-called 'Indian Problem'. On top of this, the material form that these expressions of Indigenous sovereignty took on the ground—the blockade explicitly erected to impede constituted flows of racialized capital and state power from entering Indigenous territories—must have been particularly troubling to the settler-colonial elite. All of this activity was an indication that Indigenous people and communities were no longer willing to wait for Canada (or even their own leaders) to negotiate a just relationship with them in good faith. There was also growing concern that Indigenous youth in particular were no longer willing to play by Canada's rules—especially regarding the potential use of political violence—when it came to advancing their communities' rights and interests. As then National Chief of the Assembly of the First Nations, Georges Erasmus, warned in 1988: 'Canada, if you do not deal with this generation of leaders, then we cannot promise that you are going to like the kind of violent political action that we can just about guarantee the next generation is going to bring to you'. Consider this 'a warning', Erasmus continued, 'We want to let you know that you're playing with fire. We may be the last generation of leaders that are prepared to sit down and peacefully negotiate our concerns with you' (*Toronto Star* 1988: A1).

In the wake of having to engage in one of the largest military operations since the Korean War, the federal government announced on 23 August 1991 that a royal commission would be established with a sprawling 16-point mandate to investigate the abusive relationship that had clearly developed between Aboriginal peoples and the Canadian state. Published two years behind schedule in November 1996, the 58-million dollars, five-volume, approximately 4,000-page *Report of the Royal Commission on Aboriginal Peoples* (RCAP) includes 440 recommendations which call for a renewed relationship based on the core principles of 'mutual recognition, mutual respect, sharing and mutual responsibility'. The material conditions that informed the decade of Indigenous protest that led to the resistance at Kanesatake created the political context that RCAP's call for recognition and reconciliation was supposed to pacify—namely, the righteous anger and resentment of the colonized transformed into an insurgent reclamation of Indigenous difference that threatened to *unsettle* settler-colonialism's sovereign claim over Indigenous people and our lands.

With respect to the emergent #IdleNoMore movement, although many of the conditions that compelled the state to undertake the most expensive public inquiry in Canadian history are still in place, a couple of important ones are not. The first condition that appears to be absent is the perceived threat of political violence that was present in the years leading to the resistance at Kanesatake. #IdleNoMore is an explicitly nonviolent movement, which accounts for its relatively wide spectrum of both Native and non-Native support at the moment. However, if the life of Attawapiskat Chief Theresa Spence continues to be recklessly put in jeopardy by a Prime Minister who negligently refuses to capitulate to her reasonable demands, it is my prediction that the spectre of political violence will re-emerge in Indigenous peoples' collective conversations about what to do next. The responsibility for this rests solely on the state.

The second condition that differentiates #IdleNoMore from the decade of Indigenous activism that led to RCAP is the absence (so far) of widespread economic disruption unleashed by Indigenous direct action. If history has shown us anything, it is this: if you want those in power to respond swiftly to Indigenous peoples' political efforts, start by placing Native bodies (with a few logs and tires thrown in for good measure) between settlers and their money, which in colonial contexts is generated by the ongoing theft and exploitation of our land and resource base. If this is true, then the long-term efficacy of the #IdleNoMore movement would appear to hinge on its protest actions being distributed more evenly between the malls and front lawns of legislatures on the one hand, and the logging roads, thoroughfares, and railways that are central to the accumulation of colonial capital on the other. For better and for worse, it was our peoples' challenge to these two pillars of colonial sovereignty that led to the recommendations of RCAP: the Canadian state's claim to hold a legitimate monopoly on use of violence and the conditions required for the ongoing accumulation of capital. In stating this, however, I don't mean to offer an unqualified endorsement of these two challenges, but rather a diagnosis of our present situation based on an ongoing critical conversation about how these differences and similarities ought to inform our current struggle.

The Idle No More Manifesto

Jessica Gordon, Nina Wilson, Sylvia McAdam (Saysewahum), and Sheelah McLean

We contend that: The Treaties are nation-to-nation agreements between The Crown and First Nations who are sovereign nations. The Treaties are agreements that cannot be altered or broken by one side of the two Nations. The spirit and intent of the Treaty agreements mean that First Nations peoples would share the land, but retain their inherent rights to lands and resources. Instead, First Nations have experienced a history of colonization which has resulted in outstanding land claims, lack of resources, and unequal funding for services such as education and housing.

We contend that: The state of Canada has become one of the wealthiest countries in the world by using the land and resources. Canadian mining, logging, oil, and fishing companies are the most powerful in the world due to land and resources. Some of the poorest First Nations communities have mines or other developments on their land but do not get a share of the profit. The taking of resources has left many lands and waters poisoned—the animals and plants are dying in many areas in Canada. We cannot live without the land and water. We have laws older than this colonial government about how to live with the land.

We contend that: Currently, this government is trying to pass many laws so that reserve lands can also be bought and sold by big companies to get profit from resources. They are promising to share this time. Why would these promises be different from past promises? We will be left with nothing but poisoned water, land, and air. This is an attempt to take away sovereignty and the inherent right to land and resources from First Nations peoples.

We contend that: There are many examples of other countries moving towards sustainability, and we must demand sustainable development as well. We believe in healthy, just, equitable, and sustainable communities and have a vision and plan of how to build them.

Please join us in creating this vision.

Revolutionary Acts of Nonviolence Disempower Opposition[5]

Waneek Horn-Miller

Violence is never simple; it is horrific and loaded with long-term, devastating consequences. I know this from experience and have lived it up close and personal. Imagine yourself standing on a highway as Canadian armed forces tanks roll towards you flanked by soldiers in full combat gear. Army helicopters hover above with men hanging out the sides; guns are pointed at you. You watch as Warriors scream out in anger as the tanks roll closer and closer. Women are yelling at them to 'get back!' and to us, 'stay calm!' Your heart is beating so fast as your body tries to adapt to the adrenaline coursing through your veins. You wait, hold your breath, and listen for that sound—the gunshot that will start and end it all. You are 14 years old, and your summer vacation has taken you to the middle of a war zone. You are scared, excited, and not fully comprehending what is going on. The one thing you do know is, you are unarmed and those guns are pointed right at you. You suddenly understand completely that your life could end at any second, and you wait.

It is 20 August 1990; the Canadian forces have stormed right into the disputed land where a golf course is set to expand onto a traditional burial ground. The Oka standoff would last another 27 days. I would be witness to horrific acts of violence, psychological warfare, and finally I would be stabbed in the chest, two centimetres away from my heart. Memories from that summer have both inspired me to achieve and haunted me. As I write this, my hands begin to shake as I once again feel the adrenaline flooding into me, getting me ready to run or to fight. I am writing this as an open letter. It is a window to my soul and my experiences. It is for anyone who is even hinting at violent action. In the post-9/11 world, the consequences of violent action have changed. There are new terrorism laws that have extreme implications for not only the perpetrators, but for all Indigenous people across North America.

I am reminded of watching a heated discussion, in the last days of the Oka Crisis, that violent action is not the solution. Some of the men wanted to shoot it out, guns blazing, and the women were arguing against it, telling them to keep a cool head. It was the women's role to remind them, that in the great law, it does not state that you fight till you die, but rather you fight till you win. After a long heated summer of provocation, I understood the anger those men felt and the attractiveness of a martyred death, but I was terrified watching as my life or death was being debated. In the end, the debate for life and our future won out. Witnessing that made me understand as an Indigenous person we are part of a larger community and we do not exist in a vacuum. All we do as individuals in peace and violence has a huge impact on all of us.

These memories, my new role as a mother, and my overwhelming love of all our children have infected me with a need to ensure no other 14-year-old has to face that kind of trauma. I think violent action is not the solution, and I have made it a life's mission to look for alternate ways of making change: ones based on peace, cooperation, and inspiration. Over the last few months, we have witnessed an awakening of both Indigenous and non-Indigenous peoples inspired to stand up, speak out, and act. The power of Idle No More comes from the fact that it is open to all who lend their voices for change. The potent combination of flash-mob round dances, social media, and teach-ins, has created a new generation of politicized people. It has done this because the essence of these acts is to raise awareness and because it is peaceful. People from all walks of life are drawn together, have engaged in dialogue, and are personally inspired because of the simple message: that the peaceful future of this country matters to all of us.

It is hard to miss the understandable undertone of anger and frustration; I feel this to my core. I feel anger at the incredibly damaging impact of genocidal policies like the Indian Act, intentional mis-education of the Canadian public, and resulting racism. Rage at how they have ripped at the very fabric of our nations, communities, and personal lives. It frustrates me that the most damaging legacy left is many of our people's lack of self-worth. How many see themselves only important for their anger, and their lives only worthwhile if given up in a fight. I remember a conversation I had with a reporter during Oka who asked me if I was ready to die. I said yes because if I died today, maybe my life would mean something. Looking back 23 years later, I think I have contributed more with my life than I would have with my death.

The most revolutionary act we could do is not visiting more violence on our communities, but rather to support our leaders in their fight by bringing the passion and power of Idle No More to the dismantling of the legacy of dysfunction, trauma, and violence that plagues our communities. We will disempower our opposition by ending the lateral violence expressed on each other and finally unify our nations by acts of respect, love, and peace. If our ancestors could speak to us today, they would tell us that violent action will never be fully off the table, but for the sake of our children, it should never be the first option, but rather the absolute last.

Peace and Power to all My Relations.

About the Authors
Tara Williamson, JD, is a member of the Opaskwayak Cree Nation and was raised in Gaabishkigamaag (Swan Lake, Manitoba). She holds degrees in social work, law, and Indigenous governance. Williamson was a professor at Fleming College in Peterborough and currently teaches at Trent University in Indigenous Studies.

Glen Coulthard, PhD, is a member of the Yellowknives Dene First Nation. He is an assistant professor in the First Nations Studies Program and the Department of Political Science at the University of British Columbia. He has published numerous articles and chapters in contemporary political theory, indigenous thought and politics, and radical social and political thought.

Jessica Gordon, Nina Wilson, Sylvia McAdam (Saysewahum), and Sheelah McLean are Indigenous activists and founders of Idle No More, one of the largest Indigenous mass social movements in Canadian history.

Waneek Horn-Miller is a Mohawk from the Kahnawake Mohawk Territory. She is an Olympic athlete, a sports commentator, and a motivational speaker.

Notes
1. Excerpts from *The Winter We Danced: Voices from the Past, the Future, and the Idle No More Movement*, ed. The Kino-nda-niimi Collective. Reprinted by permission of the publisher.

2. Originally published at http://decolonization.wordpress.com as 'Decolonization: Indigeneity, Education & Society', 24 December 2012.

3. On the lasting significance and impact of the Mohawk resistance at Kanesatake, see Simpson and Ladner (2012).

4. For a useful discussion of these and other examples of First Nations activism of the time, see Richardson (1989).

5. Originally published at http://dividednomore.ca/, January 25, 2013.

Chapter 11

Sex, Gender, and Nonviolent Resistance to Human Trafficking: An NGO's Response

Eileen Kerwin Jones

Introduction: Sex and Gender

Sex and gender are defining features of our common humanity. From the moment of conception and throughout one's lifetime, complex, context-specific roles and expectations regarding sex and gender shape and are shaped by all persons. According to the International Committee of the Red Cross, an organization devoted to conflict resolution on a global scale, gender can be understood as the 'culturally expected behaviours of men and women based on roles, attitudes and values ascribed to them on the basis of their sex, whereas sex refers to biological and physical characteristics'.[1]

This definition alludes to the complexity of sex and gender; it suggests that one's identity is inextricably linked to prevailing sex and gendered social practices and interactions. While conceivably central to one's sense of self, sex and gender also transcend issues of identity and are deeply infused with symbolic meaning and power. As Carol Cohn, international specialist in gender and global politics underlines, 'Gender is a way of categorizing, ordering and symbolizing power, of hierarchically structuring relationships among different categories of people and different human activities in a manner symbolically associated with masculinity and femininity' (2013: 4-5). Cohn's definition links sex and gender with inequitable power relations in society. These power relations function to include and exclude at individual and collective levels; they impact access to material and symbolic resources, security, freedom from violence, and many other human rights. It can be argued that a person's life options and general wellbeing are contingent upon adhering to the paradoxically ubiquitous, yet often invisible, construal of sex and gender. A recent conversation between American president Barack Obama and African president Uhuru Kenyatta regarding gay rights provides an example:[2] while homosexuality is illegal and punishable by fourteen years of imprisonment in Kenya, the African president dismissed Obama's concerns regarding Kenya's homophobic laws as 'non-issues'.[3] This presidential exchange encapsulates several attributes of sex and gender: they are deeply ingrained features of societies; there are no historical or cultural constants; they are socially constructed, often in hetero-normative ways that privilege two distinct sexes; they shape powerful norms regarding conventional behaviour; non-compliance with said norms is often violently prohibited.[4]

It is important to note that despite widespread knowledge of the complex realities of sex and gender, simplistic approaches often hold sway. Rigid assumptions persist notwithstanding copious amounts of academic research and global activism highlighting this complexity and the rights of gay, lesbian, and non-cisgender persons.[5] For example, sex and gender are frequently conflated and therefore largely misunderstood. Interpreted in reductionist ways, sex and gender are seen through a strict heteronormative binary of male/female, masculine/feminine, as opposed to a rich prism of human possibilities. This limited approach constrains human agency and promotes relational vulnerability of individuals and groups in multiple ways. It also normalizes (and thereby renders invisible, as evident in the presidential exchange above) violence against those who do not embrace a simplistic binary. In light of this, broad, sophisticated interpretations of sex and gender are critical for shaping effective nonviolent resistance to gender-based violence. Moreover, clear links need to be made between rigid social constructions of femininity and masculinity and gender-based violence, in order to effectively challenge this injustice and strategically empower nonviolent, transformative conflict resolution.

Methodology

In my chapter I explore the links between the social construction of sex and gender and the structural violence of human trafficking for sexual exploitation. I first situate myself as a founding member of PACT-Ottawa (Persons Against the Crime of Trafficking Humans).[6] As feminist theory and activism inform PACT-Ottawa's evolving response to human trafficking, I provide a brief overview of feminist insights on sex and gender. I indicate areas of consensus within this diverse discourse that can empower nonviolent resistance to gender-based violence, particularly sexual violence against women and girls. To substantiate the claims I make, I refer to Martha Nussbaum, a feminist ethicist and international development expert, whose work on human capabilities provides global empirical evidence detailing how males and females are not similarly situated. Because Nussbaum clarifies the interlocking ways in which violence against women systematically limits their life options, her insights provide more grounded information on gender-based violence than available from statistical data. I also refer to the womanist philosopher bell hooks, whose critique of patriarchy highlights the gender-based impacts on human agency and autonomy. As hooks links gender violence with stereotypical constructions of masculinity and femininity, her critique empowers transformative strategies for countering gender violence. In the second section, I draw upon Johan Galtung's pioneering work on violence and conflict resolution. I posit that as gendered practices and interactions are often characterized by varying degrees of domination and subordination, overcoming unjust gender relations is key to what Galtung terms positive peace. I also suggest that Nussbaum and hooks are important interlocutors with Galtung in shaping both a more robust concept of peace and more strategically effective nonviolent resistance to gender-based violence. As these feminist scholars/activists probe the deeply gendered nature of our lives, they demonstrate how the social construction of sex and gender function in the everyday production and reproduction of violence. They also signal that gender equity is key to creating enduring, violence-free societies. In the final section, I focus on Project imPACT, a recent research study conducted by PACT-Ottawa that explored human trafficking for sexual exploitation in the Ottawa area. I review its main findings and speak to the nonviolent resistance to gender-based violence Project imPACT has inspired.

Situating Myself

As a founding member of PACT-Ottawa (hereafter called PACT), a Canadian grassroots non-governmental organization established in 2004, the global problem of human trafficking is a major focus of my research, activism, and teaching. Committed to nonviolent resistance, PACT's mandate is to prevent human trafficking locally, nationally, and internationally, and to support the dignity and wellbeing of all trafficked persons. PACT's guiding principles embody a human rights approach informed by and accountable to all trafficked persons. PACT's research and activism are animated by intersectional insights into race, ethnicity, economics, geopolitics, geographical location, and history of colonization. In particular, a gender sensitive approach shapes PACT's research methodologies and strategies for nonviolent resistance. From a gender inclusive lens of inquiry, PACT uses the tools of education, advocacy, research, networking, and support services to inspire its nonviolent grassroots activism.

Feminist Perspectives on Sex and Gender: A Rich and Diverse Tapestry

Feminist scholarship has radically transformed contemporary discussions on sex and gender. It is therefore critical that grassroots organizations committed to nonviolent resistance aimed at challenging gender bias, such as PACT, are informed and shaped by this evolving scholarship. While a comprehensive analysis is beyond the scope of this chapter, I attempt a brief overview. Carol Gould's 1997 work *Gender: Key Concepts in Critical Theory* is a significant example of second wave feminists' manifold explorations into the complex links between sex and gender. From diverse and sometimes contradictory perspectives, including historical, psychoanalytical, Marxist, ecological, essentialist, lesbian, materialist, post-modern and post-structural approaches, Gould's (1997) collected work reveals the depth and breadth of feminist analyses, and invites critical (re)-thinking of sex and gender.[7] Subsequently, feminist discourses on sex and gender were expanded by queer theorists, such as Teresa de Lauretiz,[8] underlining the multiple modalities of gender oppression from the perspectives of LGBTQI+[9] persons and advocating for the deconstruction of heteronormative ideology as a human rights issue. More recently, leading transgender scholars such as Susan Stryker, called for a 'feminism that makes room for transgender people' (2008: 3). This rich tapestry of feminist research and activism underscores that adequate approaches to sex and gender presuppose critical, intersectional analyses along multiple and inclusive modalities, attentive to context-specific issues of class, race, sexual orientation, gender identity, poverty, security, colonialism, hierarchical power, human rights, and other structural oppressions.[10]

In my view, The Center for Gender Sanity's[11] approach to sex and gender as four independent continuums with multiple combinations and possibilities accomplishes this inclusive approach: it honours the diversity of feminist insights and is consistent with PACT's guiding principles.[12] In this approach, the continuum of biological sex (including external genitalia, internal reproductive structures, chromosomes, hormone levels, and secondary sex characteristics) can be thought of as observable and usually measurable phenomena with male (XY) and female (XX) points at either end. While most people ostensibly exist at either end, there is place on this continuum for everyone, and, in reality, there are individuals at every point along this continuum, including intersex people, and those with other than XX and XY chromosomal patterns. Gender identity, or one's psychological sense of self, is another continuum that transcends firm masculine/feminine domains. While there is space on this continuum for those who align themselves with the gender binary, such as cisgenders and some transsexuals, there is space for those who identify as two-spirit, trans, or neither.[13] Gender expression, or how one communicates one's gender identity, is a third continuum, with feminine and masculine at either end but with space for androgynous and gender-bending[14] persons. Sexual orientation is also on a continuum inclusive of bisexual, asexual, homosexual, heterosexual, and pansexual persons. Indeed, the

Center for Gender Sanity's spectrum of colors approach leaves room for the necessary broad interpretations of sex and gender. It is also consistent with cross-cultural research on gender diversity that indicates, 'There is no simple, universal, inevitable or "correct" correspondence between sex and gender and that the Euro-American privileging of biological sex is not universal'.[15] Moreover, this inclusive approach is key to nonviolent resistance to gender injustice, as it makes visible those who are devalued, silenced, and dehumanized due to their non-traditional sex and gender identities and expressions.

Feminist Consensus on Sex and Gender: Strategies for Nonviolent Resistance

Having provided this brief overview of feminist approaches, I submit that there are important areas of consensus that can guide nonviolent resistance to sex and gender-based violence. I detail this consensus and then demonstrate the significance of two feminist scholars and grass-roots activists in providing critical (re)-interpretations of sex and gender: the ethicist Martha Nussbaum and the womanist philosopher bell hooks. I show how critical links between sex and gender, violence and nonviolent resistance can be made by referring to Nussbaum's work on human capabilities and hooks's critique of patriarchy and gender stereotypes. I claim that understanding these links is strategically significant for shaping effective nonviolent resistance to gender-based violence.

    First, most feminists would agree that complex webs of difference exist both between and among persons identified and/or self-identified biologically and socially along the sex/gender continuums. Understanding these context-specific differences honours the uniqueness of every gendered person. It also undermines the durability of unjust hierarchical, stereotypical gender relations, thereby fuelling hope for nonviolent transformation. Second, most feminists would agree that inequitable power and meaning have often been attached to perceived biological differences in ways that negatively impact the autonomy and agency of non-dominant individuals and groups. As such, the human rights of those who have suffered gender-based inequities need to be promoted, as does insight for gender-privileged persons who (knowingly or unknowingly) have abused their power and compromised the dignity and wellbeing of others. Third, most feminists concur that while there is no generic 'woman,' women collectively as 'women' have suffered sex and gender-based injustices (albeit context-specific and non-uniform) in virtually all spheres— socially, politically, legally, economically, educationally, religiously and in health-related domains.[16] Feminists agree that cross-culturally, power and positive meaning associated with biological differences generally have not been ascribed to women, and that male gender privileging is at the root of the multiple injustices experienced by many of the world's women. The Global Gender Gap annual report consistently decries the inequitable life chances contingent on being born female.[17] However, as data on violence against women and girls are notoriously underestimated and under-reported, a more grounded method of diagnosing and addressing gender injustice is needed.[18] Fourth, most feminists would agree that despite their collective struggles against patriarchy,[19] this organizing feature of society persists cross-culturally, ensuring hegemonic males remain its principal beneficiaries. Trans-national feminists have critiqued the privileging of hegemonic, idealized males and masculinity, and the attendant devaluing of females, femininity, and other non-elite males and non-cisgender persons. Fifth, feminists share an ongoing commitment to social justice and envision what the feminist ethicist Beverly Harrison (2004: 17) once termed 'a world that would be beautiful to behold': an egalitarian, inclusive, liberated world, free from all forms of sex and gender-based violence.

Martha Nussbaum and bell hooks: Critical Insights into Gender-based Violence

Martha Nussbaum's[20] human capabilities approach provides an unprecedented way of understanding sex and gender-based violence. Nussbaum (2011) posits that respect for human dignity requires that every person experience a threshold of ten core human capabilities, which societies are beholden to secure for all citizens. Concerned about what people are 'actually able to be and to do in their everyday lives', Nussbaum's human capabilities approach allows for inter-personal comparisons of wellbeing (2011: 17-46). Thus, it is an approach that can discern inequities experienced by specific individuals and groups.

Moreover, as a grassroots feminist activist, Nussbaum (2000) grounds much of her research in the concrete struggles of impoverished women's lives. She is therefore ideally positioned to illuminate the ways in which gender-based violence against women and girls impedes their human flourishing. Nussbaum's human capabilities approach provides a normative theory: it does not explain violence against women. Rather, it helps conceptualize the pervasiveness of this problem, provides an accessible template for concretizing the myriad impacts violence has on the lives of women and girls, and gives salience to the systemic nature and multiple forms this violence assumes. It also demonstrates that the unequal life chances experienced by women and girls are on a continuum and structured into societies in harmful, albeit unique, ways. Nussbaum states, 'Many women all over the world find themselves treated unequally with respect to employment, bodily safety and integrity, basic nutrition and health care, education and political voice' (1999: 5). While accepting that some are more vulnerable to violence than others, Nussbaum claims that no woman anywhere is *ever* free of violence, the threat of, or fear of violence, and whether physical or psychological in nature, violence limits every major capability of women's lives (2005: 167-83). Nussbaum is cognizant of feminist critiques of her work, specifically regarding universalism, cross-cultural insensitivity, and the legacy of colonialism. Nussbaum accepts their validity and is vigilant of her position as a powerful Western outsider in much of her research. However, while respectful of the need to honour the uniqueness of all women, Nussbaum sees recurring patterns in their lives. For Nussbaum, mastering the commonalities of women's lives is critical to empowering their flourishing. She posits:

> The body that labors is in a sense the same body all over the world and its needs for food, nutrition and health are the same...so it is not too surprising that the female manual laborer in Trivandrum is in many ways comparable to a female manual laborer in Alabama or Chicago...that she doesn't seem to have an utterly alien consciousness or an identity unrecognizably strange, strange though the circumstances are in which her efforts and her consciousness take root. Similarly, the body that gets beaten is in a sense the same all over the world, concrete though the circumstances of domestic violence are in each society. (Nussbaum 2000: 22-23)

Nussbaum details how violence is connected to the fact that many women are deprived of the first human capability: the chance to live a life of normal length. Whether in major conflict zones, where rape is a weapon of war, or during times of 'peace',[21] women are killed by sexual violence, often at the hands of spouses and partners. Prenatally, females are disproportionably vulnerable to sex-selection abortion; if born, they are more likely to be subjected to infanticide or to die from chronic neglect.[22] Females are trafficked and coerced into sex work that often leads to lethal infections, such as HIV/AIDS; they are murdered in dowry and honour killings. In the human capability of health, Nussbaum underlines how rape exerts a momentous toll on the physical, emotional, and social well-being of inordinate numbers of females in our world,[23] particularly in light of widespread rape culture(s), wherein survivors, rather than perpetrators, are often blamed for their violation and cannot access health or legal supports. Moreover, child sexual abuse has long-term impacts on the health of girls and women, as does domestic violence. The next human capability, bodily integrity, is linked to health and includes such issues as female genital cutting, female under-nutrition, and freedom of movement. Indeed, the mobility of many women is constrained either by cultural and religious norms, or psychologically by stalking and sexual harassment, 'creating an atmosphere of threat in which all women live the entirety of their lives' (Nussbaum 2005: 167, 168-70). This capability also includes reproductive choice, a human right denied to many (particularly impoverished) women on a global scale, with the result that hundreds of thousands die every year due to pregnancy-related causes, and millions more suffer chronic disabilities.[24] Multiple forms of violence experienced by women also cripple the human capabilities of sense, imagination, thought and emotions: this squandering of creative female potential debilitates all. Nussbaum's human capability of practical reason, the capacity of women who fear or experience violence to critically reflect and plan their lives, is constrained. Likewise, the human capability of affiliation is affected by violence. Whether within one's family, or within wider spheres, such as social and political organizations, violence limits women's capacities to participate in the public realm, to say nothing of diminishing the self-confidence necessary to perceive themselves worthy of such activities. The human capability of having a meaningful relationship to the world of nature is closely linked to the capability of enjoying leisure: violence diminishes the independence of many women, their laughter, and sense of play. Indeed, as women are disproportionably charged with the manifold tasks of the informal, largely unpaid sector in all economies, their lives are often a struggle to survive, with minimal time for rest and relaxation. Regarding Nussbaum's human capability of control over one's environment, violence often silences women's voices in the political realm. It also diminishes the possibility of a rewarding career and ownership of property, the lack of which structures both their financial dependence on others and their vulnerability to experiencing violence.

Nussbaum's human capabilities approach illuminates the enormous pain and systemic suffering inflicted on girls and women in our world by gender-based violence. Evidently, men and boys, especially gay and non-cisgender males, and those of low social and economic status, may well experience personal violence. Males may also experience secondary impacts of violence against women, such as an absent or diminished mother or partner, or enforced bachelorhood consequent to the dearth of females resulting from sex-selective abortions (see, e.g., Hudson and Den Boer 2004). However, the human capabilities of boys and men are in no way constrained, nor are their lives imperilled, to the degrees experienced by girls and women in our world. The enormity of ways gender-based violence systematically impedes the wellbeing of girls and women in our world is staggering. But what fuels such ubiquitous gender-violence? Here, womanist scholar and social activist hooks' critique of patriarchy provides important insights.

'Patriarchy' is defined by hooks as 'a political system that insists that males are inherently dominating, superior to everything and everyone deemed weak, especially females, and endowed with the right to dominate and rule over the weak and to maintain that dominance through various forms of psychological terrorism and violence' (2004: 18). More-over, in addition to demeaning females and all that is culturally deemed feminine, hooks maintains that patriarchy is the 'single most life-threatening social disease assaulting the male body and spirit', rendering men 'emotional cripples' who repress all human emotion, except anger (2004: 23). She asserts that all males are 'inundated with a poisonous ped-agogy that supports male violence and domination, that teaches boys that unchecked violence is acceptable, that teaches them to disrespect and hate women' (2004: 51). As a pervasive socializing force, hooks underlines that patriarchy's logic of domination shapes all persons, including girls and women, who internalize this logic and participate in their own exploi-tation. As such, collective collaboration is required to render patriarchy visible and ultimately obsolete (2004: 24). Her insights also clarify how collective and individual violence results from patriarchal social prac-tices and interactions that link hegemonic maleness/masculinities with the power of violation, and render female/femininities relationally vul-nerable to abuse. What hooks elucidates is that hierarchical relations of domination and subordination are at the root of gender-based violence, and that their dismantling translates into strategically-sound nonviolent resistance. Moreover, in their systematic construction of male power and female vulnerability, patriarchal gender relations are latent relations of violence that need to be challenged at the symbolic level.[25] Having high-lighted the widespread gender injustices experienced by girls and women in our world and how patriarchy normalizes and reproduces these injus-tices, I turn to the pioneering work of Johan Galtung for further insights into the structure of gender-based violence.

Johan Galtung: Pioneer of Peace

The Norwegian polymath Johan Galtung is credited with advancing the-ories on nonviolence and peaceful conflict transformation. Living under German-occupied rule during World War II, the then twelve-year old Gal-tung witnessed his father's arrest by the Nazis. This experience, along with Galtung's eventual imprisonment for refusing obligatory military service, had profound impacts on him: they sowed the seeds of a rich and versatile academic and activist life devoted to nonviolent resistance, peacebuild-ing, and peace mediation (Galtung and Fischer 2013: 3-23). In particu-lar, Galtung's articulation of a typology of violence with three different categories—direct, structural, and cultural—has been used in peace stud-ies and in other disciplines.[26] According to Galtung, violence can be under-stood as an 'avoidable impairment of fundamental human needs or to put it in more general terms, the impairment of human life which lowers the actual degree to which someone is able to meet their needs below that which would otherwise be possible'.[27] Elsewhere, Galtung refers to violence as 'avoidable insults to basic human needs and more generally to life' (1990: 292). The word avoidable is key: it highlights the differences between an individual's or group's potential, versus what they actually can do and/or achieve in their lives. Any differences can be attributed to the deleterious impacts of violence. Galtung also viewed violence in terms of the harm it produces and the human needs it limits (1994: 116-46). With respect to direct violence, Galtung underlines that both the perpetrator and the victim are identifiable. For example, in intimate partner violence, an aggressor and the individual assaulted are discernible. In contrast, with structural violence, there are no obvious actors: the violence is endemic to society. Structural violence is impersonal, invisible, and normalized by social structures and everyday experiences; it results in unequal power, inequitable life chances, and 'unequal power to decide how resources are distributed in society' (1969: 171). For example, structural violence is evident in the trans-cultural poverty of women. Indeed, the adage 'poverty has a woman's face'[28] speaks to women's economic vulnerability, to the limitations of their autonomy, and to their relative lack of decision-making power in society (Farmer 2005: 40). Indeed, women and girls comprise the majority of the world's poor (Gayle and Daulaire 2007: 1297), and the life trajectories of many women are shaped by structural injustices that deny them fundamental human rights.[29] While Galtung viewed direct violence as the tip of the iceberg, he considered structural violence the larger, hidden part that is more resistant to change and rooted in wider structural and cultural systems, such as imperialism and capitalism (1994: 136). Finally, Galtung defined cultural violence as 'those aspects of culture, the symbolic sphere of our existence...that can be used to legitimize direct or structural violence' (1990: 291). Cultural violence has the effect of validating both direct and structural violence, making such violence 'look, even feel right, or at least not wrong' (1990: 291-92). Popular culture's plethora of misogynistic, sexually violent films, music, and video games are instances of cultural violence. Galtung viewed direct, structural, and cultural violence as mutually reinforcing points of a violence triangle (1996: 31). Finally, Galtung conceived of peace as both negative and positive: the former being the absence of direct violence, the latter being the presence of social justice. Galtung maintained that positive and negative peace were both necessary for violence-free societies to prevail.[30]

Galtung's far-reaching contributions to conflict resolution and peace promotion are beyond the scope of this chapter. However, significant for this chapter's focus on sex, gender, and nonviolent resistance is the importance of a peace studies/feminist alliance. This alliance has been discussed elsewhere, particularly in Catia Confortini's (2006: 333-67) comprehensive overview of Galtung's work. Confortini argues that sex and gender are key to the social construction of violence and need to be taken more seriously by peace theorists as a fundamental category of analysis in any approach to nonviolent resistance. According to Confortini, Galtung conflates and interprets sex and gender in monolithic, binary ways. Consequently, the pivotal role sex and gender play in the social construction of violence, and in the deeply gendered, hierarchical, and mutually exclusive relations of domination and subordination that normalize this violence are overlooked (Confortini 2006: 341-55). Furthermore, Confortini asserts that nonviolent resistance, devoid of gender-inclusive analyses, cannot inculcate a lasting peace (2006: 335-36). I concur with Confortini's cogent argument for a peace studies/feminist alliance. I hope to demonstrate that by integrating the feminist contributions of Nussbaum and hooks, a more robust approach to nonviolent resistance to gender-based violence can inform nonviolent grassroots activism.

Peace/Feminist Interlocutors:
Galtung, Nussbaum, and hooks

Feminist scholarship has benefited from Galtung's widely applicable work on structural violence and conflict resolution. Equally, feminist scholarship, particularly its critical analyses of sex and gender, can inform peace studies and strategies for nonviolent resistance. First, feminist analyses would encourage peace theorists to re-think gender as more than a synonym for sex. That is, re-conceptualizing gender as a context-specific social construct embodying relations of power would underscore its importance as a critical site for leveraging peaceful, nonviolent resistance. In particular, feminist analyses would elucidate the mutually reinforcing links between the social construction of masculinities and femininities and the legitimization of gender-based violence. Here hooks's understandings of patriarchy's poisonous pedagogy and its culturally idealized gender constructions are relevant. What hooks highlights are the ways in which stereotypical, binary gender constructions are at the root of gender injustice: these social constructs both depend on violence for their perpetuation and create the conditions of possibility for violence to occur. Her advocating for the strategic dismantling of idealized gender constructions is therefore significant for nonviolent resistance for several reasons. It would challenge an inherently violent logic of domination and liberate many from enforced, rigid gender binaries and expectations to experience the fullness of their humanity. It would reveal the gender injustices endured by gay, lesbian, and non-cisgender persons and thereby inform nonviolent resistance. It would alert females to internalized sexism and the dangers of adopting a patriarchal mindset (hooks 2000: 1-24), particularly its disempowering/devaluing constructions of femininity. It would liberate many males from a muted emotional life and make visible hitherto dismissed, nonviolent men for the collaborative tasks of creating new ways of living free from gender-based violence. Moreover, countering hegemonic masculinities would facilitate the dismantling of other abusive forms of dominant power, such as heterosexism and homophobia. Thus, in societies genuinely liberated from heterosexism and homophobia, these hetero-normative constraints would truly be non-issues, not because they were normalized but because they were eradicated.

Second, feminist critiques of simplistic dualisms related to sex and gender would erode other false dichotomies, such as the problematic pairings of peace/war, victim/perpetrator, private/public, subject/object. As Nussbaum has indicated in the human capabilities of health and bodily integrity, women's everyday experiences of intimate partner violence defy these simplistic binaries. Indeed, Nussbaum signals that even during public 'conflict-free' times, domestic abuse (the private war at home) continues unabated. Similarly, the oppositions of victim/perpetrator and subject/object obfuscate the everyday realities of girls and women and interfere with effective nonviolent resistance. They reinforce a misconception of women as victims, passive objects of domestic assault. In reality, active resistance and creative resilience, rather than predictable passivity, often characterize the agency and autonomy of many women (subjects) in facing the injustice of intimate partner violence. Discounting their agency and autonomy undermines nonviolent strategies that can further empower women in their efforts to seek peaceful, safer alternatives for themselves and their dependents. Clearly, feminist dismantling and re-visioning of dichotomies along wider continuums would empower peace studies by ushering in more accurate, comprehensive accounts of direct, structural, and cultural forms of violence. It would also signal the subversive spaces where nonviolent resistance to gender-based violence can flourish.

Third, Nussbaum's focus on the everyday survival struggles of girls and women in our world demonstrates the importance of re-conceptualizing gender as more than a variable in peace studies' theories of violence. Nussbaum's human capabilities approach illuminates gender as a critical axis upon which Galtung's notion of the 'avoidable constraints that interfere with life' are deeply implanted and normalized in gender-specific ways in many different contexts. Moreover, the inter-personal comparisons and trans-cultural trends Nussbaum accents make visible those most invisible, whose sufferings are predictably overlooked. The close links Nussbaum makes evident among direct, structural, and cultural violence in the everyday lives of girls and women in our world challenge any static interpretation of these typologies of violence. Nussbaum invites more flexible approaches along an interconnected continuum rather than a stable triangle and thereby expands strategies for inculcating violence-free societies.

PACT:
Nonviolent Resistance to Human Trafficking for Sexual Exploitation

This chapter has argued that feminist analyses of sex and gender can inform nonviolent resistance to gender-based violence, and that feminist and peace studies theorists are valuable interlocutors in shaping strategically sound grassroots activism. I will now demonstrate how the theoretical insights hitherto outlined can inform resilient and effective nonviolent resistance to the crime of human trafficking for sexual exploitation by presenting the results of Project imPACT. At the outset, I wish to clarify PACT's positions on two salient issues. First, while human trafficking is the second largest form of illicit trade after illegal drug sales, this serious global human rights abuse is not limited to sexual exploitation. Everyday, men, women, children, and even entire families, are trafficked and exploited for diverse reasons, including forced labour, involuntary domestic servitude, false adoption schemes, child soldiers, mail order brides, and organ harvesting.[31] No country is immune to this crime. Canadians are often astonished to realize that Canada is not only a receiving country for trafficked persons and a transit country for those trafficked from elsewhere, but also a nation where its own citizens are trafficked domestically.[32] Moreover, sophisticated, broad approaches to sex and gender are critical to understanding this complex issue. For example, not all human traffickers are male. The United Nations Global Initiative to Fight Human Trafficking (UN.GIFT) states that at least 42 percent of traffickers are female.[33] The United Nations Office on Drugs and Crime (UNODC) concurs, underlining that female traffickers are used to recruit women and girls, a tactic capitalizing on their supposedly feminine trustworthiness.[34] Second, PACT does not conflate sex work with trafficking for sexual exploitation. PACT's mandate is to prevent human trafficking and support the dignity and wellbeing of all persons exploited in this heinous way, some of whom may be trafficked and coerced into sex work.[35] PACT is committed to promoting the human rights of all marginalized people and stands in solidarity with them.[36]

Project imPACT:
Human Trafficking for Sexual Exploitation in the Ottawa Area

Project imPACT's complete report is available on the PACT website.[37] Its comprehensive analysis of human trafficking for sexual exploitation in the national capital area is beyond the scope of this chapter. However, in this section, I present five significant findings before exploring its specific insights and recommendations regarding nonviolent resistance to sex and gender-based violence.

In March 2013, PACT received funding from Status of Women Canada to explore the problem of human trafficking for sexual exploitation in the Ottawa area. Project imPACT's goals were to address the root causes of human trafficking for sexual exploitation; to respond to the needs of trafficked persons; to build partnerships with a broad range of community stakeholders and key partners; and to formulate an effective local community action plan. The research was undertaken between June 2013 and April 2014. The data was collected through round tables with front line support workers, interviews with key informants, human trafficking survivors, sex workers, one former trafficker, focus groups with youth, and online surveys with people who buy sex.

Project imPACT's findings challenged many pre-conceived notions about human trafficking for sexual exploitation. Its insights are therefore crucial for effectively responding to this illicit trade and for meeting the complex needs of trafficked persons. First, Project imPACT underlined that human trafficking for sexual exploitation is an underreported, domestic problem and does not necessarily involve transportation across national borders.[38] Indeed, this crime is occurring in the Ottawa area, where 140 cases were discovered. Ninety percent of these trafficked persons were not foreign: they were local, young, female Canadians between the ages of nine and forty (the majority were between the ages of fifteen to eighteen) from a variety of socio-economic, religious, and ethnic backgrounds.[39] Second, contrary to popular belief, youth were trafficked not within the commercial sex industry, but in informal settings, such as homes and private parties where minors are more easily concealed from police and service providers.[40] Third, the following were risk factors for being trafficked: female gender, living in foster care or group homes, economic vulnerability, Aboriginal, LGBTQI+ youth, gender stereotyping, mental health issues, sexual abuse, addiction, drug use, gang membership, homelessness and/ or unstable living conditions, lack of family support, and social exclusion. Fourth, traffickers and complicit third parties, such as some hotel owners and drivers, participate in a highly lucrative trade. A local trafficker can make between $500-$1700 per night per trafficked person—who are often coerced to meet stringent daily quotas.[41] Key respondents also concurred with the UN.GIFT's insight regarding perpetrator stereotypes: a considerable percentage of Ottawa-based traffickers and recruiters were female.[42] Fifth, Project imPACT validated the importance of PACT's organizational position regarding non-conflating sex work with human trafficking for sexual exploitation. PACT's position built alliances with sex workers, who proved invaluable in ascertaining the problem of human trafficking in

Ottawa. Sex workers' citing private, informal home parties (as opposed to commercial sex venues) as places where underage youth are more likely to be trafficked was instrumental in guiding effective responses to the trafficking of minors.[43] Project imPACT also signalled that enforcement tactics, such as police raids, often compromise the open communication and trust necessary to foster cooperative relationships with key informants, such as sex workers.[44] Clearly PACT's collaborative efforts with sex workers allowed for greater insight into the local reality of human trafficking, which will guide more effective nonviolent responses to this local crime.

Sex, Gender, Structural Violence, and Human Trafficking: The Critical Links

Comprehending sex trafficking in the Ottawa area requires a gender-sensitive lens of inquiry: this is because women and girls are significantly more vulnerable to sexual exploitation than are men and boys.[45] Here, Nussbaum's claims that trans-nationally, women and girls face significant gender discrimination and suffer from a failure of human capabilities are validated. Nussbaum's claims also elucidate the egregious dimensions of this crime: the violence of human trafficking for sexual exploitation limits every major capability of women and girls, particularly bodily integrity, health, affiliation, freedom of association, practical reasoning, control over one's environment, and living a life of normal length. In fact, key informants underlined that the deleterious physical and psychological impacts consequent to being trafficked for sexual exploitation were far reaching and included post-traumatic stress disorders.[46] Indeed, within the context of sex trafficking, Nussbaum's human capabilities approach illuminates gender as a critical axis upon which Galtung's definition of violence as avoidable constraints that interfere with life is given greater depth and strategic significance for informing meaningful responses to the complex needs of trafficked persons.

Project imPACT's gender-sensitive lens of inquiry revealed that the roots of the sexual violence in human trafficking are cultural. Key respondents signalled the gender bias animating popular culture, particularly its hyper-sexualization of young women and girls, as fuelling and normalizing sexual exploitation against vulnerable youth. Respondents also explained why underage girls are vulnerable: they are lucrative commodities in light of escalating market demands by johns for sex with increasingly younger, virginal girls.[47] Popular culture's reductionist portrayal of masculinity and femininity also was underscored as significant: two-thirds of key respondents identified the media's sexual objectification of girls and women, particularly its pervasive images of females as lacking agency, serving as props (objects) for male (subject) activities, as

salient factors. The media's construal of masculinity, wherein male domination of women and girls is normalized, and where men's agency, evident in their socially sanctioned sexual power over women and/or their
perceived roles as saviours of women, were identified as features that fed
a perfect trafficking storm. Indeed, such skewed perceptions of gender
roles and stereotypical relationships are examples of what hooks termed
patriarchy's poisonous pedagogy and what Galtung would consider cultural violence. Significantly, some respondents noted that the media's idealized portrayal of pimp and gangster culture, as well as gang culture in
general, along with the attendant eroticizing of gender-based violence,
contributed to human trafficking situations. Notable aspects identified
by respondents were also the cultural legitimization of male violence,
manipulation, and control over women and girls, who were often objec-
tively viewed as either 'the other,' or as a trafficker's property.[48] Here, the
data from Project imPACT elucidates how rigid, hetero-normative social
constructions of sex and gender are linked to endemic power relations
in society and structure relational vulnerabilities. These insights validate
hooks's critiques on gender construction, and provide critical reflection
on strategic nonviolent resistance.

Key respondents also highlighted that traffickers were adept at manipulating and exploiting these popular gender-biased perspectives to their
advantage. Traffickers were also keenly aware of the location of vulnerable girls: in shelters, group homes, bus stops, methadone clinics, and
even online through social media.[49] Specifically, the trafficker's grooming
process was noted: this extremely manipulative strategy involved a predictable pattern over several months wherein the trafficked youth was
inducted 'in the game.'[50] Attention and luxurious gift giving, invitations
to parties, where free drugs are distributed, strategic affection and promises of a better life, eventually culminate in the trafficker's psychological
control.[51] Highlighted by key respondents was the critical fact that marginalized, socially isolated girls often idealize their traffickers as romantic heroes, saving them from undesirable situations of poverty and social
exclusion. As one trafficking survivor indicated, 'For a while, it felt like
home'.[52] Consequently, the romantic dependency, false sense of safety,
love, and acceptance, as well as gratitude on the part of the trafficked
youth (who paradoxically feels safe only when in close proximity to their
trafficker, either physically or via cell phone) makes her less likely to self-
identify as being trafficked. Importantly, such misperceptions can obfuscate an exploitive situation from key service providers.[53] Once control by
the trafficker has been achieved, increasingly compromising demands are
imposed on trafficked youth, ultimately manipulating them into coerced
sex work to repay debts and/or to prove their love and loyalty, all for the
trafficker's economic benefit.[54] Ensuring trafficked youths remain socially

isolated and financially dependent on the trafficker is key to control; sexual assault, withholding basic needs, such as food and sleep, including threats of physical harm that may extend to the trafficked youth's significant others, cyber-bullying and blackmail, further reinforce compliance.[55] The trafficker's aggressive pattern of manipulation, intimidation, and dehumanization resembles situations of domestic abuse, wherein violence is interspersed with periods of affection. Consequently, trafficked youth often experience low self-esteem, confusion, feelings of entrapment, worthlessness, survival fears and, as indicated above, even complicity in their own exploitation. Resigned hopelessness to the ongoing abuse and exploitation ensues.[56]

While potentially any person can be trafficked,[57] Project imPACT identified specific individuals and groups as being more vulnerable. In particular, LGBTQI+ youth were identified: the structural violence(s) of heterosexism, homophobia, and transphobia increased their risks for being trafficked. Significantly, these forms of structural violence(s) were experienced even in shelters, where gay, lesbian, and non-cisgender youth felt unsafe and unable to access necessary supports.[58] Here, Project imPACT validated the importance of inclusive approaches to sex and gender that transcend hetero-normative binaries in comprehending gender-based violence, without which the injustices experienced by these youths would remain invisible 'non-issues.' Identifying and reaching out to LGBTQI+ youth was made possible by Project imPACT's inclusive approach to sex and gender. An intersectional analysis also allowed for insight into the fact that LGBTQI+ youth number significantly among the homeless of Ottawa.[59] Their unstable living conditions place them at greater risk: they are less likely to refuse offers of accommodation, a fact well appreciated by predatory traffickers.[60] As well, Project imPACT's intersectional approach signalled the vulnerability of Aboriginal women and girls to being trafficked for sexual exploitation. Disproportionately affected by sexism, racism, poverty, the legacy of colonial policies, and often newly arrived in the Ottawa area and devoid of both family support and the knowledge of available resources, their health and wellbeing are systematically compromised.[61] Understanding these particular vulnerabilities and seeking effective partnerships aimed at empowering these specific groups has shaped PACT's strategic nonviolent responses to human trafficking.

Sex, Gender, and Human Trafficking: Specific Strategies for Nonviolent Resistance

Project imPACT's goals to comprehend, reduce, and prevent human trafficking in the Ottawa region are being accomplished in several ways. At the outset, an inclusive, collaborative community action plan, informed and shaped by Project imPACT's main findings, was deemed essential to formulating effective, nonviolent local resistance to this serious human rights abuse. Thus, partnerships and ongoing dialogue with key community stakeholders and organizations[62] continue to shape the four pillars of Project imPACT's evolving action plan. First, raising public awareness concerning the domestic nature of human trafficking for sexual exploitation is a critical feature of the action plan; challenging prevailing myths, including perpetrator stereotypes and other inaccuracies is key to identifying and eventually eradicating this crime.

Second, as young girls are particularly vulnerable to being trafficked and sexually exploited, shaping gender-inclusive, positive, female-centred interactive educational programs, including peer-to-peer informal exchanges, are also features of the community action plan. Strategies aimed at empowering young girls by challenging popular culture's misogynistic and hyper-sexualized ideologies, is a critical part of PACT's community activism. Building coalitions with boys and men and encouraging critical re-thinking of hegemonic masculinities in relation to male mental health, also shape outreach strategies. PACT's volunteer educators are endeavouring to create sex/gender positive cultures, both inclusive of, and informed by, persons with diverse gender identities and expressions, akin to the Center for Gender Sanity's spectrum of colors approach. As such, exploring issues of sexual consent, healthy sexualities and gender identities, challenging the gender-policing and stereotyping inherent in rigid hetero-normative approaches to sex and gender are being highlighted. Raising awareness about the injustice and harms of internalized sexism, homophobia, and transphobia animate the cooperative workshops currently unfolding in diverse venues—including shelters, group homes, youth organizations, colleges, and local high schools.

Whenever possible, this nonviolent resistance is conducted in collaboration with trafficking survivors. The insights afforded by these courageous, resilient individuals add credibility and relevance to the collective learning process, and ensure PACT's accountability to those most marginalized. In addition, digital activism is being cultivated through media literacy approaches that encourage digital citizenship and netiquette, and raise awareness of privacy and safety concerns in relation to social media, cyber-bullying, and cyber-misogyny. Highlighting the ubiquitous and multifaceted problems of gender-based violence, especially violence against Aboriginal women and girls, and strengthening existing laws and women-centred programs aimed at reducing violence against women, is another dimension to Project imPACT's community action plan.

Third, in light of the research data, trained PACT volunteers are working closely with the Ottawa Coalition to End Human Trafficking. Guiding frontline workers, including health care professionals, counsellors, educators, social workers, and other community service personnel on identifying trafficked youth and recognizing the obfuscating form their vulnerabilities sometimes assume are key. This includes detailed information on the highly manipulative grooming process traffickers employ in which trafficked youth perceive themselves as willing participants and/or complicit, and therefore guilty, of the abuse they suffer. This task, like many hitherto mentioned, is difficult and evolving: trafficked youth, whose agency and autonomy have been severely compromised, require astute, trauma-sensitive, compassionate support workers. Finally, outreach and partnership is the fourth pillar of Project imPACT's community action plan. This collaborative nonviolent activism is built on partnerships established through the research study, and aims to continuously reach out to more at-risk girls, including sex workers, LGBTQI+ youth, Aboriginal women, and the public in general.

Conclusion

I return to Carol Cohn's definition of sex and gender. Indeed, Project imPACT has elucidated the multiple ways power relations aligned with sex and gender function within human trafficking for sexual exploitation. Project imPACT's research has shown that this issue is a deeply gendered, local crime, and a concrete example of violence against women, girls, and more specifically, against Aboriginal and LGBTQI+ youth. Project imPACT has underscored the strategic utility of sophisticated, feminist intersectional analyses of sex and gender: these analyses have clearly mapped the problem of human trafficking for sexual exploitation in the Ottawa area and have deepened peace theorists' insights into direct, structural, and cultural forms of gender-based violence. In so doing, they have guided PACT in shaping robust strategies of nonviolent resistance and grassroots activism that honour Galtung's notion of peace. Project imPACT provides an important anchor from which further grassroots community activism and nonviolent resistance to this serious human rights abuse can flourish.

About the Author
Eileen Kerwin Jones has a background in public health, midwifery, and ethics. She has worked nationally and internationally in the fields of health and education and is a founding member of PACT-Ottawa, a Canadian NGO challenging contemporary slavery and human trafficking. She teaches in the Humanities Department of John Abbott College, Montreal, CA, where she is the Coordinator of the Certificate in Women's Studies and Gender Relations.

Notes

1. This definition is used by many national and international agencies engaged in conflict resolution globally. See, for example, ICRC (2004: 7).

2. I do not position America and Kenya in dichotomous ways as first/third world, civilized/uncivilized nations, because of their varying stances on gay rights. Indeed, progress toward the rights of LGBTQI+ individuals in America has been very recent, slow, and uneven. While gay marriage is now legal in America, many states adhere to traditional conceptions of marriage (see, e.g., Roberts 2015: 5). However, having lived in Kisumu, Kenya, I regularly witnessed overt homophobia. In a 2013 poll, 90 percent of Kenyans were against homosexuality (see, e.g., Wesangula 2015, at http://www.theguardian.com/global-development-professionals-network/2015/jun/29/homophobia-in-kenya-nairobi-prejudice-acceptance.

3. See Lee and Vogt (2015), at http://www.wsj.com/articles/president-obama-praises-africa-in-kenya-summit-speech-1437820696.

4. See Gender Spectrum (2015), at http://www.genderspectrum.org.

5. A non-cisgender person is one whose gender identity does not coincide with the ascribed gender role given at birth. See UTexas (2008), at http://www.utexas.edu/student/housing/pdfs/staff/LGBTQ_Vocab.pdf, accessed 27 July 2015.

6. PACT-Ottawa was founded after a 2004 workshop sponsored by the Canadian Religious Conference and Kairos Spirituality-for-Social-Justice Centre, entitled *Trafficking in Women and Children: A Lucrative Multinational Business: What is Our Response?* A grassroots organization, PACT-Ottawa has about thirty volunteers; it is a member of the Chrysalis Anti-Human Trafficking Network, the Ottawa Coalition to End Human Trafficking, the Coalition for an Ontario Task Force, the Committee Against the Sexual Exploitation of Children, the Canadian Council for Refugees (CCR), and is affiliated with Zonta International. Incorporated in 2007 as a non-profit corporation, PACT-Ottawa elects a working board of directors to oversee its operations. See PACT-Ottawa (2004), at http://www.pact-ottawa.org.

7. For example, Gould's book includes Simone de Beauvoir's seminal work *The Second Sex* (1953), inviting women to break from oppressive gender bonds, Luce Irigaray's radical deconstruction of patriarchal hegemony in *This Sex Which Is Not One* (1985), Carol Gilligan's ethical challenge to male-dominated moral meaning in 'Moral Orientation and Moral Development' (1987), Sara Ruddick's feminist standpoint theory in 'Maternal Thinking' (1980), positing a peace politics based on women's inherently peaceful maternal nature, Karen Warren's eco-feminist perspectives linking ecology with feminism in 'The Power and Promise of Ecological Feminism' (1990), Patricia Hill Collins's womanist stance, underlining the relevance of race-sensitive, intersectional approaches in 'Black Feminist Thought' (1991), and Judith Butler's postmodern perspectives in 'Gender Trouble' (1990), viewing gender as performative and open to subversive (re)-interpretation.

8. For a key text on queer theory, see Sedwick (1990).

9. The acronym LGBTQI+ stands for lesbian, gay, bisexual, trans, queer/questioning, and intersex, and the '+' stands for other groups within the queer community.

10. While this work focuses on sex and gender, feminist analyses of violence against women require an intersectional analysis attentive to the multiple jeopardies of women's lives, including structural oppressions related to race, class, ethnicity, socio-economic status, and colonization. Feminists are indebted to womanist scholars, such as Kimberlé Williams Crenshaw (1997: 245-64), for underlining

the critical importance of intersectionality in all feminist methodologies. PACT's research methodologies are informed by this scholarship.

11. See Center for Gender Sanity (2001–2011), at http://www.gendersanity.com.

12. See PACT-Ottawa's guiding principles (2012), at http://www.pact-ottawa.org.

13. Cisgenders and cissexuals self-identify with the sex and gender they were assigned at birth. 'Trans' is an umbrella term for persons whose gender identity is different from what they were assigned at birth. Trans persons may be transgender, transsexual, FTF, FTM, crossdresser, butch, fairy, stud, bulldagger, gender nonconforming, and gender queer. Two spirit persons are Indigenous North Americans who display both masculine and feminine characteristics and do not fit neatly into Western transgender categories. See LGBT Community Centre of New Orleans (2014), at http://www.lgbtccneworleans.org.

14. 'Gender bending' is an umbrella term describing someone who does not conform to conventional gender roles and norms. For an exploration of gender bending within the Latina/o population, see Hernandez-Truyol (2008: 1283-31).

15. See Mazurana-Proctor (2013), at http://www.fletcher.tufts.edu/~/media/Fletcher/Microsites/World%20Peace%20Foundation/Gender%20Conflict%20and%20Peace.pdf.

16. It is interesting to note that while most structural violence theorists see gender as an independent variable, medical anthropologist, physician, and structural violence theorist Paul Farmer has long challenged this view as evidenced in his work on female susceptibility to HIV/AIDS (Farmer et al. 1996).

17. The Global Gender Gap 2015 report identifies the relative gaps between men and women across four key areas: health, education, economy, and politics. It signals that if a person is born today, s/he will be 80 years of age before the gender gap is closed in 2095 (Global Gender Gap, 2015, at http://www.agenda.weforum.org/2015/03/gender-gap-calculator-2015/).

18. For example, many international and national organizations, such as the RCMP, no longer give statistics on human trafficking of women and girls due to the clandestine nature of this crime and the silence of victims. See RCMP (2014), at http://www.rcmp-grc.gc.ca/ht-tp/q-a-trafficking-traite-eng.htm#q3. This also echoes a key finding of the Statistics Canada report (2010), at http://www.statcan.gc.ca/pub/85-561-m/2010021/appendix-appendice3-eng.htm.

19. Two classic feminist works on patriarchy are by Lerner (1986, 1994). See also hooks (July 25, 2004), at http://imaginenoborders.org/pdf/zines/UnderstandingPatriarchy.pdf.

20. Martha C. Nussbaum is a major feminist figure in political philosophy, ethics, law, economics, and international development. Her human capabilities approach has been strongly critiqued by some feminist scholars as universalistic and insensitive to cross-cultural differences. This critique is beyond the scope of my chapter. Nussbaum maintains that the threshold of capabilities she proposes is a rubric of social justice that ideally can be adopted in national constitutions. It is meant to be a basis for thinking about basic human entitlements that should be experienced by all persons to ensure a life of human dignity. Nussbaum's list of basic human capabilities include life, bodily health, bodily integrity, senses, imagination and thought, emotion, practical reason, affiliation, relation to the world of nature (including play and leisure), and control over one's environment.

21. 'Peace' is in quotes because the war at home and intimate partner abuse overwhelmingly claims the wellbeing of women and children in the absence of external

conflict (Vagianos 2015, at http://www.huffingtonpost.com/2014/10/23/domestic-violence-statistics_n_5959776.html).

22. Nussbaum has collaborated with the Nobel Prize winning economist, Amartya Sen, on the problem of 'missing women' because of sex-selective abortion. They estimate that skewed sex ratios in many countries indicate there are approximately 100 million missing females in our world (2010: 12-13, 77-80).

23. While the majority of rapists are men, I do not infer that all men are inherently violent, or that some men have not experienced physical and sexual violence from women. While the majority of men are not violent, statistically, men perpetrate most violent acts worldwide, either against women or men. For a discussion on male, masculinity, and violence, see Douglas (1993).

24. The World Health Organization (WHO) estimates that every day 800 women die from preventable causes related to pregnancy and childbirth. The greatest reason for adolescent deaths in Majority World countries is pregnancy. See WHO (2014a), at http://www.who.int/mediacentre/factsheets/fs348/en/.

25. In addition to the work of hooks, I am indebted to Cilja Harder's critical analysis of gender relations explored in her 2011 article at http://www.berghof-foundation.org/fileadmin/redaktion/Publications/Handbook/Articles/harders_handbook.pdf.

26. These disciplines include sociology, anthropology, and clinical medicine. See Ho (2007: 7).

27. See Galtung (1975: 110-11).

28. This is a common statement referring to the trans-cultural economic vulnerability of many of the world's women. See Mendoza (2010), at http://www.ipsnews.net/2010/02/development-asia-lsquopoverty-still-has-a-womanrsquos-facersquo/.

29. The poverty of women is ubiquitous. Seventy percent of the 1.3 billion persons who struggle to survive on less than $1 US per day are women. See Chen and Vanek (2005), at http://www.unifem.org/attachment/products/POWW2055, accessed 30 May 2010; Fitzgerald (2010: 20). Even in Canada, the poorest of the poor are women, particularly single parents (mostly mothers) raising children, elderly women living on their own, Aboriginal women, women from racialized communities, women with disabilities, and recent women immigrants. See Townson (2009), at http://www.policyalternatives.ca/publications/commentary/canadian-women-their-own-are-poorest-poor.

30. See Galtung (1967), at http://www.transcend.org/files/Galtung_Book_unpub_Theories_of_Peace_-_A_Synthetic_Approach_to_Peace_Thinking_1967.pdf.

31. There is a growing body of research on the multiple ways people are trafficked in our world. A recent article in an international newspaper detailed the trafficking of Rohingya Burmese refugees in the Thai fishing industry; the products from this slave labour serve a global market, including North America. See Stokes et al. (2015: 32-33). See also Bales (2009); Cacho (2012); Jones (2013: 101-43).

32. See Perrin (2011) for an exploration of human trafficking in Canada. See also *Avenue Zero*, a National Film Board documentary by Hélène Choquette, which contains interviews with trafficked persons in Canada (2009), at http://www.nfb.ca/playlists/global-issues/viewing/avenue_zero.

33. Most traffickers also share the same nationality as their victims. See UN.GIFT (2007), at http://www.unglobalcompact.org/docs/issues. Recent cases before the court in Ottawa involving female traffickers, including three teenage girls charged with human trafficking in 2012, validates this statement.

34. UNODC (2012), at http://www.unodc.org/unodc/en/human-trafficking/prevention.html.

35. See PACT-Ottawa (2012), at: www.pact-ottawa.org. (PACT's position on sex work is part of their guiding principles and has been their position since 2012.)

36. Amnesty International's recent vote to promote the human rights of sex workers is consistent with PACT's commitment to promoting the human rights of all marginalized groups. See Amnesty International (2015), at http://www.amnesty.org/latest/news/2015/08/global-movement-votes-to-adopt-policy-to-protect-human-rights-of-sex-workers.

37. The full report of 'Project imPACT' is available online: PACT-Ottawa (2015), at http://www.pact-ottawa.org. The project team who conducted the research in 'The Local Safety Audit Report: Towards the Prevention of Trafficking in Persons and Related Exploitation in the Ottawa Area', were lead author Elise Wohlbold, co-author Katie Lemay, and project director Christina Harrison Baird. In November 2015, PACT-Ottawa received the Community Program Award for Crime Prevention at Ottawa's 7th Annual Community Safety Awards. Project imPACT was signalled for its exemplary contributions in the areas of community safety and crime prevention.

38. Wohlbold, Lemay, and Baird (2014: 16), at http://www.pact-ottawa.org.

39. Wohlbold, Lemay, and Baird (2014: 2-3, 16), at http://www.pact-ottawa.org. The research found no foreign individuals trafficked into Canada. As indicated, the majority of trafficked youth were from the local area; some were trafficked from other parts of Canada.

40. Wohlbold, Lemay, and Baird (2014: 19-20), at http://www.pact-ottawa.org.

41. Wohlbold, Lemay, and Baird (2014: 38), at http://www.pact-ottawa.org. It was estimated that with 140 trafficked persons identified in the Ottawa area, human traffickers in the national capital area are potentially making as much as $25.5 million per year.

42. Wohlbold, Lemay, and Baird (2014: 2-3, 35-36), at http://www.pact-ottawa.org.

43. As one service provider stated: 'The people who recognize trafficking the fastest are sex workers, so they need to be at the table because they are really good allies' (Wohlbold, Lemay, and Baird, 19-20, 30-31, 2014, at http://www.pact-ottawa.org).

44. Wohlbold, Lemay, and Baird (2014: 18-19, 52), at http://www.pact-ottawa.org.

45. Wohlbold, Lemay, and Baird (2014: 25), at http://www.pact-ottawa.org.

46. Wohlbold, Lemay, and Baird (2014: 40), at http://www.pact-ottawa.org.

47. Wohlbold, Lemay, and Baird (2014: 21, 26), at http://www.pact-ottawa.org.

48. Wohlbold, Lemay, and Baird (2014: 23, 26), at http://www.pact-ottawa.org. While the links between gangster culture, gangs, and human trafficking are contested and not straightforward, many respondents, particularly social service providers, claimed its significance in sex trafficking situations.

49. Wohlbold, Lemay, and Baird (2014: 15, 24, 27), at http://www.pact-ottawa.org.

50. As one former trafficker interviewed indicated, 'In the game you don't ask, you just do what you are told by your man'. Once trafficked (i.e., 'in the game'), there are very limited options for escape, hence the urgent need for meaningful, timely interventions and alternatives. Wohlbold, Lemay, and Baird (2014: 36), at http://www.pact-ottawa.org.

51. Wohlbold, Lemay, and Baird (2014: 16, 27-29), at http://www.pact-ottawa.org.

52. Wohlbold, Lemay, and Baird (2014: 15), at http://www.pact-ottawa.org.

53. Wohlbold, Lemay, and Baird (2014: 29, 41), at http://www.pact-ottawa.org.

54. Wohlbold, Lemay, and Baird (2014: 29), at http://www.pact-ottawa.org.

55. Wohlbold, Lemay, and Baird (2014: 41), at http://www.pact-ottawa.org.

56. Wohlbold, Lemay, and Baird (2014: 31), at http://www.pact-ottawa.org.

57. A young trafficking survivor clarified this point during a recent PACT training session. She stated that anyone could be trafficked: 'If you care about anyone or anything, traffickers will find this out and use it against you, to lure you in.'

58. Wohlbold, Lemay, and Baird (2014: 22), at http://www.pact-ottawa.org.

59. One key informant stated that as many as 50 percent of homeless youth across Canada identify as LGBTQI+, which makes them exceedingly vulnerable to multiple forms of exploitation. This figure concurs with Canada-wide research. See Wohlbold, Lemay, and Baird (2014: 21-22), at http://www.pact-ottawa.org.

60. Wohlbold, Lemay, and Baird (2014: 13), at http://www.pact-ottawa.org.

61. Wohlbold, Lemay, and Baird (2014: 21), at http://www.pact-ottawa.org.

62. Crime Prevention Ottawa, The Ottawa Police Service, St Joe's Women Centre, the Ottawa Coalition to End Human Trafficking, as well as health care workers, counsellors, Aboriginal organizations, frontline workers, sex workers, shelters, youth centers, immigration services, and local politicians are among the partnerships and organizations involved in the implementation of Project imPACT's community action plan.

Chapter 12

Women Seeking Safety:
Nonviolent Responses to Intimate Partner Violence

Catherine Holtmann

Introduction

The feminist movement in Canada and elsewhere is a process of systemic change with the aim of establishing egalitarian gender relationships in the public and private spheres. In its collective and public form, feminism is a nonviolent movement for structural and ideological change. One area of particular concern to feminists is the problem of violence against women, particularly within intimate relationships. Feminist resistance to intimate partner violence has taken a variety of forms. Intimate partner or domestic violence has been the subject of much academic research from a variety of disciplinary perspectives. There is a network of research centres devoted to better understanding all forms of domestic violence at universities across Canada.

The Religion and Violence Research team is a collaborative research partnership at the Muriel McQueen Fergusson Centre for Family Violence Research at the University of New Brunswick. For over 20 years the team has conducted numerous social-scientific studies across North America, Europe, and the Caribbean with clergy, church women, shelter workers, therapeutic professionals, seminary students, as well as men of faith who have acted abusively.[1] This research at the intersection of religion, gender, and domestic violence has shown that despite the religious rhetoric of peace, love, and family values, faith groups have been slow to acknowledge the prevalence of intimate partner violence in their midst, have failed to recognize that many religious homes are not safe places, and have not considered the safety of women.

As a research assistant with the team, I conducted two studies: one that examined resources for domestic violence amongst Catholics in Canada (Holtmann 2013a: 139-59), and another that involved Christian and Muslim immigrant women in the Maritime provinces of New Brunswick and Prince Edward Island (Holtmann 2013b). This chapter explores elements of the nonviolent feminist and religious responses to intimate partner violence beginning with a definition of intimate partner violence and some statistics outlining its prevalence globally and in Canada. It continues with an overview of the Canadian feminist movement's work on the problem of intimate partner violence, as well as some of the responses developed in the subfield of religion and domestic violence. The latter half of the chapter introduces the results from my own research program, which can further assist religious groups and shelter workers to help women of faith in seeking safety as they join in the collaborative work of nonviolent resistance to intimate partner violence.

Defining Intimate Partner Violence

The United Nations (UN) defines violence against women as, 'Any act that results in, or is likely to result in, physical, sexual, or psychological harm or suffering to women, including threats of such acts, coercion or arbitrary deprivation of liberty, whether occurring in public or private life'.[2] This is a comprehensive definition in that it includes not only acts of physical and sexual violence but also the threat of these kinds of violence as well as the causes of psychological harm or suffering. Globally, women aged 15 to 44 are more at risk of experiencing violence perpetrated by their current or former intimate partners than suffering from cancer, car accidents, war, and malaria.[3] The UN has declared domestic violence to be the most common form of violence against women—more prevalent than violence perpetrated by strangers or violence that occurs from civil unrest or war.[4] Intimate partner violence goes by many names, including domestic violence, family violence, spousal assault, and wife abuse. Some examples of actions typically associated with intimate partner violence include name calling and putdowns; constant monitoring of a woman's activities; deliberately isolating a woman from friends and family support; asserting complete financial control over a woman; neglecting a woman's emotional needs; physically abusing a woman, such as slapping, biting, hitting, shoving, and choking; and forcing a woman to have sex or engage in sexual acts with which she is uncomfortable.

The Prevalence of Intimate Partner Violence

Based on evidence gathered in 79 countries, the World Health Organization (WHO) estimates the global prevalence rate for intimate partner violence at 30 percent, with some countries reporting rates as high as 70 percent.[5] The global prevalence rate is in line with research that has taken place closer to home. Canada was the first Western country to undertake a dedicated national survey on violence against women. The 1993 Violence Against Women Survey (VAWS) in Canada estimated that 29 percent of women 18 years or older who had ever been married or in a common-law relationship had experienced some form of physical or sexual violence in their lifetime (Johnson and Dawson 2011: 67). Analysis of data from the more recent General Social Surveys (GSS) on Victimization indicates that the prevalence of domestic violence in Canada has remained steady for the past decade (Statistics Canada 2011). In the GSS, women who have been victimized report multiple incidences of violence in an intimate relationship, with sexual assault, choking, or being threatened with a gun or knife being the most frequent forms of abuse reported. Intimate partner violence is deadly and Canadian women are most likely to be killed by someone with whom they have had an intimate relationship. In 2008, 52 percent of the solved homicides of women were perpetrated by former or current partners (Johnson and Dawson 2011: 123). While all women are vulnerable to domestic violence, a combination of social and individual factors have been identified as increasing their risk of being victimized, and these include attitudes and beliefs that support violence against women, age, race/ethnicity, socio-economic status, and personal histories (Johnson and Dawson 2011: 75-85). For example, in Canada, Aboriginal women are twice as likely to report experiences of intimate partner violence (Statistics Canada 2005: 11).

Responding to Intimate Partner Violence

Responses to the widespread social problem of intimate partner violence are tied to the theoretical explanations for the violence and there are many theoretical debates as to why the problem persists (Gill 2006: 47-66; Fong 2010: 8-28). Feminist theory roots intimate partner violence within the patriarchal structuring of gender in which men maintain power and control over women through social institutions. According to Sylvia Walby, violence is not merely a tool of patriarchal power but is itself an institution that creates and maintains gender inequalities (2009: 191-217). Intimate partner violence is a manifestation or consequence of gendered systems of power (economic, political, cultural), which are both structural and ideological (Hunnicutt 2009: 553-73). An intersectional feminist theoretical framework considers the intersection of multiple structures when conceptualizing women's lives, including ethnicity, class, sexual orientation, ability, and religion in addition to gender. The precise configuration of these intersections and their impacts on specific groups of women who experience intimate partner violence depends on local contexts. The intersection of multiple structures does not necessarily mean that there is a higher prevalence of domestic violence amongst particular groups, but it does have consequences for understanding the complexity of the women's experiences. This theoretical approach to intimate partner violence also acknowledges that women exercise agency within structures of domination and have access to multiple sites of power (Hunnicutt 2009: 566). Intersecting structures create both complex inequalities and valued differences. Women occupy multiple subject positions or identities and can simultaneously be victims of intimate partner violence yet part of a dominant social group (Collins 2000).

When considering the range of Canadian women's responses to domestic violence, the responses have certainly been individual, as women have survived the violence that for many years was simply considered a normal part of marital relationships. Just the fact that women are surviving what is now considered a global pandemic of violence is an indication of the strengths they possess. However, individual women do act violently, as the GSS data also include Canadian men's experiences of violence by their intimate partners. Most of the violence perpetrated by women is in response to the violence of their partners. Individual women also resist violence by utilizing a variety of nonviolent strategies, including compliance, deception, exposure reduction, outreach to informal social networks, accessing public services, and leaving the relationship (Paterson 2009: 124).

The collective feminist response to domestic violence has been nonviolent and two-pronged in that it involves providing direct services to victims of intimate partner violence, as well as the work to change the social structures, institutions, and ideologies that foster gender inequalities. As feminist groups recognized the need to assist women in seeking safety in violent intimate relationships, the first shelters opened up in 1973 in Vancouver, British Columbia; Calgary, Alberta; and Saskatoon, Saskatchewan. Women and their children can find temporary respite from violent partners at a shelter—usually up to a month. In the early years, many shelters operated as feminist collectives and workers encouraged women seeking safety to engage in a process of both personal and political change during their stay (Proffit 2000: 132).

Shelters initially relied on donations from the local community in order to operate, but the VAWS provided the evidence needed to convince federal and provincial governments to allocate funding for women's shelters as well. Today there are more than 550 shelters and transition houses across the country (Johnson and Dawson 2011: 86). In addition to providing refuge for women and children seeking safety from men who act violently, contemporary shelters provide short-term counselling, outreach for women who choose not to live at a shelter, advocacy for former residents, and specialized services for older women (Tutty 2006). The shelter model of nonviolent resistance is not appropriate for all women, especially for those from ethnic, immigrant, and other visible minority groups (Rupra 2010: 134-46). This is because contemporary shelters assume an individualist model of identity for women that subordinates the collectivist values and practices that minority groups often have. Many women who seek safety at a local shelter end up returning to their violent partners because of their socio-economic vulnerability. This vulnerability is a result of the stratification of Canadian society along the lines of gender, ethnicity, religion, and class.

Changes to the criminal justice system have been another significant focus of the feminist response to intimate partner violence in Canada. Pro-arrest and pro-charge policies, also known as no-drop policies, mean that when police respond to a call and find evidence of domestic violence, they are obligated to arrest the offender, and it is the responsibility of the Crown to press or stay the charges. Additionally, the criminal justice system includes specialized family violence courts, victim services, and batterer treatment programs. Other aspects of the nonviolent feminist response to the problem of domestic violence in Canada include working for pay equity and changes to public social policy, such as the availability of low income housing and affordable child care.

In recent years, however, there has been a steady erosion of many of the Canadian social welfare policies that have helped women to cope with the effects of social stratification on the basis of gender, ethnicity, and class. The current federal government has shifted to gender-neutral discourse in addressing what it calls family violence. In 2006, the Conservative government announced that the Status of Women Canada would no longer use the word 'equality' in any of its lists of goals, and in 2007, federal funding was cut for the National Association of Women and the Law, a feminist organization promoting the equality of women through legal education, research, and law reform advocacy (Dekeseredy 2011). Budget cuts have impacted public health programs and other social services that have aided women who seek safety from violence in their intimate relationships.

The Religious Response to Intimate Partner Violence

In comparison to these collective nonviolent feminist strategies for social change, religious groups have been slower to respond to the problem of intimate partner violence. Feminists have been quick to condemn patriarchal religions outright as supporting ideologies of male dominance of females—a key aspect of the feminist theoretical approach to understanding the root causes of domestic violence. Sociological research into women's lived religious practices, as opposed to the teachings of religious institutions, has shown that women within conservative religious traditions are not merely oppressed under the domination of men but also exercise agency within structures of subordination (Gallagher 2003; Kaufman 1991). In a study of women in a variety of Christian denominations in the United States, the researchers referred to the women's strategy of dealing with the patriarchal elements of their faith tradition as 'defecting in place' (Winter et al. 1995). This strategy enables women in patriarchal religions to use the resources of their faith in working nonviolently for social change on a day-to-day basis (Mahmoud 2006: 177-221; Bullock 2012: 92-112). Research at the intersection of religion, gender, and domestic violence reveals that there are factors within religious women's beliefs and practices that contribute to their vulnerability when violence is a part of their intimate relationships.

Christianity and Islam are religious traditions within which members adhere to a tremendous diversity of institutional structures, practices, and beliefs. This diversity is influenced by theological positions—from conservative to liberal—as well as by ethno-cultural differences. For many Catholics and Muslims, ethnicity is intertwined with religion to such an extent that it is difficult to distinguish between the two (Bramadat 2005: 1-29). Among conservative Christians and Muslims, there is a strong emphasis on the importance of families, and the primary responsibility for keeping families together has traditionally been placed on women's shoulders (Chernyak and Barrett 2011: 1-24; Penner 2000). According to the religious concept of complementarity, the role of wives is centred in the private realm of the home, and the role of husbands is in the public realm of paid employment. This subordinate role of women in marriage has been justified using sacred texts, such as passages in the Bible or verses from the Qur'an and Hadith. Religious explanations for male domination of women in marriage can increase religious women's vulnerability to domestic violence by making it more difficult for deeply religious women to distinguish between conflict and abuse. This can prevent them from seeking help from family, friends, religious leaders, or secular professionals. The disclosure of domestic violence can raise intense feelings of shame, guilt, embarrassment, and spiritual anguish for Christian and Muslim women (Nason-Clark 1997; Mojab 2012: 115-34).

The religious texts that appear to support the subordination of women are the source of contemporary debate among Muslims and Christians (Ammar 2007: 516-26; Kroeger 2011: 3-11). However, most women of faith have not heard a public message from their religious leaders condemning domestic violence, nor are they aware of alternative interpretations of sacred texts (Kulwicki et al. 2010: 727-35; IMA 2014). These vulnerabilities do not necessarily increase the prevalence of domestic violence amongst religious families but they make it more difficult for religious women to seek safety when violence is identified and must be addressed. Religious responses to domestic violence are not separate from secular feminist responses, but need to be part of a collaborative nonviolent response at all levels of society (Nason-Clark and Holtmann 2013).

There are religious teachings and practices within Christianity and Islam that can be drawn upon in collective and individual nonviolent responses to domestic violence. Religious texts include passages that outright condemn violence and injustice, as well as offer encouragement to victims of domestic violence (Nason-Clark and Kroeger 2010). Women throughout history have rooted their work for social justice in their religious traditions and movements for social change. Services for the poor in many parts of the world are still supported almost exclusively by faith groups (Krane et al. 2000: 1-18). Women's formal and informal support networks operate within many religious congregations and often under the radar of religious leaders (Beaman-Hall and Nason-Clark 1997:176-96). The act of prayer itself encourages women to seek help in the face of problems (Barata et al. 2005: 1132-50). When religious leaders publically condemn violence on the basis of their religious traditions, their words can assist women to seek safety for themselves and for their children (Nason-Clark et al. 2013). In her book, *The Cross and Gendercide* (2014), Elizabeth Gerhardt argues that what is needed is a prophetic theology of the cross that condemns violence against women as sin and promotes active nonviolent resistance among all Christians. This is not simply a moral or ethical side issue but is central to the Christian confession of faith. Sabra Desai and Zehra Haffajee call for a re-examination of the Qur'an in order to free it from patriarchal ideology to 'decolonize and reclaim Islam as a way of influencing social change as it did in the time of the Prophet' (Desai and Haffajee 2011: 133).

Responding to Intimate Partner Violence amongst Christian and Muslim Immigrant Women

As mentioned in the introduction, my research program incorporates the experiences of immigrant women into existing feminist research on religion and intimate partner violence and involves a comparison between Christian and Muslim women. Changes to Canadian immigration policies in the 1970s increased the diversity of ethnic origins among the population and today, one in five Canadians are foreign born.[6] In 2010, I interviewed 30 Catholics in three dioceses across Canada about the resources available to victims of intimate partner violence. Participants included clergy, laity employed in administration and pastoral care work, as well as women working in shelters and women's centres. This research heightened my awareness of the growing number and ethnic diversity of immigrant Catholics. This led to doctoral research with immigrant women in the Maritimes. In 2012, I spoke with 58 Christian and 31 Muslim women, as well as 22 public-service providers, through interviews and focus groups.

My research indicates that the specifics of a local context are important when considering the vulnerabilities of Christian and Muslim immigrant women. Large urban centres in Canada attract higher numbers of immigrants, and the greater density of any single ethno-religious group provides new immigrant women with more opportunities to build a social network with those who share a common worldview and language. For example, some urban Catholic parishes are able to serve congregants with Latin American or East/Southeast Asian ethnic origins and have priests who can celebrate mass in their native tongue. In contrast, in the Maritimes there are relatively few immigrants. Each city in New Brunswick and Prince Edward Island has only one mosque. Finding a common language amidst the wide range of ethnic diversity of Muslims in Maritime cities presents a significant challenge to religious leaders, especially when it comes to passing on important information about local public services. Even with this information, however, Muslim women in the research indicate that they are most likely to seek help from a friend or relative if their relationships become violent. When their social networks are small, immigrant women's vulnerability to isolation is high, which means that some women may be overly reliant on abusive spouses.

There is internal and external pressure on members of immigrant groups not to talk about problems. Members of minority immigrant groups already face stigmatization, and it is risky to raise the issue of intimate partner violence because it can confirm stereotypes held by native-born Canadians that males within some ethno-religious groups are inherently violent. Filipina temporary foreign workers who participated in the research in the Maritimes indicated that they would feel ashamed if their parish priest talked to them about the problem of intimate partner violence during a homily in mass. The women are very focused on getting permanent resident status so that they can continue to provide a measure of economic security for their families, and they do not want to jeopardize their opportunities for Canadian citizenship. They want to handle marital problems amongst themselves. Even if an immigrant woman did seek help from a shelter in the Maritimes, because the immigrant population is so small, many shelter workers are unprepared to respond to their particular vulnerabilities, especially when it comes to providing translation or culturally sensitive strategies for nonviolent change.

The danger of social isolation is present for all immigrant women when the density of their ethno-religious groups is low, but this vulnerability is even more pronounced for Muslim women in the research. Their isolation is compounded by the intense public scrutiny of Muslims in Canada after the violence of 9/11, as well as Islamophobia.[7] Women in the research who choose to wear a veil, headscarf, or hijab are subject to constant questions and comments from strangers, especially from men. Sometimes they are yelled at by strangers passing on the street. This kind of treatment results in an inward turning of Muslim families and groups in order to shield women and girls from harassment. The protective attitudes of Muslim males can be interpreted by outsiders as evidence of patriarchal control, but the women do not describe it this way. These experiences of discrimination against Muslim women by non-Muslims in the Maritimes increase their vulnerability when their marital relationships are in fact violent, justifying the males' abusive control and making it even less likely that the women will trust public service providers.

Many of the immigrant women who participated in the research are living in transnational family situations. Some of them had come to Canada for their children's education. This is part of a strategy in which mothers are single parenting and running the Canadian households while their husbands continue to work and support their families from their country of origin. Some of the women are pursuing university degrees as international students or employed as temporary foreign workers—both groups of women are maintaining contact on a daily basis through social media with family members who remain in their countries of origin. Transnational situations also include frequent travel between two countries with vastly different social contexts. Women in these situations are coping with the structuring of gender, ethnicity, class, and religion in two societies at the same time. In the case of South Korean mothers, for example, the women are proud of the skills that they are learning, their English language competence, and increased sense of independence. But they are acutely aware of how the loss of their husbands' social status in both contexts is impacting their marital relationships. The marital tensions created by transnational family situations, particularly for newlyweds or couples with young children, is another vulnerability facing immigrant women who experience intimate partner violence, making it difficult for them to ensure their safety for fear of jeopardizing their own or their children's future.

These vulnerabilities of Christian and Muslim immigrant women in cases of intimate partner violence—the low density of immigrant groups in particular social contexts, the pressure on immigrants not to disclose problems, Islamophobia, and transnational family situations—can and must be considered by religious groups in Canada if they want to respond appropriately to women suffering from abuse in their midst. The research also identified specific religious resources that can be harnessed for this purpose.

Many religious groups acknowledge the complexity of the marital relationship and the need for social support throughout its duration. In Catholic churches across Canada, for example, marriage preparation courses

are mandatory for all couples. The research found that marriage preparation courses for Francophone Catholics include well developed and
explicit information about the cycle of violence in relationships. This is
not surprising given that the Assembly of Quebec Bishops were the first
religious leaders in the country to condemn publicly intimate partner violence (SACAQB 1989; see also Holtmann 2013a: 139-59). Francophone Catholic marriage preparation courses require engaged couples to talk about
abuse and, in one case in the research, the facilitators arrange presentations from criminal justice, advocacy, and shelter workers in the local
community. Facilitators of marriage preparation courses who took part
in the research admitted that most couples preparing for marriage had
already been living together. Providing information on the cycle of abuse
and the reality of intimate partner violence at the time when couples
are formalizing their religious commitment to each other helps them to
reflect upon their current patterns of interaction, make changes if necessary, and heighten their awareness of the resources available to them
should their relationship already show signs of abuse or become violent.

Marriage preparation courses are an important resource in the response
to domestic violence amongst immigrants in religious groups. Making
them a mandatory requirement means that couples with weak ties to
social networks are introduced to a broader range of people from the local
community as well as information about public services. Marriage preparation courses are especially valuable to immigrant couples who come
from unstable social contexts of civil and political unrest. A shelter worker
who had immigrated as an international student indicated that people in
her church may not have observed healthy relationship patterns in their
birth families because of constant situations of struggle. Many immigrant
women choose to settle in Canadian society because of its stability and are
eager to practice values of peace, equality, and respect. For them, immigration marks a new start, and the women's desire to embrace change is
a quality that can be emphasized during marriage preparation courses.

There is a lot of critique about the Catholic process of marriage annulment, but my research highlights that there is also a wealth of knowledge
about the dynamics of domestic violence among those who minister to
individuals in marriage tribunals. Most of those who work within the tribunals are either clergy or women religious (e.g., women who are part of
religious orders). There is evidence that women in religious orders that
are international in scope are training their members in Canadian interpretations of canon law and thus bringing a more complex understanding of gender and domestic violence to the countries in which they work.
An annulment of a marriage can only be sought by an individual after the
couple has been legally divorced. This in itself is important information
for most Catholics who have been led to believe that the church is against

divorce in all circumstances. Through the retelling of their life history, along with testimony from those who know them well, the annulment process sets out to determine if there were impediments to either of the individuals' full participation in the sacrament of marriage. Evidence of experiences of abuse prior to the marriage is a legitimate ground for an annulment. A nun who had worked in a marriage tribunal for almost 30 years suggests that the deep listening and confidentiality that she practiced during the annulment process is a model that can be implemented in parish life. The immigrant women who participated in the research want more Canadian-born friends—they have a deep desire to connect with others and to have people they trust listen to their stories of struggle.

It was on the basis of their education and professional credentials that women were able to immigrate to Canada, and the study participants are acting strategically in order to provide a better life for themselves and their families. Many of these women are at the forefront of the settlement process and experiences of adversity were not new. Religious narratives in Christianity and Islam provide them with hope and support in the journey of overcoming adversity. For example, a Korean woman indicated that it was in her bible study group that she was able to share the agony she experienced in being unemployed for more than two years before finding a job. For other women, the Christian narrative of Jesus's liberation from suffering through membership in a community that practices love of neighbour led to their post-migration conversion.

A central narrative of Islam is about the Prophet Muhammad, an honest and moral man whose faith led to his being chosen to be a messenger of God, despite his lack of social prestige. He spoke out against injustice and oppression. An international graduate student indicated that her decision to leave her job in Egypt and uproot her husband and children was because she was fed up with dealing with corruption. She feels that they can be better Muslims in Canada because they can practice their religious values of honesty and hard work. Although she misses her extended family and worries about them, she has more hope for the future here.

For immigrant women who experience intimate partner violence or reach out to those in their social networks who disclose abuse, the religious narratives of the journey from suffering and injustice to liberation and freedom from oppression can be very powerful resources for change. They can provide hope when the going is very difficult and the assurance that women are not alone in their struggles. But religious immigrant women need help in distinguishing between the suffering that results from difficult choices made for a better future and the suffering that is a result of spousal violence. These are two different types of suffering. Women who are abused by their husbands suffer from injustice. The distinction between different types of suffering can help immigrant women to deal with the intense shame that often accompanies disclosure. It is important that the process of healing from abuse allows religious women to renegotiate the stories, symbols, and practices of their faiths so that they can come to a deeper understanding of this very difficult yet potentially profound stage in their social and spiritual journey.

Members of many Muslim and Christian religious groups across Canada are busy providing practical assistance to immigrant families in negotiating the various legal, medical, educational, economic, and political systems of which they were a part, while at the same time offering spiritual resources for the journey ahead. These groups can also become involved in the painstaking and nonviolent work of assisting immigrant women in seeking safety in situations of domestic violence, as well as the long-term work of advocating for social justice for ethno-religious minority groups. Leaders in these groups must have the courage to denounce openly intimate partner violence as a social injustice on the basis of their religious traditions, initiate conversations amongst their members about what constitutes healthy and nonviolent intimate relationships, and model professional relationships of equality.

The prevalence of intimate partner violence in Canada indicates that the feminist nonviolent movement for gender equality and social justice is as necessary now as when it began. Perhaps it is even more important today, given the increased ethno-religious diversity of the population in recent years that demands responses to intimate partner violence that incorporate the impact of intersecting structures of gender, ethnicity, religion, and class on the lives of women. The contemporary nonviolent response to intimate partner violence will be most effective when it is collaborative, involving representatives with secular feminist perspectives and leaders from different religious groups who have been trained in best practices of responding to victims of abuse while at the same time incorporating the resources of their faith traditions, as well as survivors. This collaborative response must continue to address both the structural aspects of inequality as well as the immediate needs of women seeking safety from violence.

About the Author

Catherine Holtmann, PhD, is an associate professor in the Sociology Department and the Director of the Muriel McQueen Fergusson Centre for Family Violence Research at the University of New Brunswick in Fredericton, New Brunswick. Her research interests lie in the areas of religion, gender, ethnicity, immigrants, and domestic violence. Holtmann is a member of the RAVE (Religion and Violence E-Learning) Project research team.

Notes

1. The results of much of this research have been incorporated into online resources for use by religious leaders, survivors, and others who accompany religious victims and perpetrators, and can be found on the Religion and Violence E-Learning or RAVE Project website: http://www.theraveproject.org. Links to scholarly books and journal publications based on the results of these studies are also available on the website.

2. UN General Assembly (1993), at http://www.un.org/documents/ga/res/48/a48 r104.htm.

3. UN (2011), at http://www.endviolence.un.org.

4. UN (2008), at http://endviolence.un.org/.

5. WHO (2013), http://www.who.int/reproductivehealth.

6. Statistics Canada (2007), at http://www.statcan.ca.

7. Islamophobia is a process of 'othering' in which fears are projected onto a minority group within society in order to make members of dominant groups feel safe. The 'other' embodies all of those qualities that members of dominant groups judge negatively, such as irrationality, gender inequality, and violence. Korteweg refers to this as 'the process of abjection—the psychic casting out of what is other in order to define ourselves as free from that which is abhorrent' (2012: 138). For further analysis of the impact of Islamophobia on Muslim women in Canada, see Zine (2012); Korteweg and Selby (2012); Kazemipur (2014).

Chapter 13

Instrumentalizing the Ambiguity of Violence in the *Carré Rouge*: The Quebec Student Crisis of 2012

Marie Boglari and Martin Samson

Introduction

In 2012, the *carré rouge*—the little red felt square representing the student movement against postsecondary tuition hikes—morphed into a broader social justice movement, which questioned the political status quo in Quebec. This social movement faced the hard task of actualizing its values and ideals while broadening its social justice project with other movements. The current chapter will argue that the relationship between the *carrés rouges* (people wearing the red felt square symbol)[1] and nonviolence is ambiguous. This is because it is rooted in a social discussion on violence that was inscribed in a complex ideological web of normative and discursive acts. This web affected the ambiguity of the *carrés rouges'* position towards certain acts of nonviolence, which was then instrumentalized in order to maintain the status quo. In this sense, the dominant sociopolitical elite's response to the *carrés rouges* is a perfect example of how directly engaging the Quebec population's social imaginary can be used to transform the discourse on counter-hegemonic social movements through the use of the highly connoted rhetoric of violence, speech acts, and emotion-driven symbolism.

The chapter is divided in three parts. In the first part, we will assess the ideological context in which the ambiguity towards violence developed. We will analyze the student organization's values, their involvement in the 2012 student crisis, and the symbolic meaning these values conferred to the symbol of the *carré rouge* and to those wearing it. In the second part, we will analyze how an ambiguity toward violence emerged in the *carrés rouges*. Within this analytical framework, we will then break down the transformation of the *carrés rouges'* nonviolence, civil disobedience, and social-justice symbolic capital into that of irresponsibility, intimidation, and violence by the producers of the dominant ideology (Bourdieu and Boltanski 2008).

The Ideological Context: Violence

The Quebec student crisis of 2012 is not an event that took place *ex nihilo*. It is the result of a long sociopolitical history. This particular context may be said to have started with the freezing of tuition fees in 1968 and the evolution of discourse around the necessity and inevitability of new measures on a tuition hike in the 1990s.[2] It was in 2005, however—when the Quebec Liberal government made cuts in the higher-education budget and reduced the financial aid available for students—that the student movement started to organize, educate, and resist what was perceived as a threat to accessible education for all. In 2010, a similar threat was announced by the Quebec Liberal government. The prospective tuition hike once again united the students in an unequal fight against the government.

Facing this new sociopolitical issue, the Broad Coalition of the Association for Student Union Solidarity (CLASSE), the Federation of College Students of Quebec (FECQ), and the Federation of University Students of Quebec (FEUQ) decided in 2012 that they would unite and strike. This was to show their disagreement with the Quebec Liberal government's decision to hike tuition fees by roughly 75 percent within five years. These three main student organizations shared three important values, which were decisive for the future of the *carrés rouges*.

The first value they shared is the importance of fighting for their vision of a better, more accessible higher education system and the recognition of the student population's contribution to society. Secondly, these organizations stated that they could achieve their aims through political and militant action. The CLASSE went further by basing its mission statement on the motto of the Association for a Unionist Student Solidarity (ASSÉ):[3] 'combative student unionism through dynamic mass action and mobilization'. This value entails that the student organizations are not fighting only for the students they represent but for the welfare of all students in Quebec. The third value the student organizations shared was the principle of direct or semi-direct democracy. This principle is articulated first by protecting and fighting for human rights in fundamentally democratic ways and second, by allowing power-sharing and fair and direct voting within their own organizational structure.

The student organizations' vision of education, active involvement, collective responsibility, and democracy led to their strong reaction to the government's tuition fee hike. This measure was seen as implementing an elitist model of postsecondary education, which compromised social justice through the denial of the right to education for all. As a consequence, after a series of internal votes taken from the different student associations from 7 February 2012 to the symbolic date of 22 March 2012,[4] all three student organizations declared a general student strike, and demanded negotiations with the government. Picket lines were set up and protests took place in different cities (Montreal, Quebec, Gatineau, and others), which helped students bring awareness to their cause and rally other members of civil society. The *carrés rouges* movement was born.

The *carré rouge* symbol used in previous student protests was adopted in order to create unity and recognition among members of the student movement. The red felt square—the *carré rouge*—became not only the symbol of the students participating in the general strike. It also became the symbol of the values for which the 2012 student movement was fighting. If in 2004, the *carré rouge* was used in protests demanding more social justice, the 2005 student strike associated it clearly with the phrase, 'on est carrément dans le rouge' ('we are completely indebted'). This was also the first meaning of the *carré rouge* in the 2012 student strike. Aside from this phrase, the *carré rouge*'s meaning has been left intentionally open and vague, which had the advantage of uniting many causes under one symbol. Therefore, as more and more social movements supported the student strike and the movement broadened, the *carré rouge* came to embody values of democracy, social justice, and nonviolent action, and of an alternative society that values education (Chiasson et al. 2012: 34-35).

Moreover, the symbol of the *carré rouge* does not only signify democratic values, social justice, and nonviolence. It has also come to define the social identity of the group wearing the symbol of the *carré rouge*. This is how the people wearing the *carré rouge* became the '*carrés rouges*'. In line with Alberto Melucci's definition of 'social movement', which goes further than Alain Touraine's (1978), we maintain that the collective identity of the *carrés rouges* was constructed through the clear statement of the conflict with the Liberal government and by the solidarity emerging within the collective nonviolent action—represented by the *carré rouge*— taken in breach of the mainstream system (Melucci 1996: 28; Neveu 1996). There is thus a community of strangers who were transformed from me and you into us and we through the power of the *carré rouge* as a connector (Fortin 2013: 518, 525-26). The symbol of the *carré rouge* transformed the student movement into a revitalized political class of active citizenship. It is exactly this phenomenon of legitimate active citizenship based on the three values listed above that the government, mass media, and members of the civil society tried to dismantle and discredit. They did so by producing a structure of delegitimizing discursive formations that contained two major axes:

- The first axis consisted of attacks by the mass media and the government on the legitimacy and nonviolent symbolic capital of the *carrés rouges*. While normatively grounding their arguments and actions on precise democratic principles, this movement was deemed violent on the grounds that its radical democracy was impeding other people's fundamental rights and liberties, which were inscribed within liberal democracy.

- The second axis concerned the transformation within the media sphere of the *carrés rouges'* fighting-spirit image. This spirit was rooted in principles of solidarity, collective responsibility, social justice, and radically creative action, which led to strong discourse and action. Even if these actions and discourses were nonviolent, the spirit behind them was clear: the *carrés rouges* were resisting. This fighting spirit was therefore exploited in a way to reorient the debate not on tuition fees and higher education but on the violence and radicalism surrounding the student movement.

How then did the *carrés rouges* defend their ideas against discursive acts based on these two axes? They did so by clarifying their positions on violent acts and on the diversity of tactics principle, which contributed to further the debate. The clarification of their positions is explored in the next section.

The Ambiguity of the *Carrés Rouges'* Standpoint on Violence

The 2012 student crisis in Quebec led to a great diversity in nonviolent tactics. Many festive protests and an upsurge in artistic projects were seen, especially in the city of Montreal. Slogans, banners, and graffiti on walls or on the streets succeeded in spreading the students' message and raising awareness in the general public. Other nonviolent actions also took place: the sit-in in the office of the Minister of Education Line Beauchamp, the nude-demonstrations and saucepan-demonstrations, the use of mascots such as anarchopanda or rebel-banana, and, of course, the symbolic *carré rouge*, to name a few. These have all contributed to a nationwide dialogue on what the future of education, students, and social justice should look like.

The creativity and thoughtfulness of the nonviolent actions, as a lipdub video[5] and other online artistic creations can attest,[6] were tarnished by violent confrontations between police and protesters and other dangerous protest acts, such as the throwing of rocks on cars on the highway or bags of bricks placed on the rails of a Montreal metro line.[7] Such behaviour stems from what we could call two shortcomings of the *carrés rouges*: (1) they tried to answer the criticisms and (2) they failed to foresee the shift in topics by the government and mass media. Their answers to criticism were embedded in their ideological point of view and did not resonate with the public as valid counterarguments.

The first shortcoming is linked to an ambiguity about the definition of (non)violence within the *carrés rouges* and more generally, its meaning for protest movements. As such, the student organizations came up with various definitions of violence, which negatively impacted the coherence and scope of the nonviolent methods used. The student spokespersons and organizations were pushed to the wall by the government when the latter declared it would negotiate with the student spokespersons from the FECQ and FEUQ but not with the CLASSE, unless this organization condemned the acts of violence committed by the *carrés rouges*. The FECQ was very clear on what they considered 'violent action': all forms of violence, brutality, vandalism or intimidation,[8] and the FEUQ added that it condemned all criminal acts and all violence committed during protests.[9]

The CLASSE was accused by Line Beauchamp (Minister of Education when the protests started) and former Minister of Education Jean-Marc Fournier of a pathological incapacity in regards to speaking out against violence.[10] Moreover, their affiliation to the principle of diversity of tactics was seen as a justification for the slip-ups that happened during protests. This situation forced the CLASSE to clarify its position on violent acts and to adopt a resolution condemning deliberately perpetrated physical violence, except in the case of legitimate defence. Furthermore, stating its desire to fight with the population and not against it, the organization added that citizens who were not involved should not be the target of protesters.[11] However, the CLASSE made it clear that violence and intimidation could not be equated with civil disobedience acts such as blockades, sit-ins, protests, and picket lines.

Despite the efforts made by the student organizations to clarify their definitions of violence, they did not succeed in convincing the mass media and the government of the intrinsic nonviolent character of their endeavour. The mass media and government continued to equate the *carrés rouges*' fighting spirit and will for change with radicalism and violence, basing their arguments on some cases of broken windows and altercations between police and protesters.

The second shortcoming of the *carrés rouges* is linked to the principle of diversity of tactics. According to Janet Conway, this principle articulates the requirement that all activists not publicly criticize or rule out in advance any method used by other activists (2003: 510-11; see also Shantz 2012). This principle is based on the value of solidarity between diverse groups acting within the same nonviolent framework. The diversity-of-tactics principle is a concept that has historically contributed to blurring the lines between violent and nonviolent action.[12]

Consequently, the public debate quickly shifted from the actual issue at hand (the tuition fee hike) toward a debate about the violent content of the student crisis and the heterogeneous and out-of-control character of the student movement.[13] Furthermore, the reduction of the diversity-of-tactics principle to violence can be understood as a shortcut taken by politicians fearing that their position in the power relation with the *carrés rouges* was being undermined by legitimate direct-democracy and nonviolent action. This semantic shortcut nevertheless succeeded in questioning the collective responsibility and legitimacy of every action taken by the *carrés rouges* in order to weaken and disrupt this movement's strength and unity.

Weaving Violence in the Symbol of the *Carré Rouge* and the Advancement of the Neoliberal Political Agenda

By crafting a violent image of the *carré rouge* symbol—and the protestors who wear it—in the mass media and the public sphere, the social movement saw its symbolic nonviolent capital fundamentally transformed. Consequently, the image associated with its activists was also transformed into that of a motley crew of egotistical self-absorbed brats,[14] nostalgic parents, and grandparents reminiscing about a utopian socialist past, and, as police officer Stéphanie Trudeau,[15] better known in Quebec media as Matricule 728, put it: feces-eating, dirty hippies, and guitar players.

In this section, we will break down the very definition of violence, which was woven into the *carré rouge* by the Quebec Liberal government and mass media for political and ideological purposes. First, we will analyze the implementation of the neoliberal definition of personal responsibility contra collective responsibility through a specific conceptualization of the notion of fair share. Second, we will analyze the Liberal government's production of a definition of violence, which was created in concordance with the primacy of individuality over collectivity, and with the necessity of discrediting collective measures of protest and direct political action initiated by the *carré rouge* social movement.

The Concept of Fair Share

We argue that the *carrés rouges* as a nonviolent social movement needed strong ties of solidarity in order to gain all its strength to face the neoliberal cultural hegemony of the Liberal government, to put it in more Gramscian terms (Gramsci 1971). Moreover, the *carré rouge* also embodied collective responsibility through its ideological substance: to reaffirm the society's collective responsibility towards democratic, just, and accessible postsecondary education.[16]

This articulation of social responsibility is opposed to the government's neoliberal definition of 'responsibility'. Consequently, the tuition hike was publicized as a way to restore justice to taxpayers by relieving education's collective economic burden[17] through making students more individually responsible and active in paying their fair share for their education. This ideological 'fact', articulated through the government's neoliberal *nova lingua*, became a reified concept of fair share as individual responsibility, which was conveyed profusely in the public sphere by mass media without ever being given a meaning (Boltanski and Chiapello [1999] 2011; Bihr 2007). Doing your fair share was never clarified, nor was its measures ever clearly defined except for the promotion of individual responsibility at the expense of its collective counterpart.

The Institute for Socioeconomic Information and Research (IRIS) raised the debate on the definition of 'fair share' to counteract the dominant rhetoric that was rooting itself in Quebec's social imaginary. Quebec Finance Minister Raymond Bachand was comparing two different postsecondary education systems: the one prior to 1968 that was elitist, and the State-funded system put in place during the decade of 1968–78 (Martin and Tremblay-Pépin 2012: 13). This unspoken bias demonstrates two simultaneous dynamics. The first and most apparent is the gradual retreat from the welfare state, which characterizes Quebec's post-Quiet Revolution context.[18] The second dynamic relates to the ideological and electoral purpose of the fair-share concept as delegitimizing the student movement's demands while also appealing to certain taxpaying demographics that had finished their university education prior to or not much later than 1968–78. By appealing to these demographics, the Liberal government tried to rally support in the upcoming elections of 2012.

The general semantic matrix in which the fair-share argument evolved gradually erased the conceptual boundaries of personal and collective articulations of social, economic, and moral responsibility. It proceeded to a reductive logic of commodification stating that, if one is not willing to pay for one's education, as for any other service, one should either be excluded from the use of postsecondary education or be considered illegitimately wanting to have access to an education. According to this logic, one would then be contributing to the economic burden of provincial taxpayers.

As a by-product of this appeal to a generation, the once social and ideological conflict took on a new dimension: that of an intergenerational social issue in which the baby boomer and X generations were perceived to be in opposition to the spoiled, child-king Y generation student protesters. This resulted in a general social uneasiness in which both violence and the discourse on violence could easily take shape.

Intimidation and Violence as the Hindering of Personal Freedom

Because of the general uneasiness alluded to in the previous paragraph, the social discourse seems to have shifted during the protests from the question of education and the fair-share rhetoric towards that of intimidation and violence. For example, *Influence Communication*'s Caroline Roy[19] claims that at the beginning of the conflict, 79 percent of the articles about the student strike touched on the growth of tuition fees, whereas at the end, the percentage dropped to only 4 percent. This research also states that in mid-May 2012, 39 percent of these articles talked about massive detentions, riots, and violence surrounding the conflict more than the social justice and ideological nature of the conflict itself.

This turn to violence was a direct result of the prolongation of the conflict, which evolved into a crisis because of the strengthening of the government's refusal to negotiate and of the discourse about violence that emerged in a context of heightened and radicalized relationships. On one side, the government was supported by socioeconomic leaders, parts of the population, the legal system, and a militarized police force, which was frequently being solicited to act during protests. On the other, the *carrés rouges* were exhausted and frustrated by many months of daily and nightly protests and diverse political actions,[20] while remaining mostly unacknowledged by the government.

Far from being a natural progression or outcome, this context of violence was fostered semantically by the Quebec Liberal government's use of an intimidation and violence related speech-act. This speech-act was first implemented by Premier Jean Charest, who respectively stated on 1 and 10 April 2012 that the protesters were attacking him and not his ideas.[21] Moreover, he added that as with politicians, students opposed to the *carré rouge* should not be bullied or intimidated by protesters.

This paved the way for the deceptive use of emotion-driven symbolism, which was blatant in one of the Premier's press conferences when he asked: 'In what kind of society would we live in if we accepted that people be intimidated because they wanted to study?'[22] Both this speech-act concerning violence and intimidation and the general political discourse's semantic structure contributed to delegitimizing the democratically supported picket line, amongst other tactics. They also contributed to radically reducing positions within the debate's spectrum to the Manichean formula of either you are with us or you are with the violent intimidators. The space given to the intimidation and violence rhetoric started to fade away after Culture Minister Christine St-Pierre had to make a public apology following her statement that Fred Pellerin[23] had the right to wear the *carré rouge*, but that she and a great majority of Quebecois knew what this symbol meant: 'intimidation, violence, and also that it prevented people from studying'.[24]

From the beginning of April to the end of June, the rhetoric of violence and intimidation and emotion-driven references to victimization were used in order to delegitimize the movement and its actions. Because every direct action taking place in the streets and on postsecondary education grounds was seen as impeding the pro-tuition-hike students' fundamental rights to attend classes, the very act of protesting became synonymous with violence in the government's eye. Consequently, universities and the College of General and Professional Education (CÉGEPs) became the micro-social spaces of ideological but also physical opposition between *carrés rouges* and pro-hike students. Furthermore, it was in these spaces that the symbolic reference to pro-hike students as hostages in their own homes took form.

It was on that particular issue of tuition hikes that the picket lines on university and college premises, the blocking of streets and bridges, and the clanging of pots and pans at eight o'clock every night for fifteen minutes were portrayed as infringing on individual rights and disturbing the social order or the very fabric of society. Ergo, to protect the individual rights of the students and citizens, political and legal measures had to be taken. For students, the use of injunctions made possible by special law number 78[25] ensured the legal right to attend one's classes, and therefore rendered illegal any picket line or measure impeding that right. As for the citizens' fundamental right to social order, the creation and enforcement of the P-6 regulation in Montreal gave police the power to declare any protest illegal if it contained more than 50 people, if the route was not preapproved by police, or if it contained any masked protesters. Both measures were used as tools to suppress protests and the activists' direct collective actions. By doing so, these measures were also undermining the *carré rouge*'s power relation with the government.

The Liberal government's definition of 'violence' delegitimized the *carrés rouges* by portraying their actions as violations of individual human rights and as intimidation, which is a form of psychological violence. Moreover, it finally succeeded in closing the debate on tuition fees by announcing elections. As the safeguard of democracy, the use of elections to suppress the *carrés rouges* can be seen as further undermining its legitimacy by affirming that direct nonviolent actions cannot be a legitimate vector of the will of the people.

Conclusion

In light of this analysis of the transformation of nonviolent resistance into violent action by sociopolitical actors during the 2012 student crisis in Quebec, we can say that the *carré rouge* was a social movement that, because of its sociopolitical social-justice project, came to threaten the status quo implemented by the Quebec Liberal party. Although its direct actions were based on the general conception of nonviolent principles, the fact that the *carré rouge* did not position itself clearly within the conceptual ambiguity towards violence and nonviolence from the beginning of the strike made way for the Liberal government's instrumentalization of violence for its own benefit. Not only did it use certain events and actions in order to exemplify violence without giving it a clear definition, the government and mass media proceeded to the use of a specific conceptualization of fair share and a vague yet constant rhetoric of intimidation and violence in order to render obsolete the need for a clear definition of violence and to impede the critical assessment of violence in the public debate.

As the literature on nonviolence clearly states, far from being defined as mere contemplation and inaction, nonviolence requires strong normative grounds and praxis in order to achieve social transformation (Freeman 1966: 228-54; Rawls 1999; McCarthy et al. 1997). Consequently, where and how does one cultivate the normativity and praxis of resistance in an age of moral relativism? Weaving a strong network of solidarity and social responsibility between social movements seems to be a good avenue to pursue this cultivation. In this sense, could the *carré rouge* become the symbol of a *new* New Left nonviolent social movement of resistance? As long as neoliberal hegemony acts to suppress conflict by delegitimizing civil disobedience and resistance to its social project, the Gramscian counter-hegemonic historic bloc will need to go further in its reflections on radical creativity and citizenship, but also on the normative grounds on which the broadening of an inclusive movement of active resistance can flourish and thrive.

About the Authors

Marie Boglari is a PhD candidate in Conflict Studies at Saint Paul University in Ottawa, where she teaches BA-level courses on social justice and alternative dispute resolution. Her thesis consists of a qualitative study on the impact of ethnic and nationalist discrimination on the actors of conflict.

Martin Samson is a PhD candidate in Conflict Studies at Saint Paul University in Ottawa. His thesis focuses on a theoretical and literary analysis of emancipation and conflict through the philosophical and sociological thought of Michel Freitag (1935–2009). Samson teaches BA-level courses on social justice, climate change, and the world-ecological crisis at Saint Paul University, and conflict studies at Discovery University, an outreach university in partnership with Saint Paul, the University of Ottawa, and the Ottawa Mission.

Notes

1. The *carrés rouges* term will be used throughout the chapter as a reference to all members of the movement.

2. Association pour une Solidarité Syndicale Étudiante (2005: 11).

3. In December 2011, ASSÉ founded the CLASSE as a temporary organization meant to organize the strike against the tuition fees hike. See CLASSE (2011), at http://www. bloquonslahausse.com/laclasse/a-propos/.

4. On March 22, 2012, more than 100 000 protesters marched in Montreal. Organizers considered it would be one of the important protests in Québec's history. Breton (2013), at http://www.lapresse.ca/actualites/dossiers/conflit-etudiant/201302/12/01-4 621045-greve-etudiante-le-vote-qui-a-donne-le-ton.php; Radio-Canada (2012) at http:// ici.radio-canada.ca/nouvelles/societe/2012/03/21/001-manifestatoin-nationale-etudiants.shtml.

5. Verodagg (2012), at http://www.youtube.com/watch?v=9YVprVrnfZ0.

6. Lisée (2012), http://jflisee.org/category/mouvement-etudiant/printemps-erable -2/un-conflit-creatif/. Even if this is the blog of a Parti Québécois politician, it is a good example.

7. Chouinard (2012), at http://www.ledevoir.com/societe/education/347550/greve-etudiante-carton-d-invitation.

8. FECQ (2012), at http://www.fecq.org/nouvelles/la-fecq-denonce-les-gestes-de-violence-tant-du-cote-des-forces-policieres-que-des-etudiants/.

9. Ici Radio Canada (2012), at http://ici.radio-canada.ca/nouvelles/societe/2012/ 04/18/002-etudiants-conflit-mercredi.shtml.

10. Chouinard (2012), at http://www.ledevoir.com/societe/education/347550/greve-etudiante-carton-d-invitation.

11. TVA Nouvelles avec Agence QMI (2012), at http://tvanouvelles.ca/lcn/infos/ national/archives/2012/04/20120422-113731.html. See also Ici Radio Canada (2012), at http://ici.radio-canada.ca/nouvelles/societe/2012/04/22/002-fecq-utlimatum-classe. shtml.

12. We will not enter the philosophical debate on the precedence of violence or nonviolence (see Weil 1981). It nevertheless needs to be accepted that violence and nonviolence are relational concepts, and the definition of one will affect the scope of the other. See also Mellon and Semelin (1994 12-18); Sharp (2009: 22, f1).

13. For example, see Ici Radio Canada (2012), at http://ici.radio-canada.ca/nouv elles/societe/2012/04/26/001-conflit-etudiant-jeudi.shtml.

14. Lagacé and Mason (2012), at http://www.theglobeandmail.com/news/politics/ quebec-students-legitimate-strikers-or-self-absorbed-brats/article4104939/.

15. Ici Radio Canada (2012), at http://www.radio-canada.ca/regions/montreal/20 12/10/10/004-matricule-728-spvm-arrestation.shtml. See also *La Presse* (2014), at http:// www.lapresse.ca/actualites/justice-et-affaires-criminelles/201403/21/01-4750129-matricule-728-accusee-de-voies-de-fait.php.

16. A model put in motion by the Parent Report in 1963 (Parent 1965).

17. Richer (2012), at http://www.lapresse.ca/le-soleil/affaires/actualite-economique/201203/11/01-4504478-que-chacun-paye-sa-juste-part-plaide-bachand.php; Boivin (2012), at http://www.lapresse.ca/le-soleil/actualites/ politique/201203/06/01-4503059-bachand-deposera-son-budget-le-20-mars.php?utm_ categorieinterne=trafficdrivers&utm_contenuinterne=cyberpresse_vous_suggere_4504478_article_POS1.

18. The Quiet Revolution is a period of fundamental social change in Quebec history, taking place during the 1960s and 1970s, and characterized the baby boomer generation's socio-demographic weight. It was marked by a strong secularization movement, the nationalization of natural resources, and a strong nationalist or sovereignty movement. For a more detailed overview of the role of the Quiet Revolution in Canadian politics, see Guindon (1996), at http://www.ropercenter.uconn.edu/public-perspective/ppscan/71/71026.pdf.

19. See Blatchford (2012), at http://journalmetro.com/dossiers/conflit-etudiant/80682/la-crise-etudiante-interesse-a-letranger/.

20. From the beginning of the student strike to 8 May 2012, 184 protests took place in the city of Montreal alone. See Duchaine (2012), at http://www.lapresse.ca/actualites/dossiers/conflit-etudiant/201205/08/01-4523017-le-conflit-etudiant-a-fait-des-centaines-declopes.php. It is also estimated that the seven-month-long strike made way to roughly 700 protests. See Benesaieh (2013), at http://www.lapresse.ca/actualites/dossiers/conflit-etudiant/201306/04/01-4657804-printemps-erable-382-arrestations-1711-interpellations.php.

21. The exact quote is as follows: '*Les attaques personnelles, ça ne résonne jamais très bien. L'enjeu, ce n'est pas ma personne. L'enjeu, c'est l'avenir du Québec*' (2012), at http://www.lapresse.ca/actualites/education/201204/01/01-4511427-droits-de-scolarite-lavenir-nest-pas-dans-le-gel-dit-charest.php.

22. The original text is as follows: '*On ne doit pas céder le pas à l'intimidation*', *a affirmé le premier ministre, avant de se demander: "Dans quelle sorte de société on vit, si on accepte que des personnes sont intimidées parce qu'elles veulent aller étudier?"*' (Ici Radio Canada 2012, at http://ici.radio-canada.ca/nouvelles/societe/2012/04/11/003-beauchamp-boycottage-etudiant.shtml).

23. A Quebec artist nominated for knighthood by the *Ordre national du Québec* in June 2012 (Journet 2012, at http://www.lapresse.ca/actualites/politique/politique-quebecoise/201206/13/01-4534514-christine-st-pierre-sexcuse-pour-ses-propos-sur-le-carre-rouge.php?utm_categorieinterne=trafficdrivers&utm_contenuinterne=cyberpresse_vous_suggere_4534228_article_POS1).

24. Translation by authors (*Le Devoir*, 8 June 2012, at http://www.ledevoir.com/politique/quebec/352008/fred-pellerin-refuse-l-ordre-national-du-quebec).

25. Bill 78 is an Act to enable students to receive instruction from the postsecondary institutions they attend (39th legislature, second session, 18 May 2012).

Part IV

Nonviolence and Ecological Concerns

Chapter 14

Being in 'Rights' Relationship with Animals:
The Importance of Political Visibility for Animals

Nathan Townend

Introduction

Humans are extremely violent towards animals; yet, constructing an intelligent path towards nonviolence involves more than simply addressing at face value the specific kinds of ethical violations that humans commit against animals. Indeed, activist and academic conversations that aim to advance concepts like nonviolence, spirituality, and social transformation bring into focus that our choices as individuals, cultures, and societies are conditioned by many often conflicting ideas, some of them conscious, many of them less so. Given this reality, the issue of advancing nonviolence in relation to animals is not as simple as choosing an alternative to violence; first, we must recognize that nonviolence means choosing to recognize the need to *think* differently.

Certainly human behaviour, such as how humans treat animals, can be informed by ideologies deeply imbedded in our cultural psyches, and violent, destructive ones seem particularly difficult to erode. Thus, a focus on a number of political and theoretical conversations helps to lay the foundations for the burgeoning discussion of animals and nonviolence. Here, the aim is to provide one of many possible configurations that draw out some of the larger historical, contemporary, and intersectional nuts and bolts for advancing nonviolence and animals. More specifically, I aim to reveal that when it comes to animals and nonviolence, what is at stake is the extent to which humans regard animals as members of a moral community that is both politically visible and safeguarded. Once again, the issue is not simply a matter of how humans treat animals; rather, how we treat animals reveals how we think about them and how we conceive our responsibilities towards them. The scope and limitations of those responsibilities form the most appropriate boundaries within which to discuss animals and nonviolence.

Moral Schizophrenia

The current stance of Euro-western peoples towards animals can be characterized by what Gary Francione terms as a 'moral schizophrenia', or a fundamental disparity 'between what we say we believe about animals, and how we actually treat them' (2004: 108). Sue Donaldson and Will Kymlicka (2011: 3) cite a 2003 Gallup poll that found that 96 percent of Americans favour some limits of animals' exploitation—a result that stands in contrast to the fact that 'we bring billions of sentient animals into existence for the sole purpose of killing them' and do so in increasingly cruel and intensive ways (Francione 2004: 132). Animal research and factory farming are two very large-scale examples that highlight this fundamental disconnect and help to explain why an exploration of political theory is apropos. Critically, Francione argues that our moral schizophrenia is 'related to the status of animals as property, which means that animals are nothing more than *things* despite the many laws that supposedly protect them' (2004: 108).

In the context of animal research, according to the Canadian Council on Animal Care (CCAC), in 2009 over 3.4 million animals were used for scientific purposes in Canada. This figure represented an increase from 2.3 million in 2008.[1] These animals included mice, rats, dogs, frogs, cats, rabbits, hamsters, guinea pigs, monkeys, fish, birds, pigs, and many others. Gruesome tales from the bowels of the research laboratory include the story of Pablo, recounted by Marc Bekoff in *The Emotional Lives of Animals*. Pablo, a chimpanzee who was otherwise known as CH-377, lived out his days in a New York University laboratory. He was caged and subjected to being darted 220 times, undergoing 28 liver biopsies, two bone-marrow biopsies, and two lymph-node biopsies; enduring four injections for an experimental hepatitis vaccine; and receiving 10,000 times the lethal dose of HIV.[2] To bring it closer to home, for those who may have companion animals, imagine the following: your cat companion receives a pre-surgical injection cocktail of drugs. Then your cat is anaesthetized and placed in a head and body brace; the upper vertebrae are removed to expose the nerves of the spinal column. Sections of the spinal cord are damaged or removed and then your cat is kept alive for seven to nine days after this surgery. After this period, your cat is again anaesthetized and returned to the brace. The spinal cord is once again exposed and the scar tissue that has formed over the previous week is removed. Following this, your cat is put on a respirator, given an injection causing paralysis, and injected with various kinds of staining fluids that are allowed eight to ten hours to spread through tissues. Finally, your cat is killed by lethal injection and the tissues are harvested for study.[3]

Such stories would offend most people's basic ethical sensibilities. It might be fair to suggest that most of us are aware that animals suffer and that this suffering is largely inflicted by humans; most people would be troubled by this awareness. When hearing stories like Pablo's or seeing images like the undercover footage of Delimax Veal farm workers kicking cattle, most people perform some combination of responses, such as bursting into tears, yelling at the television set, or sighing in despair and disbelief.[4] Regardless of the unique way in which individuals respond, most do so from a moral position that boldly declares, 'This is not right!'

Yet, in spite of this kind of awareness and accompanying outrage, the situation for animals continues to worsen. The dramatic increase in animals used for scientific purposes between 2008 and 2009 is a tiny demonstration of the larger reality that billions of dollars in governmental and corporate funding are continually poured into discovering new ways to exploit animals. At the same time, the meat industry continues to farm animals in ever more intensive conditions. According to the United Nations (UN) report, *Livestock's Long Shadow* (2006), meat production is expected to double by 2050. Considering that in 2011 humans killed 56 billion animals per year, this prediction seems almost unfathomable. Thus, it would appear that Francione's charge of moral schizophrenia is correct. Indeed, something does not seem to add up: if most people are outraged at the kinds of cruelty endured by animals like Pablo, then how is it possible that more such lives of misery are exponentially increasing?

The Importance of Political Theory

The answer to the above question can be partially understood with reference to Will Kymlicka and Sue Donaldson's political theory of animal rights. In their ground-breaking work, *Zoopolis—A Political Theory of Animal Rights*, Donaldson and Kymlicka define three different categories of positions that the majority of people occupy when discussing animals: welfarist, ecological, and basic rights (2011: 3).[5] Their framework helps to capture a broad spectrum of philosophical and political opinion, and accordingly, can assist us in underlining the critical deficiencies in thinking that contribute to our moral schizophrenia.

The welfarist position has a long track record. Nocella II et al. observed:

> As a modern development, the philosophical, moral, and ethical foundation of animal advocacy can be traced back to the great Eastern religions of Jainism, Buddhism, and Hinduism, along with numerous early Western philosophers such as Pythagoras, Hesiod, and Draco, each calling for the protection of non-human animals in some manifestation. (Nocella II et al. 2014: xxi)

During the nineteenth century, organizations such as the Society for the Prevention of Cruelty to Animals (SPCA), founded in England in 1824, and the Royal Society for the Prevention of Cruelty to Animals (RSPCA,

1840) began to appear as public intellectuals and politicians such as William Wilberforce, religious leaders such as William Cowherd, and ordinary members of the general public began to espouse moral and ethical concerns about the humane treatment of animals. The central ethos of the welfarist tradition can be characterized by the idea that humans have a moral responsibility to ensure that animals are treated in a way that minimizes unnecessary suffering and that egregious instances of cruelty should be addressed punitively. In terms of the legal framework surrounding the treatment of animals, the welfarist principle has been the most popular and most influential; hence, legislation such as the Animal Welfare Act of 2006 exists in the UK.[6]

In the contemporary context, issues of animal welfare are hotly contested in a number of arenas. These include farming, research, zoos, circuses, aquariums, hunting, and other instances of sport and leisure (such as horse riding), and so on. There is significant diversity of opinion regarding which arenas are acceptable in principle. For instance, someone might claim that whilst zoos, circuses, and aquariums are unacceptable, farming (meat production) and research are okay. Inevitably, the intellectual justification for whichever combination is adopted becomes inconsistent if the welfare of the animals is truly the criterion of judgement. For example, how does one justify caging a rabbit for therapeutic research as acceptable, yet caging the same rabbit for cosmetic research as not? If the animal subject is the starting point, and the full extent of sentience is accounted for, then these distinctions become moot. However, these distinctions *are* made, and in spite of their philosophical precariousness, they continue to inform the animal welfare legislation.

This seeming theoretical dilemma is avoided when one appeals to the claim that animal interests are ultimately subordinate to human interests. The distinction between the uses of rabbits in cosmetic versus therapeutic research supposedly becomes rational when one considers that whilst cosmetic research is not strictly necessary, therapeutic research is because it benefits the greatest number of humans. The idea that humans matter intrinsically more than animals is often entirely taken for granted, as something that seems to make sense to everyone. Western jurisprudence has reflected this idea in almost all major pieces of legislation in recent history. Take, for example, this statement from the Quebec Court of Appeal case of *R. v. Menard* (1978):

> Thus men, by the rule of s402 (1)(a), do not renounce the right given to them by their position as supreme creatures to put animals at their service to satisfy their needs, but impose on themselves a rule of civilization by which they renounce, condemn and repress all infliction of pain, suffering or injury on animals which, while taking place in the pursuit of a legitimate purpose, is not justified by the choice of means involved.

'Without necessity' does not mean that man, when a thing is susceptible of causing pain to an animal, must abstain unless it be necessary, but
means that man in the pursuit of his purposes as the superior being, in
the pursuit of his wellbeing, is obliged not to inflict on animals pain, suffering, or injury which is not inevitable taking into account the purpose
sought and the circumstances of the particular case. In effect, even if it is
not necessary for man to eat meat and if he could abstain from doing so,
as many in fact do, it is the privilege of man to eat it. (Quebec 1978)

There is much to unpack in this statement about meat eating. Firstly,
there is the almost deliberate theological language of rights that are given
to humans as supreme beings. The problem with the theological language
is that it inscribes a decidedly anthropocentric view, and thus perpetuates
the problem of animal concerns becoming subject to human desires. Secondly, the document also seems to hint at the Kantian view that 'he who
is cruel to animals becomes hard also in his dealings with men' (Kant 1963:
240). In other words, the rule of civilization that humans impose on themselves, which would cause them to renounce cruelty, is simply about cultivating moral lives that promote the ethical treatment of other humans;
there are no moral obligations owed to animals. Most critically in this view,
animals are fundamentally at the disposal of humans, even if the purposes
of use are not strictly necessary. As far as the law is concerned, as long as
an act of animal use is not solely intended for the purposes of cruelty, then
the actual level of cruelty that the act inflicts is by and large not indictable.

Hence, on 4 September 2014, the US Senator for Oklahoma, Jim Inhofe,
was able to hold a live pigeon shoot as a fundraising event for his re-
election campaign.[7] Although the occasion involved the gratuitous shooting of 1,000 pigeons for no practical purpose, Inhofe had the law firmly
on his side because the shooting of pigeons (and leaving them on the
ground to writhe in pain and full of lead) was an occasion to raise money.
Even if it were not, Inhofe would still have been legally within his rights
because pigeon-shooting is a recognized sport, and as a leisure activity it
can claim, however loosely, to be about something other than cruelty for
cruelty's sake. The questions of how, why, and by whom these privileges
are bestowed on humans remain largely unanswered in a secular political or legal context; what is clear is that humans consider that they have
the right to use animals, and by extension, have the right to *own* animals.
Thus, in a Nova Scotia Small Matters case, *Savoie v. Dowell*, a case over the
custody of a dog, the judge declared, 'At law, dogs are property. The "best
interest of the dog" is not a concept any more relevant to the law than
would be the best interest of the motorcycle in a dispute over a Harley-
Davidson' (Nova Scotia 2009: §8).

Understanding the paradox represented by the dual increases in human
concern for animal welfare and the levels, rates, and variety of cruelties

committed against animals is to see that the problem is not that people are unaware of animal suffering. This is important to note because there are many, particularly members of animal welfare groups, who put forward arguments that suggest if only people knew more about what cruelty animals suffer, there would be greater change. These arguments fail to take into account that most people are reluctant to address the fundamental status quo as it is enshrined in law: that humans have the right to use and to own animals. The principles of animal welfare and anti-cruelty laws have 'no meaningful application to animal interests if they are the property of others' (Francione 2004: 25). Ultimately, 'the profound inconsistency between what we say about animals and how we actually treat them is related to the status of animals as our property' (Francione 2004: 116). Thus, transitioning to a basic rights position can offer a way forward.

Moving towards a Rights Position

At the present time, animals are politically invisible. This is not to say that there are not visible and influential political organizations that advocate animal welfare and animal rights. Thinkers like Peter Singer (1983) and Tom Regan (1983) helped to bring about the advent of the animal rights movement in the 1970s and 1980s and the movement has since enjoyed widespread profile and popularity. However, although most Western governments have an environment portfolio and environmental issues have significant legislative traction, by contrast no government has an animal portfolio. In fact, no major political party, including the Green Party of Canada, has a platform or policies that refer explicitly to animals. Animal issues are rather almost exclusively dealt with in the context of anti-cruelty and welfare legislation; yet, we have established that this approach is ineffectual in so far as it is too slow to adapt to the ever-rapid increases in animal exploitation. It also fails to address the fact that as long as *animal* interests are subject to *human* interests, animals will continue to suffer unspeakable cruelty.

The subjection of animal interests to human interests is precisely why the basic rights position begins from the idea that an effective ethical framework is one in which animals are acknowledged as 'bearers of certain inviolable rights' (Donaldson and Kymlicka 2011: 4). In order to become truly politically visible, animals need political rights that are not subject to human desires. There are many different approaches to articulating what this means. Some approaches are weaker in the sense that they put forward simpler rights for animals that operate within the existing exploitative model. For instance, someone of a weaker animal-rights position might claim that chickens have the right to dust-bathe; more vigorous versions of animal rights would make statements that animals have a right not to be killed, and would thus oppose the exploitative model outright. The approach I wish to follow, that of Donaldson and Kymlicka, begins from and builds upon a more robust rights position. Inevitably, I must pass over much of the discourse on animal rights that has taken place over the last 40 years. To mitigate this intellectual violence, my use of Donaldson and Kymlicka's work—currently at the cutting edge within animal rights theory—is intended as a way to go beyond certain impasses of the last several decades of debate.

Firstly, then, Donaldson and Kymlicka foreground the principle of inviolability, which implies 'that people's right to life is independent of their relative contribution to the overall good, and is not violable in the service of the greater good' (2011: 22). This idea stands in contrast to the utilitarian view that morality is the obligation to bring about the greatest good for the greatest number of people—an obligation that can involve the sacrificing of a few for the sake of many. However, since the advent of human rights, the utilitarian view has become largely peripheral in the human context, but it is very much alive and well in the animal debate. In the human context, the principle of inviolability forms the basis of most ethical structures from bioethics to international law; hence, minorities are recognized as possessing equal rights to everyone else. As Donaldson and Kymlicka point out, however, 'the assumption of most mainstream contemporary Western political theory is that the community of justice is coextensive with the community of human beings' (2011: 24). In other words, rights are by definition reserved for humans. Why is this the case?

Historically, rights have been assigned only to humans because only humans possessed personhood, defined in terms of that which supposedly 'makes humans special' (Varner 2012: 134). Following from Descartes and other Enlightenment thinkers, these (supposedly) exclusively human characteristics have often been a routine list of cognitive capacities, such as reason-rationality, inter-subjectivity, and emotional intelligence. Up until quite recently, these exclusions seemed almost self-evident. With the arrival of contemporary animal sciences like ethology, which accept Darwin's idea that differences among species are those of degree rather than kind, the gap between humans and animals is closing. We now know that many species display immensely sophisticated cognitive abilities, and likewise many have inter-subjective experiences of the world. Yet, attempting to prove that animals deserve to be in the 'club' on this basis is an unfair way to go about obtaining animal rights because it neglects identifying a fundamental philosophical discrepancy. That is, when dealing with sentient humans, 'we do not assign degrees of basic human rights or inviolability according to differences in mental complexity, intelligence, or emotional or moral range' (Donaldson and Kymlicka 2011: 30).

Indeed, the premise of inviolable rights is precisely to protect the most vulnerable, who in many instances lack the very cognitive capacities we would demand of animals. When it comes to humans, we recognize that, 'moral status does not rest on judgements of mental complexity, but simply on the recognition of selfhood' (Donaldson and Kymlicka 2011: 30). That particular selfhood is determined merely by there being a vulnerable self, 'someone home' whose life 'can go better or worse as experienced from the inside' (Donaldson and Kymlicka 2011: 30). Animals overwhelmingly pass this test, and so the insistence on forcing animals to pass certain other cognitive tests to acquire rights is merely an attempt to keep animals disenfranchised and can only be achieved by 'hollowing out the theory [of inviolable rights], making a mockery of the idea of protecting the vulnerable and the innocent' (Donaldson and Kymlicka 2011: 30).

The question then becomes whether animals are to be afforded negative rights or positive rights, or some combination of both. The strict abolitionist approach, such as that of Francione, essentially argues that humans should leave animals alone, and that currently domesticated animals should be allowed to become extinct.[8] Others, such as Martha Nussbaum, argue that in fact, 'respect for nature should not and cannot just mean just leaving nature as it is, and must involve careful normative arguments about what plausible goals might be' (2004: 311). This conversation is a deeply complex one that would require another chapter. The most important thing to take away from this discussion is that from a basic rights perspective, the status quo simply will not do and is deeply flawed. Moreover, Donaldson and Kymlicka's discussion of human rights in particular brings the crucial problematic distinctions between humans and animals into focus.

The Need for and Challenge of New Visions

Critics of the political approach above will argue that 'it is often through the language of human rights that empire is accomplished today' (Razack 2088: 148). Therefore, animal rights can likewise appear as something of Western genus, which neglects the cultural diversity that exists with respect to animals and the relationships humans ought to have with them. Donaldson and Kymlicka point to Indigenous cultures as potentially obvious objectors, given that many of them have hunted and trapped animals for millennia as part of their culture. To be sure, the cry for cultural exemptions is commonplace at the negotiating table of human rights, and given that Donaldson and Kymlicka bind animal rights to the same inviolable and universal premises of human rights, then animal rights will inevitably experience a similar process and destiny. In the case of human rights, history has indicated that in spite of cultural variations (which are significant and cannot be adequately resolved here), there has nevertheless been instances when shared global priorities have gained real traction.

Take, for example, the Convention on the Elimination of All forms of Discrimination Against Women (CEDAW) adopted by the UN General Assembly in 1979. Considering the significant variation of cultural attitudes worldwide concerning the role of women, this convention would have seemed as farfetched at that time as proposing a similar one on animal rights is today. Yet what achievements like CEDAW demonstrate is that 'whether members of a society endorse human rights is not predetermined by their primordial cultural DNA, but rather is determined by their ongoing judgment about which of their diverse moral sources are worthy of allegiance' (Donaldson and Kymlicka 2011: 46).

This kind of concentrated intellectual and spiritual work has been underway for some time in fields such as religion and ecology, where many religious traditions have attempted to revise classical theologies and rediscover forgotten sources of wisdom that help to produce a more ecologically benign or enhancing outlook. As Mary Evelyn Tucker says of religion, 'While grounded in foundational beliefs and practices, [religions] have never been static, but have always both effected change and been affected by change in response to intellectual, political, cultural, social and economic forces' (2003: 12). This statement is true not just of religion but also of the full variety of cultural forms. Given this, it becomes possible to suggest, as Donaldson and Kymlicka do, that, 'the view of animals as vulnerable selves who need the protection of inviolable rights is one that is accessible to all societies from within their diverse moral sources and cannot be treated as the unique property of any one culture or religion' (Donaldson and Kymlicka 2011: 49).

The above discussion of political theory and rights discourse helps to flesh out the practical contours of why animals are exploited and likewise what are the most available, practical steps forward. Moreover, political theory has broad intellectual traction and any potential social transformation will only endure if it enjoys a solid intellectual and philosophical footing. However, an additional dimension, implicit in Francione's concept of moral schizophrenia, is a clash of worldviews, in between which most of us find ourselves. That is to say, the way in which many of us increasingly experience the world conflicts with the way in which we continue to be *taught* to experience the world. Thomas Berry once said of the environmental movement that if it 'has not yet achieved its full efficacy in confrontation with the industrial vision, it is not primarily because of the economic or political realities of the situation, but because of the mythic power of the industrial vision' (2006: 31). This is true for the animal rights movement also.

Just as humans are repulsed by environmental degradation, they appear to be repulsed by animal cruelty; yet, the mere expression of repugnance has not been enough to curb either environmental or animal exploitation. This is because deep in our cultural psyches many of us are still wedded to a worldview that regards only humans as having rights and those rights include the use and ownership of animals and the natural world—a worldview continually reinforced by powerful, non-democratic forces, such as the fossil-fuel industry and global corporations. Hence, human exploitative behaviour seems the stronger partner in the clash of worldviews; domination and exploitation have been practically and intellectually imbedded in our cultural psyche for thousands of years—an interconnected web of coherence in which we remain caught.[9] Disentangling this strand or that will not be enough; rather, an entirely different way of understanding the world is necessary. The political rights theory of Donaldson and Kymlicka is a philosophically compelling way to tackle the problem of animal cruelty and exploitation, yet it should be a strand in a larger web of approaches to nonviolence, within newer visions of human activity in the world.

Conclusion

Martin Luther King Jr once said, 'Injustice anywhere is a threat to justice everywhere' (1963: 24). This notion becomes all the more compelling when animals are understood as a concern of justice. When animals are excluded from being vulnerable persons to whom are owed rights to life and the most basic of protections, the entire edifice of inviolable rights is in serious jeopardy. In the very recent past, women were not persons and, thus, had no legal rights; neither were racial minorities, the mentally or physically disabled, nor lesbian, gay, bisexual, transgendered, or queer persons.[10] The more comprehensive recognition of personhood (which includes these diverse groups of people), and by extension the possession of inviolable rights, has been critical to both the illumination and overcoming of systemic injustice.

Critical theories have been hard at work over the past century to render visible the kinds of injustices that allow for violence and exploitation. Although political empowerment is by no means the only way, it is among the more important ways to address violence and exploitation. Indeed, rights discourse is a banner around which the global community is increasingly mobilized. Although effective nonviolence clearly involves many additional steps, many of which are discussed in this book, animals are significantly behind on almost all fronts. As in the human case, I do not imagine that affording rights to animals will conclusively eliminate violence against them, but it will be an important step, just as it has already been an important step in the human world. Therefore, the way forward in nonviolent action must be less about picketing the next animal research lab—although that is important—and more about developing intellectually sound and persuasive political theories, which can then be applied to existing legal frameworks to see animals enfranchised as persons and afforded distinctive rights not subject to human desires.

Ultimately animals are not at humans' disposal, and their interests are not fundamentally subject to our human interests. Rather, animals 'have their own subjective existence, and hence their own inviolable rights to life and liberty, which prohibits harming them, killing them, confining them, owning them, and enslaving them' (Donaldson and Kymlicka 2011: 40). Clearly this position has radical consequences for human activity: 'respect for these rights rules out virtually all existing practices of the animals use industries, where animals are owned and exploited for human profit, pleasure, education, convenience, or comfort' (Donaldson and Kymlicka 2011: 40). Francione affirms that 'our moral compass will not find animals while they are lying on our plates' (2004: 134). As Paul Waldau states, 'it is deeply mistaken to claim that our sole community is and can be humans alone', and rights discourse is a clear reflection of this truth (2013: 196).

About the Author

Nathan Townend has been working for the past ten years as a scholar, farmer, social activist, and politician in Ontario. His academic work has centred on religious responses to environmental crisis, and more recently on understanding how religions continue to influence human relationships with non-human animals.

Notes

1. University of British Columbia (2014), at http://www.animalresearch.ubc.ca/research-process-3-more.html.

2. The case of Pablo is recounted in Bekoff (2007).

3. This was an actual experiment conducted at Queen's University in Kingston, Ontario, and is recorded in Fenrich and Rose (2011: 3240-58).

4. *The Star* News Staff (2014), at http://www.thestar.com/news/investigations/2014/04/19/abuse_of_veal_calves_unveiled_by_hidden_camera.html.

5. The ecological approach will not be discussed here in any detail as Donaldson and Kymlicka (2011) persuasively argue that the broad spectrum of ecological approaches typically reinscribes or reconstitutes the same basic philosophical discrepancy of why humans possess inviolable rights that are an acceptable restraint on practical ecological goals (e.g., we do not accept the culling of humans) and animals do not (e.g., most ecologists accept that culling animals viewed as part of invasive species is an acceptable means to ecological holistic ends).

6. UKPGA (2006), at http://www.legislation.gov.uk/ukpga/2006/45/contents.

7. The shoot was recorded on film by an investigator from an animal activist group

SHARK (Show Animals Respect and Kindness) who infiltrated the event (SHARK 2014, at http://www.sharkonline.org/.

8.   Critics of this approach refer to its potential for 'species apartheid' and argue that it is neither ethical nor practical, given that humans do not in fact live separately from animals as part of the natural world. Moreover, many argue, as Donaldson and Kymlicka (2011) do, that humans have particular responsibilities towards domesticated animals that are distinct from those towards wild animals.

9.   In a far more wide-ranging discussion of this theme in relation to animals, Adams (1990) intersects the exploitation of animals with the exploitation of women in the context of the historical roots of patriarchy and the emergence of domination (see also Donovan and Adams 2007).

10.   It should be noted that in many parts of the world this is still the case.

Chapter 15

Deep Green Violence:
Our Animal Bodies as Sites of Resistance

Todd LeVasseur

Introduction

In this chapter I situate the phenomenon of nonviolence and its historical, ethical, and political implications within the emerging eco-crisis. I take as valid consensus science that suggests humans broadly[1] have precipitated both the planet's sixth mass extinction event and triggered new climatic and oceanic regimes, both of which, from an evolutionary point of view, are going to become increasingly inimical for most extant life forms, including our own. Within this discussion, I want to explore the development of radical environmentalism, focusing especially on Deep Green Resistance. This group specifically challenges many preconceived notions of what counts—tactically, ethically, and strategically—in nonviolent social movements given the larger context of the eco-crisis. It is my hope that this discussion might generate a space for those who both study and practice nonviolence to entertain tough decisions that historically might be seen as taboo avenues of inquiry. This taboo, or at least silently discussed space, might become more critical and might need to become more public, as the human-induced environmental trajectory of the planet presages a very troublesome, radically impoverished future.

Radical Environmentalism

Radical environmentalism is an outgrowth of North American, and especially US, forms of environmentalism.[2] Progenitors to radical environmental actions, such as torching and defacing billboards in the American desert Southwest, can be traced to the 1950s. The *modus operandus* of the movement, however, is the essayist, novelist, and eco-philosopher Edward Abbey's 1975 publication of *The Monkey Wrench Gang*. This novel features an entertaining yet fictitious account of four eco-saboteurs motivated by perceptions of an intrinsically sacred and sublimely beautiful Southwestern desert being systematically destroyed by development, especially for coal, nuclear, oil, rangeland, and residential/tourism reasons. In large part, the book is a summary of Abbey's own views and moral justification for acts of eco-sabotage that he himself clandestinely committed in the region.

As Abbey wrote elsewhere,

> There may be some among the readers of this book, like the earnest engineer, who believe without question that any and all forms of construction and development are intrinsic goods, in the national parks as well as anywhere else, who virtually identify quantity with quality and therefore assume that the greater the quantity of traffic, the higher the value received. There are some who frankly and boldly advocate the eradication of the last remnants of wilderness and the complete subjugation of nature to the requirements of—not man [sic]—but industry. This is a courageous view, admirable in its simplicity and power, and with the weight of all modern history behind it. It is also quite insane. (Abbey 1968: 47)

In this passage, we encounter key tenets of radical environmentalism, including a widely held conviction regarding the intrinsic and often sacred value of the natural world, where such value is present despite possible instrumental uses of this world for human ends. Such views of a sacred, intrinsically valuable natural world are also often mixed with a concomitant concern with the destruction of a pristine, unspoiled wilderness by urbanization and industrialization of the American landscape.[3] Important, especially given the theme of nonviolence, is Abbey's political and ideological critique of the US's and industrial civilization's telos or end game, which is a manifest destiny of perpetual growth that comes at the expense of the natural world, and ultimately and ironically, of human survival. Thus, for Abbey, replacing the natural world in which we evolved with the detritus of industrial civilization and seeing this as beneficial, desirable, and good, is literally insane. This key conviction has mobilized the tactics, ethics, and political critiques of radical environmentalism since.

While a cult classic to this day, Abbey's *The Monkey Wrench Gang* played a pivotal role in the development of subsequent forms of radical environmentalism, including the development of Earth First!, whose four founders were directly informed by Abbey's writing (see, e.g. Taylor 2005: 2561-66). Dave Foreman, one-time editor for *The Earth First! Journal* and co-founder of Earth First!, the leading radical environmental group of the 1980s and the 1990s until the onset and rise of the Earth Liberation Front and Animal Liberation Front, even generated a field manual for 'monkeywrenching'. This term is radical environmental parlance for various forms of property destruction undertaken in defence of the natural world.

In the book's 'Forward!' [sic], Abbey uses an analogy of a stranger invading the reader's home, threatening the family. In such a scenario, 'the householder has both the right and the obligation to defend himself [*sic*], his family, and his property by whatever means are necessary... Self-defense against attack is one of the basic laws not only of human society but of life itself, not only of human life but all of life' (1993: 3). Readers should note a few key moves in this passage as here again, Abbey provides justification for the ethics, tactics, and political philosophy of radical environmentalism with deep implications for discussions about nonviolence. First, he generates a naturalistic fallacy, but one that he accepts: all life defends itself from attack, so human individuals and/or communities, as evolutionary animals, also have the right to protect themselves from attack. Abbey calls this self-defence a basic law of life.

Second, Abbey points out that in this process of self-defence, those defending themselves are justified in using whatever means are necessary. For radical environmentalists, such means have historically been at odds with historically privileged tactical nonviolent actions, especially the strident practice of property destruction advocated by some radical environmentalists. Their justification is that in order to save wilderness, which is conflated with the self and thus home, radical environmentalists are ethically and tactically allowed to use whatever means are necessary to self-defend their ecological home from the attacks of industrial civilization.[4]

Such views are echoed by Foreman, who in chapter 1 of *Ecodefense*, offers key insights into strategic monkeywrenching. His purpose in generating this list of insights that begins the field manual is to recognize that radical environmentalists should embrace other tactics more often associated with nonviolent protests aimed at social change. However, given the slow and at times anaemic success rates of such movements, coupled with the rapid destruction of our wilderness home, sometimes moving beyond typical nonviolent actions are morally justified and politically beneficent. Foreman writes that monkeywrenching is individual; targeted; timely; dispersed; diverse; fun; not revolutionary; simple; and key, deliberate, and ethical (1994: 9-11). On this last attribute, he states,

> Monkeywrenchers are very conscious of the gravity of what they do. They are deliberate about taking such a serious step... Monkeywrenchers—although nonviolent—are warriors. They are exposing themselves to possible arrest or injury. They remember that they are engaged in the most moral of all actions: protecting life, defending Earth. (Foreman 1994: 11)

Here, Foreman is building on Abbey's ethical justification of self-defence. He also adds to it, calling such self-defence the most moral of all actions, with Earth First!ers and other monkeywrenchers being warriors for life. Notice, too, that Foreman describes actions such as spiking trees that are to be logged; engaging in arson; sugaring the gas tanks of bulldozers;

pulling up survey stakes in areas to be developed; and other forms of property destruction as nonviolent. For radical environmentalists, the distinction about nonviolence does not hinge on property destruction, which is seen as tactically (it saves nature, it hurts the bottom line of companies destroying nature, it raises awareness) and ethically (defending Earth, defending one's home) justified, but on whether or not an action will hurt another human (historically seen as not tactically or ethically justified for most radical environmentalists).

Deep Green Resistance and Decisive Ecological Warfare

It is upon the above historical trajectories that contemporary radical environmentalism is built. The movement is now a pan-global phenomenon, ranging from Indigenous resistance to globalization to urban punks liberating minks from fur farms in England to food activists uprooting test plots of genetically engineered plants around the world. What has grown since the start of Earth First! in the early 1980s is the consensus science about what industrial, carbon-based human lifeways are doing to the habitat fitness of planet Earth, where the survival of all terrestrial and aquatic species is increasingly at risk. Radical environmentalists have a detailed political critique in which such 'omnicidal assault' on the planet is premeditated and systematically undertaken by 'powerful and greedy forces, above all, by transnational corporations, national and international banks, and G8 alliances [for which] these menacing foes are part of a coherent *system* rooted in the global capitalist market currently in the final stages of the privatization and commodification of the natural and social worlds' (Best and Nocella 2006: 8). Importantly, and *pace* Abbey's conjecture that unchecked growth at the expense of the natural world, our home, is insane, is the analysis that 'the very concept of "civilization" is problematic as Western cultures have defined it in antithesis to everything wild, non-domestic, animalic, primal, emotional, instinctual, and female, all forces to be subdued and conquered' (Best and Nocella 2006: 9).[5]

Two things should be noted about the above: first, while Best and Nocella prefer the term 'revolutionary environmentalist', I will use the more common term, 'radical environmentalist'. Second, radical environmentalists contextualize their actions within the larger conviction, based on their reading of politics and the anthropological record, that civilization is built upon endemic, often hidden forms of violence that target the Other. Furthermore, civilization is built on systemic exploitation and violence (see Derrick Jensen's premises below), and thus, to end the destruction of the natural world, this system must be stopped by any means necessary. This is a key insight that becomes the basis of radical environmental tactics in regards to property destruction. In other words, civilization is built upon entrenched hierarchies of what ecofeminists call the 'logic of domination', in which binary dualisms are established that conceptually codify and justify the oppression of minority voices and bodies. These possible voices and bodies range from those in the natural world (seen as inferior to the human world) to women (seen as inferior to men) to non-whites (seen as inferior to whites) to the privileging of human culture and society (often assumed to be based on capitalism) over non-human communities.

Given the above dualisms and view of civilization, coupled with concerns about an intrinsically valuable natural world being rapidly altered and destroyed, I want to condense my focus. For the remainder of this chapter, I want to investigate what I take to be the most extreme voices of extant radical environmentalism found today and explore the implications their tactics have on the concept and practice of nonviolence. Here, I want to focus immediately on the tactics, ethics, and political philosophy of Derrick Jensen, Lierre Keith, and Aric McBay, as articulated in their movement manifesto, *Deep Green Resistance* (DGR) (2011).

In this book, the public face and voices of DGR advocate that readers participate in both aboveground and underground activities to bring about what they call decisive ecological warfare. Taken from their website about the book, the authors write:

> Decisive Ecological Warfare (DEW) is the strategy of a movement that has too long been on the defensive. It is the war cry of a people who refuse to lose any more battles, the last resort of a movement isolated, co-opted, and weary from never-ending legal battles and blockades. The information in the DEW strategy is derived from military strategy and tactics manuals, analysis of historic resistances, insurgencies, and national liberation movements. The principles laid out within these pages are accepted around the world as sound principles of asymmetric warfare, where one party is more powerful than the other. If any fight was ever asymmetric, this one is.[6]

This chapter is in many ways shaped by my own trajectory struggling with the implications raised by the above analysis of DGR and their call for DEW. The struggle largely results from the implications of their position, which I feel must be taken seriously by those engaged in issues devoted to nonviolence. This is because of the urgency with which they justify their tactics, their reading of power dynamics on the global stage, and the unapologetic tone they take with expressly advocating actions that might strike many people who would otherwise be sympathetic to their concerns as being far too violent.

First, in regards to the quote shared above, notice that their position builds upon the 'warrior' call of Foreman and the frustration felt by revolutionary environmentalists Best and Nocella. We see that DGR is, therefore, situated in long-standing radical environmentalist tributaries. More so is the fact that their tactics and strategy are based upon a nuanced understanding of violence. For those in DGR, violence is a product of interlinked oppressions, including those of imperialism, neocolonialism, racism, and misogyny, which together make up a larger system that is not redeemable by votes, economic pressure, or creating self-sufficient sustainable 'lifeboats' outside industrial civilization (Keith et al. 2011: 79). Their definition of violence is built upon distinctions between the violence of hierarchy vs. the violence of self-defence, in which 'The violence of hierarchy is the violence that the powerful use against the dispossessed to keep them subordinated' (Keith et al. 2011: 80); violence against people vs. violence against property, in which 'Destroying property can be done without harming a single sentient being and with great effect to stop an unjust system' (Keith et al. 2011: 81); and violence as self-actualization, especially based on male entitlement vs. violence for political resistance. Given we are all moral agents, we must navigate understandings of violence and actions that are either violent or that defend against violence within a larger context of hierarchy and imperialism, through which, to use their understanding and rationale for strategic violence,

> We can decide when property destruction is acceptable, against which physical targets, and with what risks to civilians. We can decide whether direct violence against people is appropriate. We can build a resistance movement and a supporting culture in which atrocities are always unacceptable; in which penalties for committing them are swift and severe; in which violence is not glorified as a concept but instead understood as a specific set of actions that we may have to take up, but that we will also set down to return to our communities. Those are lines we can inscribe in our culture of resistance. That culture will have to include a feminist critique of masculinity, a good grounding in the basics of abuse dynamics, and an understanding of posttraumatic stress disorder. We will have to have behavioral norms that shun abusers...[a] support network for prisoners...and an agreement that anyone who has a history of violent or abusive behavior needs to be kept far away from serious underground action. (Keith et al. 2011: 83)

DGR posits that vertical violence is endemic to civilization, but not to humans and societies *per se*. Rather, those in DGR focus on one way of living: that based on hierarchy. DGR points to the onset of the agricultural revolution as the beginning of our unsustainable, hierarchical path. For DGR, civilization today is now global, with the violence of hierarchy, patriarchy, racism, imperialism, and neocolonialism stretching throughout the globe, impacting all terrestrial and aquatic habitats and thus all organisms. For DGR, the only way to counteract this violence is by building a culture of resistance committed to aboveground and underground acts of DEW.

Some symptoms cited of the violence of fossil fuel and agricultural revolution-based hierarchical industrial civilization include the potential for up to a possible 16-degree Celsius temperature increase by 2100; the reality that 100 to 200 species are killed a day, for up to 73,000 a year, with almost half of all species threatened with extinction due to industrial civilization; that 80 percent of the world's old growth forests and 90 percent of large fish in the ocean are gone; that the breast milk of mammals have carcinogens; that one of three women and one of seven men are sexually assaulted in their lifetimes; and that the acidification of the oceans is killing plankton, which may cause humans to asphyxiate as plankton is actually the biggest producer of oxygen on the planet. When taken together, such figures, backed by sophisticated models and forms of measurement, especially when compared to baseline historical records that predate the agricultural revolution as well as the industrial revolution, are for those in DGR indeed insane.

For these reasons, those in DGR call this an 'omnicidal system', as it destroys landbases in their entirety (Keith et al. 2011: 14). For DGR, this destruction is guaranteed because by definition such destruction is seen as success in the eyes of industrial, patriarchal capitalism. Such omnicidal activity is also a manifestation of the political and social organization of global civilization, which those in DGR claim is mechanized; urban; based on a division of labour and social stratification; militarized; predicated on perpetual growth; defined historically by collapse; hierarchical and centralized; undergoing steadily increasing forms of behaviour regulation; sold to largely passive recipients via monumental architecture and propaganda; and lastly, making the planet uninhabitable for humans and the majority of our non-human kin. They conclude,

> The dominant culture isn't only a serial killer—it's also an amnesiac. Entire species and biomes are not just wiped out, but forgotten. And worse, they are deliberately erased, scratched out of history. People don't recognize this culture's pattern of ecocide because they don't mourn for all that has already been lost, been killed. (Keith et al. 2011: 79)

DGR urges their readers and sympathizers to realize that we are losing our icecaps, a stable atmosphere below 350 ppm of carbon dioxide, biodiversity both aquatic and terrestrial, and the last window of time we have to make a truly sustainable society, all so Exxon and Halliburton and a few others can reap record profits in this short blip of geological time and of human history. Their strong, pointed political critique is based upon recognizing that the violence of the state and here, the corporate-military-industrial state, against the natural world is justified and propped up by economic incentives, and that this violence will not willingly stop by those who profit from this destruction. This last is a key insight, as according to

DGR, the *only way* to get the destruction of our planet to stop, and thus the destruction of the rest of the life forms who live on this planet, is to actively stop industrial civilization through any means necessary, meaning asymmetrical DEW.

Violence (?) and Tactics

I begin this section by borrowing an insight from the anthropologist Talal Asad, who writes, 'A secular state does not guarantee toleration; it puts into play different structures of ambition and fear. The law never seeks to eliminate violence since its object is always to *regulate* violence' (2003: 8). According to radical environmentalists, the state regulates violence so that those in the Global North benefit at the expense of the Global South and at the expense of the planet and the rest of all life forms. Such benefits are based on the rest of the life forms, which have as much right to their homes as we do to ours, which are in the midst of the sixth extinction crisis brought about by a way of living that is based on the most extreme forms of violence ever seen for 10,000 years and growing. This reality and attendant analysis makes me question our roles as animals dependent on certain environmental parameters for our continued survival. It should also present a strong occasion to pause and deeply question our own identities and understanding of nonviolence, given that most of us reading this book, as well as those who are committed to nonviolence, are probably predominantly liberal, progressive in our politics, and who are, understandably, champions of nonviolence. Lastly, most of us are willing to work with the state and want to eschew property destruction while working to create social change.

I think DGR and their call for DEW prompt us to ask a key question: what are we obligated to do to stop this omnicidal destruction? If Jensen is correct (see below premises), then we must deal with the reality that we are surrounded by state-sponsored violence, especially against the natural world, and this state violence will never willingly be stopped by those in power. So, what are we to do? This is the question radical environmentalists attempt to answer and their insights in regards to various discussions and strategies about nonviolence might be hard for us to stomach. Given what is at stake (our survival), these insights at least deserve our sustained and honest discussion, with responses ranging anywhere from active and sophisticated rebuttals to tacit agreement.

Jensen is the most prominent eco-anarchist writing today against civilization, and in his book *Endgame*, he shares 20 premises about industrial civilization.[7] Because of space constraints, I can only share some key ones, which, similar to DGR, point to a systematic form of violence that we often do not recognize. This form of violence is much more maladaptive to our own survival chances, and I argue that moving forward, Jensen's premises must be factored into any political, ethical, and tactical discussions of nonviolence.

Jensen's first premise is 'Civilization is not and can never be sustainable', because 'Our way of living—industrial civilization—is based on, requires, and would collapse quickly without persistent and widespread violence', his third premise.[8] This leads to his fourth premise:

> Civilization is based on a clearly defined and widely accepted yet often unarticulated hierarchy. Violence done by those higher on the hierarchy to those lower is nearly always invisible, that is, unnoticed. When it is noticed, it is fully rationalized. Violence done by those lower on the hierarchy to those higher is unthinkable, and when it does occur is regarded with shock, horror, and the fetishization of the victims.[9]

This leads to premise 5:

> The property of those higher on the hierarchy is more valuable than the lives of those below. It is acceptable for those above to increase the amount of property they control—in everyday language, to make money—by destroying or taking the lives of those below. This is called 'production'. If those below damage the property of those above, those above may kill or otherwise destroy the lives of those below. This is called 'justice'.[10]

Another key premise derives from premise 5 and in part gives rise to the impetus behind the present chapter, as the implications are unsettling and I feel deserve to be grappled with. Jensen's claim in premise 6 is:

> Civilization is not redeemable. This culture will not undergo any sort of voluntary transformation to a sane and sustainable way of living. If we do not put a halt to it, civilization will continue to immiserate the vast majority of humans and to degrade the planet until it (civilization, and probably the planet) collapses. The effects of this degradation will continue to harm humans and nonhumans for a very long time.[11]

Jensen offers another key premise, 8, which is:

> The needs of the natural world are more important than the needs of the economic system. Another way to put Premise Eight: any economic or social system that does not benefit the natural communities on which it is based is unsustainable, immoral, and stupid. Sustainability, morality, and intelligence (as well as justice) require the dismantling of any such economic or social system, or at the very least disallowing it from damaging your landbase.[12]

And premise 15 is: 'Love does not imply pacifism'. And finally, premise 19 is: 'The culture's problem lies above all in the belief that controlling and abusing the natural world is justifiable'.[13] Taken together, Jensen and DGR broadly argue that we live in a hierarchical culture in which hegemonic violence is allowed to flow only one way, and this defines the culture, and the impacts of this are a destroyed planet.

If love does not imply pacifism, and if we are animals, then our bodies become sites of resistance to the violence of industrial civilization. The question becomes: who are we as animals on a planet with other kin and what are our duties to our biological family, given they are under systematic assault? In Abbey's terms, do we have a right to defend our home, and in Foreman's terms, are we called to be warriors for Earth who are guided by his vision of strategic monkeywrenching?

As a writer, teacher, activist, and, importantly, an animal living in increasingly brittle and degraded habitats that are being destroyed, I personally do not have an answer to these questions, except to note that I largely agree with the analysis—political, economic, social, and ethical— of DGR.[14] Furthermore, the emerging scientific record matches up with 10,000 years of a clear trajectory that echoes Jensen's premise 6: this culture is not redeemable or sustainable, and things are about to get even more perilous once carbon dioxide and methane from the last 20 years begin to impact our climate. So what do we do? What counts as nonviolence and violence if we are worried about defending our beloved? What counts as violence and nonviolence if we want to try to halt the sixth largest extinction crisis? What tools are at our disposal, what tactics should we adopt, and what conversations do we need to have about violence and nonviolence given what is at stake—which may include our own species' survival as well as the wellbeing of our progeny for the rest of our time here as a species on Earth?

Active Resistance

There are no easy answers to the above questions and nothing redeeming about possible scenarios that may include human extinction and the extinction of up to half of other life forms sometime in the coming decades. Instead, I want to end this chapter and add to the volume's discussion about nonviolence by drawing on insights from the eco-phenomenologist and neo-animist, David Abram. In an articulate essay 'Reciprocity', Abram relates that while kayaking through Alaska, he had a deep encounter with migrating salmon and their bodies. As the proverbial totem species of the Pacific Northwest, Abram relates how salmon unite the ocean and land, people and nature—they teach wonder, humility, the importance of place and bioregion, and also, especially, a form of ethics. For Abram, this form of ethics is reciprocity, based on the sacrifice of the salmon back to the rivers and other-animal bodies that make up the ecosystem where their own young will be born. Abram titles this insight of reciprocity the 'silver rule', based on the silver scales of the salmon,[15] and writes,

If you wish to receive sustenance from the land, then you must offer sustenance to the land in return... Most specifically, never take more from the living land than you return to the land—not only with nourishing offerings and propitiations, but also with prayers and praises—gifting the breathing earth with your eloquence, honoring the sensuous and sentient surroundings with the heartfelt gratitude of your songs and your dances, feeding the more-than-human world with your grateful attention. (Abram 2004: 77-94)

I want to pose to the readers of this book that this silver rule might require us to think about our tactics, about what counts as gratitude, about what counts as prayer and hymn and dance and grieving and mystery and love, if we realize we live within an omnicidal culture built on 10,000 years of systematic destruction of our home. What actions might we have to take, might we be compelled to take, to turn our animal bodies into sites of resistance and reciprocity with the mystery of life, in order to defend our beloved home, Earth? There are no easy answers for this on a personal level for myself, but for DGR and other radical environmentalists, the answers are clear: we must resist the endemic violence of industrial civilization with whatever means are necessary.[16] This is because:

Resistance is a simple concept: power, unjust and immoral, is confronted and dismantled. The powerful are denied their right to hurt the less powerful. Domination is replaced by equity in a shift or substitution of institutions. [However,] most people are not psychologically suited to the requirements of resistance. The sooner we accept that, the better. (Keith et al. 2011: 167)

This last insight is what makes DGR and their call for DEW problematic for traditional conceptions of nonviolence: they call for active resistance, both aboveground and underground. Their aboveground strategies for DEW are on more familiar terrain in regards to tactics of nonviolence: boycotts and social shaming and noncooperation, staging marches and sit-ins, letter writing, permaculture and organic farming, filing lawsuits, and creating a public culture of resistance. It is their call for clandestine cells operating underground, with strategic, premeditated actions (which may have to be armed) specifically targeted in an effort to destroy, incapacitate, and ultimately dismantle and render inoperable nodes of industrial power so that a ripple effect of industrial collapse occurs, which are most likely psychologically offsetting for many. In their ideal vision, a secretive group of DEW soldiers, working in isolation from one another for security measures, plan and then undertake attacks on transport, oil lines, cell towers, the stock exchange, ports, and energy grids. DGR's hope is that enough resistance fighters in various parts of America (and the world) are working to target vulnerable infrastructure, using *Deep Green Resistance* as a manual. In DEW, when one group acts, another shortly acts elsewhere targeting the infrastructure that powers the industrial civilization that they claim is violently destroying the planet.

In their understanding, 'Ultimately, success requires direct confrontation and conflict with power; you can't win on the defensive' (Keith et al. 2011: 263). If radical environmentalists are correct in arguing that success is averting, or at least slowing the eco-crisis, and if by definition allowing industrial civilization and its inherent violence to continue keeps such success from occurring, then future forms of nonviolence may have to grapple with the reality of having to confront and enter into violent conflict directly with power. DGR asks those who care about life, who have compassion and concern about rejecting all forms of injustice, to be open to the legitimacy of underground acts of decisive ecological warfare, in which for them our animal bodies become sites of active resistance to planetary omnicide.

About the Author

Todd LeVasseur, PhD, is a visiting assistant professor in the Religious Studies Department at the College of Charleston in Charleston, South Carolina, where he is also the Environmental Studies Program Director. His research focuses on the interactions between cultural values and the natural world. LeVasseur has had a variety of journal articles and book chapters published on topics ranging from sustainable agriculture to climate change to eco-linguistics.

Notes

1. I say 'broadly' to recognize the extreme differences, past and present, of colonial and imperial trajectories as well as issues of gender, class, and race, and how these relate to resource use, population size, and other factors that contribute to the eco-crisis.

2. For an early critique of this geographical outlook, see the works of Ramachandra Guha (2000).

3. On the fetishization of wilderness by early radical environmentalists and the environmental movement more broadly, see Cronon (ed., 1996).

4. For insights on divisions that developed through the 1980s and that continue to this day within Earth First! on tactics and ethics regarding property destruction, see Taylor (2005: 519-21).

5. Best and Nocella use the term 'revolutionary environmentalism' to signal the call for a more robust, confrontational form of environmentalism that stands in solidarity with communities of colour, Indigenous resisters, and feminist and social revolutionary movements, all of which are justified because, 'Increasingly, calls for moderation, compromise, and the slow march through institutions can be seen as treacherous and grotesquely inadequate. With the planet in the throes of dramatic climate change, ecological destabilization, and the sixth great extinction crisis in its history, "reasonableness" and "moderation" seem to be entirely unreasonable and immoderate, as "extreme" and "radical" actions appear simply as necessary and appropriate' (2006:

10). As an author who is daily exposed to such environmental metrics in the course of my teaching and research, and who is a champion of environmental justice, I am extremely sympathetic to the above sentiments. Indeed, it is precisely such a revolutionary environmentalist view that problematizes nonviolent tactics, as it seems obvious that the nation-state and international treaties as well as the capital-industrialist world are impotent in their abilities to generate human lifeways that are both just and sustainable. Such a reading may become even more pronounced as we head towards a four-degree Celsius temperature increase by 2100. For more on this, see my discussion on Deep Green Resistance.

6.   Deep Green Resistance (n.d.), at http://www.deepgreenresistance.org/en/deep-green-resistance-strategy/decisive-ecological-warfare.

7.   Jensen (2006), at http://www.derrickjensen.org/work/endgame/endgame-premises-english/.

8.   Jensen (2006), at http://www.derrickjensen.org/work/endgame/endgame-premises-english/.

9.   Jensen (2006), at http://www.derrickjensen.org/work/endgame/endgame-premises-english/.

10. Jensen (2006), at http://www.derrickjensen.org/work/endgame/endgame-premises-english/.

11. Jensen (2006), at http://www.derrickjensen.org/work/endgame/endgame-premises-english/.

12. Jensen (2006), at http://www.derrickjensen.org/work/endgame/endgame-premises-english/.

13. Jensen (2006), at http://www.derrickjensen.org/work/endgame/endgame-premises-english/.

14. For important criticisms of Deep Green Resistance, see LeVasseur (forthcoming).

15. And thus not to be confused with the Confucian Silver Rule.

16. I want to point out the distinction that, having read and taught Deep Green Resistance in a seminar on radical environmentalism, as stated I agree with their ethical, political, and tactical analyses. I also recognize that their three scenarios of the future are plausible and worthy of sustained discussion: (1) no DEW warfare occurs, so the earth is rapidly destroyed, leading to failed states and final strangleholds of industrial power; (2) aboveground actions (see below) occur, somewhat slowing eco-collapse, but that does not halt the inevitable; and (3) active aboveground and underground (see below) actions become sustained and concerted, with inevitable repercussions for those in power, leading to DEW in very real terms. DGR feels this final scenario is the only one that might halt the eco-crisis, possibly giving future generations a chance to restore the planet. For those in DGR, the sooner we enter into stage three of DEW, the better. However, I personally am ambivalent, seeing both pros and cons of DEW as articulated in their missive. Having invited other viewpoints represented by both activists and scholars to my class, the reader should recognize DGR has many critics and others advocate equally plausible tactics to help halt and reverse the eco-crisis. Such discussions are beyond the scope and space allotted for this chapter, but I encourage readers to not only read *Deep Green Resistance* and grapple with its implications for nonviolence; but also actively seek out criticisms of DGR and DEW.

Chapter 16

Nurturing Peace by Subverting
Violence in the Larger Community*

Paul Waldau

Introduction

Each individual reading this chapter possesses a set of abilities I wish to invoke. These eminently human faculties—which can also be thought of as aptitudes, inclinations, skills, or possibilities—are our remarkably robust capabilities for caring about others. Throughout human cultures, a central question has been: who might these others be? As I suggested in 2011:

> Concern for others is such an ancient theme that scholars often have identified it with the very beginning of religion. The best-selling scholar Karen Armstrong in her 2006 book *The Great Transformation* observed how care about all living beings became a hallmark of the important time in prehistory called the Axial Age. During the period from 900 BCE to 200 BCE, ancient religious sages in China, India, Israel, and Greece taught that 'your concern must somehow extend to the entire world... Each tradition developed its own formulation of the Golden Rule: do not do to others what you would not have done to you. As far as the Axial sages were concerned, respect for the sacred rights of *all beings*—not orthodox belief—was religion'. (in Waldau 2011: 132-33)

'Who might these "others" be?' is in fact the root question of ethics in a most important sense. In essence and in practice, ethics is, most directly and simply, an answer to the question: who are the others about whom I should care? There are more elaborate forms of this question, to be sure, such as: who are the others about whom I should care, given that I have finite abilities and there are, as a practical matter, many other limits on this special ability?

This connection of any human being to others is indeed a most basic skill, and efforts to promote peace among nations are widely known examples of this human ability. The academic field of peace studies might be thought by some to offer an expansive answer to ethics and its 'who are the others?' root question. Here, I argue, we must push for more, asking the field of peace studies to recognize that the work done to date in its name has been tragically narrow. I have in mind the standard human-centred explanation of peace that has, with regard to the goal of *ahimsa*, been self-defeating because it characteristically has been silent on humans' many direct and indirect harms to nonhumans. By 'direct harms' I mean violence intentionally inflicted by an actor on specific individuals (such as that which occurs in one-on-one combat or the killing done in slaughter-houses). By 'indirect harms' I mean those that flow from a chosen action but which the actor does not notice or take seriously, examples of which include institutionalized forms of violence that harm humans, or the destruction of a diverse living community because a local human community builds yet another shopping centre termed 'real estate development' and 'progress'.

Our species cannot nurture true peace by focusing on harms to humans alone. Ignoring violence done beyond the species lines reinforces humans' ability to harm other living beings whether human or nonhuman. In effect, ignoring violence to nonhuman individuals and their communities *trains* humans to be violent and self-focused.

Nurturing Peace, Subverting Violence: Our Larger Community

When the idea of nurturing peace among our planet's species is advanced by acts of subverting violence in *all* its forms, the community that can emerge has been described by an insightful geologian, Thomas Berry, as humans' larger community: 'Indeed we cannot be truly ourselves in any adequate manner without all our companion beings throughout the earth. The larger community constitutes our greater self' (2006: 5).[1]

Each human is, in fact, a member of a series of nested communities that run from each family, neighbourhood, local community, and eco-niche to nation(s), species, home continent, and thus our membership in the larger, Earth-inclusive community. Consider how concern for any number of these nested communities within our larger community advances nonviolence, and thereby teaches us and others a key theme around which the Saint Paul University conference was organized—nonviolence can be, as Gandhi and others have noted, a weapon of the strong. Protecting others through nonviolence, whether they are members of our most local community or citizens of our larger community, can demonstrate, as Gandhi modelled so well, that deploying nonviolence can be a tool of the strong. As they have lived out the ideals of nonviolence and *ahimsa*, Gandhi-inspired activists, such as Martin Luther King Jr, have explored how these tools also enhance spirituality and social transformation (see, e.g., Sharp 1973; Sharp and Paulson 2005).

How do we accomplish such nonviolence? For, this is an extraordinary goal in a world in which reports of humans harming humans are an everyday occurrence. In answering this question, I wish to contribute to our collective awareness in multiple ways, not the least of which is helping us all to see what it is that prompts so many humans to continue with violent acts against human others.

In this chapter, I suggest an answer and a path to nonviolence that will seem unusual to some. This is because most of us now live in industrialized or developing societies that are beset by a profoundly dysfunctional human-centredness promoted in a manner that harms not only nonhumans but, ironically, humans as well (Waldau 2013a: 7-9). To solve the dysfunctions, imbalances, and injustices created by what I have come to call 'human exceptionalism' (i.e., holding humans superior to and thus rightly entitled to privileges over all else in our more-than-human world) (Waldau 2013a: 6-9, 144-49), I wish to underscore the value of understanding the heartbeat of nonviolence encapsulated in a phrase from Mahatma Gandhi's *Non-Violence in Peace and War* (1972) that today is often quoted by Thich Nhat Hanh, the well-known Vietnamese Buddhist monk: 'There is no path to peace—peace *is* the path. Acting peacefully in a human-centred world is a challenge, in part, because so many living beings today are marginalized in our societies that purport to protect humans' (in Waldau 2011, 2013a). Given this challenge, I first wish to send the message that it is more than crucial—it is truly foundational—that we work at stopping violence by humans against other humans. In sending this message, I choose to affirm the foundational nature of nonviolence by taking our insights to what might be called their natural limits. That is, I apply them as widely as we can in the local, altogether real places where each of us lives our daily lives.

When taking nonviolence to its natural limit in this way, something becomes clear: the key to understanding the issue of human-on-human violence is, ironically, to look beyond the species lines for ways that we train ourselves to be violent. There are some corollaries to recognizing this key. One is that any gathering that hopes to engage the value of nonviolence that, to meet this end, confines discussion to *only* human-on-human violence is *bound to fail*. Indeed, such a human-focused conference would *ab initio* be a failure, because violence is best understood as a most virulent cancer: if one does not address its multiple metastases, that is, the development of secondary malignant growths at a distance from a primary site of the disorder, then the cancer of violence will continue to arise within us, returning again and again in ugly forms that kill a wide variety of life, including both humans and nonhumans. To understand violence, one needs to be open-hearted enough to see that violence has long taken myriad forms.[2]

To illuminate these insights, I ask the readers to remain as local, personal, and in the moment as possible. Local human-on-human violence occurs in far more than the all-too-familiar forms of domestic violence and violent crimes against strangers.[3] Structural and other forms of collective violence (that is, forms of violence in which a social institution or some other social structure harms citizens by preventing them from meeting their basic needs) also occur in local forms. For example, a dominant group of humans can establish in a local community a political or economics-related system under which the dominant group establishes and maintains power over other humans in that same community who do not enjoy access to policymaking or law enforcement mechanisms that the dominant group monopolizes (Krug et al. 2002).

An illuminating example of staying local was used regularly at the May 2014 Nonviolence: A Weapon of the Strong conference convened in Ottawa, Canada. Conference participants repeatedly referred to another form of violence that played a major role historically in the Ottawa locale and that today continues to play out socially, politically, and personally for local citizens. This is the harsh violence that is inevitable during a powerful people's colonization of lands occupied by another people. The history of conquest of colonized lands is an ugly one that still holds sway today in the ways that modern nation-states such as Canada, the US, Australia, China, Russia, Brazil, and many others subordinate Indigenous peoples.[4] This is one reason that participants in this conference regularly heard the recurring affirmation from speakers that we meet on Anishinaabe Algonquin land. Such affirmations of the local world and its history are surely a move in the direction of noticing and taking seriously the historical violence by which one human group has displaced another. This recurring reference to the local place and its history modelled well an honesty about some of the human-on-human violence that has beset our larger community.

To solve such problems is no easy task. One key to seeing possible solutions has already been hinted at above: understanding the issue of human-on-human violence *requires* that one look beyond the species line to discern the many ways that our forebears trained themselves (and thus us as well) to be violent. Acknowledging that much of the very worst of human-generated violence has been practiced on the more-than-human world and its other-than-human citizens is not a popular idea in today's world, however. Many citizens of modern industrialized states have been trained to think of domination of the more-than-human world as a right conferred on humans through mechanisms such as natural law, modern legal systems, constitutional documents that founded these nation states, and the acts of a divinity that made this world primarily for humans (see, e.g., Waldau 2011: ch. 2, 7, 3013a: ch. 4-8).

Such training prevents many people today from understanding the range of our human propensity for violence; without frankness about this range, it is almost impossible to work together to solve this moral short-coming. Said simply, communal work toward realistic solutions that reduce our own species' tendencies to violence requires us to see all of our forms of violence. It is, in fact, an ancient insight that when a human harms a living being (whether human or not), it is easier to harm again another being (whether human or not).[5] There is a tragic bottom line here: practice harm to living beings and you will be desensitized to other beings. Humans have suffered a lot because of the callousness that humans have toward nonhumans, and nonhumans have suffered terribly because of the insensitivities that humans have toward each other.

This insight underscores why talking only about human-on-human forms of violence is, in a multispecies world, arguably just another kind of violence. This species-centred form of violence has something in common with the indirect forms of violence to humans done by our own human institutions; just as human-on-human violence can be indirect, institutionalized, and carried out collectively at the level of one culture harming another, so too indirect forms of violence can be perpetrated on the natural world and its nonhuman citizens, nations, communities, families, and individuals.

By mentioning indirect forms of violence, I do not mean to play down the far more obvious and direct forms of violence. Cruelty is well known in today's world—for instance, how we produce food for ourselves in factory farming is, as noted below, increasingly a matter of deep concern. Further, direct harms to treasured nonhumans like dogs, cats, horses, and other nonhumans that we bring into our homes are still very common. Laws are beginning to be enforced and even expanded, however. In the US, for example, the vast majority of states have expanded the penalties available to a court that convicts an individual of cruelty to a nonhuman animal (Waldau 2011, 2013a: ch. 5).

In conjunction with learning how common direct violence against non-human animals has been and remains, one learns that certain forms of violence are not only tolerated but importantly, actively promoted within modern societies. If one acknowledges this phenomenon, and if one takes seriously the risk that forms of violence are, as some contemporary sociologists put it, linked or interlocked (Nelson 2011: 369–414), one can appreciate the sociological data confirmation that when harms to nonhumans are allowed, harms to humans are nearby, and vice versa. Because different forms of violence can reinforce each other, a society that tolerates one form of violence is asking for more forms of violence because those who use violence to dominate others are often indiscriminate when it comes to choosing additional targets.

The connection between one kind of violence and another is so common that the presence of certain kinds of violence can be used to assess the likelihood of other kinds of violence. A 1997 study of women's shelters in the US found that 85 percent of women in the shelter disclosed that there had also been pet abuse in the home. Sixty-three percent of children in these shelters talked about animal abuse at home. A 1983 study showed that abused animals were found in 88 percent of homes of families in which child abuse occurred (Ascione et al. 1997: 205-18; DeViney et al. 1983: 321-29).

The upshot is that cruelty at home begets not only more cruelty within the family but also cruelty that eventually reaches beyond the home. This cruelty also reaches across generations, because children of batterers all too often go on to commit the same kind of violence. Cruelty at home also reaches across the species line as well. Consider one feature of breaking this pattern: if the cycle of abuse can be interrupted, not only existing people and nonhuman animals benefit, but future generations do so as well. In a very real way, leaving any kind of oppression unaddressed threatens to allow violence to raise its ugly head again in the future. Some researchers note that there will be no reduction in family violence until all victims—human and nonhuman alike—receive satisfactory protection from our laws (Lacroix 1999).

Peace Studies Beyond the Species Line as a Sign of Strength

For these reasons, I argue that acknowledging nonviolence to nonhuman animals is a tool of the strong. Such an acknowledgment affirms an encompassing understanding of nonviolence and also opens up those wisdom-fostering and compassion-generating forms of life we call 'spiritual' and 'ethical' that, in turn, foster conditions that are far more conducive to human thriving than are the conditions fostered by human exceptionalism (2013a: ch. 11, 12).

For some, such as those engaged in many of the academic departments with titles like Peace Studies, my topic of animals may seem to come from the most removed margins of our ethical vision. Animal protection is indeed a topic marginalized in my own culture's (US) policy discussions, education, mainline businesses, and religious institutions. This is, interestingly, yielding somewhat (see, e.g., Waldau 2013a); although—and let me not overstate this—the situation is ably summed up by Matthew Scully, a prominent US political commentator who was the senior speechwriter of President George W. Bush, at the beginning of a bestselling 2002 book: '[N]o age has ever inflicted upon animals such massive punishments with such complete disregard, as witness scenes to be found on any given day at any modern industrial farm' (2002: x).

One might think that it is true only for nonhuman animals that today's times fit Dickens's classic description: 'It was the best of times, it was the worst of times'. There remains any number of tragic ways in which this claim is also true of certain problems inside the species line. For example, Daniel J. Goldhagen opened his 2009 book, *Worse than War: Genocide, Eliminationism, and the Ongoing Assault on Humanity*, by explaining his title in this way: 'Our time, dating from the beginning of the twentieth century, has been afflicted by one mass murder after another, so frequently and, in aggregate, of such massive destructiveness, that the problem of genocidal killing is worse than war' (xi).[6] Goldhagen's descriptions lead him to conclude, 'mass murder and eliminations are among our age's defining characteristics' (2009: 55). One particularly tragic set of problems has been, as already noted, the harms visited in the last two decades upon the Indigenous, small-scale societies still in existence.

A peace advocate might be tempted to argue that because of such human-on-human harms, we should surely work on human problems first. Such a claim, understandable though it may be, is misguided. Harms to *all* living beings, for the reasons stated above, are interlocked, linked, and mutually reinforcing. This recurring insight was invoked in the conference by the opening prayer of Albert Dumont whose words reflected that many Indigenous peoples continue to teach insights in the spirit of peace with all beings called to mind by the Axial Age sages millennia ago.

This is not a notion, of course, that prevails in many circles of modern industrialized societies. For this reason, some readers will perhaps not know of the developments I discuss. I hope I can convince you that the terrible problems of human-on-human violence are a particularly vile form of a larger problem, namely, how each human chooses to treat the living beings in each's local world—as neighbours or as enemies, as members of other nations or as vermin, as subjects or as objects, as members of our larger community, or unwelcome trash-animals whose sole value is that they serve some human-centred purpose.

Although it is common for many advocates who promote peace and condemn violence to concentrate *solely* on human-on-human problems, that strategy is incomplete. For this reason, I chose in this peace studies conference to talk about issues that go beyond the species line. Others did this as well, although sometimes not so explicitly as I do here. For example, a number of presenters who come from cultures or local communities where the question of relationship to the Earth's other living beings is part of story and song and common sense, pointed out either explicitly or implicitly that getting across the species line is one of the features of human life that make us fully human. In the Power, Ecology, and Healing panel, Heather Milton Lightening's reference to 'all my relations' was followed by a challenge to get such an encompassing understanding into our heads and hearts. Very much in the spirit of this insight,

Ramin Jahanbegloo[7] mentioned prescriptive nonviolence as a moral ideal and imperative based on the sanctity of living creatures. Christopher Hrynkow[8] in the Spirituality, Ecology, and Nonviolence panel displayed the cover of Elise Boulding's *Cultures of Peace* (2000), which features many different nonhuman animals portrayed in the series of paintings on the Peaceable Kingdom artwork of the early nineteenth century US folk painter Edward Hicks.

Thus, in the spirit of Lightening's recurring observation that the challenge is to have the conversation, I seek in this written form of my presentation to push individuals and communities in the modern world to use that suite of abilities for caring with which I opened this essay. Again, each of us has these skills and possibilities within us, such that whenever we enter a room, walk in the natural world, or teach a child, we arrive at that task with these abilities fully intact.

For this reason, I go beyond *only* human-on-human violence, as horrible and morally reprehensible as this recurring form of violence is. Frankly, I have come to see any exclusive focus on humans as problematic—it is what I have referred to elsewhere as 'the fallacy of misplaced community' (Waldau 2013a: 16, 18, 249, 302). For the same reason, I do not in this chapter speak about only human-on-*nonhuman* violence, for that, too, would be radically incomplete. Both human-on-human violence and human-on-nonhuman violence remain today at a fevered pitch. Both come in direct and indirect forms, and both arguably continue to be major failures of the human spirit.

Reflection

Given the human-on-human harms so many humans practice, it is no surprise that concern for humans is high on our caring list. The root question, 'who are the others?', however, pushes us much further than concern for familiar human others. It pushes us to call out the many failures to notice, then take seriously the many harms done to unfamiliar human groups who have long been marginalized. With only minimal work, we can deploy our powerful human abilities to care about others in ways that help us recognize harms whether they are direct or indirect. Among privileged and protected humans, as among those we refer to as educated, there remains much ignorance, some of it willful and self-inflicted, about the harms that follow directly or indirectly from our choices. As great as our considerable ignorance is about harms to other humans, our ignorance about human-on-nonhuman harms and the harms themselves are far more profound. Consider how one observer of Africa in the last few decades describes human problems first and then concludes with a short sentence about the nonhuman dimension that is as revealing as it is chilling:

> In the course of this quarter century, I've watched as the continent—at least its sub-Saharan part—has suffered inexorably escalating misery and depredation. Its population has exploded, but standards of living have continued a remorseless and accelerating decline. Every time I visited, it was hard to imagine that things could get worse for ordinary people, and yet every time I returned, that was indeed the case. Civil wars, genocide, starvation, killing epidemics, and kleptocratic and/or sadistic rulers have been the order of the day. For the most part, aid projects only worsened the situation by lining the pockets of corrupt politicians or displacing the primitive but effective structures of village life, while offering no alternative.
>
> For wildlife the decline has been even more precipitous. (Linden 2011: 79)

It is noteworthy that the former (human-focused) topic is discussed sometimes in important circles, but that the latter problem (wildlife decline), both in its specific African manifestation and in its more general manifestation around the world, seems rarely a matter of discussion in our primary educational institutions, public policy circles, laws, or mainline religious institutions. This is the fallacy of misplaced community-inaction, a by-product of human exceptionalism narrowing down concern to one of our nested communities even as it ignores others. There are, however, community circles in which awareness of a wide, multispecies array of harms is keen. These circles include concerns of many Indigenous peoples about the harms done to Mother Earth or Turtle Island by industrialized societies,[9] the worldwide animal protection movement, and its larger, even more successful cousin known as the environmental movement (Waldau 2013b: 27-44).

In other words, the lifeways of some societies continue to be organized by the insight that the larger community constitutes our greater self. This wisdom, in the almost three millennia since it was advanced by the Axial Age sages, has often been forgotten. Humans, however, have again and again felt the need to notice and take seriously the other-than-human members of our Earth community, and thus, individuals and groups have repeatedly rediscovered, developed, and nurtured the key insight that we are members of a more-than-human community. Of course, again and again the descendants of those who rediscovered this insight have ignored and eventually forgotten this insight entirely. Thankfully, however, the rediscoveries seem to be in our very nature, such that the importance of noticing and taking other living beings seriously has again and again resurfaced. In the twentieth century, for example, some have framed the issue as one of our human possibilities, as is the case with Viktor Frankl, who asserted that 'self-actualization is possible only as a side-effect of self-transcendence' (1992: 115). Going beyond the notion that individual self-actualization is important is the recurring insight that meeting this same challenge is crucial at the species level. History, therefore, seems to suggest that many members of our species have felt a strong *need* to make community with the more-than-human world. One of the best known statements in the academic world is the key mid-twentieth century insight of Aldo Leopold that our species needs to evolve 'from conqueror of the land-community to a *plain member and citizen* of it' ([1948] 1991: 240).

There are, of course, many such affirmations here in the early twenty-first century. One current claim is that our own health is benefitted if and when we 'go wild'. Harvard Medical School's John Ratey and his co-author Richard Manning use this exhortation as the title of a book that asserts that we are wild animals. Ratey, a medical doctor, urges us to see how our self-focus (i.e., our focus on only ourselves and our species) has caused problems: 'Much of the damage that we inflict on ourselves, on others, and certainly on the natural world stems from extreme adherence to the notion of human exceptionalism' (in Ratey and Manning 2014: 8).[10] Ratey and Manning thereby give us a prescription for health and flourishing that contrasts greatly with the diseases of civilization that the subtitle of their 2014 book calls out. Similar reasons for concern about human-centric life appear in what Richard Louv has been saying for decades, namely, that what is at stake is the healthy and full cognitive development of our human children. This is the message of Louv's ground-breaking 2005 book, *Last Child in the Woods*, which carries the subtitle *Saving Our Children from Nature-Deficit Disorder*.

Our Daily World and Personal Realms

In the conference's multiple sessions, a particular richness and diversity prevailed. Presenters were welcomed even though they used many different ways of talking. For example, some used activist rhetoric even as some spoke in academic terms, and others manifested the important concerns typical of peace-studies work that has long focused on wars and harms to marginalized human groups. Throughout, there was a willingness to dialogue and, above all, listen fully and generously to each other. Further, as is typical of interdisciplinary conferences, there were those moments in which one could renew personal connections with longtime friends, just as there were moments when a new acquaintance's or unknown speaker's commitment to see violence in all its ugly forms fostered responsible thinking about real problems faced around the world today.

What was also clear at this conference was that the human-centred mantra: *all* humans matter, is often mere political rhetoric masking a much narrower agenda by which a privileged elite holds power for its own benefit and to the exclusion of many others. For example, consider the shortfall between, on the one hand, the *inclusivist* language of the American

Declaration of Independence's assertion that 'all men are created equal' and, on the other hand, the *exclusivist* political realities that upheld slavery, racism, and sexism for several centuries. Such masquerades are possible because superficial talk invoking themes of universality all too easily is allowed to disguise exclusions that harm both human and nonhuman others.

As for the question of harms to the living beings outside our own species, recall Linden's chilling words, 'For wildlife the decline has been even more precipitous' (2011: 79). Historically, much discourse about peace has not addressed the seemingly constant violence that is needed to maintain industrialized society's complete domination over the Earth, other animals, and even marginalized humans. Having become psychologically adjusted to our species' constant production of violence, many now assume that domination over the more-than-human world is a well-deserved human privilege.

The question of the many failures of mainline institutions to address the harms our species has done, is now doing, and will in the future no doubt continue to visit upon many nonhuman animals is sometimes called 'the animal question', which can mean either 'the set of issues arising for us in connection with all those nonhuman animals *out beyond the species line*' or, alternatively and more scientifically, 'the issues arising because of the inevitable intersection of human animals and nonhuman animals in our shared, more-than-human world' (Waldau 2013a: 16-18).[11] Raising the animal question provides an opportunity to point out that what has been called violence has sometimes been conceived in unconscionably narrow and human-centred ways. Such a narrow framing has been supported by the fact that, as an historical matter, the vast majority of our discussion in the last several hundred years in humans' largest and most dominant societies—as measured by the words of educators, philosophers, religious leaders, and civic leaders—has dealt with morality overwhelmingly with regard to humans *alone*.[12]

From Lose-Lose to Win-Win

It has been argued that whenever a human community shuts out its neighbouring nonhumans, both lose. Likewise, whenever humans find ways of living with other animal communities, both win. These insights have arisen constantly in human society and, just as often, have been forgotten. Here are two instances from different cultures in which this wisdom was stated eloquently: 1) Chief Luther Standing Bear in 1933 observed, 'the old Lakota...knew that man's heart, away from nature, becomes hard; he knew that lack of respect for growing, living things soon led to lack of respect for humans too' (1998: 205-6); and 2) the twentieth-century US naturalist

Joseph Wood Krutch said, 'Whenever man forgets that man is an animal, the result is always to make him less humane' (1949: 186). In both comments one can discern the same insight that drives Berry's suggestion that we cannot be truly ourselves in any adequate manner without all our companion beings throughout the earth, *precisely because* that larger community constitutes our greater self. One can also detect echoes of such wisdom in Ratey's suggestion that much of the damage that we inflict on ourselves, on others, and certainly on the natural world is rooted in extreme adherence to the notion of human exceptionalism.

The most virulent human-centrednesses are, then, lose-lose propositions that impoverish both us and the world's other animals by robbing each of their potential. On the nonhuman side, of course, the many benefits of survival and a healthy community are, from the surviving animals' perspective, obvious. On the human side, because much is at stake in developing more balanced views, a long list can be compiled by looking at history and many different cultures that have noticed and treasured our earth's biodiversity and, in response, developed respect of the kind offered above by Standing Bear, Krutch, and Berry, all of whom stand in the tradition of the Axial Age sages. These traditions are the wellspring of the claim that nonviolence is a tool of the strong, even as it fosters spirituality and social transformation. The deep peace of such nonviolence projects an imagined future onto those communities that foregrounds noticing other animals and taking them seriously.

When we embrace nonviolence, the strikingly important benefits that accrue on the human side, which complement those accruing on the nonhuman side, are easier for us to assess in detail, and they are surprisingly diverse (Waldau 2013a: 9, 16, 56). There are those that arrive in daily life when we recognize our larger community and greater self: we stop inflicting damage on ourselves (Ratey and Manning 2014); we grow in our sense of place and our greater self as we notice our nonhuman neighbours and take them seriously (Berry 2006); we help our children develop cognitive abilities (Louv 2005); and we teach them wisdom when we give them a chance to take charge of their own lives and their connections with nonhuman others. As said by (Sioux) Francis Teton Densmore:

> Let a man decide upon his favorite animal and make a study of it... let him learn to understand its sounds and motions. The animals want to communicate with man, but *Wakan-Tanka* does not intend they shall do so directly—man must do the greater part in securing an understanding. (Densmore 1918: 172)

James Fernandez reiterates Densmore's ancient wisdom:

> Meditation on animals and our relations with them must be very nearly the oldest and most persistent form of human pensiveness; it is doubtful

that we could ever really adequately know our identity as humans if we did not have other animals as a frame for our own activity and reflectivity. (Fernandez 1995: 8)

In education, the benefits of noticing other animals include development of 'educational forms that prompt rich human thinking and imagination' (Waldau 2013a: 16). Why might this be so? When human hearts and minds are hospitable to forms of compassion that strengthen character, the result is not only character building but also an enrichment of the human mind and creative impulses. In addition, much happens when science is done under the motto 'question everything',[13] for then key reflective capabilities like critical thinking flourish. This is particularly evident in the newly emerging field of animal studies, which 'puts students in challenging contexts (human-centered or not) and thereby creates one opportunity after another for self-actualization through self-transcendence and connection to a larger, more-than-human community' (Waldau 2013a: 16).

These benefits stand in stark contrast to the myriad forms of human selfishness fostered by intentionally ignoring other animals in one's locale or the larger world. The win-win approach produces virtues and a robust ability to be concerned for others that contrast markedly with the exclusivist values and virtues that prevail under human exceptionalism regarding other animals. The latter produces a lose-lose world dominated by a self-inflicted ignorance about other animals' realities that is only too congenial to human arrogance and callous insensitivities, while the former produces the win-win combination of awareness and caring.

For these very reasons, broad notions of caring for others and working for peace produce a deep acknowledgment of one's membership in a series of nested communities that go well beyond the human species. These in turn produce 'the benefits of enhanced critical thinking skills and self-actualization through self-transcendence [which] stand opposite self-indulgence and other self-aggrandizement' that stunt human depth and breadth (Waldau 2013a: 16). The result is:

> Connection to our larger community contrasts well with ignorance-driven forms of the exceptionalist tradition that prompt so many of our species to commit what might be called the fallacy of misplaced community—in essence, the notion that the human species alone should be our focus. (Waldau 2013a: 56)

This suite of benefits leads to far greater possibilities of 'self-actualization through self-transcendence' (Frankl 1992: 115) because it fosters 'developed compassion, strengthened character, enrichment of mind and imagination, and enhanced critical thinking skills' (Waldau 2013: 56). This is why challenges to the exceptionalist tradition can draw strength from several domains—the most obvious is realism about other animals' abilities and the harms our worst forms of human-centredness are doing to nonhumans.

The First of Three Stories

I include a series of stories to help the reader map how humans today are walking the terrain beyond the species line. These stories illustrate both potential and risk, especially as they circle around and near the observable realities of other living beings. They also help us see and reflect upon how each of us has been educated for or against (that is, toward or away from) noticing our own animality and that of the living beings outside our own species. Above all, they provide an exhortation for all of us to move beyond the dysfunctional exceptionalisms that ignore the ascertainable realities of many nonhuman animals and their communities.

The first story, which is about an Anglican bishop's encounter with some nonhuman animals, is revealing about the background values inculcated in many modern citizens by virtue of their having been educated in the post-Enlightenment industrialized societies of the modern world. Charles Gore, the English bishop who succeeded Darwin's famous critic Samuel Wilberforce, took personal time to visit the London Zoo, which was at the time the cutting-edge entertainment in the thriving capital of the most powerful empire in the world. After viewing the zoo's chimpanzee exhibit, the bishop commented that the sight of the zoo's captive chimpanzees made him

> ...return an agnostic. I cannot comprehend how God can fit those curious beasts into his moral order... When I contemplate you, you turn me into a complete atheist, because I cannot possibly believe that there is a Divine Being that could create anything so monstrous. (in Sagan and Druyan 1992: 272)

Gore was apparently feigning atheism, for he continued to serve as a bishop in a Christian denomination that asserts a wise God freely chose to create the very chimpanzees who had been removed from their natural world in order to be displayed for the bishop and other visitors to the London Zoo. What Gore was *not* feigning was his belief that he and all other humans were, are, and always will be *qualitatively* different from chimpanzees or any other nonhuman animal.

Yet, by one respected measure, Gore was not all that *quantitatively* different from the 'so monstrous' chimpanzee that sparked this peculiar passage. Our contemporary science of genetics revealed in the mid-1980s that human and chimpanzees are extraordinarily similar in terms of genetic material (Sibley and Ahlquist 1984: 2-15). The figures usually given are 98.4 percent for human/chimpanzee similarity. Subsequent work has suggested that the similarity in the *active* parts of the genetic coding mechanism (as opposed to the inactive, 'junk' part of our DNA) is well *over* 99 percent. In fact, chimpanzees and humans are closer genetically to each other than are two hard-to-distinguish bird species such as the red-eyed vireo and the white-eyed vireo, which are 97.1 percent identical, and closer to each other than are African elephants and Asian elephants (Fouts 1997: 55, 57).

Given that DNA is so hard to see, we might dwell instead on another feature of Gore's experience, namely, the quality of the education he received during his zoo visit, for it is tellingly revealed in his strong negative reaction. The bishop's perception of the chimpanzees was, no doubt, seriously prejudiced by the captive circumstances themselves, for the individuals he saw had been extracted from a complex social and ecological niche whence they originated. These living beings were, plainly and simply, exhibited out of context for the British public's benefit, whether that be edification, education, entertainment, or something else entirely. Before moving on from this salient fact, the reader should engage with what this means existentially for all involved: social beings torn from familial, communal, and ecological contexts. This is no simple reality and it surely is ethically charged, for such captivity requires coercion and domination by humans, which is, from the standpoint of the captive animals, brutal and impoverishing relative to the natural world amidst their own kind.

Gore, perceptive primate that he was, could not have missed the meta-message of the zoo's basic presentation, namely, that his and other humans' education was deemed by someone more important than the captive chimpanzees' freedom to pursue their individual and social needs. He seems not to have noticed that his own worldview could have supported the claim that captivity was contrary to God's purpose, since captivity was not the order initially established by what Gore believed was a divine architect of the universe.

What is even more important is that even if this moral leader had reacted positively to the captive chimpanzees he saw in the London Zoo, he would not have seen them in their home or in terms of their larger ecological, social, and cultural contexts—it has been a major contribution of the science of primatology to search out our cousin great apes' actual realities in *their natural contexts*, and then describe these findings as honestly and dispassionately as good science will allow. The 1994 book, *Chimpanzee Cultures*, reveals that the prized word 'culture' has for decades been widely used for *all* chimpanzee groups (Wrangham et al.). One author in that collection says plainly, 'The last two decades have witnessed a paradigmatic change in our thinking about the behavior of animals' (van Hoof in Wrangham et al. 1994: 267). Equally passionate efforts have been directed toward elephants, cetaceans, and many other animals.[14]

Gore's extraordinary reaction might be explained in other ways, too. For example, it might be explained as an attempt to distance himself from the obvious but uncomfortable fact that he, too, is an animal (Midgeley 1973: 111-35). Sheer ignorance and prejudice might also explain the bishop's comment or the collision between, on the one hand, the deep-seated conviction in Western cultures that humans are set apart from the rest of nature and, on the other hand, the increasing scientific evidence that many of the animals we cage are extraordinary individuals, and some are very much like us in dozens of morally significant ways (see, e.g., Griffin 2001; Bekoff 2007). On the particular issue of consciousness in other animals, consider an observation about consciousness by one of the foremost thinkers today, Daniel Dennett, and place this comment amidst a secular debate in which many have regularly and vehemently denied consciousness to any nonhuman animal:

> Again a curious asymmetry can be observed. We do not require absolute, Cartesian certainty that our fellow human beings are conscious—what we require is what is aptly called *moral* certainty. Can we not have the same moral certainty about the experiences of animals? I have not yet seen an argument by a philosopher to the effect that we cannot, with the aid of science, establish facts about animal minds with the same degree of moral certainty that satisfies us in the case of our own species. (Dennett 1995: 693)

Dennett's observation provides a reason to return to Gore's question about how God can fit those curious beasts into his moral order. Gore was, both by virtue of his general cultural heritage and through the training he received as a member of the Anglican religious establishment, inclined to see the captive chimpanzee individuals as radically different from humans, that is, stemming from different roots (*radix* is Latin for 'root'). Thus, he ignored not only the obvious similarities—many are clearly there if you look at all carefully—he also ignored the obvious fact that, through the power relationship of captivity, *we* have subordinated *them* and thereby fitted them into *our* moral and religious order.

To be provocative and radical (in the sense, again, of going to the *radix* or root), we can ask some simple questions, such as 'Why was the good Bishop Gore so negative?' Had he been prepared by his culture to notice and take seriously any of the chimpanzees' obvious similarities to humans, or had he been trained to dismiss them *ab initio*? Further, why did Gore ignore an altogether relevant feature of his Christian heritage, namely, his awareness that Christianity claims that God had intentionally chosen to make these very creatures *and had pronounced them good*, for the first chapter of the Bible's first book (Gen. 1) again and again emphasizes that creation was good. In fact, verse 31 concludes the chapter with: 'And God saw everything that he had made, and behold, it was very good'.

Another Take on Encountering Our Cousin Apes

A second story helps us see that not everyone suffers from the same exceptionalist heritage that blinded Gore. *Kweli ndugu yanga* was a phrase uttered spontaneously by Dian Fossey's guide, Manuel, when, after searching for free-living gorillas, both Fossey and Manuel encountered their first free-living gorilla family (Mowatt 1987: 14). The situation was a tense one, of course, for both Fossey and Manuel had heard stories about gorillas that included some potentially misleading accounts of their viciousness. On this day, Fossey and Manuel were able to approach a gentle group as the family fed. Spying them for the first time, Manuel exclaimed, *Kweli ndugu yanga!* Although this Swahili phrase translates mechanically into English as 'truly (*kweli*) my (*yanga*) kin (*ndugu*)', Manuel's excited utterance is more truly captured by the freer translation, 'Surely, God, these are my kin' (in Mowatt 1987: 14). Fossey herself said, 'These words in Swahili, whispered by the awestruck Manuel, who was also seeing his first gorilla, summed up exactly what I was feeling' (in Mowatt 1987: 14).

Manuel's simple but altogether connecting and remarkable utterance contrasts wonderfully with the negativity of Gore. Further, it begs questions about the attitude of citizens in industrialized countries, for it captures so much that those schooled in primary and higher education have lost of the world about us. In effect, this story captures—the word is chosen advisedly—a very different, altogether disruptive and dismissive attitude about the living beings around us. It is an attitude that now dominates in more than education but also law and other public policy circles, business, and mainline religious institutions in the developed world. Public policy, law, and mainline education reflect something of the spirit of Pope Pius IX, who led the Catholic tradition from 1846 to 1878, and is reported to have told the anti-vivisectionist Anna Kingsford, 'Madame, humankind has no duties to the animals', and then backed up his assertion by 'vigorously' opposing the establishment of a society for the protection of animals in Rome (in Gaffney 1986: 149). This is, in effect, the set of values that dominates the cultural terrain walked by modern consumers.

More on the Local Cultural Terrain of 'Advanced Industrialized Societies'

A third story provides more about this modern terrain as it has been shaped by a deeply dysfunctional human exceptionalism. The following court-based exchange in a trial of one of the 50 US states reveals key features of the modern US legal system. Scully describes the context of his story as follows:

Just how bereft of human feeling that entire industry has become was clear at a municipal court case heard in Warren County, New Jersey, in the fall of 2000. A poultry company, ISE America, was convicted of cruelly discarding live chickens in trash cans. The conviction was appealed and overturned, partly on the grounds that ISE America (short for International Standard of Excellence) had only six employees overseeing 1.2 million laying hens, and with workers each left to tend two hundred thousand creatures it remained unproven they were aware of those particular birds dying in a trash can. (Scully 2002: 285)

The exchange in the court went as follows:

Lawyer (for the corporation): We contend, Your Honor, that clearly my client meets the requirements [of the law]. Clearly it's a commercial farm. And clearly the handling of chickens, and how chickens are discarded, falls into agricultural management practices of my client. And...we've litigated this issue before in this county with respect to my client and how it handles its manure...

The Court: Isn't there a big distinction between manure and live animals?

Lawyer: No, Your Honor. Because the Right to Farm Act protects us in the operation of our farm and all of the agricultural management practices employed by our firm. (Scully 2002: 285-86)

The judge's common-sense query, 'Isn't there a big distinction?', reflects a widely held belief characteristic of many people today, and thereby reveals that there are vestiges of decency regarding unnecessary violence that still have a certain traction in daily conversation patterns. But conversations in legal, political, and economic circles are dominated by a conception of nonhuman animals as property and therein deny that violence to such property is a social problem, even in the flagrant situations of factory farming. Consumers of such products are, simply said, trained not to care. A decade ago, Michael Pollan framed the issue as one of intentional forgetting, a version of self-inflicted ignorance:

What is perhaps most troubling, and sad, about industrial eating is how thoroughly it obscures all these relationships and connections. To go from the chicken (*Gallus gallus*) to the Chicken McNugget is to leave this world in a journey of forgetting that could hardly be more costly, not only in terms of the animal's pain but in our pleasure, too. But forgetting, or not knowing in the first place, is what the industrial food chain is all about, the principal reason it is so opaque, for if we could see what lies on the far side of the increasingly high walls of our industrial agriculture, we would surely change the way we eat. (Pollan 2006: 10-11)

The problem of humans turning away from such harms and the mental habits fostering such extensive violence haunts many approaches to peace studies that choose to forget, that is, intentionally choose not to notice, let alone take seriously, the violence visited upon chickens and food animals such as pigs, cattle, and many other domesticated mammals. When such realities are ignored rather than frankly acknowledged, profoundly important learning and unlearning dynamics are missing in our exploration of realities. The meta-messages to students in readings, classrooms, and lectures become one-dimensional, foregrounding violence to humans even as great violence remains an integral part of daily acts like eating. Consider how a speech on the floor of the US Senate in 2001 framed such a facile dismissal of violence to food animals as morally troubling:

> Our inhumane treatment of livestock is becoming widespread and more and more barbaric... A 23-year-old Federal law...requires that these poor creatures be stunned and rendered insensitive to pain before this [slaughter] process begins. Federal law is being ignored. Animal cruelty abounds. It is sickening.[15]

The situation in the US today remains the same, such that there still is little to no state and federal protection for the vast majority of non-humans that our society is impacting, namely, farm animals. The fact that such extensive harms exist throughout our societies but are ignored says much about what we consider as violence and peace. Ironically, the opportunity to teach key features of contemporary legal systems, the values that drive our education and public policy, and our tolerance of institutionalized violence in violation of the law on the books (which, of course, is unenforced) says much about the human-centred vision that dominates calls for peace now.

Learning and Unlearning Dynamics

Working with the appraisal that Scully indicated above—'No age has ever inflicted upon animals such massive punishments with such complete disregard, as witness scenes to be found on any given day at any modern industrial farm'—makes clear that we live amid violence. The resulting complacency of a consumerist public desensitizes everyone and it cannot be too surprising that many consumers remain uncaring about the lives they impact. What can be the integrity of discussions of *ahimsa* that turn their backs on such extensive, intentional, and unnecessary violence? What can be gleaned from the fact that *cruelty is the norm*, for it is known *even if not acknowledged openly* that 'massive punishments...inflicted upon animals with such complete disregard' dominate public policy, law, and education (Scully 2002: x).

But keep in mind that there is good news as well: Scully also claimed, 'No age has ever been more solicitous to animals, more curious and caring' (2002: x). This caring has been evident in the emergence of a field called 'animal law' within legal education over the last few decades. In 2000,

Harvard Law School offered its first animal-law course, called Animal Rights and taught by a leading proponent of specific legal rights for certain nonhuman animals. The Harvard course was the direct result of petitions for such a course that were signed year after year by scores of students at this high-profile law school. From 1977, when the first such course in the US was taught at Seton Hall Law School, to 2000, fewer than a dozen such courses were offered at US law schools. But when Harvard Law School announced its course, the American legal education establishment took notice. So did the media, and courses in animal law multiplied rapidly in law schools around the world—within the following decade, the number of such courses increased tenfold in the US. Such an increase would be significant in any educational field, of course, but this development was particularly noteworthy for a variety of reasons. First, the demand for new courses was driven almost solely by students. Second, the development took place at a level of education (law schools) characterized by an entrenched tradition of open discussion that is among the most developed in modern education circles.

The developing student demand is anchored in 'a deeply personal dimension of connection with nonhuman animal individuals themselves' (Waldau 2013a: ch. 1). There are almost 200 accredited law schools in the US. In a single decade, the number of these graduate-level professional schools offering an animal-law course shifted from fewer than a dozen to more than two-thirds (including virtually every one of the 15 most prestigious schools). This shift is inherently interesting, but the inauguration of such courses because of student petitions is most telling: students want education that is relevant, and students find open discussion of industrialized societies' present treatment and future possibilities with other animals to help them consider what sort of changes would foster the kind of compassion-intensive society in which they would like to live (Waldau 2013a: 114-15).

There is even more good news: the demand for courses involving nonhuman animals is spreading. Throughout the academic world, inquiries regarding humans' relationship to the more-than-human world have developed on their own again. A good example is the Harvard summer term course, Animals: Religion and Ethics, which combines inquiries about humans' spiritual side with our ethical connection to the living beings around us. As with the animal-law courses, such courses are relevant to the ethics of caring in daily lives. Further, such courses are a very effective vehicle for teaching ecological understanding. The field of animal studies can be understood to be 'more than a discipline—it is in reality a megafield whose sweep is broad in response to the great diversity of ubiquitous nonhuman life and the astonishing complexities of the human-nonhuman intersection' (Waldau 2013a: 301).

Collectively, the emergence of a concern to be connected to the natural world challenges the fundamental separation of humans from other animals that promotes human exceptionalism. Awareness of our larger community is, in fact, a reaffirmation of an ancient preoccupation. When many consider the diverse ways in which humans are in relationship with others whether human or non-human, it is not surprising to find 'animals make us human' themes, such as those that drive Deborah Bird Rose's *Dingo Makes Us Human* (1992) or Temple Grandin and Catherine Johnson's *Animals Make Us Human* (2009). The roots for such values can be seen in ecologist Paul Shepard's (1978) *Thinking Animals: Animals and the Development of Human Intelligence:*

> Animals are among the first inhabitants of the mind's eye. They are basic to the development of speech and thought. Because of their part in the growth of consciousness, they are inseparable from a series of events in each human life, indispensable to our becoming human in the fullest sense. (Shepard 1978: 2)

Anticruelty sentiments, although often overridden by the property status of nonhuman animals in all modern legal systems, have ancient roots and thus are persistent and diverse. As a scholar of Hinduism points out, 'The term "nonviolence" (*ahimsa*) originally applied not to the relationship between humans but to the relationship between humans and animals' (Doniger 2009: 9). What is at stake in recognizing both present capacities to care about others and their ancient roots is our taking responsibility for choosing a future:

> Now to the very heart of the wonder. Because species diversity was created prior to humanity, and because we evolved within it, we have never fathomed its limits. As a consequence, the living world is the natural domain of the most restless and paradoxical part of the human spirit. Our sense of wonder grows exponentially: the greater the knowledge, the deeper the mystery and the more we seek knowledge to create new mystery. (Wilson 1984: 10)

Our larger community, then, is within the sphere in which we act—we can promote peace, or we can think of ourselves as at war with the natural world. The latter is a distorting image fostered by some, such as Philo of Alexandria, who about the time of Jesus argued that humans are in a continuous war with other animals 'whose hatred is directed...towards...mankind as a whole and endures...without bound and limit of time' (1968: 85).

We have an alternative in our caring about others and in our desire to live in a peaceable kingdom. Consider the power suggested by the observation that, 'every choice we make can be a celebration of the world we want to live in'.[16] This is both a power and a burden, of course. It is a door through which human self-actualization may be accessed. Passing through this door is no easy challenge, for as one insightful person put it, 'It's hard enough to start a revolution, even harder still to sustain it, and hardest of all to win it. But it is only afterwards, once we've won, that the real difficulties begin' (Ben M'Hidi in Pontecorvo 1966).

Such a revolution is needed in peace studies, basic and higher education, public policy, law, economics, scientific exploration, environmental ethics, and much more—in other words, in our daily lives and local worlds. Our choices in these personal domains, as well as our activism to change education, law, and public policy, will project an imagined future onto our children and succeeding generations. Will we project violence or *ahimsa*? This is the unavoidable question for each person and her or his personal choices.

My personal hope is that concern for our larger community can help us self-actualize, surmount the dysfunctional and arrogant forms of human exceptionalism, and thereby reinvigorate education, ethics, and peace studies; spark deep interest in nonviolence of an encompassing sort; and foster deep appreciation of our larger community as well as connection with the nested communities in which each of us belongs.

About the Author

Paul Waldau, PhD, is an educator, scholar, and activist working at the intersection of animal studies, law, ethics, religion, and cultural studies. A professor at Canisius College in Buffalo, New York, he is the Director of the Master of Science graduate program in Anthrozoology, for which he has been the lead faculty member since the program's founding in 2011. He has completed five books, the most recent of which are: *Animal Studies—An Introduction* (2013) and *Animal Rights* (2011).

Notes

* This chapter is based on a keynote lecture at the conference, Nonviolence—A Weapon of the Strong: Advancing Nonviolence, Spirituality, and Social Transformation, Saint Paul University, Ottawa, Ontario, 8-11 May 2014.

1. The term 'geologian' is appears at http://thomasberry.org/publications-and-media/thomas-berry-selected-writings-on-the-earth-community (accessed 26 May 2016).

2. For a typology of the types of human-on-human violence, see World Health Organization (2016) at http://www.who.int/violenceprevention/approach/definition/en/. While this typology does not include human-on-nonhuman violence, the variety and scope of different kinds of violence are easy to discern in this human-focused typology.

3. For more on the variety and prevalence of different forms of human-on-human violence described here, see Krug et al. (eds.) (2002), at http://www.who.int/violence_injury_prevention/violence/world_report/en/.

4. See for example, Goldhagen, who observes, 'More groups of Indigenous peoples have likely been destroyed during our age than in any other comparable time period' (2009: 54).

5.   Regarding the ancient insight connecting human-on-human violence to humans' violence to nonhuman animals, see Thomas (1983: ch. 4). Thomas mentions ancient Athenians, Old Testament sources, the work of Thomas Aquinas, and the eighteenth-century figures William Hogarth and Immanuel Kant. Thomas summarizes, 'But this view did not originally reflect any particular concern for animals; on the contrary, moralists normally condemned the ill-treatment of beasts because they thought it had a brutalizing effect on human character and made men cruel to each other' (1983: 150-51).

6.   The opening sentence in Goldhagen's preface states, 'Hundreds of millions of people are at risk of becoming the victims of genocide and related violence' (xi). A short second paragraph describes some places of extreme risk, and then the third paragraph is the one quoted in the text.

7.   See Jehanbegloo's chapter 2 in this volume.

8.   See Hrynkow's chapter 9 in this volume.

9.   See, for example, Dumont (2007) or Idlenomore (2016), at http://idlenomore.ca.

10. The afflictions of civilization referred to in the subtitle are listed and explained starting at page 39 in Ratey and Manning (2014).

11. See Waldau (2013a: 16-18) for my argument that the second description of the issue is the more scientific description.

12. Two different sources that argue that traditional ethics has been overwhelmingly anthropocentric are Jonas, '[A]ll traditional ethics is anthropocentric' (1984: 4) and Gustafson (1981: 96-97).

13. This is the motto of the Science Channel (2016), at http://www.sciencechannel.org (accessed 26 May 2016).

14. For a summary of the complexities of these animals, see Waldau (2001: ch. 4). Detailed arguments about cetaceans appear in White (2007) and about elephants in Chadwick (1992).

15. Byrd (2001), at http://www.nyshumane.org/articles/speechSenatorByrd.htm.

16. This quote is commonly attributed to Frances Moore Lappe and Anne Lappe, at https://www.changingworld.com/every-choice-we-make-can-be-a-celebration-of-what-we-want-francis-moore-lappe-anne-lappe-art-by-jennifer-hewitson-printed-on-recycle-paper.html.

Part V

Nonviolence and Future Directions

Chapter 17

Wondering about Wonder as an Antidote to Our Violence against Earth

Simon Appolloni

Introduction

> Instead of entering into communion with such powers of the universe,
> our modern industrial civilization seeks to triumph over these wild forces
> that have dominated the affairs of the planet from earliest times. Indeed
> it does sometimes seem that we have conquered the wild though our
> inventions... We have intruded into the composition of the atmosphere.
> We have damned the great rivers of the world. We have diminished the
> inherent fertility of the soils of the Earth thinking that we were bringing
> about an improvement. (Berry 2001: 200)

It is not hyperbole to state what many scientists and environmental
thinkers have been saying for some time now, that humans have become
a geological force.[1] The aggregate effects of our modern industrial civilization, while having yielded many fruits, have also brought about the
destruction of rainforests, the acidification of oceans, the depletion of
aquifers, the degradation of soils and waters, the damming of rivers, and
the pollution of the atmosphere. Humans have the ignoble distinction
of being the cause of the sixth major extinction in Earth's history. The
sheer volume in which chemicals, such as nitrogen and phosphorous, flow
into waters because of agro-industrial processes (mainly fertilizers leach-
ing into rivers), as well as from sewage and fossil-fuel burning, is making
large bodies of water anoxic (devoid of oxygen), thereby killing marine
life (Rockström et al. 2009: 1-32). I am calling these injurious, destructive
forces what they are: violent.

Why is it that our modern industrial civilization—as a whole—seemingly
countenances these violent actions it perpetrates against Earth? A possible response, whose ethos undergirds this chapter, comes from cultural
historian Thomas Berry, who maintains that our modern civilization on
the whole currently lacks a sense of communion, a sense of intimacy with
the world around us, which, in turn, has fostered a view of the world as
containing mere objects to be exploited (in Swimme and Berry 1992: 243).

Yet, Berry also suggests that the capacity to foster that sense of communion, thus cultivating nonviolent expressions of being on Earth, actually lies within us as a primordial emotion: wonder.

Berry is not alone in promoting the significance of wonder; a number of authors, such as Mary Evelyn Tucker (2003), Brian Swimme (2011), and Celia Deane-Drummond (2006), corroborate the significance he affords it. While these three ecologically minded thinkers hold differentiated understandings of wonder, each in various ways is influenced by Berry's writings, and each, along with Berry, maintains that when fixed at the natural world, wonder can serve as a corrective, neutralizing the violence that our modern civilization perpetuates toward the environment. Ultimately, this primordial emotion within us can serve as a guide and impetus to stop us from destroying and to encourage us to protect the environment. Put another way, from what all four suggest, wonder could serve as an antidote to our violence against Earth.[2]

If this is the case, and it is my sense that it is, much is not clear. In what manner, for instance, can wonder serve as a guide and impetus to help steer us away from our destructive path and to foster a communion with the natural world? With the exception of Deane-Drummond, the authors above are not entirely clear about the process in which wonder fosters a communion with Earth. If wonder is elemental to who we are as a species, as the authors above suggest, what happened to it that seemingly has kept our modern industrial civilization indifferent to the violence it has perpetrated against the natural world?

Finally, these four authors suggest—and not incorrectly—that wonder remains fixed at the natural world. Yet, if we affirm humans to be truly part of the natural world (as ecologists and evolutionary scientists have been stressing for some time now), why should our gaze of wonder remain fixed solely at the natural world? Should wonder's gaze not also focus on the human, as part of the natural world? These are the questions I will be investigating within this chapter. In addressing them, I will demonstrate how this emotion can nurture a wisdom that motivates us to respect the natural limits of Earth's resources, recognize our limits to know the world with certainty, and ultimately take responsibility for the violence perpetrated against the environment. Moreover, when wonder's gaze is also focused on human individuals and communities as part of the natural world, there arises the possibility of fostering a more integral approach to creating nonviolent expressions of being on Earth.

This exploration is but a preliminary discussion of wonder and violence. Yet, evoking wonder, as Berry, Swimme, and Tucker do, and trying to understand its processes, as Deane-Drummond does, appear timely and crucial endeavours. The wealth of data scientists have accumulated on climate change, species loss, and the depletion of fresh water seems to be doing little to counter the violence of our modern industrial ways (Dean-Drummond 2013: 73). Knowledge, it would seem, is not enough. What Berry is suggesting is that perhaps it is time to pay attention to more visceral connections humans can foster toward the world about us—feelings that arise from wonder that could help us relate to the planet in a nonviolent way.

While relatively little has been written about wonder in relation to violence against Earth and its potential for fostering intimacy between humans and the natural world, fortunately, much has been written about wonder as a potent emotion by a number of philosophers and critical thinkers, each inquiring how and to what degree this emotion can spur our understanding of the world around us. Hence, along with the works of Berry, Tucker, Swimme, and Deane-Drummond, I will consider what some contemporary theorists are saying about this emotion. To begin, it will be helpful to understand the violent paradigm of our modern civilization.

Establishing the Contours of a Violent Paradigm

I refer to violence here as the intentional use of physical force by humans against individuals and/or communities that results (whether knowingly or unintentionally) in damage, injury, some form of deprivation, or even death. The individuals and communities are not only humans. I extend individuals and communities to include flora and fauna and ecosystems across the planet. To be sure, some violence is unavoidable. For example, when we mine, we destroy parts of the Earth. Notwithstanding this reality, a distinction needs to be made between need and greed. Mining for coal, for instance, when renewable energies readily present themselves, is unnecessary. Moreover, when entire mountain tops are levelled to extract this fossil fuel, the act becomes senseless.[3] Erupting volcanoes and earthquakes are also violent, destroying entire ecosystems and human communities. I distinguish here between these naturally occurring violent phenomena and the anthropogenic pressures on the Earth systems brought about by our modern industrial civilization. The former is an integral dimension of how the planet functions; the latter is human-constructed violence, and when spurred by greed and apathy, is senseless.[4]

For example, when Bill McKibben declared in 1989 that we have arrived at the 'end of nature', he was underlining the degree to which the human presence has inexorably marked 'every inch of the planet' (xix). Scientists now refer to our current geological era as the Anthropocene to underscore the extent that anthropogenic pressures on Earth systems are at a point at which the possibility of sudden and catastrophic planetary environmental change cannot be ruled out (Rockström et al. 2009: 2). Through this senseless violence, humans have become a geological force or, as Berry more aptly labels, an affliction of Earth and even a demonic presence (1988: 209). Instead of entering into communion with the natural forces that have created the wondrous world around us, our modern industrial civilization has sought to conquer them, as the quote from Berry that opens this chapter attests. In keeping with a medical metaphor, one might say that humans are detrimental to the health of the planet and a dangerous poison to life.

There is an important irony to consider when making this claim. That humans are injurious to the health of the planet does aptly convey the violent essence of human *actions*, but it does not necessarily assign a violent essence to *human nature*. In fact, the destruction of the natural world has been carried out largely by good people and ostensibly for noble reasons: the betterment of life for humans and our offspring (Berry 1996). Moreover, not all cultures and peoples are equally indictable for this offence. Liberation theology, along with more constructive ecological responses to the preferential option for the poor, has revealed that much of the appropriation, destruction, and alteration of life has been carried out predominantly by the industrialized countries of the North (Scharper 2013: 169, 214 f39). In other words, our violence could be considered a disorder of our civilization, brought about by a portion of the human family whose cultural system too often coerces us to indulge our desires and deny biotic realities.

Wonder and Its Role

Wonder is an intriguing and complex human emotion that we experience, evoking images from childlike awe-inspiring surprise at the sight of butterflies landing on our chests to amazement at extraordinary occurrences—such as a falling star—to the arousal of puzzlement, reverence, and even fear or foreboding, to the primordial mystery of existence, when gazing at an erupting volcano, for instance. Wonder's influence on humans has been the subject of much discussion by reflective thinkers throughout the ages. Plato placed wonder as central to all philosophical thought.[5] Yet, despite his praise for it, wonder has received an ambivalent reception from subsequent thinkers. Francis Bacon, for instance, viewed it as broken knowledge, which ought to diminish as scientific investigation progresses (in Hepburn 1984: 137). Descartes accepted its usefulness, as it prompts us to focus on phenomena that surprise us; yet, he cautioned us to rid ourselves of wonder soon after, because it could have us dwell in a state of astonishment, which, he surmises, disinclines a person to investigate the causes of things and to arrive at clear ideas (in Rubenstein 2008: 15). By the eighteenth century, Deane-Drummond (2006: 5) informs us, wonder became associated with a dull stupor, the hallmark of the ignorant and barbarous.[6]

Today, there is a resurgence of wonder amongst many thinkers in a more positive light. Specifically, for my purpose here, some are promoting wonder for its spiritual-ethical implications, that is, its capacity to foster a particular relationship with the natural world. Rachel Carson adeptly captures this aspect of wonder when she says, 'I believe that the more clearly we can focus our attention on the wonders and realities of the universe about us, the less taste we shall have for destruction' (2008: 559). It is precisely this distaste for perpetrating senseless violence toward Earth that Berry, Tucker, Swimme, and Deane-Drummond wish to have us develop—and by 'us', I mean humanity in general, but specifically those humans engrossed in the wonders of modern industrial civilization.

Tying together insights from religion and psychology, scholar Robert C. Fuller ascribes an indispensable evolutionary function to wonder, arguing that this emotion elicits a more-than-physical reality and, therefore, enhances our capacity to understand deeper patterns in the way the universe unfolds. By bringing our attention to our surroundings, Fuller argues, wonder essentially helps humans to consider life from new perspectives. This open-ended or heuristic approach to life, he suggests, perhaps explains how humans have been able to adapt to various challenging climates and living situations throughout history. But it is not just an open-ended approach to life that wonder can elicit. Fuller maintains that because of its potential to elicit belief in a more-than-physical reality, wonder can also serve as a defining element of spirituality, which he defines as 'a person's motivation to align his or her life with some kind of higher order' (2006: 2). This last point has significance for how we understand religion, Fuller notes. He points to the work of theologian Friedrich Schleiermacher who, contending with the onslaught of anti-religion Enlightenment thinking in the early nineteenth century, had suggested that religion (which for Schleiermacher was Christianity), evokes a 'feeling of absolute dependence' (in Fuller 2006: 3). Writing well over a century after Schleiermacher, German theologian Rudolph Otto in *The Idea of the Holy* (1958) develops more fully the spiritual-ethical import of wonder. Otto speaks about the inexpressible mystery (Latin: *mysterium*) that is at the same time terrifying (*tremendum*) and fascinating (*fascinans*). It is this sense of wonder, Otto asserts, that explains why a person can feel a sense of communion with the numinous or holy.

Very much inspired by Otto's conception of wonder, Berry goes further with this emotional state, suggesting that experiencing wonder is one of our main purposes for existence. 'While the universe celebrates itself in every mode of being', Berry writes, 'the human might be identified as that being in whom the universe celebrates itself and its numinous origins in a special mode of conscious self-awareness' (1999: 19, 166). Berry sees wonder, then, primarily as the means through which we open ourselves to the 'numinous mystery that is being revealed to us' (1988: 221). This arguably religious experience can be both benign, such as a sunset viewed from a back porch on a clear day, or terrifying, such as a high-magnitude earthquake or being rolled under the sea by a breaking wave. These experiences—both benign and (natural-occurring) violent moments, Berry avers—can evoke admiration, mystery, and a sense of the sacred, and, most importantly for him, they can foster an intimate human relationship with the natural world.

In their collaborative work, *Journey of the Universe*, Tucker and Swimme affirm Berry's understanding of wonder. They argue that wonder is one of our most valuable guides on our journey into the future as human beings. Specifically, they argue that by wondering at the roughly 14-billion-year expansion and evolutionary development of the universe, we realize we are children of the stars and, hence, part of a cosmic community (2011: 113-14). While Berry emphasizes wonder's ability to evoke within us a 'world beyond human explanation' (2002: 15), Swimme and Tucker emphasize wonder's ability to affirm our belonging to the universe. Through wonder we awaken an understanding that we are Earthlings and that the story of the universe is also *our* story.

Looking at wonder somewhat differently, as a 'heightened psychological and emotional state engendered by different experiences' albeit with the religious sense espoused by Berry, Celia Deane-Drummond views wonder as an important phase in our continuous development of wisdom (2013: 71). Deane-Drummond draws our attention to the early saints and mystics who, in sensing 'a pregnant sense of the world infused with the presence of God', experienced 'a strong sense of wonderment' (2013: 74). In a similar manner, she maintains, focusing our wonder on not only the pleasant but the disturbing aspects within the natural world can help nurture a prudence within us that has us respect the natural limits of Earth's resources and take responsibility for the harms we are causing to the environment (Deane-Drummond 2006: 14).

Notwithstanding their distinct perspectives on the role of wonder, Berry, Swimme, Tucker, and Deane-Drummond seem to elevate wonder as a key pathway into what it means to be human. In all cases, wonder is not just another emotion, but the means by which humans can regain a sense of communion with the natural world. But how might wonder actually accomplish this task? Our authors all stress that the natural world demands a more-than rational response, which is no doubt why Berry maintains that wonder finds its greatest expression through moments of child-like innocence (1999: 16). They also all share a sense that the process wonder inaugurates has waned at this time of history for one reason or another or that it has become prevented from effecting any transformation within us (Swimme and Tucker 2011: 101-4; Berry 2002: 15;

Deane-Drummond 2006: 1-6). It is only Deane-Drummond, however, who delves to any length into the actual process of moving from wonder to a sense of communion. How might we understand this movement?

How Wonder Might Function

Philosopher Jerome A. Miller applies the metaphor of a hinge to describe the emotional and cognitive movement that wonder initiates. He suggests wonder serves as a gateway to the unknown 'that turns [our] attention away from the immediately present toward what can only be known through questioning' (Miller 1992: 38). There is a sense with Miller that wonder operates at a never-ending threshold stage as a continuous point of departure into the unknown. Yet, absent from this understanding is any sense that knowledge of what we are experiencing should be the goal of the wonderer. In other words, the point is not to get us through the door, but to experience the throe of opening it, even if it is 'awe-full and terrifying' (Miller 1992: 51). By allowing ourselves to become entangled in this throe of wonder, Miller suggests, we experience even familiar objects as mysteries. In this manner, redolent of Otto's *mysterium tremendum fascinans*, wonder evokes characteristics of a religious experience, as it has us marvel at what stands before us: the realization that we are before the other as other, which evokes a reality that is ultimately recognized as sacred (Miller 1992: 84).

The term 'throe' seems fitting because the process entails allowing ourselves to be vulnerable to the unknown as it presents itself before us. Evocative of how Berry speaks of child-like moments, Miller likens this experience to a child on the verge of opening a door to a secret room: 'What fascinates the child, and terrifies her at the same time, is the unknown in its very character as unknown' (1992: 35). The child is transfixed in a 'dreadful play between withdrawal and venturing, retreat and longing, reluctance and urgency, delay and hastening' (Miller 1992: 36). Tucker also articulates this appreciation of mystery and its corresponding sense of agonizing struggle, suggesting that the reluctance we feel could arise from the fear that the unknown could consume us (2003: 54). Philosopher William Desmond assigns a fitting label of 'too-muchness' to these moments (2012: 274). These are flashes of astonishment at experiences of the world before us that we are unable to measure—encounters that at times can seem more than we can bear. While Berry goes as far as to say that it is especially in the natural-occurring violent moments that the human imagination awakens and humans find fulfilment (1999: 51), it is certainly not only the dreadful aspects of nature that cause us to retreat. The crucial first step, it would seem, lies in beholding what is before us as mystery, for within nature, as Tucker maintains, 'beauty and death [are] inextricably intertwined' (2003: 54).

If the first phase is to acknowledge mystery before us, Deane-Drummond underlines the subsequent need to attend to the agonizing struggle the mystery initiates. In fact, the capacity to remain steadfast and dwell in wonder, especially in the presence of that which horrifies us, is actually the basis for fostering harmony with the suffering experienced by all living beings in the natural world. Based on her reading of Simone Weil, Deane-Drummond's understanding of wonder resonates to a large degree with that of Miller. In order to attend to this struggle, a certain steadfastness is required when experiencing the natural world—one that 'does not flinch in the face of suffering, for it perceives that hidden beauty within' (Deane-Drummond 2013: 77). As Miller states above, this is wonder with a religious sense; yet for Deane-Drummond it is one disciplined by love or justice requiring an 'extreme attention' not unlike that which one would give in deep prayer, and not only to the good but also to the bad and the ugly (2013: 77, 76).[7]

Knowledge about the mystery is not the goal. Rather, it is the actual *experience* of wondering—remaining steadfast in the throes of wonder, even when it destabilizes our conceptions of the world—that matters first and foremost. This is the continuous point of departure into the unknown of which Miller speaks. For this reason, Deane-Drummond posits the need for wisdom—one that disciplines our wonder so that we remain attentive to the experience, even with the agony it might evince. The wisdom she has in mind, however, transcends anthropocentric boundaries and incorporates a close study of phenomena and all creatures—a way of thinking 'not just about human culture, but an integration of those insights into alternative cultures, such as that found in social animals' (Deane-Drummond 2006: 14). Such a wisdom, she maintains, reminds us of our human capacity for self-deception. Indeed, have we not in fact deceived ourselves into thinking that in the process of diminishing the inherent fertility of the soil, we were bringing about an improvement? For Deane-Drummond, this is why wisdom and wonder must work in a synergistic manner, forming what she terms an 'imaginative intellect' (2006: 14). Figuratively speaking, wisdom has wonder look into a mirror with frank honesty. Wonder, in turn, reminds wisdom that there is more to learn, that the search for wisdom is never ending. It would seem then, that the process requires both a discipline *and* a certain humility that cause us to suspend our thoughts, deny our egos, and hold back our domineering desires. In so doing, we are forced first and foremost not to overcome our ignorance, but to acknowledge it.

It is becoming clearer how wonder might foster a greater intimacy with the natural world. Wonder turns our attention away from the immediately present and makes us mindful of what is being offered to us. It terrifies us, yet we stay still before it, not trying to evade the fear it instills in us. And if we allow ourselves to respond to it with creativity as it presents itself, we are better able to transcend our individual worlds and occasion the possibility, as Berry says, of being 'present to the Earth in a mutually enhancing manner' (1999: 55). A cheetah capturing a gazelle that feels the fangs penetrate into her neck, a volcano spewing ashes, a star-filled night, a warm breeze: these are natural forces that we recognize as being not only terrifying but sacred. From this point, we pay attention in love in order to respond to the phenomenon before us as it is, and not as we wish it to be. Deane-Drummond sees this process leading to the development of an ethical stance toward the natural world that concedes limits to what we can do and should do. We develop, as Carson puts it, less taste for the destruction of the natural world. Moreover, as Deane-Drummond suggests, paying attention to the suffering of another creature—to the gazelle captured by the cheetah, for instance—can lead to 'an experience of solidarity with those who suffer alongside a protest against that suffering, including that inflicted by humans on other creaturely beings' (2013: 80).

Whither Wonder Today?

What happened to wonder that has kept our civilization as a whole indifferent to the senseless violence we have committed toward the natural world? If wonder is primordial for us as humans, what has happened to it? Berry laments in one of his writings:

> The main difficulty in human affairs in these opening years of the twenty-first century seems to be the loss of our sense of wonder, our sense of the sacred, our sense of play and laughter, our inability to respond to the dawn or sunset, the loss of our vision of the stars... So now my hope is that the wonder we experienced in childhood will return to quiet our restless souls in this new age of anxiety that has descended upon us. (Berry 2002: 15)

Some possible answers to this question about wonder have already been suggested above. In a sense, when we wonder, it is what we do *not* do that really matters: we do not try to tame or manage what is before us, nor do we try to avoid it or flinch, even when it instills fear within us. Quite possibly, as Miller and Deane-Drummond attest, our modern industrial civilization demonstrates a discernible distaste for being vulnerable to the unknown as it presents itself before us. Perhaps the too-muchness of the violence that we witness in the natural world is the reason why we seek to tame it. Consider, for instance, evolutionary scientist Richard Dawkins (1998), who presents wonder as an important and necessary ingredient for making science. Dawkins argues that wonder is a spirit that moves great scientists. His wonder, however, excludes the very possibility of an other-than-physical realm of reality and is grounded in a deterministic materialism. Moreover, Dawkins underlines that only science adequately translates wonder into effective engagement with the environment. His view of wonder, then, is not only materialist but elitist, as it denotes scientists as the primary wonderers of our time.[8] A closer examination of this point will help explain what I mean.

William Desmond suggests that it is precisely such a materialistic approach to wonder that explains why it has waned: it has become blocked, its porous flowing-nature clogged from unfolding into ever deeper mystery (2012: 288). Tucker and Swimme share this analysis, stating that a deterministic materialism as evidenced today by scientists like Dawkins, as well as an inadequate understanding of time have disconnected us from the rhythms of Earth only to tether us to the ticking of a clock. From the sixteenth century on, Tucker and Swimme inform us, the idea of the universe as a vast machine was gaining popularity. Matter became viewed as passive or inert, devoid of subjectivity. It is this reductionist view that has led to the clear-cutting of vast amounts of forests and the cruel treatment of animals. After all, it was believed that only humans possessed thoughts and feelings. Time became mechanical and disconnected from the rhythms of daily existence, and eventually, 'Our systems of housing, transportation, agriculture, and commerce [became] intertwined and... constructed without significant reference to the patterns of organic life of the enveloping ecosystems' (Swimme and Tucker 2011: 108). There is no sense within this framework that life required hundreds of millions of years to bring forth the complex world we have today. In short, Tucker and Swimme suggest that we have trained our minds to focus elsewhere. The materialist, mathematical approach was presumed to exhaust the process of being and knowing. Moreover, this approach is considered today as the one and only approach, making ourselves the measure of what perplexes us. This is scientism, which Desmond argues has led to 'a kind of sclerosis of astonishment' in which 'the world is stripped of the qualitative textures of sensuous communication and becomes bare, neutral thereness'—a worthless other with no value in and for itself (2012: 288, 289). The synergy between wisdom and wonder, of which Deane-Drummond speaks, has ceased to work. There is no mystery. Certain knowledge is imminent.

And perhaps this belief that certainty is at hand is the crux of the matter. Philosopher Mary Rubenstein points out that when Descartes cautions us to emancipate ourselves from wonder after it has served its purpose, he does so because he believes we shall have thereafter arrived at our goal: determinate knowledge of things (2008: 14). Echoing the sentiments of Miller and Deane-Drummond above, Rubenstein maintains that modernity has repressed wonder, tried to domesticate it.[9] She is adamant that a 'particular kind of mastery that proceeds by means of *certainty* and exceptionless appropriation' is inimical to wonder (Rubenstein 2008: 8). In other words, we can appropriate the world around us with impunity, as there is nothing sacred about it. Wonder is relegated to that initial impetus by which humans will eventually master the unfamiliar. However, 'Wonder', she concludes, 'either keeps itself open, exposing itself to the raging elements, or it shuts itself down, shielding itself against all uncertainty within the comfortable confines of the certain, the familiar, and the possible' (Rubenstein 2008: 5).

In this light, it seems more accurate to conclude that it is not just scientism or mechanical time that is misguided. Any political, social, theological, or economic construction of reality that retreats from the process of wondering, announcing that we have arrived at certainty, is naive. Declarations that we know how to manage ecosystems or introduce safely new chemicals into the air, or that we are confident that damming yet another river is harmless, are delusional. Such self-deception has led us to conquer the wild. It has led us to believe with a certain assuredness that the massive, overcrowded, and intensive-confinement systems of our modern industrial agriculture—in which animals are eating, sleeping, giving birth, and nursing in tiny concrete or metal-slatted floors—do not cause them grave suffering (Valen 2006: 570). Moreover, the situation is doubly problematic: we remain indifferent to the violence we have committed to the natural world because we have repressed the very emotion that could enable us to see the inherent value of it. In short, the communion with the natural forces we seek not only *begins* but also *endures* with wonder. Put another way, the antidote to violence is not a one-time prescription but necessarily a ceaseless, albeit painful, remedy.

The potential for transforming our senseless violent modern industrial system through wonder is promising. Specifically, when wonder is focused on the natural world, humans can nurture a wisdom that allows us to respect the natural limits of Earth's resources, recognize our limits to knowing the world with certainty, and ultimately take responsibility for the violence perpetrated against the environment, thereby placing our energies on searching for nonviolent ways of living with the natural forces around us.

Broadening the Horizon of Wonder

There is good reason to believe that this understanding of wonder as an emotion can and should also engender within us the will to take responsibility for the violence we perpetrate against human individuals and communities around the globe. Consider, as a brief venture into this line of thinking, the sentiments expressed by *New York Times* columnist Thomas Friedman about the relationship between climate change and the violence occurring in Syria. Friedman has been documenting how extreme weather, which caused the worst drought in Syria's modern history, has helped to induce its current revolution and crisis. Friedman interprets the uprising almost like a recipe: take one part climate change phenomenon, one part repression, add a douse of a corrupt and uncaring regime, and you get 'young people and farmers starved for jobs—and land starved for water' (2013). Add some communal reflection, and you have youth radicalized to do violence. Similar connections, Friedman states, have been drawn between wildfires fuelled by record temperatures and drought in Russia in 2010, the resulting rising food prices, and the Arab Spring.

The above scenario suggests a profound interconnectedness between natural-occurring violence and anthropogenic senseless violence.[10] It also points to the organic unity of the planet. Conflict studies professor and ecofeminist theologian Heather Eaton aptly underscores that 'persistently speak[ing] of humans and "the environment" is ridiculous in the face of planetary dynamics, evolutionary processes, and emergent complexities' (2013: 116). Quoting Vladimir Vernadsky, she employs a fitting metaphor for humans as 'walking talking minerals' (Eaton 2013: 115). Consider the implications of this thinking: if we truly affirm that we emerged from Earth and exist as part of an organic whole, and if we recognize the intricate way in which the human forces and the natural forces on Earth are interconnected and interrelated, then it seems inauthentic and otherwise misguided to focus our wonder and its great potential for ending our violent ways solely on the non-human world.

Indeed, why should our sense of wonder begin and endure fixed solely on the putative natural world? It makes little sense to consider the violence we perpetrate against the Earth without simultaneously considering the violence we perpetrate against humans and human communities. The two, it seems, are integrally interconnected. Certainly, if wonder is acknowledging the other, as we have seen above, then that other can be a fellow human. This is not new thinking.[11] Writing some 30 years ago, philosopher R. W. Hepburn, in a manner resonating with Carson's thinking, suggests, 'The more intense a person's wonder at the human brain, so inadequately modelled by any of our favoured mechanical analogies, the less bearable becomes the thought, for instance, of wantonly putting a bullet through it or crushing it with a rifle-butt' (1984: 145). It appears prudent with this understanding to broaden our focus of wonder to include the human. The question at hand then, is whether wondering at the human could make a difference in our relationship with the other-than-human world. And the answer appears to be yes.

The significance of this affirmation for ending our violence against Earth as an organic unity must be stressed. If we were also to focus wonder on the human, specifically, for example, on those human communities comprising the Alliance of Small Island States (AOSIS),[12] we would first realize that these small-island and low-lying coastal countries are subject to intensifying storms and droughts, sea level rise, and ocean acidification. Were our attention to remain focused, we might nurture a wisdom that has us recognize and take responsibility for the suffering these states are enduring from the inaction by the larger global human community on climate change. In other words, we might gain the solidarity that Deane-Drummond mentions above with these humans and cease perpetrating violence against their very existence. What I am suggesting here is that by broadening the horizon of wonder to include humanity and its communities, we might be able to end not only the violence we perpetrate against other humans, but perhaps put an end more comprehensively to the violence we perpetrate against Earth as an organic whole.

The good news is that this line of thinking has been gaining ground and is increasingly acknowledged by environmental thinkers and theorists of human conflict. Stephen Bede Scharper, for instance, in recognizing that the poor are often excluded from the environmental decision-making process, has exposed the interrelated trajectories of poverty, social justice, and environmental despoliation. 'Environmental devastation', he states, 'emerges out of (and contributes to) the unequal conditions of power that characterize the world' (2013: 170). Applying his analysis to the Syrian crisis Friedman describes, Scharper vividly describes the reality for millions of individuals and countless communities in the Middle East.

From a different standpoint but along the same line of reasoning, Mennonite conflict transformation practitioner and theorist John Paul Lederach presents an interesting account that caused him to recognize the integrated manner in which we ought to approach violence and conflict amongst humans. When presenting his framework to a group of Mayan Indigenous people in Guatemala, a traditional priest voiced to him an important deficiency in its process for building peace. The priest told Lederach that his approach to ending violence and fostering peace was 'missing one overarching element' (2005: 140). Lederach was initially puzzled and could not imagine which political, economic, or historic piece he had omitted from his presentation. The priest explained:

> Your framework is missing the earth and skies, the winds and rocks. It does not say where you are located. In a traditional Mayan view, if there is a problem in the community, the first thing we would ask is: Did you greet the sun today? Did you thank the earth for the corn? It is not the only thing, but it is the first. We always must know where,...what place and time, we are located. (Lederach 2005: 140)

In our globalized, interconnected, and not always just world, if wonder is to serve as an antidote to the violence we perpetrate against Earth, then we should begin by recognizing humans as an organic constituent of Earth—even if we have become its affliction—and broaden the horizon of wonder to include the human.

Conclusion

In this chapter, I have examined wonder as an important emotion that could serve as a corrective to the violent modern industrial ways, developing within us a distaste for the destruction of the entire Earth community. To realize wonder's potential, the process of how we wonder must be respected. It must never cease, never flinch in the face of the terror it sometimes presents to us, and it must work in tandem with a wisdom that is inclusive of the entire Earth community—a wisdom that keeps in check our capacity for self-deception. Perhaps the greatest self-deception we hold is the belief that we can arrive at certainty about the primordial mystery of existence. Conceivably, this is why so many important thinkers in the past and today have been ambivalent about wonder: it asks us to be in a constant state of vulnerability before the unknown. Our modern civilization has opted to try to master the unknown rather than be open to the numinous mystery of existence.

As a child I recall my mother, when addressing the concerns and problems of the world, often quoting a passage from poet Robert Browning's *Pippa Passes*: 'God's in His heaven, All's right with the world!'[13] It struck me some years later that while perhaps reassuring, this passage and its sentiment can be a double-edged sword. All is *not* right with the world; nor is all wrong with it either. Certainly, as Berry says above, we are in desperate need of quieting our restless souls in this age of anxiety. But in so doing, I think that we must also resist the temptation of thinking that we are certain about God and where God might be. Perhaps the secret in trying to quiet our restless and anxious souls is to pay attention in wonder, but not as we wish the universe—and God, for that matter—to be, rather as they are.

About the Author

Simon Appolloni, PhD, currently teaches as a sessional instructor at the University of Toronto, Humber College, and Brock University. His research investigates the relationships humans nurture with nature—often through a religious lens and/or through the appropriation of new science—with a view to finding avenues of harmonious living amongst humans and between humans and the natural world.

Notes

1. From the Royal Swedish Academy of Science, for instance, see Steffan, Crutzen, and McNeill (2007: 614-21). For environmental thinkers, see Swimme and Tucker (2011: 102).

2. This is, in fact, the idea behind the medical term 'antidote': 'an agent that neutralizes a poison [which is any substance that is injurious to health or dangerous to life] or counteracts its effects' (*Stedman's Medical Dictionary* 2005). It is this sense of counteracting that I wish to stress here.

3.   McQuaid, (January 2009), at http://www.smithsonianmag.com/ecocenter-ene rgy/mining-the-mountains-130454620/?all. The Environmental Protection Agency esti- mates that the decades of practicing mountaintop removal mining within the Appala- chian bioregion could be responsible for destroying or degrading almost twelve percent of forests and burying over a thousand miles of streams.

4.   Berry, Swimme, and Tucker note similar distinctions in their writings; see Swimme and Tucker (2011: 101). In chapter 3 of their book, Swimme and Berry outline the difference between humans creatively dealing with the constraints of the universe throughout history and our more recent attempts to relate to it by 'destroying resis- tance, denying intrinsic cost, and magnifying the intensity of all its desires' (1992: 57).

5.   Plato 'Theaetetus', *Plato 12*, ([1921] 1987), at http://www.perseus.tufts.edu/hop per/text?doc=plat.+theaet.+155.

6.   Notwithstanding this, as historian of science Holmes tells us (2008: xvi), there was a period in between the Enlightenment period of science and the Victorian period, a period of less than 70 years, when men and women voiced a subtle reaction against the idea of a purely mechanistic universe. In this unique short interval, which he labels the age of romantic science, scientists embraced wonder, talking about the mysterious energies that flowed and the organic nature of change.

7.   Deane-Drummond (2006: 14) is, in fact, critical of Miller's work for overlooking this aspect. Without wisdom, she reasons, philosophy is simply open to the throes of wonder and could become unhinged.

8.   Dawkins (1998) holds that mysteries—such as a rainbow—do not lose their poetry because they are solved. In fact, he sees the solution as being more beautiful than the puzzle. While knowing about a rainbow and how it forms, it is my contention here that the rainbow is always more than our grasp of it.

9.   There is a marked similarity between Miller's and Rubenstein's philosophical approaches worth noting here, explained in large measure by the fact that both are influenced by the thinking of Martin Heidegger. Heidegger was the first thinker to challenge the Western philosophical metaphysical tradition for conferring the status of being only on that which can be represented or calculated by humans. Miller and Rubenstein seem to be following a post-Heideggerian way of approaching the world, which opens us up to the other before us without, however, attempting to colonize it. This approach, Rubenstein avers, raises the represented and representer over the actual happening of being that constitutes them: 'Attentive only to what is repre- sentable', she says, 'metaphysics is incapable of thinking the unrepresentable event that sets representation in motion. This steady fall into 'calculative-representational thought' eventually gives rise to the curse and blessing of modern technology' (Ruben- stein 2008: 17).

10.   I am cognizant that by labelling climate change as a natural-occurring violence, it seemingly overlooks its anthropogenic cause. In this light, I refer to the effects brought about by a warming climate as being natural-occurring, while not denying humanity's role in bringing about this phenomenon.

11.   Roesch-Marsh (2003: 305-27) points out how the philosopher Levinas consid- ered wonder within this ethical dimension. Ironically, Levinas downplayed the import of focusing wonder on the natural world.

12.   AOSIS is a coalition of 44 small island and low-lying coastal countries that, according to their website, 'share similar development challenges and concerns about the environment, especially their vulnerability to the adverse effects of global cli- mate change. It functions primarily as an ad hoc lobby and negotiating voice for small

island developing States (SIDS) within the United Nations system' (2015, at http://aosis.org/).

13. Browning (1906 [1841]), at http://www.archive.org/stream/pipppasseswithan00browuoft/pipppasseswithan00browuoft_djvu.txt.

Chapter 18

Music and Nonviolence:
Reflections on Possibility and Hope

Lauren Michelle Levesque

Introduction

> Let's recognize that music can be (and has been) both a repository for his-
> tory and a shaper of other possible futures, and that its power—symbolic
> or otherwise—resides precisely in its refusal to be aligned with any and all
> forms of reductive thinking... Music's capacity to unsettle fixed systems of
> understanding, we suggest, is precisely what enables hope and dialogue.
> (Fischlin and Heble 2003)

The scholarly examination of the arts in nonviolent social and political
change is not new. Studies have explored the contribution of music to the
education of activists and the general public, the constitution of social
movement identities and alternative cultures, as well as the generation
of energy and feelings of solidarity during marches, meetings, and rallies
(see, e.g., Eyerman and Jamieson 1998; Rosenthal and Flacks 2011). Singing in particular has been recognized as integral to various nonviolent
social movements, including the American Civil Rights movement and the
movement against the Soviet occupation of Estonia (Kattau 2010: 107-18;
Tusty and Tusty 2008).

Despite the recognition of the integral role music and other art forms
play in nonviolent campaigns, Marty Branagan, an Australian Peace Studies lecturer and activist, suggests that the arts are an 'under-theorised
part of nonviolent praxis' (2013: 187). This chapter is a modest attempt
to address some of this under-theorising. My objective is to examine the
ways that music can provide an innovative framework to think about nonviolence. In particular, through an in-depth discussion of music, I hope to
spark interest in the many ways that this art form can contribute to nonviolent social and political change.

My starting point is a question that Branagan raises about the possibility of replacing national militaries with nonviolent civilian defence
forces (2013: 63-65). Contemplating this possibility, he asks: 'What could

nonviolence achieve if it was better resourced and more widely under-stood?' (2013: 64). For the purposes of this chapter, I reframe Branagan's question in relationship to music: What can be achieved when individuals and communities seek to understand, support, and appreciate nonviolence through music? What can music bring to these processes of understanding, support, and appreciation?

The chapter is divided into three sections. First, I discuss definitions of nonviolence, including nonviolence as creative energy espoused by Gandhian scholar and practitioner Michael N. Nagler (2004, 2014). Second, I examine music as a source of insight and as an act of social imagination using the term 'musicking', coined by scholar and music educator Christopher Small (1998). In the final section, I reflect on some of the challenges and implications of thinking about nonviolence through music.

Principled Nonviolence as Creative Energy

Nonviolence can be understood in multiple ways. When spiritual ideals are considered a defining characteristic, nonviolence is often described as a principled nonviolence (Jahanbegloo 2014: 1-88). 'Principled nonviolence' has been identified as a commitment to do no violence under any circumstance. This commitment involves both the ways people think about nonviolence and how their ideas are implemented. To underscore this point, religious studies professor Ira Chernus cites Mahatma Gandhi, Dorothy Day, and Martin Luther King Jr, among others, as exemplars of the commitment to thought and action intrinsic to a principled nonviolence (Chernus 2004: 1-2, 91-110, 145-81).

For scholars such as Gene Sharp, however, principled nonviolence can be distinguished from 'nonviolent action' or 'nonviolent struggle'. Sharp suggests that nonviolence is a technique used in people-power movements throughout the twentieth century (2005: 20-21). He explains: 'Nonviolent struggle is identified by what people do, not by what they believe' (Sharp 2005: 19). This distinction has two purposes. First, it recognizes that nonviolence is not necessarily defined by spiritual or religious ideals.[1] Second, the distinction underscores that nonviolence is not passive but active, meaning that it is a struggle for which activists may have to lay down their lives. Experts in nonviolence Peter Ackerman and Jack DuVall observe:

> It is often assumed that the choice of nonviolent resistance is made for moral reasons, but the historical record suggests otherwise. Most who used nonviolent action in the twentieth century did so because military or physical force was not a viable option. Some simply lacked sufficient arms to mount a violent revolt; others had recently seen a violent insurrection fail, with devastating results for life and property. But since

peoples' most vital interests were at stake, and because they were determined to take down rulers or laws that withheld their rights, they were
impelled to take up other, nonviolent weapons. Those who used nonviolent actions in our stories did not come to make peace. They came to fight.
(Ackerman and DuVall 2000: 5)

Sharp, Ackerman, and DuVall are correct in acknowledging that nonviolence is not defined solely by spiritual or religious ideals. I also agree
with their assessment that nonviolence is a struggle to persuade others
that alternatives to violence and war are viable means to pursue social
and political change. Taking these points into account, I understand nonviolence, alongside Chernus, as a commitment to do no violence under
any circumstance. Spirituality can define this commitment or not but
it is not passive. Conceptions of nonviolence as 'relentless persistence'
that emerged in Latin America speak to this active element (Boff 1991: x).
Adolfo Pérez Esquivel comments:

Nonviolence is not passivity or conformism... It is a spirit of prophecy, for
it denounces all sundering of a community of brothers and sisters and
proclaims that this community can only be rebuilt through love. And it is
a method—an organized set of ruptures in the civil order so as to disturb
the system responsible for the injustices we see around us. (Esquivel in
Cortright 2008: 223)

That principled nonviolence is characterized by a drive to disrupt resonates with understandings Nagler engages within his works. He argues
that relying on violence to address societal conflicts and/or issues reveals
'a serious lack of imagination' (Nagler 2004: 190). Nonviolence can disrupt
this lack of imagination by encouraging individuals and communities to
seek out new and/or different ways of thinking and acting (Nagler 2004:
191-92). In this conceptualization, nonviolence becomes a creative energy
that can fuel a search for alternatives.

For example, nonviolence acts as this fuel by interrupting common
reactions of anger and hostility in circumstances in which activists are
confronted by physical challenges and/or threats (Cortright 2009: 128-
30). Historian of peace and fellow Gandhian scholar David Cortright states:
'Instead of energies clashing as they do in violent conflict, the contending forces in a nonviolent struggle interact and are able to learn from one
another' (2009: 128). This statement suggests that nonviolence can be
viewed as a meeting of energies through which normative ways of thinking and acting are unsettled. A consequence of this meeting can be the
opening of possibilities and options not only for those utilizing nonviolence but also for those who are in opposition to this creative energy.

Discerning these possibilities and options, however, takes time and
requires a willingness to learn in the long term, as Cortright hints. Nagler
also observes: 'There is no quick and easy way to become nonviolent. It

calls for constant effort and becomes a lifelong challenge' (2014: 8). Music is one avenue through which individuals and communities can pursue this challenge.[2] More specifically, I propose that conceptualizations of music as sources of insight and as acts of social imagination can provide innovative ways for thinking about nonviolence as a creative energy. As a source of insight, music affords individuals and communities with a space to consider their options. As an act of social imagination, music can reveal that such options are particularly powerful when collectively created and enacted.

Music as a Source of Insight and as an Act of Social Imagination

Like nonviolence, music can be defined in multiple ways. In this chapter, I define music through an examination of Small's term, 'musicking'. By examining the term in-depth, I do two things. First, I take up Nagler's idea that discerning nonviolent possibilities and options takes time and a willingness to learn. Second, by taking up this idea, I demonstrate the complex and multidimensional ways that music can intersect with nonviolence beyond the context of marches, rallies, and/or campaigns. Let me turn now to Small's ideas.

Musicking as a Source of Insight

Musicking is described as participating in a musical performance in any capacity (Small 1998: 9). This participation includes rehearsing, performing, listening, and dancing as well as activities such as the provision of materials for performance and the sale of tickets. Thus, musicking comprises 'all participation in a musical performance, whether it takes place actively or passively, whether we like the way it happens or whether we do not, whether we consider it interesting or boring, constructive or destructive, sympathetic or antipathetic' (Small 1998: 9). In this understanding, even listening to a recording can be an important act of musicking that gives meaning to a performance.

The idea of musicking is significant for several reasons. First, as a verb, it is a reminder that musical meaning is not fixed in a score or a song's text but in its performance (Small 2011: ix-x). Musicking, in other words, is an action (Small 2011: x). Placing the emphasis on action implies that performance is not a secondary concern for those seeking to understand this human phenomenon. Rather, performance should be considered at the centre of such understandings (Small 1998: 185).

Second, Small's concept draws attention to the relationships that are brought into being in musical performances. These relationships, in his opinion, are the root or foundation of musical meaning (Small 2011: xi). He explains:

> Musical meanings, then, are concerned with relationships, the relation-
> ships of our world as we believe they are and as we believe they ought to
> be. And since how we relate is who we are, we can say that in musicking
> we are exploring, affirming, and celebrating who we are, or at least who
> we think we are, in relation to fellow humans, to the world and even per-
> haps to the supernatural world—if the supernatural is a part of our con-
> ceptual world. (Small 2011: xiii)

Another way to understand this explanation is that musicking provides participants with a space to explore, affirm, and celebrate how they
relate to the world. By providing this space, musicking becomes a source
of insight into the ways people interact. Stated differently, musicking is a
human encounter that shapes and reshapes 'our landscape of human relationships', including the ways in which people come together to dream up
and live out constructive social and political change (Small 2011: xii-xiii).

Analyzing this human encounter in the particular is important (Small
1998: 49). This is because understandings of the complex interplay of relationships in musical performances differ according to context. Small comments: 'A work of art "means" whatever the beholder, in whatever "here"
or "now" they might find themselves, think it means' (2011: ix). Such contingency is not considered an obstacle, however. It is a means for innovative thinking on particular acts of musicking (Small 1998: xv). To foster
this thinking, Small asks: '*What does it mean when this performance takes
place at this time, in this place, with these participants?*' (1998: 10, emphasis
original). His question highlights at least three sets of relationships that
create meaning in musical performances.

The first set concerns the relationship between the participants and the
physical setting (Small 1998: 193). Inquiring into this relationship reveals
that the physical setting in which a musical performance takes place has
the power to guide human behavior (Small 1998: 20). For example, in a
Western style concert hall there is often a sense of crossing a threshold
into another world when participants move from the foyer to the performance hall (Small 1998: 24). The building's design gives the impression
that social interaction takes place in the foyer and contemplative reception of the music occurs in the hall (Small 1998: 25-27). By adhering to or
challenging these physical parameters, participants create an imaginative
space in which to envision or re-envision their relationships. The point
is that both the physical setting and the imaginative space created give
meaning to the performance and its reception.

The second set of relationships highlighted by Small's question is
among those taking part in a performance (Small 1998: 193). This idea—
that meaning is created in the relationships between those participating—
challenges notions of performance as predictable, inevitable, and static
(Small 1998: 46). The reality is that the meaning of musicking changes as

individual and communal tastes change (Small 1998: 91, 133). The relevant point is that, echoing Nagler's description of nonviolence as creative energy, understandings of this musical encounter cannot be reduced to a single relationship or activity. All relationships and/or activities generated as part of a performance have the potential to contribute to its meaning. These meanings evolve, fall silent, and perhaps re-emerge depending on who is participating at any given moment and where.

Finally, the third set of relationships is between the sounds that are made by the performers (Small 1998: 193). For example, what meaning is generated through the relationships between different vocal lines? Attending to these relationships is important because, as Small suggests, they model the complexity and dynamism of life (Small 1998: 200). Sonic relationships are here understood as metaphors that enable an experience of deep interdependence. He writes:

> When we perform, we bring into existence, for the duration of the performance, a set of relationships, between the sounds and between the participants, that model ideal relationships as we imagine them to be and allow us to learn about them by experiencing them. The modeling is reciprocal, as implied by the three words I have used persistently through this book: in exploring we learn, from the sounds and from one another, the nature of relationships; in affirming we teach one another about the relationships, and in celebrating we bring together the teaching and the learning in an act of solidarity. (Small 1998: 218).

Musicking as an Act of Social Imagination

By using the term musicking, Small hoped to provide people with a way to explore the multiple relationships possible in musical performances (1998: 10). He believed that cultivating awareness of musicking's 'ever widening spiral of relationships' could give people a renewed sense of what music can do (Small 1998: 210). More specifically, he hoped that people would come to understand musicking as a space where they could live out the relationships they wanted to see in their everyday lives (Small 1998: 46, 50). In this sense, the term presents music as an encounter that is dynamic and relational and can provide insights into and experiences of interdependence.

As though echoing this hope, Janet Sarbanes discusses musicking in her analysis of a Greek musical subculture known as *rebetika* (2006: 11-35). *Rebetika* is a blend of Greek and Turkish influences and in the early twentieth century was associated with marginalized urban milieus such as hashish dens.[3] In the context of this subculture, musical performance became a space for what Sarbanes calls 'social imagination' (2006: 20-21). Social imagination captures what is implicit in the verb 'musicking'. This is the idea that music is a highly collaborative act, meaning that it involves 'the integration of people doing different things' (Sarbanes 2006: 21). Along-side exploring, affirming, and celebrating the relationships they would like to see in their everyday lives, people also use musicking to contest these relationships.

For instance, *rebetika* involved the construction of alternative identities and communities that resisted normative perceptions of what it meant to be Greek. This meant dressing in Turkish costumes and participating in customs such as drinking, dancing, and smoking hashish (Sarbanes 2006: 19-22). Through these various activities, those who performed *rebetika* contested simplistic understandings of Greek identity. By musicking, they gained the insight that to be Greek could also include the exploration, affirmation, and celebration of Turkish influences (Sarbanes 2006: 31).

In another example, a 2003 Clash tribute concert is characterized as a highly collaborative and contesting act of musicking (see, e.g., Lynskey 2010: 339-58; Phull 2008: 139-64).[4] Kevin Dunn remarks:

> On stage, the bands—all many years younger than I—were using the songs to make sense of the world; to make sense of what was happening around them. It was clear to them, it was clear to the kids in the audience, and it was clear to me that we were living in extremely dangerous times. The in-between song banter reflected this—comments about President George W. Bush, remarks about American fascism, concerns about the impending war on Iraq, and pleas to register to vote. The kids in the club were using the Clash, much as I did years before, to help them understand the world they were inheriting. (Dunn 2005: 264)

At the concert, Dunn was struck by the ways in which Clash fans used musicking to make sense of their engagements with and experiences of the world. More pointedly, in the space provided, participants used song, dance, and conversation to voice their opposition to the former Bush administration's decision to go to war in Iraq. In a sense, the *performative* space of the concert became an *imaginative* space and, thus, a source of insight into the ways people could oppose the war.

By engaging with these spaces, those present participated in an act of social imagination. They re-conceptualized their relationships to each other and to their government. For Dunn, the act sparked reflections about how to integrate his roles as an engaged citizen and as an international relations scholar (2005: 272). The point I wish to make is that, through concert musicking, spaces were created for the insight that he could be both.

Dunn's description resonates with Small's and Sarbanes's ideas. They include understanding musicking as a highly collaborative act that mirrors the complexity, multifacetedness, and interconnectedness of people's relationships with each other and the world. Musicking is also theorized as a space where those participating can experiment with how they envision and enact these relationships. In this way, musicking contributes to the ways people understand their engagement with themselves and the wider world: what that engagement can look, sound, and feel like in particular contexts. In relationship to the arguments discussed in this chapter, the questions arise: What happens when these ideas are applied to engagements with nonviolence? What challenges and implications emerge from this application?

Understanding Nonviolence Through Musicking: Challenges and Implications

Given the various understandings of nonviolence and music that I have discussed, it is evident that these are complex and multifaceted human phenomena. They are conceptualized at least as spaces to which people from diverse backgrounds and experiences can contribute. Challenges arise, however, in how these phenomena intersect in pursuits of constructive social and political change, in particular when musicking is conceived as a means through which to play and experiment with nonviolence.

One challenge is the need for safe spaces where people can explore music and through this exploration, tap into nonviolence as a creative energy. Briefly defined, safe space can be understood as a location in which those present feel physically and emotionally protected, where they feel they can experiment and take risks, and where they feel a sense of solidarity with fellow participants (Hunter 2008: 5-21). Community-based peacebuilding programming can offer such a space, as Lesley J. Pruitt (2013) argues in her research on music, gender, and youth in Northern Ireland. As part of this programming, music was used by youth from diverse backgrounds to experiment with different understandings of their identities and relationships (Pruitt 2013: 115-40). In the process of this experimentation, the actual spaces where the programming was taking place were reconstituted into what Pruitt calls 'common ground'. She observes, however, that creating this common ground was not always straightforward:

> Programs aimed at building peace through music then ought to take into account local needs and preferences to ensure that the work is relevant and worthwhile. At the same time, they also need to take care to avoid (re) creating space in a way that supports or further inflames conflict... Questions of how and where space is shared are important to building peace. (Pruitt 2013: 117)

Pruitt's statements imply that using musicking as a source of insight and/or as an act of social imagination to explore nonviolence is not simply a matter of finding a physical location where people can gather to play and/or experiment. It is also not a matter of presenting a group of individuals with instruments and instructions to get creative. Attention needs to be paid to what safety, inclusivity, and accessibility mean for different groups in different contexts. If these dimensions of music and space are not considered, then the experiences offered may be alienating and potentially contribute to an escalation of tensions rather than their reduction.

If musicking is used as an innovative theoretical framework, flexibility and interdependence become important aspects of creating such safe spaces for play and experimentation with nonviolence as a creative energy. To underscore these notions in the context of peacebuilding, scholar and practitioner John Paul Lederach uses the image of a web of relationships to approach constructive social and political change (2005: 75-86). He writes:

> This whole endeavor of making a web requires a deep commitment to innovation and flexibility. The end result and the process of creating the end result are characterized by a capacity to adapt to shifting contours, ever-changing environments, and unexpected intrusions. A web, therefore, can never be thought of as permanent, fixed, or rigid. The spider's genius lies in its ability to adapt, reshape, and remake its web of connections within realities presented in a given space. (Lederach 2005: 83)

Within this web and in the context of pursuing peace, individuals can take up a diversity of roles (such as activist, artist, educator, thinker), depending on their particular talents and the particular conflicts and/ or issues they are confronting. Acknowledging that flexibility and interdependence hold the web together can encourage people to engage with nonviolence, for example, in their own unique ways. One result, as literature on singing within US peace activism suggests, is an enlarging of not only a group's sense of solidarity but also its sense of empowerment (Brooks 2010: 56-71).

When using musicking to reflect on nonviolence, however, another challenge emerges. This is its ambiguity. Musicking is not innately nonviolent. It has been used to incite and sustain conflict and violence in various contexts (Baker 2013: 409-29). Recognizing this dimension of musicking is important because it belies simplistic and/or overly optimistic understandings of the art form's contribution to constructive social and political change (Garcia 2014: 24-51). To use Nagler's phrase, learning about musicking takes time. Such learning and relearning are, therefore, integral to the creation of spaces where individuals and communities utilize this art form to try on nonviolent ways of being in the world (Pruitt 2013: 147).

For example, scholars and arts advocates Daniel Fischlin, Ajay Heble, and George Lipsitz (2013) propose that improvised musicking is both a source of insight and an act of social imagination into civil and human rights discourses and experiences. Reflecting on the importance of flexibility and interdependence, they write:

> Improvisation calls into being questions of responsibility, rooted etymo-
> logically in the word *responsible*, that is, answerable or morally account-
> able for one's actions, driven by the responsibility to respond. Being
> responsible, as we've intimated earlier, requires deep, careful listening.
> You need to hear to respond. You need to account for what the other
> really has to say in order to be responsible, that is, to account morally
> and ethically for your own actions in relation to others. Improvisation
> is a key staging ground of this form of encounter, a key crucible through
> which the event-horizon of infinite possible encounters is addressed, per-
> formed, imagined. (Fischlin et al. 2013: 239, emphasis original)

The idea that improvisation is a key staging ground and a key crucible
suggests that those participating not only have access to a space where
they can imagine but also simultaneously experience infinite possibilities.
This simultaneity, a merging of imagination and experience in real time
through face-to-face encounters, is one reason why improvisation is considered a vital sonic practice with deep social and political implications.
As stated, among these implications is a sense that other ways of being in
the world are possible (Fischlin et al. 243).

The understandings of musicking and nonviolence explored in this
chapter point to the ways theoretical engagements with these human
phenomena can also be approached as dynamic, flexible, and interdependent. This is because they can also be conceived as spaces where disruption, play, and experimentation are encouraged. Speaking of Gandhi's
understanding of nonviolence, Mark Juergensmeyer writes: 'Just as there
are laws of nature, reasoned Gandhi, there are laws of harmonious living.
Our task is to seek them out, to "experiment with truth" the way a scientist might use a laboratory' (2005: 19). Theory, when considered in this
light, becomes a space that can generate creative possibilities and options
for transformation in relationship to both music and nonviolence.

Conclusion

In this chapter, I have engaged with Branagan's suggestion that the
arts are an under-theorised dimension of nonviolent praxis. I demonstrated that an in-depth understanding of music reveals its potential
to act as an innovative theoretical framework through which insights
about nonviolence may be cultivated. Such insights include ideas on
the challenges of creating safe spaces where individuals and groups
can play and experiment with nonviolence as a creative energy. I also
suggested that the ambiguity and complexity of music provide insight
into nonviolence as not only a creative energy but also one that is flexible and interdependent, constituted by a range of contexts, people, and
relationships.

To return to my initial questions: what can be achieved when individuals and communities seek to understand, support, and appreciate nonviolence through music? What can music bring to these processes of understanding, support, and appreciation? One answer is that music, when understood as a source of insight and an act of social imagination, can encourage individuals and communities to step out of their fixed systems of understanding, including our conventional ways of understanding music as nonviolent praxis and vice versa. This stepping out, as Small, Pruitt, Fischlin, Heble, and Lipsitz imply, can result in an appreciation of different identities, perspectives, and/or relationships. Music can bring forward, in other words, possibilities and options that may not have been contemplated otherwise. In doing so, it fosters hope in the prospects of nonviolent and constructive social and political transformation, if only for the length of a song, an album, or a concert.

About the Author

Lauren Michelle Levesque, PhD, is a lecturer at Saint Paul University, Ottawa, Canada, where she teaches courses on spirituality, feminist ethics, and trauma, healing, and reconciliation. Levesque was a 2013–2014 postdoctoral fellow with the Improvisation, Community, and Social Practice project housed at the University of Guelph, Guelph, Canada. Her research interests include nonviolence, arts-based research, and creative modalities of grassroots peacebuilding.

Notes

1. It should be noted that commitments to do no harm in any circumstance emerge from secular as well as religious ideals, as Jahanbegloo points out in his book (2014: 56-76). Chernus (2004: 182-91) also acknowledges this possibility by discussing the life and work of Barbara Deming, an influential theorist of principled nonviolence in the United States.

2. Other art forms such as contact improvisation have been used as an avenue through which to understand aspects of nonviolence (see, e.g., Goldman 2007: 60-74).

3. Grove Dictionary Online, at http://www.oxfordmusiconline.com.proxy.bib.uottawa.ca/subscriber/article/grove/music/51102.

4. The Clash was a British punk band formed in 1975. The punk movement emerged in Britain and the US at a time when each country was experiencing economic, social, and political hardships, including rising inflation, high unemployment, and racial tensions. The music spoke to a sense of having no options for a better future among youth. The Clash was one of the iconic bands of the late 1970s and early 1980s.

Chapter 19

The Case for Child Honouring*

Raffi Cavoukian

Introduction

Across three decades, people and events have transformed a children's troubadour singing life-affirming songs for the very young into a global troubadour and advocate not only for children but also for a viable future we all might share. My new songs still celebrate life and our global family, but now my appearances are before older audiences that include college students,[1] parents, educators, economists, policy makers, and professionals from many walks of life. My work is now part of a bigger quest that seeks to answer the question: *How can we turn our troubled world around, and work toward creating a nurturing world fit for all children?* It has moved me to 'sing' a new paradigm into being: a compassionate revolution I call Child Honouring.

Since the 1970s, we have witnessed a rapid shift in societal mores and in planetary health, with serious consequences for children and families. In Canada and the United States, an increasingly violent and sexualized media culture reaches younger and younger kids. Alcohol and drug use, casual sex, and bullying have become prevalent among preteens and teens, and pandemic numbers of child sexual abuse cases are a grave concern. The gap between rich and poor has widened and more families live in poverty. Alongside these worrisome trends, by the mid-1990s, books such as *Our Stolen Future* (Colborn et al. 1996) and *Raising Children Toxic Free* (Needleman and Landrigan 1994) detailed the pervasive chemical contamination in the biosphere and in our bodies, as well as young children's unique vulnerability to toxic chemicals. They revealed something profound: Chemical pollution is so prevalent worldwide that every baby is now born at risk.

The unique susceptibility of infants to even the minutest doses of toxicants[2] led me to wonder in what other ways they were most vulnerable. I explored the interrelated factors that impact early childhood, connecting the dots between economic and environmental conditions and their effect on child health and learning: for example, between a living wage and family nutrition, between accessible child care and employment prospects for single parents, and between the way paper is bleached and the state of breast milk. Over the past decade, in consultation with a broad range of experts in diverse fields, I developed an integrated philosophy that addresses the personal, cultural, and planetary conditions that affect formative human development.

Child Honouring is a vision of hope and renewal in response to a time of unprecedented social and ecological breakdown worldwide. It is a metaframework for addressing the major issues of our time and for redesigning society towards the greatest good by meeting the priority needs of the very young.

A Theft of Futures

> Losing my future is not like losing an election or a few points on the stock exchange. (Severn Cullis-Suzuki, age twelve. Earth Summit, Rio De Janeiro, 1992)

For a civilization and planet in systems failure, metaphors abound: the end of empire, a new *Titanic* headed for disaster, downed canaries in a coal mine. To me, our current unsustainable state on a globe with failing life support adds up to a colossal theft, a theft of futures—the futures of our children. How have we let this happen? The following stark warning in 1992 by the Union of Concerned Scientists was formally endorsed by 1,670 distinguished senior scientists (among them 104 Nobel laureates of many disciplines) from 71 countries from China to Chile, India to Ireland, the US to the UK. But governments and the mass media ignored it:

> We the undersigned, senior members of the world's scientific community, hereby warn all humanity of what lies ahead. A great change in our stewardship of the earth and the life on it is required, if vast human misery is to be avoided and our global home on this planet is not to be irretrievably mutilated.[3]

Despite the technological gains in the 50-plus years since I was a boy (space missions, instant communication, nanotechnology), our lives are still haunted by the demon of nuclear weapons and a hideous global arms trade. True, we have made tremendous advances in medicine, engineering, and science, and in life expectancy. Car engines start reliably. We have all sorts of material comforts. We are finally generating solar, wind, and hydrogen power. We can see sharp close-up images of the landscape on Mars. And yet, in the human mission to make peace on Earth, to care for the less fortunate, and in our stewardship of the planet, we are losing ground.[4]

Rachel Carson's *Silent Spring*, published in 1962, was hailed as a brilliant wake-up call. But by 1990, mass demonstrations that put Earth on the cover of *Time* magazine (Planet of the Year) failed to produce substantive change in business, the engine that drives society. Sustainable development, a key phrase at the 1992 Earth Summit, has not lived up to its promise. In *Earth in the Balance*, Senator Al Gore (before he became US Vice-President), urged a green Marshall Plan for Earth's revival, but ecology-as-central-organizing principle was not heard of again.

The birth of a responsible commerce movement and the growth of ethical investment funds have not yet shaken business-as-usual. With corporate globalization we have witnessed the accumulation of money and markets at all cost. The 1990s, a period of record corporate profits, saw massive job losses coupled with a greater-than-ever income gap between rich and poor. With communism's demise, capitalism's triumph turned global commerce into a 24/7 gold rush. For all the admirable work of so-called civil society (tens of thousands of non-governmental organizations [NGOs] worldwide), no countervailing idea has emerged to slow the worldwide shopping frenzy.

Since the grassroots uprising during the World Trade Organization's 1999 meeting in Seattle, millions have marched worldwide to protest the global money cartel and the financial organizations (such as the International Monetary Fund and World Bank), whose loans and programs often hurt the countries they are supposed to help. This response to globalization's excesses is one sign that a tipping point may be near.[5] E .O. Wilson, one of the world's most respected and influential scientists, likened the antiglobalization outcry to the Earth's immune system rising up to expel a disease: 'The protest groups are the world's early warning system for the natural economy. They are the living world's immunological response' (2002: 188).

Among progressives, some anticipate a global economic collapse; they doubt that anything less will precipitate systemic change. Many, however, are forming local living economies to proactively grow networks of local entrepreneurs whose goods and services both build community and offer a safety net in case of international supply and distribution shortages.[6]

The onset of global warming brings the end of the fossil fuel era, and with it the need for a quick turn to clean energies to avert unimaginable hardships. Fortunately, there is an infinitely renewable energy within each one of us: in the pulse of the human heart, in the boundless love we feel for our children and grandchildren, there is a tremendous power that, when tapped, can turn this world around.

The Child-Honouring Lens

We are conducting a vast toxicological experiment in which the research animals are our children. (Philip Landrigan, professor of pediatrics, Mount Sinai School of Medicine, New York)

> The feeling appropriate to an infant in arms is his feeling of rightness, or essential goodness...that he is right, good and welcome in the world. (Jean Liedloff, *The Continuum Concept*)

Across all cultures, we find an essential humanity that is most visible in early childhood—a playful, intelligent, and creative way of being. Early experience lasts a lifetime. It shapes our sense of self and how we see others; it also shapes our sense of what is possible, our emerging view of the world. The impressionable early years are the most vulnerable to family dynamics, cultural values, and planetary conditions. At this critical point in the history of humankind, the irreducible needs of all children can offer a unifying ethic by which the cultures of our interdependent world might reorder their priorities.

Child Honouring is a vision, an organizing principle, and a way of life—a revolution in values that calls for a profound redesign of every sphere of society. It starts with three givens: first, the primacy of the early years—early childhood is the gateway to humane being. Second, we face planetary degradation unprecedented in scope and scale, a state of emergency that requires a remedy of equal scale and that most endangers the very young. And third, the crisis calls for a systemic response in detoxifying the environments that make up the ecology of the child. This is a children-first approach to healing communities and restoring ecosystems; it views how we regard and treat our young as the key to building a humane and sustainable world. It is neither about a child-centred society in which children rule, nor a facile notion of children being all things nice, and it has nothing to do with permissive parenting; none of these is desirable. Child Honouring is a global credo for maximizing joy and reducing suffering by respecting the goodness of every human being at the beginning of life, with benefits rippling in all directions. It is a novel idea—organizing society around the needs of its youngest members. Just as startling is the finding of neuroscience that a lifetime of behaviours is significantly shaped by the age of four, and that, developmentally speaking, the preschool years are more important than the school years.[7] In the words of Stanley Greenspan and Stuart Shanker, founders of the Council of Human Development, 'Early childhood is the most important time in a human being's development'.[8]

What does it mean to honour children? It means seeing them for the creatively intelligent people they are, respecting their personhood as their own, recognizing them as essential members of the community, and providing the fundamental nurturance they need in order to flourish. As formative growth is simultaneously affected by the personal, cultural, and planetary domains, sustainability strategies must take all three into account.

Children are not a partisan concern, and Child Honouring is not pitted against person or ideology. Its allegiance is to the children and their families. It speaks emphatically for the birthright of the young of every culture to love, dignity, and security. At the same time, it encompasses the whole of life; first years' benefits trickle upward and enrich later years. It takes people of all ages to co-create humane societies. The focus on early life simply underscores a key developmental tenet. In fully honouring children, we would honour the lifelong web of relations that brings them forth and sustains them. Child Honouring involves honouring all life, and ultimately means living in reverence with the mystery of creation. In our quantum universe where everything is interrelated, the child is a 'holon'—something that is both whole and a part of something bigger. Just as in quantum physics observation affects outcome, so too in human relations, with respect to the very young, regard shapes development. How we regard a child is the vital mirror with which that child's innate potential comes alive.

Children who feel seen, loved, and honoured are far abler to become loving parents and productive citizens. Children who do not feel valued are disproportionately represented on welfare rolls and police records. Much of the criminal justice system deals with the results of childhood wounding (the vast majority of sexual offenders, for example, were themselves violated as children), and much of the social-service sector represents an attempt to rectify or moderate this damage, which comes at an enormous cost to society. Most of the correctional work is too little, too late.

Child Honouring is a corrective lens that, once we look through it, allows us to question everything from the way we measure economic progress to our stewardship of the planet; from our physical treatment of children to the corporate impact on their minds and bodies; from rampant consumerism to factory schooling. It offers a proactive developmental approach to creating sustainable societies. As a creed that crosses all faiths and cultures, Child Honouring can become a potent remedy for the most challenging issues of our time.

At stake for our species is nothing less than the right to be human, the right to remain human in the magical world that gives us life—before it's too late. Babies today carry toxic chemicals barely known 50 years ago, born into a degraded biosphere. That is the extent to which business-as-usual has failed children, both worldwide and here at home. It has endangered their wellbeing and undermined family life, as Sharna Olfman's book *Childhood Lost* (2005) dramatically reveals. The moral imperative is to undo the damage wherever possible and to take action to restore children's diminished futures.

Urgently we need to create a culture of deep compassion, one in which the primacy of the early years guides public policy, the admired life blends material sufficiency with more noble aims, and our children learn to become responsible global citizens. We need to create a culture in which corporate ingenuity is redirected to profit all shareholders of the planet, and in which our economy (as a subset of nature) becomes a means to this end, not an end in itself. We need to create a culture in which the good life speaks not to purchasing power but to the quality of our existence—our relationships with one another, between cultures, and with Nature. We need a culture that puts self-confidence ahead of consumer confidence and affirms developmental health as the true wealth of nations.

But how do we get there? Eminent thinkers such as Lester Brown, Maurice Strong, Hazel Henderson, Vandana Shiva, Amory Lovins, and others have written important books on a range of economic, cultural, and environmental breakthroughs that, in my view, are practical and much needed. But I want to stress that effective strategic planning must embrace—as a priority—the universal needs of the very young. Their wellbeing will comprise the true test of all our efforts.

Covenant and Principles

One morning in late 1996, the phrase 'Child Honouring' woke me up from a sound sleep. In that pivotal moment, I realized that all my years of singing and talking with young children, learning all I could about child development—and then of watching, with growing alarm, the disintegration of communities and the deterioration of our planet—had been a preparation of sorts, a way of showing me the link between the state of the world and the health of its children. I knew I had to speak out in a new way on behalf of the world's young. This sparked a dialogue with people in a wide range of disciplines.

On New Year's Eve, 1998, on the University of Virginia campus, an important part of the Child Honouring vision emerged. I had been visiting with Bill McDonough, then dean of architecture, who began his sustainable-design course each year with the question: how do we love all the children? McDonough spoke of the importance of not imposing remote tyranny on children to come, of society's current activities not compromising their future lives. This was the same message I had heard twelve-year-old Severn Cullis-Suzuki deliver in 1992 at the Earth Summit in Rio de Janeiro. Later that night, I pulled a copy of the US Declaration of Independence from a bookcase and began reading. In those pages, there was no mention of children. I wondered what a similar emancipatory proclamation about them might say, and began writing what became 'A Covenant for Honouring Children'—a declaration of duty to this and future generations.

An early supporter of the covenant was Philip Landrigan, a pediatrician and director of the Center for Children's Health and the Environment, who invited me to speak at the New York Academy of Medicine. After a day of scientific and medical presentations, my talk 'Child Honouring: The Loving Challenge' was greeted with a rousing ovation. Encouraged, I accepted invitations to speak at Parliament Hill in Ottawa and at a number of conferences, including the World Bank's 'Investing in Our Children's Future'. At Harvard, I spoke of Child Honouring as the next ecological paradigm, stressing its integrated nature as expressed in the following piece I began writing in Virginia:

> *A Covenant for Honouring Children*
> We find these joys to be self-evident:
> That all children are created whole, endowed with innate intelligence,
> with dignity and wonder, worthy of respect.

The embodiment of life, liberty and happiness, children are original blessings, here to learn their own song. Every girl and boy is entitled to love, to dream, and to belong to a loving 'village'. And to pursue a life of purpose.

> We affirm our duty to nourish and nurture the young, to honor their caring ideals as the heart of being human.
>
> To recognize the early years as the foundation of life, and to cherish the contribution of young children to human evolution.
>
> We commit ourselves to peaceful ways and vow to keep from harm or neglect these, our most vulnerable citizens.
>
> As guardians of their prosperity we honour
> the bountiful Earth whose diversity sustains us.
> Thus we pledge our love for generations to come. (Cavoukian 1992)

The following Child Honouring principles elaborate the essential themes of the covenant and suggest a way to embrace the young of every culture as treasure and inspiration. Taken together, they offer a holistic way of reversing the deterioration of natural and human communities, thereby brightening the outlook for our children and the world we share. They also form a basis for a multifaith consensus for societal renewal based on the universal and irreducible needs of the very young:

> *Respectful Love* is key. It speaks to the need to respect children as whole people and to encourage them to know their own voices. Children need the kind of love that sees them as legitimate beings, persons in their own right. Respectful love fosters self-worth—it i+s the prime nutrient in human development. Children need this not only from parents and caregivers, but also from the whole community.

Diversity is about abundance: of human dreams, intelligences, cultures, and cosmologies; of earthly splendours and ecosystems. Introducing children to biodiversity and human diversity at an early age builds on their innate curiosity. Not only is there a world of natural wonders to discover, but also a wealth of cultures, of ways to be human. Comforted by how much we share, we're able to delight in our differences.

Caring Community refers to the 'village' it takes to raise a child. The community can positively affect the lives of its children. Child-friendly shopkeepers, family resource centers, green schoolyards, bicycle lanes, and pesticide-free parks are some of the ways a community can support its young.

Conscious Parenting can be taught from an early age; it begins with empathy for newborns. Elementary and secondary school curricula could teach nurturing parenting (neither permissive nor oppressive) and provide students with insight into the child-rearing process. Such knowledge helps to deter teen pregnancies and unwanted children. Emotionally aware parents are much less likely to perpetuate abuse or neglect.

Emotional Intelligence sums up what early life is about: a time for exploring emotions in a safe setting, learning about feelings and how to express them. Those who feel loved are most able to learn and most likely to show compassion for others. Emotional intelligence builds character and is more important to later success than IQ. Cooperation, play, and creativity all foster the EQ needed for a joyful life.

Nonviolence is central to emotional maturity, to family relations, to community values, and to the character of societies that aspire to live in peace. It means more than the absence of aggression; it means living with compassion. Regarding children, it means no corporal punishment, no humiliation, no coercion. First do no harm, the physicians' oath, can apply to all our relations—it can become a mantra for our times. A culture of peace begins in a nonviolent heart and a loving home.

Safe Environments foster a child's feeling of security and belonging. The very young need protection from the toxic influences that permeate modern life—from domestic neglect and maltreatment to the corporate manipulations of their minds and the poisonous chemicals gaining access to their bodies. The first years are when children are most impressionable and vulnerable; they need safeguarding.

Sustainability means living in a way that does not compromise the lives of future generations. It refers not merely to conservation of resources, renewable energy development, and antipollution laws. To be sustainable, societies need to build social capacity by tapping the productive power of a contented heart. The loving potential of every young child is a potent source for good.

Ethical Commerce is fundamental to a humane world. It requires a revolution in the design, manufacture and sale of goods, supported by corporate reforms, triple bottom line business, full-cost accounting, tax and subsidy shifts, and political and economic cycles that reward long-term thinking. A child-honouring protocol for commerce would enable a restorative economy devoted to the well-being of the very young.

The contributors to *Child Honouring: How to Turn This World Around* include leading thinkers in the fields of psychology, education, economics, business, governance, and religion. Together, they show how the universal human symbol and reality—the child—can inspire a peacemaking culture for our world.

Onward! Making a Vow: Living the Covenant

Nelson Mandela's call to 'turn this world around, for the children'[9] is the plea of this century, the cry of humanity's elder on behalf of the young on every continent. And yet, never in history has there been a revolution inspired by the growing child. Child Honouring seeks to spark just that: a compassionate reglobalization towards a child-friendly world that would benefit everyone.

Whatever the future brings, in best-case scenarios or the worst—natural calamities, terrorist strikes, wars, rising sea waters—we have a duty to the children. How can Child Honouring, as a moral imperative, grow to be understood, shared, and engaged worldwide? It will take the whole village: parents and educators, CEOs and policy makers, grandparents and graduates, social justice and human rights activists, non-governmental organizations and students, professors and health professionals, scientists and faith leaders.

No belief system is more vital than a child's need to believe in the love of his or her caregivers and community. May our love for children activate the joyful power of possibility. In a number of ways, let me play to your imagination.

Scene 1: Bionomy

In April 2020, the lead article in both the *Online Bionomist* and in the United Nations Bionomic Report reads:

> The bionomy[10] shows robust signs of restorative energy, the Living Planet Index is in recovery mode, and for once, all indicators signal the overall turn towards sustainability that bionomists have predicted. The tax shift has been an unqualified success, sparking a reversal of decades-old destructive subsidies and practices. The Well-Being Index, established in every country, is a welcome change.

This future article touches on what today's business news could be reporting. It goes on to read:

The Humane Cultures indicator has been very active: A multifaith consensus on an initiative to end child beating has garnered widespread reaction and surprising levels of cooperation. After a passionate speech by the 85-year-old Dalai Lama in Vancouver, the Council of Children's Commissioners worked round the clock to reach agreement with the Young Catholics and the Muslim Youth League, and thus secure the pan-religious accord. This 2020 gathering of the World's Parliament of Religions has been named by the Global Center for Child Honouring as the recipient of its twelfth annual Humane Stewardship award.

The present is the ground that shapes our futures. Sixty years—six decades—is long enough for nuclear bombs to hold us for ransom and now to threaten us again, is too long to keep measuring societal progress with the wrong tools,[11] and is far too long for electing 'I'll grow the economy' politicians on false premises for false promises. Forty-five years is too long to ignore Eisenhower's warning about the military-industrial complex. Fear-induced realpolitik has bullied and pillaged the world far too long, and oil industry dominance has run its course. Two thousand years is far too long for money vendors to rule the temple, for money to have the upper hand, for children to be for sale, for human potential to falter.

May the immeasurable currencies of compassion accumulate (with interest!), actualizing and maximizing society's loving potential. This is the age of Real Magic: organic foods and fibres, smart money, hydrogen and hemp, infinite sunshine. Make room for the playful child, for love of life, to lead the way. Come feel the glory of Nature, our Creation mystery day and night, Universe of a bijillion stars. Tend the heart-mind, groom the garden. Wizards: light up the 'muggle' culture! Individuate, meditate, activate. Put your soul to work.

Scene 2: A Child Shall Lead Us

If a thing must be done, it can be. (Eleanor Roosevelt)

The global human family faces a basic conflict of interest: between a child's right to breathe and a corporation's limited liability protection by which it can do unlimited harm to that child and to all children. Imagine your infant (or grandchild) in a heroic stand-off, your David against the multinational Goliath, with nothing more than a moral slingshot—a reasonable right to breathe, play, and grow up in a non-toxic world.

In the multinational child, the multinational corporation has met its match: the universal child, essential human of every culture, the spirit of humanity.

Your Honour:
   My people come from no single country, they are in all of them;
they come from a space and time called childhood,
the place of our common origins; they have no vote,
no way to sway their fate except with the play of their eyes,
their curiosity, their songs, their dance, and their drawings;
for centuries these people have struggled for recognition, to take their
rightful place in communities, as part of the evolving intelligence of our species.
   These small and impressionable members of our human family,
Your Honour, they look up to you and the parental society
and believe you love them more than anything;
they expect you to rule in their favour;
as apprenticing adults, they are acutely sensitive to example,
they need consistency and fairness,
they are easily confounded by double standards,
hurt and demoralized by grown-up cynicism.
   Do you remember how it felt to be their age, Your Honour?
   The children are counting on you.
   In a genuinely human court, the child would prevail. The soulful cor-
poreal being would easily prevail against the heavy-footed rootless multinational, the soulless abstract entity, the pathological habit run amok. In
the court of humane ethics, 'Honour the child, serve its communities and
its habitat' would be the clear directive. For a theft of futures, guilty as
charged, the sentence might mean revocation of corporate license, ump-
teen years of community service, untold forms of retribution. A time to
come clean.
   Throughout the world, the young of the human family—the untapped
power of our species—must be seen, heard, and respected. The primacy of
the early years must become the key tenet by which to redirect our societies towards peace. Addressing children's universal needs can emerge
as the new standard by which compassionate cultures tilt their priorities
towards families and communities. *A vibrant 'first ecology' is the systems key
that opens lifetimes of change towards restoring our planet's life supports and
securing a viable future.*

Scene 3: The Power of Personal Acts

In this chapter, you have read about the emotional growth of the mind, the
unique vulnerability of the first years, every infant's foundational need
for respectful love and bonding. And you have read about the corporate
assault on children's minds and bodies—the bottom-line thinking that has
poisoned our planet and imperiled us—about the theft of our children's
futures. No spiritual tradition or holy book condones such a culture. Ask
yourself: if it's morally and ethically repugnant to exploit children and
undermine families, why is it legal? And now ask: am I complicit? Does my
conscience condone this? What am I prepared to do about it?
   We do not have decades in which to sue the chemical industry and
other multinationals for redress: some systems thinkers say we have but

20 to 25 years to set the course decisively for humanity. We can and we must engage every democratic forum available—to challenge, for example, political candidates to make sustainability the foundation of their platforms, and to make child-friendly, pro-family policies the focus of their corporate commerce agenda. There is no better way to tell wizards from muggles.

A defining moment in history is no time for paralysis or pessimism. Apartheid, the Soviet Empire, and the Berlin Wall have come and gone. So too will the global money-complex decline and fall, by will or by Nature. The obsession with money has been killing us. Maximizing capital has cost us the world. Delete the notion of maximizing capital. Let us maximize goodwill. Put money back in its place. Curb its excesses. Redefine its role. Let the children breathe.

Imagine a compassionate revolution that invites you to dance! Imagine trading the warrior archetype (spiritual or other) for the lover: the lover in you who loves life. The early troubadours of the twelfth and thirteenth centuries were lovers. In an age of male savagery and marriages for territory and power, the troubadours' writings of love for the sake of love were revolutionary, as were their concepts of chivalry and the gentle man.

Mandela's triumph was that of a lover: of freedom, of his people, of South Africa, of an important idea. His life has been an epic tale of ennobling love. During his confinement, he held his captors captive!—by his Gandhian dignity and by his faith in the possible. In a previous century, those who achieved the unthinkable abolition of slavery in the US knew it was time. They did not get stuck on feasibility, thinking 'Oh, it'll never work—the economy's built on slaves'. They knew it was time for an untenable situation to end. So too, the colonization of the child psyche must end.

Each person's inner nature longs to be known and to act in life's play cast as itself. Centuries apart, Socrates and Shakespeare said respectively, 'Know thyself' and 'To thine own self be true;...thou canst not then be false to any man' (*Hamlet*, act 1, scene 3). We need institutions built around that fundamental psychological value—authenticity, authentic being, true authorship of ourselves. A child only wants us to be real, to be truthful—is that not what we keep asking of the child?—to be true.[12] Is that not what you want in whomever you meet?

The sweetest freedom is creative: freedom—not from, but towards something. When children can be free to be their true selves, we too are freed: free to enable more love, more joy, and more creativity. We want to remake ourselves in the image of intelligent Nature, our loving human nature reclaimed and celebrated.[13]

Scene 4: 'Resisto Dancing'—An Invitation to Beluga Grads (BGs)

Dear Beluga Grads: You're Invited to Dance!
'Resisto Dancing'[14] is my graduation song for you, a fusion of Maslow,
Goldman, Dylan, Shakespeare, and hip-hop... Remember Abraham Maslow's
saying, 'Healthy individuation requires resisting unhealthy enculturation',
and Emma Goldman's, 'If I can't dance, it's not my revolution'.
The best dancers have a strong core,
a middle that lets them leap and turn with ease.
A child needs a strong middle too; we all do.
A sense of self as lovable and love-able, with potent conscience,
a power that's response-able—the lover, powered with a joy for life.
Resisto dancing, to keep your love alive...
to keep your songlines open and hummin'

You are neither alone, nor a drop in the ocean: you are the ripple, the wave, the gathering swell at a historic turn of the tide. In this age, the spirit of King and Gandhi are very much with us in the likes of Jane Goodall, Arundhati Roy, Howard Zinn, Naomi Klein, Desmond Tutu, Louise Arbour, Stephen Lewis, and Wangari Matthai, and in the distinguished voices of this anthology. We must become the change we seek in the world, Gandhi said. Lead by example, as best we can.

Riane Eisler's partnership ethic begs us to live it in our intimate relations, to weave a loving legacy from the strands of our daily lives. David Korten's Earth Community comes alive in every acre of farmland converted to organics, every restaurant devoted to local foods, and every family devoting a portion of its food bill to buying organic; every business transformed.

We turn this world around with every call, fax, or email to an elected official praising a sustainable action or supporting change; every publisher, nongovernmental organization, and state government that switches to chlorine-free paper[15]; every material designer who opts for nontoxic threads and dyes; every municipality that votes to ban pesticides; every school greening its playground; every Roots of Empathy classroom; every mosque where a woman leads prayers (as happened in Toronto); every cop or politician who stands up to corruption; every act of personal integrity.

Calling All Grads: Choose your *resisto*, and dance up the 'hood! Shake those sillies out. Keep a clear head and make positive waves. Belugas swim in pods...hmm, BG pods and podcasting...podsinging and pod-pals...pod-punning! Podruple your power.

Scene 5: The World We Want

From 80 countries, 400 eight-to-twelve-year-olds at a 2002 environmental conference in Victoria, British Columbia, joined me in singing the chorus of 'Turn This World Around',[16] my Mandela-inspired song. As I have heard repeatedly from children of many cultures, there was in these diverse young people an overwhelming desire for *all* children to live in a healthy world, a world of diversity and peace.

Towards this end, there is much that universities can and must do. Good news from my part of the world: the University of Victoria (UVic) and the University of British Columbia (UBC) are engaged in a variety of child-honouring initiatives. In the last two years, UVic has held a Colloquium on Child Honouring (which led to a Child Honouring task force), infused its teacher training program with the Covenant and Principles, held a seminar on children's rights with Irwin Cotler, Canada's justice minister, and created the World We Want Global Arts Project.[17]

The latter initiative grew from an exercise in paintbrush diplomacy: a children's art exhibit shown at UVic, with drawings from the children of Victoria and those of Iraq and Afghanistan, with the help of the Canadian military, who distributed art supplies overseas. There is immense power in these drawings, in the visual play of a child's soul and longing. Stunning use of colour and composition along with a purity of heart produced a moving exhibit, as the drawings' titles might suggest: 'I like to be a bride one day'; 'Let peace prevail in every country' (from Iraq); 'Young woman in a *burqua* is caged like a bird'; 'Mothers that are educated can teach their children well'; 'Land mines have caused death and dismemberment to many children' (from Afghanistan); and the one by Stephanie Chong (Grade seven, Victoria) entitled 'Make Peace: Do It For the Children went on to say: 'The theme of my artwork is peace...because that's the way I want the world to be. I drew two doves carrying a peaceful world. I also drew a sun in my poster because I think the sun represents a new beginning... STOP WAR NOW!'

At UBC, the Human Early Learning Partnership (HELP) is a pioneering, interdisciplinary research partnership that is directing a world-leading contribution to new understandings and approaches to early child development. HELP director Clyde Hertzman has been mapping the early development indicators of communities that correlate with positive outcomes in later life and has provided useful research for Mary Gordon's Roots of Empathy program. Centres of higher learning can inspire their own students by taking steps to become sustainable communities. A switch to using chlorine-free paper would be a significant step forward and set an example for other sectors. Multidisciplinary Institutes for Child Honouring could become hubs for advancing the next generation of research questions on Child Honouring's multiple facets.

Scene 6: GNN—Good News Network

The shake-up of bottom-line values can help correct media's depressing 'if it bleeds it leads' habit, in itself a distortion of news. A worldwide good news network could be an effective media engine for delving into the myriad stories on Child Honouring as embraced and practiced in diverse cultures and could serve to broadcast the inspirational acts of both individual youths and youth groups.[18]

Breaking News: The World Youth Parliament urges the world's billionaires to make legacy gifts to the world's children. Among their proposals: green computer production and recovery, neighbourhood Sunpower Hubs, energy efficiency contests, hemp newsprint and papers, and a superfund for cleaning up toxic waste sites. In a developing story, influential public figures are speaking out for the need to decommercialize childhood. At a press conference in New York, Larry King, Bill Gates, Oprah Winfrey, Shania Twain, and J. K. Rowling echoed the call of child development experts in urging lawmakers to ban advertising and marketing to children.

Headlines: Extra, Extra—Imagine…

UN Human Rights Commission recognizes the young child as MVP.[19]
China's internet youth initiative forms Global Green Youth Corps.
Bono and Nobel Laureates on hunger strike for free AIDS remedies.
Stunning gains for Progressive Party in U.S. congressional elections.
Windfall Profits Superfund powers Africa's recovery and revival.
Human Security Network oversees huge reductions in military budgets.
Children of every country singing Mother Earth anthems.
United States, India, and China pledge massive CO2 reductions to combat global warming.
With expanded powers, International Criminal Court targets corporate polluters.
In J. K. Rowling's new book, children rescue the real magic of the real world.
Ecopreneurs mark 10th anniversary of Fair Trade's makeover of Free Trade.

Choose your passion, invent your own headlines and work to make them come true.

A Circle Where We All Belong

Awakening to full humanity, we dare to ask any and all questions:

Who gave money the power to poison the world? Courts, governments, voters.
Who gave money the power to poison our food? Courts, governments, voters.
Who gave money the power to exploit the children?
Who has the power to turn this around?

We need new words and ideas to help us get through our global survival drama. Left, Right, Liberal, Radical, Conservative, Environmentalist: these labels cannot help us deal with interrelated issues like children's asthma and the toxic load of belugas, domestic violence and the soul erosion in our youth, international politics and dwindling freshwater supplies. This also has to be said: there is no such thing as 'the environment', a phrase that objectifies and alienates the living community of Nature from ourselves. It keeps us from feeling directly connected to the real world that we literally eat, drink, and inhale. To pretend we do not is madness.

We are meant for glory, not for misery, for reaching to our highest dreams when basic needs are met. The faces of Armenian, Japanese, Gabonese, Tibetan, Salish, Irish, Iranian, and indeed all children are animated by the same emotions. In every culture human tears fall the same, and smiles look the same. Remembering this, we can truly celebrate differences in the human mosaic. Let nations compete, if they want, in acts of kindness and compassion. They have no logical or moral rationale for keeping billions of people from life's table.

Child Honouring recognizes both the real suffering and the real joys in living and seeks to end the unnecessary suffering caused by ignorance. Is there not enough everyday tragedy in life without blind ignorance adding more? If ignorance is our greatest sin, then we all have our share. Let it be our common enemy, our only enemy. Conscious living and spiritual growth is what we are born to learn.

The child-honouring society I imagine would show love for its children in every facet of its design and organization. It would uphold the basic human rights of every child, and corporal punishment would be a thing of the past. No child would live in neglect or lack access to health care. Kids would not be alone after school playing violent computer games, eating junk food, waiting for a parent to get home. You would see family support centres in every neighbourhood. Working with the young would be valued and well rewarded. Universally available child care facilities would be staffed by trained professionals. We would have more schools and teachers, smaller class sizes, and a range of learning options from which families might choose. The arts would loom large, and from a young age we would teach child development as a primary subject as fundamental as reading, writing, and arithmetic. Children would learn early on about the importance of empathy and the basics of nurturing parenting.

A child-honouring world would honour the central place of women in life. To address the dramatic rise in children's asthma and the body burden of toxic compounds, mother's milk legislation would detoxify the chemical industry. We would breathe better thanks to strict clean-air laws. Bionomics would accelerate a full-fledged renaissance in business. We would have a triple bottom-line bionomy that factors social and environmental considerations into full-cost market pricing; a quality-of-life index that measures what matters most; subsidy and tax shifts towards clean energies, sustainable practices, and innovative enterprise; and political cycles not financed by corporations or geared primarily towards re-election. We would have a culture that rewards elected representatives for long-term wisdom rather than short-term power.

A child-friendly protocol for commerce would breathe new life into public health. Organic farmers would play a leading role in protecting the world's food security. Engineers would compete for child-friendly designs using the most benign chemical compounds and manufacturing processes. Corporate charter reforms would herald a new dawn in which CEOs and shareholders would be truly accountable to the public good. Released from the Midas curse, we could be free to work towards our highest aspirations.

Humanity must choose its future in a race against time. The compassionate revolution needs you. Make a vow to live by Child Honouring principles in your own life and to infuse them in our institutions. Let the transformative power of Child Honouring enrich our commons and strengthen the global civil society. Join the wave to restore our children's stolen future, to make this the world of their dreams as well as ours.

About the Author

Raffi Cavoukian is a renowned Canadian singer, songwriter, music producer, author, and child and peace advocate. In a career spanning four decades, Cavoukian has refused commercial endorsements or direct advertising to children. He developed principles for Child Honouring, including a website, a Centre (Salt Spring Island, British Columbia), a book, and now a global movement that views honouring children to be the best way to create ecologically sustainable, peacemaking cultures. Of his many books is the *Lightweb Darkweb: Three Reasons to Reform Social Media Before It Reforms Us* (2013). He is the recipient of three honorary degrees and numerous honours, some of which are the Global 500 Roll, the Order of Canada, and the United Nation's Earth Achievement Award.

Notes

* Excerpts from Cavoukian and Olfman, *Child Honouring: How to Turn This World Around* ([2006] 2010); 'Introduction: The Case for Child Honouring' and 'Onward! Making a Vow: Living the Covenant' reprinted with permission from the publisher.

1. This includes beluga grads, the young adults who as children sang 'Baby Beluga'. I wrote this song in 1979 after seeing a beluga whale at the Vancouver Aquarium; in 1980 it became the title song of my fourth album.

2. The old thinking was 'the dose makes the poison'. Recent findings show that exposure to even parts per billion or parts per trillion of some toxicants wreaks havoc on fetal development, including the endocrine system.

3. Union of Concerned Scientists (1992), at http://www.actionbioscience.org/environment/worldscientists.html.

4. United Nations Environment Programme (2000), at http://www.unep.org/geo2000/ov-e/index.htm.

5. The *New York Times* referred to the 15 February 2003 worldwide antiwar out-pouring of some 15 to 30 million people as a 'second global power'.

6. One of these is the Business Alliance of Local Living Economies (BALLE), which was cofounded by David Korten and Judy Wicks (at http://www.livingeconomies.org for more information).

7. Although people can and do change throughout their lives, it is much harder to alter the core emotional patterns of one's earliest years. What's more, a strong positive foundation at the start of life can help mitigate the wounding of later trauma.

8. At http://www.councilhd.ca.

9. In 2000, Mandela, Graça Machel, and UNICEF launched the Say Yes for Children campaign.

10. 'Bionomy' means 'the stewardship of the biosphere'.

11. Never thus intended, according to Simon Kuznets and (later) Robert F. Kennedy.

12. 'I wish that everyone could be exactly who they really are', from the song 'Whatever You Choose' (Rattray and Cavoukian 1995).

13. David Loye's book, *Darwin's Lost Theory of Love* (1998), reveals that survival of the fittest was a minor theme; Darwin's main idea was what he called 'the moral agency of man': humans as biologically social, relational, and loving creatures. This is also the view of biologist Umberto Maturana of Chile.

14. Full lyrics available at raffinews.com.

15. All books of New Society Publishers are on chlorine-free paper, as are all of Troubadour's books, and the paper used by Rounder Music (and Universal Music in Canada) for our music packaging. The Atkinson Charitable Foundation (Toronto) has made the switch. Praeger Press agreed to print the first edition of my book, *Child Honouring: How to Turn this World Around*, on chlorine-free paper. Doing so reduced the dioxin output produced by chlorine bleaching of pulp. This is one tangible way we can detox mothers' milk. Going chlorine-free is a litmus test of understanding the link between purchasing choices and public health.

16. 'Turn This World Around' (Cavoukian and Creber 2001).

17. At http://www.digitaltao.ca/testarea/latwww2/index.html.

18. Ryan's Well; and the international organization founded by Jane Goodall, Roots & Shoots.

19. MVP: Most valuable and vulnerable players, needing priority protection.

Chapter 20

Violence, Nonviolence, Anti-violence, and Contra-violence in Environmental Education Practice

Richard Kool

Introduction

Environmental Education (EE) emerged in the late 1960s and early 1970s as a domain of professional educational practice growing out of earlier incarnations of nature education and conservation education. Concerns driving the development of the field were expressed by one of its founders, Clay Schoenfeld, in one of the first syntheses of literature in that nascent field:

> The spirit of the seventies is a spirited concern for environmental quality. We are figuratively and literally sick and tired of a mis-development of America that diminishes daily the quality of the human experience: water pollution; air pollution; soil erosion; forest, range and wetland deterioration; waning wildlife; urban sprawl; pre-empted open spaces; vanishing wilderness; landscapes scarred by highways, litter, noise, and blight—a not so quite crisis of decreasing beauty and increasing contamination that threatens not only the pursuit of happiness but life itself. (Schoenfeld 1971: 11)

From this quotation, we can see that from the beginning of EE, a concern was articulated about violence against nature—a violence that in 1971 was troubling because that violence, that 'mis-development', diminished the quality of the human experience, decreased beauty, threatened the pursuit of happiness, and threatened life itself. Much of this litany seems quite naïve by today's standards, quite local, and in some ways even trivial. How can we compare global climate change and carbon dioxide loading of the atmosphere, ocean acidification, and the sixth great extinction with highways, litter, noise, and blight except to say the impacts noted in the 1970s were harbingers of what was to emerge 40 years later? Schoenfeld, however, never called what concerned him and the other founders of EE 'violence', and neither do most practitioners today.

I work in a field suffused by an awareness of violence and yet the word is rarely used. Violence is virtually never found in our professional

literature and I imagine is rarely uttered by teachers engaged in EE practice.[1] Among our founding documents is the Tbilisi Declaration, the product of an intergovernmental conference organized by UNESCO and UNEP
in 1977. This and other documents never mention human violence against
nature but simply talk about issues and problems. A literature search of
the major journals in the discipline produces nothing of relevance about
the relationship between EE and violence. The term 'nonviolence', for
example, comes up in fewer than ten out of hundreds of papers in our
major journals since 1997, and is found in the context of statements such
as: 'To promote environmentally conscious behaviors, teachers should
impart humanistic values such as social responsibility, compassion, nonviolence, and equality' (Kastenholz and Erdmann 1994: 19). Violence does
not show up in a single title at the annual meetings of the North American
Association for Environmental Education over the past five years.

Every day, environmental and sustainability educators talk about pollution, extinction, carbon-loading of the atmosphere, ocean acidification,
and unsustainability. What are these but an expression of the outcomes
of violence? Even when, as educators, we talk about and then go into natural settings with our students and experience the beauty, wonder, and
awe of the natural world, we know that what we study, admire, and live in
appreciation of is under various kinds of existential threats from human
violence; and while we might talk about threats, we rarely seem to understand those threats in terms of the threat of violence.

An Understanding of Violence

Violence is a term with a wide variety of meanings. For example, the
World Health Organization (WHO) states that violence is:

> the intentional use of physical force or power, threatened or actual,
> against oneself, another person, or against a group or community, that
> either results in or has a high likelihood of resulting in injury, death, psy-
> chological harm, maldevelopment or deprivation.[2]

It is understandable that the WHO, focused as it is on human health, would
have such a strongly anthropocentric definition of violence. Another definition is provided by peace scholar Johan Galtung, who originally stated,
'I see violence as avoidable insults to basic human needs, and more generally to life, lowering the real level of needs satisfaction below what is
potentially possible' (1990: 292). Later, and in a more expansive consideration, he redefines violence as

> any avoidable insult to basic human needs, and, more generally, to *sen-*
> *tient* life *of any kind, defined as that which is capable of suffering pain and can*
> *enjoy well-being,* lowering the real level of needs satisfaction below what is
> potentially possible. (Galtung 2013: 35, emphasis added)

Galtung extends his conception of violence significantly beyond human consideration to include individual sentient members of the biosphere and notes that beyond the four classes of basic human needs that violence violates—survival, wellbeing, freedom, and identity or meaning—'the needs of the non-human rest of nature; the *sine qua non* for human existence' should likely be added to his typology (2013: 36).

Humans can and do enact violence on the rest of non-human nature, reducing the potential for both human good and the good of non-human nature as well. And while the forces of nature—both biotic and physical—are powerful and can do great damage to humans and non-humans alike, the forces of nature do not, in Galtung's consideration, exhibit violence. Natural systems do what natural systems do and we would be wrong were we to talk about predation, for example, as violence. The intent of a predator is to preserve life; there is no intent to insult.

In this regard, it may not be useful to argue about which groups of pre-industrial humans did or did not enact violence against non-human nature or whether, in Galtung's sense, there was an intent to insult. I also believe that we should be extremely careful about painting all modern human activity as violent, while at the same time, romanticizing traditional peoples' activities everywhere. Not all human actions in the world should be seen as enacting violence against nature, and teachers should not be giving children that frame of understanding for human activity in the world through environmental education programs. Not all cultures through time have lived lives of environmental violence and, to be clear, not all traditional peoples lived sustainable lives in harmony with nature (see, e.g., Diamond 2005; Wright 2004). It makes as much sense to me to say that violence towards nature is part of our genetic makeup as to say it is part of the nature of a lion or a moose. However, today and at least since the Industrial Revolution growing out of European cultures,[3] many humans have enacted violence against nature in three ways that Galtung describes: direct, structural, and cultural.

He talks about 'direct violence' as the outcome of an actor with intent to commit violence; humans do exhibit direct violence towards nature through their intent. Direct violence is something that humans are capable of doing, and in an environmental context, can occur in deeds such as slaughtering rhinoceroses for their horns or grizzly bears for their pelts, knowingly dumping toxic materials into watercourses, strip mining, or creating toxic tailing ponds at the tar sands operations in northern Alberta.

Galtung also talks about 'structural violence' as the result of human systems that cause violence either through intent or unintentionally, or through what we do or what we fail to do. To Galtung, structural environmental violence would be more insidious [than direct violence], not intended to destroy nature but nevertheless doing so by the pollution and depletion associated with modern industry, leading to dying forests, ozone holes, global warming etc. What happens is transformation of nature through *industrialization*, leaving non-degradable residues and depleting nonrenewable resources, combined with a world encompassing *commercialization* that makes the consequences invisible to the perpetrators. (Galtung 1990: 294)

Galtung finishes his typology with 'cultural violence' as the result of social legitimization and justification of direct or structural violence (1990: 294). As members of an industrialized culture, we are complicit in cultural violence because we enjoy the legitimization and indeed, the expectation of structural environmental violence being perpetrated on our behalf, yet more often than not, hidden from our view and our consciousness. In that context, the commission of culturally permitted environmental violence is part of what Kelly Levin and colleagues refer to as a 'super wicked problem' (2012: 123). Such problems have 'wicked' attributes (Rittell and Webber 1973), which are characterized as being 'more complex, rather than just complicated—that is, [a wicked problem] cannot be removed from its environment, solved, and returned without affecting the environment' (Grint 2008: 12). The added super features are that, for this class of wicked problems, 'time is running out; *those who cause the problem also seek to provide a solution*; the central authority needed to address it is weak or non-existent; and, partly as a result, policy responses discount the future irrationally' (Levin et al. 2012: 123, emphasis added).

While few of us may intentionally commit direct environmental violence in this sense (although many of our actions on a smaller scale are clearly direct forms of violence), it seems those of us in highly industrialized and technologically advanced societies are unavoidably complicit in both the structural environmental violence of our society through our daily living, as well as in its cultural legitimization through our acceptance of the long-term social and political structures that actively defend and maintain the necessity of environmental violence. Interestingly, Galtung relates these three forms of violence in a revealing temporal analysis: 'Direct violence is an event; structural violence is a process with ups and downs; cultural violence is an invariant, a "permanence"...remaining essentially the same for long periods, given the slow transformations of basic culture' (1990: 294). For Galtung, it is clear that while we have to work at reducing all levels of violence, the invariant of cultural violence must be the critical leverage-spot we need to work on to reduce the other two as, according to Galtung, 'cultural violence makes direct and structural violence look, even feel, right—or at least not wrong' (1990: 291). And it is in these three domains of violence that the field I have worked in for many years—a field that concerns itself with educating in, about, and for the environment (Lucas 1972)—should be explicitly invested. Unfortunately, it isn't.

Environmental Education and the Silence Around Violence

For many educators, it seems that presenting the language of violence as part of an analysis of contemporary environmental issues is anathema. Indeed, many of the governmental and corporate supporters and sponsors of today's environmental education programs in Canada are committing the most egregious direct violence against the environment, benefiting from the structural violence we condone and the cultural violence that suffuses it all. For example, the Alberta Council for Environmental Education,[4] an important and influential organization that does excellent work in Canada and is run by people I deeply respect, receives their major financial support from Cenovus ('we're committed to being a responsible developer of one of Canada's most valuable resources—the oil sands'), Conoco Phillips ('we are poised to become Canada's leader in the discovery and responsible development of our oil and gas assets'), Encana ('a leading North American energy producer that is focused on growing its strong portfolio of diverse resource plays producing natural gas, oil and natural gas liquids'), Tervita ('we deliver on our value promise—minimizing impact, maximizing returns—for customers and partners in oil and gas, mining, industry, community and government'), and Suncor ('a Canadian integrated energy company. It specializes in production of synthetic crude from oil sands'). These companies are all directly involved with the Alberta tar sands developments, oil pipelines, and, in general, facilitating the movement of fossil carbon deposits from the ground ultimately into greenhouse gases deposited into the atmosphere.[5]

Another Alberta based and very successful environmental non-governmental organization (ENGO), Inside Education, has at its highest level of funding partnership a list of 13 companies that includes British Petroleum (BP) ('one of the world's leading integrated oil and gas companies'), the Canadian Association of Petroleum Producers ('Canada's oil sands industry will provide a secure source of energy, reduce its impact on the environment and provide economic benefits to society while developing this globally significant resource'), Cenovus, Connacher ('a growing integrated crude oil and natural gas company with a focus on producing bitumen and expanding its *in-situ* oil sands projects'), Devon ('a leading independent oil and natural gas exploration and production company'), Encana, and Suncor.

As governments in Canada have backed away from funding ENGOs delivering EE programs and many right-wing politicians led by the current Prime Minister, Stephen Harper, see environmentalists as 'radicals'[6] and 'public enemies',[7] organizations trying to deliver programs are forced to curry favour with the only other part of society with disposable funds: the wealthy corporate players in the fossil-fuel industry. In this context, environmental educators associated with ENGOs such as those mentioned above might be able to talk about environmental issues and problems, but I can only imagine that talking about environmental violence might not be appreciated by some of their larger corporate sponsors.

As environmental educators, we do have our traditional responses to environmental violence (which is never named). Quite often in schools, these responses include advocacy of a 3Rs response (reduce, reuse, recycle), while some teachers or programs will encourage advocacy activities such as letter-writing campaigns. The seeming emphasis on personal responsibility and the accompanying feeling of shame or guilt for our culturally sanctioned violence is part of such responses, along with efforts to bolster hope and overcome apathy (see, e.g., Kelsey and Armstrong 2012; Kool 2010; Lertzman 2008; Ojala 2007, 2012). But if environmental violence surrounds us, how can and should we talk about forms of environmental nonviolence with our students?

Environmental Education, Nonviolence, and Anti-violence

The themes of the conference at which this chapter was originally presented related to the power of nonviolence and, clearly in some contexts, environmental nonviolence as a potential response to the violence we see around us. A response discussed and/or enacted with our students to what we see as direct environmental violence could be direct environmental *nonviolence*. As individuals, we can resolve to reduce or eliminate—which clearly is nearly impossible to do if we are to remain members of our technological society (Ellul 1966)—our direct violence, as difficult or impossible as that is for many of us to do. Few of us wake up in the morning with the intent to commit violence against nature. While I do, for example, get on airplanes and burn natural gas at home, my daily commute is a fossil-free one, and so I try to convince myself I can look my students in the eye—once I shower with solar-heated water after my bicycle ride—and talk about personal nonviolent decisions we can make.

While I have to see that getting on my bike is better than getting into a car every day, I am clear that my actions make little direct impact on the amount of anthropogenic carbon dioxide released into the atmosphere globally, which in 2014 was 44 Gigatons (Le Quéré et al. 2015). My commute is a nonviolent response to my more general practice of what I would like to think of as low-level environmental violence that I could, were I to choose to do so, lower even more. As educators, we can help our students from where they are, with whom they are, and with the tools available to them, to look for nonviolent responses to direct environmental violence. This may not be enough, however, as the structural and cultural forms of environmental violence cannot be confronted in ways as simple as, for example, getting on my bicycle or eating sustainably-harvested seafood. For some teachers and students, there is a sense that perhaps we must get involved in environmental *anti-violence* as nonviolence may not be enough. Anti-violence begins to target those structural and cultural forms of environmental violence through an examination of and actions against those political and economic structures that compel many of us to engage in violence.

A range of anti-violence responses to stop direct environmental violence may include acts of engaged citizenship (Dalton 2008; McBeth et al. 2010), such as attempts at community restoration and transformation—for example, Transition Town[8] approaches—and range from activities such as countering voter suppression to participating in demonstrations or engaging in civil disobedience. Whether my colleagues running fossil-fuel funded ENGOs could talk about anti-violence is not clear. The question remains: would their funding partners continue to support them if, as a result of the programs they present, young people decided to take an anti-violence and pro-citizenship stance and work publically and forcefully against environmental violence that might involve working against the funders of the programs from which they are learning?

Structural violence and cultural violence are different and far more difficult to confront than direct forms of violence. Structural environmental violence is something that we are all part of, as previously argued. While many of our students and colleagues have no choice but to get in carbon-producing vehicles every morning, eat factory-produced chicken eggs, or arrive to a conference via fossil-fuel-using forms of transportation, I wonder how many of us are comfortable with the cultural justifications that allow this form of violence to occur.

My issue is that while EE's analysis may extend to understanding the structural and cultural aspects of environmental violence, our prescriptions tend to go back to ways of stopping direct violence but often through what might be somewhat trivially direct means and small projects, projects that either cannot or will not examine the larger issues of structural or cultural violence. Within the world of most K-12 environmental educators, I would argue, we have not been able to confront structure and analysis with prescriptions that seem to be anywhere near effective relative to the scale of the problems we face. While there are wonderful scholars and graduate academic programs that do deal with critical issues and analysis, confronting structural environmental violence means confronting real economic and political power, and schools are neither authorized nor expected to teach students how to confront power and change systems.

While as teachers, we may feel that we have few opportunities to offer responses that might be categorized as anti-violence, we could at least help to reveal what is going on around us to our students, colleagues, communities, and ourselves. Sprinkling, so to speak, the pixie dust of revelation to reveal the now-hidden nature of the systems of structural and cultural violence that are driving our culture in such a destructive manner, we can help to expose what is going on economically, environmentally, and socially and what, in a culturally and age-appropriate manner, could be a range of actions and responses in a variety of spaces, including the home, the school, the natural world, and community, and in a variety of contexts that would necessarily involve the political. At the same time as providing these opportunities for responses and revealing spaces and contexts for action, educators must also be open to the directions and insights of our students and our communities. This openness to possibility and direction is something that we can all do. As Gandhian activist Rajagopal P. V. (2014) explained, if we are to make nonviolence a powerful tool for change, we have to be with the people, learn from the people, and act with the people at their speed and level.

Yet as noted earlier, sometimes all we can do is move in small ways. Sometimes as teachers, students, and community members, all we have available to us are small things, as we are not in a position to exert the power necessary to change society and culture. If the structures of society keep us from being nonviolent and we have few opportunities as educators to engage in anti-violence, what we can ask of our students, as collaborators with us, is to engage in what I will tentatively call *contra-violence*.

Environmental Education and Contra-violence

'Contra-violence' could be seen as the acts we can do to counteract and attempt to undo, and not just minimize, the violence that our individual actions within our culture inflict on the environment. Within the realm of EE, we can refer to these acts as 'environmental contra-violence'. With intent, we can do more than only *not* do violence and work to change systems that drive us towards environmental violence; we can also engage in acts of healing, of restoration and regeneration, and of planting the seeds of regrowth and hope. There are skills that need to be taught to do this work of *undoing* violence, and environmental educators are in a good position to enhance students' abilities and their sense of agency to engage in the problems that surround us (see, e.g., Bandura 2006; Newman and Dale 2005). As teachers, we can help our students to identify the three forms of violence that Galtung articulates, see how they impact the world, and then foster a discourse that talks about, imagines, and then practices the three alternative praxes I have proposed.

Working within an environmental contra-violence context, there are culturally acceptable injunctions about the obligation to engage in ecological restoration (Higgs 1991), a very clear form of contra-violence. Gretel van Wieren talks about 'ecological restoration as public spiritual practice' and 'argues that one of the ways in which restoration practice reconnects humans to nature is in a spiritual-moral sense. In addition to performing ecological work, restoration performs sacred work and serves as a form of public witness; and it can engender spiritual-moral experiences within participants' (2008: 237). This work of restoration is something that we can advance as educators: we can teach the science necessary to understand the meaning and impact of our actions and at the same time, teach the moral correctness of a contra-violent approach to environmental violence.

While schools might not want to bring religious teachings into the classroom, many children attending schools will come from religious backgrounds that have strong statements about contra-violent pro-environmental behaviours (van Wieren 2013). Were we to be religious educators or brave enough to bring religious topics into a secular classroom, I believe we would not find it hard to connect with the religious orientations of many of our students. Or perhaps we can see education, as did the great mathematician and metaphysician Alfred North Whitehead, as religious in itself:

> The essence of education is that it be religious... A religious education is an education which inculcates duty and reverence. Duty arises from our potential control over the course of events. Where attainable knowledge could have changed the issue, ignorance has the guilt of vice. And the foundation of reverence is this perception, that the present holds within itself the complete sum of existence, backwards and forwards, that whole amplitude of time, which is eternity. (Whitehead [1929] 1949)

One could say that contra-violence is a duty we could strive to inculcate in students and in ourselves even as we work to influence events with the people around us and with the tools and power at our disposal. And our work in this context, while perhaps small, can still be done with reverence.

The conception of ecological restoration as a means of countering the ecological violence we perpetrate is easily found in our religious traditions. While I am not a religious scholar, it was not hard to find sources such as those citing the Prophet Muhammad, who said: 'Whoever plants a tree and diligently looks after it until it matures and bears fruit is rewarded' (in Religion and Conservation Biology 2008). Similarly, Othman Abd Ar-Rahman Llewellyn wrote:

The Prophet Muhammad, on whom be blessings and peace, declared that fructifying the earth is a profoundly ethical act:

Whoever revives dead land, for him is reward in it; and whatever any creature seeking food eats of it shall be reckoned as charity from him.

There is no Muslim who plants a tree or sows a field, and a human, bird, or animal eats from it, but it shall be reckoned as charity from him. (Llewellyn 1984: 31)

While through these few quotations the Prophet is speaking about positive actions, Judaism has injunctions against direct environmental violence in the teachings of *bal taschit*, meaning 'do not destroy' (see, e.g., Friedman and Klein 2010; Nir 2006; Wolff 2009). These teachings are related to the prohibition, found in Deuteronomy 20:19, against the destruction of fruit trees during times of military siege: 'when you besiege a town for many days, waging-war against it, to seize it: you are not to bring ruin on its trees by swinging-away (with) an ax against them, for from them you may eat. For are the trees of the field human beings, (able) to come against you in a siege?' (Fox 1995: 941).

There is also the positive injunction of *tikkun ha-olum*, having a range of meanings often revolving around the conception of 'repair of the world' (Cooper 2013) or 'improvement of society' (Rosenthal 2005), which is derived from Midrash Ecclesiastes Rabbah 7:13, an early rabbinic commentary:

When God created the first human beings, God led them around the Garden of Eden and said: 'Look at my works! See how beautiful they are— how excellent! For your sake I create them all. See to it that you do not spoil and destroy My world; for if you do, there will be no one else to repair it.' (Friedman and Klein 2010)

Many secular as well as religious environmentalists, environmental scientists, and educators have also been deeply moved by and encouraged by Pope Francis's 2015 encyclical on climate change.[9] They are also encouraged by both his understanding of the science involved and his call for necessary action.

Conclusion

I believe that as educators, we must be involved in the transformation of our culture—one that seems simply to accept environmental violence as normal and necessary. While we can and likely must work over the long term to change systems and structures that facilitate the three forms of environmental violence, we can and must act in pro-environmental ways, as small as they might be, and together with others engage in similar acts. Confronting the violence in which we are complicit and then in small ways pushing against what we ourselves cannot change as an individual, yet can transform as a society, are acts of potential meaning making.

As Viktor Frankl learned from his experiences in Nazi concentration camps, we have available to us three ways of creating meaning. First 'is by creating a work or by doing a deed' (Frankl 1984: 170). In this sense, works of nonviolence, anti-, and contra-violence are acts of meaning making. Second, Frankl states that meaning is created by 'experiencing something or encountering someone' (1984: 170). This claim points to the understanding that our work as educators is never done in isolation but always with others. Finally, in the face of unavoidable suffering, Frankl affirms that 'even the helpless victim of a hopeless situation, facing a fate he cannot change, may rise above himself, may grow beyond himself, and by so doing change himself' (1984: 170). Our actions may be small, tiny even, and yet, we can change ourselves as we each do our own small thing, even if that is all we can do.

A sense of hopelessness seems to run through the deep emotional lives of many involved in environmental protection and societal transformation. The tasks are so great and the power moving us in unsustainable directions so pervasive that many of us are challenged by a sense that no matter what we do, it will not be enough. Individually, this may be very true. Yet, confronting environmental violence does mean that we have to *do* something, and in that doing of something, we may find a way to remember our personal agency, and in that remembering, we can develop a sense of efficacy in our ability to do something that is within our power and through working in solidarity with others.

As educators, we can strive to encourage our students to accept the responsibility of reducing, resisting, and then working to undo the damage we collectively have created wherever we are, with the people around us, and with the tools available. Healing, restoration, and the awareness of an obligation to and the power to help in the healing of a damaged world can be profoundly rewarding activities and should be a natural part of our educational life from early childhood to old age. Our individual attempts at healing may be incommensurate with the wound to be healed, but it moves us spiritually towards the right direction. These deeds allow us to fulfill the injunction made by Rabbi Tarfon in the second century CE, who wrote: 'You are not obliged to complete the work [of the repair of the world], but neither are you free to evade it' (Pirkei Avot, 2003).

About the Author

Richard Kool, EdD, founded the MA program in Environmental Education and Communication at Royal Roads University in Victoria, British Columbia, in 2003. His interests have ranged widely, and his publications include studies on ciliated protozoans, whales and dinosaurs, museum education and exhibits, and pedagogical, psychological, and philosophical dimensions of environmental education.

Notes

1.   Yet a foundational article (Harris 2004) on peace education clearly sees environmental education as a vehicle for peace.

2.   See 'Health Topics/Violence' (2014b), at http://www.who.int/topics/violence/en/para 1.

3.   It should be noted that European cultures are not alone in enacting violence against nature (see, e.g., Tuan 1968; Tuan and Tuan 1970).

4.   Online, at http://www.acee.ca.

5.   All quotes from corporations mentioned are taken directly from their corporate web pages or secondary sources: British Petroleum (http://www.bp.com/en/global/corporate/about-bp/bp-at-a-glance.html); Canadian Association of Petroleum Producers (http://www.capp.ca/canadian-oil-and-natural-gas/oil-sands/what-are-oil-sands); Cenovus (https://www.cenovus.com/about/); Connacher (http://www.pageinsider.com/connacheroil.com); ConocoPhilips (http://www.conocophillips.ca/who-we-are/Pages/default.aspx); Devon (http://www.devonenergy.com/about-us); Encana (https://www.encana.com/about/): Suncor (https://en.wikipedia.org/wiki/Suncor_Energy); Tervita (http://www.tervita.com/about-us/overview).

6.   See Babad (2012), at http://www.theglobeandmail.com/report-on-business/top-business-stories/joe-oliver-taints-all-with-talk-of-environmentalists-radicals/article 4085710/.

7.   See McQuaig (2012), at https://www.thestar.com/opinion/editorialopinion/2012/06/04/stephen_harper_government_turns_environmentalists_into_public_enemies.html.

8.   See, for example, Transition Network, at https://www.transitionnetwork.org.

9.   See 'Encyclical Letter *Laudato si*' (2015), at http://w2.vatican.va/content/francesco/en/encyclicals/documents/papa-francesco_20150524_enciclica-laudato-si.html.

Bibliography

A Force More Powerful. 'Homepage' (n.d.), at http://www.aforcemorepowerful.org/ (accessed 10 February 2016).

Abbey, Edward. *Desert Solitaire: A Season in the Wilderness*. New York: Simon and Schuster, 1968.

—*The Monkey Wrench Gang*. New York: Avon Books, 1976.

—'Forward!' In *Ecodefense: A Field Guide to Monkeywrenching*, 3rd edn., ed. Dave Foreman and Billy Haywood, 17-19. Chico, CA: Abbzug Press, 1993.

Abram, David. 'Reciprocity'. In *Rethinking Nature: Essays in Environmental Philosophy*, ed. Bruce Foltz and Robert Frodeman, 77-94. Bloomington, IN: Indiana University Press, 2004.

Ackerman, Peter, and Jack Duvall. *A Force More Powerful: A Century of Nonviolent Conflict*. New York: Palgrave, 2000.

Adams, Carol. *The Sexual Politics of Meat*. New York: Continuum, 1990.

Albert Einstein Institution. 'Homepage' (2016), at http://www.aeinstein.org/ (accessed 10 February 2016).

Alberta Council for Environmental Education. *ABCEE* (n.d.), at http://www.abcee.ca (accessed 10 April 2014).

Alliance of Small Island States (AOSIS). 'About AOSIS' (2015), at http://aosis.org/ (accessed 13 November 2015).

Altman, Nathaniel. *The Nonviolent Revolution: A Comprehensive Guide to Ahimsa—The Philosophy of Dynamic Harmlessness*. Longmead, UK: Element books, 1988.

Ammar, Nawal. 'Wife Battery in Islam: A Comprehensive Understanding of Interpretations'. *Violence against Women* 13 (2007): 516-26.

Amnesty International. 'Global Movement Votes to Adopt Policy to Protect Human Rights of Sex Workers' (2015), at http://www.amnesty.org/latest/news/2015/08/global-movement-votes-to-adopt-policy-to-protect-human-rights-of-sex-workers (accessed 11 August 2015).

Amster, Randall, Elavie Ndura-Ouédraogo, and Michael N. Nagler. *Exploring the Power of Nonviolence: Peace, Politics and Practice*. Syracuse, NY: Syracuse University Press, 2013.

Aquinas, St Thomas. *Summa Theologica*, 61 vols. Cambridge: Blackfriars, 1964–81.

Arendt, Hannah. *Crises of the Republic*. New York: Harcourt Brace Jovanovich, 1972.

—*On Revolution*. London: Penguin Books, 1990.

—*The Human Condition*. Chicago, IL: Chicago University Press, 1998.

—*Between Past and Future: Eight Exercises in Political Thought*. New York: Penguin Books, 2006.

Asad, Talal. *Formations of the Secular: Christianity, Islam, Modernity*. Stanford, CA: Stanford University Press, 2003.

Ascione, Frank R., C. V. Weber, and D. S. Wood. 'The Abuse of Animals and Domestic

Violence: A National Survey of Shelters for Women Who Are Battered'. *Society and Animals* 5.3 (1997): 205-18.

Association pour une Solidarité Syndicale Étudiante (ASSÉ). *Recueil de Texte sur l'Histoire du Mouvement Étudiant* (2005), at http://www.asse-solidarite.qc.ca/wp-content/uploads/2013/02/histoire-du-mouvement-etudiant-hiver-2005.pdf (accessed 7 October 2013).

Attenborough, Richard (dir.). *Gandhi*. 1982. DVD. Columbia Pictures.

Ayer, A. J. *Language, Truth and Logic*. London: Victor Gollancz, 1936.

Babad, Michael. 'Joe Oliver Taints All with Talk of Environmentalist, Radicals'. *The Globe and Mail* (9 January 2012), at http://www.theglobeandmail.com/report-on-business/top-business-stories/joe-oliver-taints-all-with-talk-of-environmentalists-radicals/article4085710/ (accessed 21 June 2016).

Baker, Catherine. 'Music as a Weapon of Ethnopolitical Violence and Conflict: Processes of Ethnic Separation During and After the Break-up of Yugoslavia'. *Patterns of Prejudice* 47.4/5 (2013): 409-29.

Bales, Kevin. *Modern Day Slavery*. Oxford: One World, 2009.

Ball, Christine. 'The History of the Voice of Women—*Voix des Femmes*—The Early Years'. PhD dissertation. University of Toronto, Toronto, ON, 1994.

Bandura, Albert. 'Toward a Psychology of Human Agency'. *Perspectives on Psychological Science* 1/2 (2006): 164-80.

Barata, Paula, Mary Jan McNally, Isabel Sales, and Donna Stewart. 'Portuguese Immigrant Women's Perspectives on Wife Abuse: A Cross-Generational Comparison'. *Journal of Interpersonal Violence* 20 (2005): 1132-50.

Bartkowski, Maciej J. *Recovering Nonviolent History: Civil Resistance in Liberation Struggles*. Boulder, CO: Lynne Rienner, 2013.

Baum, Gregory. *Amazing Church: A Catholic Theologian a Half-Century of Change*. Maryknoll, NY: Orbis, 2005.

BBC News Staff. 'Israel-Palestinian Violence: Israeli killed in Beersheva Bus Station Attack' (2015), at http://www.bbc.com/news/world-middle-east-34567988 (accessed 18 October 2015).

Beaman-Hall, Lori, and Nancy Nason-Clark. 'Translating Spiritual Commitment into Service: The Response of Evangelical Women to Wife Abuse'. *Canadian Woman's Studies* 12 (1997): 176-96.

Bekoff, Marc. *The Emotional Lives of Animals: A Leading Scientist Explores Animal Joy, Sorrow, and Empathy, and Why They Matter*. Novato, CA: New World Library, 2007.

Benessaieh, Karim. 'Printemps Érable: 382 Arrestations, 1711 Interpellations'. *La Presse* (5 June 2013), at http://www.lapresse.ca/actualites/dossiers/conflit-etudiant/201306/04/01-4657804-printemps-erable-382-arrestations-1711-interpellations.php (accessed 24 September 2013).

Berry, Thomas. 'Ethics and Ecology'. Paper presented at the Harvard Seminar on Environmental Values, Harvard University, Cambridge, MA (April 1996), at http://www.earthcommunity.org/images/Ethics%20and%20Ecology%201996-Edited.pdf (accessed 1 May 2013).

—*The Dream of the Earth*. San Francisco, CA: Sierra Club Books, [1988] 2006.

—*The Great Work: Our Way into the Future*. New York: Bell Tower, 1999.

—'Response to the Essays'. *Worldviews: Environment, Culture and Religion* 5.2 (2001): 198-222.

—'Wonder'. *The Ecologist* 32.6 (2002): 38.

—'Loneliness and Presence'. In *A Communion of Subjects: Animals in Religion, Science, and*

Ethics, ed. Paul Waldau and Kimberley Patton, 5-10. New York: Columbia University Press, 2006.

Best, Steven, and Anthony J. Nocella II. 'Introduction: A Fire in the Belly of the Beast: The Emergence of Revolutionary Environmentalism'. In *Igniting a Revolution: Voices in Defense of the Earth*, ed. Steven Best and Anthony J. Nocella II, 8-32. Oakland, CA: AK Press, 2006.

Bharadwaj, L. K. 'Principled Versus Pragmatic Nonviolence'. *Peace Review: A Journal of Social Justice* 10.1 (1998): 79-81.

Bihr, Alain. *La Novlangue Néolibérale*. Lausanne, CH: Éditions Page Deux, 2007.

Biko, Stephen. *We Write What We Like: Celebrating Steve Biko*, ed. C. van Wyk. Johannesburg, ZA: Wits University Press, 2007.

—*I Write What I Like*, ed. Aelred Stubbs. Johannesburg, ZA: Picador Africa, 2009.

Blatchford, Andy. 'La Crise Étudiante Intéresse à l'Étranger'. *Metro* (28 May 2012), at http://journalmetro.com/dossiers/conflit-etudiant/80682/la-crise-etudiante-interesse-a-letranger/ (accessed 24 September 2013).

Bloquonslahausse. 'À Propos' (2011), at http://www.bloquonslahausse.com/laclasse/a-propos/ (accessed 25 September 2013).

Bock, Joseph G. *The Technology of Nonviolence: Social Media and Violence Prevention*. Cambridge, MA: MIT Press, 2012.

Boff, Leonardo. 'Foreword'. In *Relentless Persistence: Nonviolent Action in Latin America*, ed. Philip McManus and Gerald Schlabach, vii-xi. Eugene, OR: Wipf & Stock, 1991.

—*Cry of the Earth, Cry of the Poor*, trans. Philip Berryman. Maryknoll, NY: Orbis Books, 1997.

—*The Prayer of Saint Francis: A Message of Peace for the World Today*, trans. Philip Berryman. Maryknoll, NY: Orbis, 2001.

—*Francis of Assisi: A Model for Human Liberation*, trans. John W. Dierckmeier. Maryknoll, NY: Orbis, 2006.

—*Virtues for Another Possible World*, trans. Alexander Guilherm. Eugene, OR: Cascade Books, 2011.

—'An Unworthy Servant in the Service of Francis', trans. Francis McDonaugh. *The Tablet* (27 June 2015).

Boivin, Simon. 'Bachand Déposera son Budget le 20 Mars'. *La Presse* (6 March 2012), at http://www.lapresse.ca/le-soleil/actualites/politique/201203/06/01-4503059-bachand-deposera-son-budget-le-20-mars.php?utm_categorieinterne=trafficdrivers&utm_contenuinterne=cyberpresse_vous_suggere_4504478_article_POS1 (22 September 2013).

Boltanski, Luc, and Ève Chiapello. *Le Nouvel Esprit du Capitalisme*. Paris: Gallimard, [1999] 2011.

Bond, Brian. *The Pursuit of Victory from Napoleon to Saddam Hussein*. Oxford: Oxford University Press, 1996.

Boulding, Elise. *Cultures of Peace: The Hidden Side of History*. Syracuse, NY: Syracuse University Press, 2000.

Bourdieu, Pierre, and Luc Boltanski. *La Production de l'Idéologie Dominante*. Paris: Raisons d'Agir, 2008.

Boutilier, Beverly. 'Educating for Peace and Cooperation: The Women's International League for Peace and Freedom, 1919–1929'. Master of Arts dissertation, Carleton University, Ottawa, ON, 1998.

Bowler, Kate. *Blessed: A History of the American Prosperity Gospel*. New York: Oxford University Press, 2013.

Bramadat, Paul. 'Beyond Christian in Canada: Religion and Ethnicity in a Multicultural Society'. In *Religion and Ethnicity in Canada*, ed. Paul Bramadat and David Seljak, 1-29. Toronto ON, CA: Pearson Longman, 2005.

Branagan, Marty. *Global Warming, Militarism, and Nonviolence: The Art of Active Resistance.* New York: Palgrave MacMillan, 2013.

Bristow, William. 'Enlightenment'. In *The Stanford Encyclopedia of Philosophy*, ed. Edward N. Zalta (2011), at http://plato.stanford.edu/archives/sum2011/entries/enlightenment/ (accessed 10 October 2015).

British Petroleum. 'BP at a glance' (2016), at http://www.bp.com/en/global/corporate/about-bp/bp-at-a-glance.html (accessed 21 June 2016).

Brookfield, Tarah. 'The Fasting Granny vs. the Trudeau Government: Demanding an End to the Canadian Presence in Vietnam'. In *Worth Fighting for: Canada's Tradition of War Resistance from 1812 to the War on Terror*, ed. Lara Campbell, Michael Dawson, and Catherine Gidney, 187-98. Toronto ON, CA: Between the Lines, 2015.

Brooks, Jeneve R. '"Peace, Salaam, Shalom": Functions of Collective Singing in U.S. Peace Activism'. *Music and Arts in Action* 22 (2010): 56-71, at http://musicandartsinaction.net/index.php/maia/article/view/antiwarsongs (accessed 30 June 2012).

Browning, Robert. *Pippa Passes* (1906 [1841]), at http://www.archive.org/stream/pipppasseswithan00browuoft/pipppasseswithan00browuoft_djvu.txt (14 November 2015).

Bullock, Katherine. 'Toward a Framework for Investigating Muslim Women and Political Engagement in Canada'. In *Islam in the Hinterlands: Muslim Cultural Politics in Canada*, ed. Jasmine Zine, 92-112. Vancouver, BC, CA: UBC Press, 2012.

Bush, George W. 'Bush Makes Historic Speech Aboard Warship'. *CNN* (2003), at http://www.cnn.com/2003/US/05/01/bush.transcript/ (accessed 23 June 2016).

Bush, Jeb. 'Bush says Pope Should Stay out of Climate Change Debate' (2015), at https://www.youtube.com/watch?v=Zj7LcxQQX7k (accessed 3 July 2015).

Business Alliance of Local Living Economies (BALLE) (2012), at http://www.livingeconomies.org (accessed 1 January 2012).

Buttrick, George Arthur, ed. *The Interpreter's Bible*. New York: Abingdon-Cokesbury Press, 1952.

Byrd, Robert C. 'Speech' (2001), at http://www.nyshumane.org/article-speaking-up-for-animals-speech-by-senator-robert-c-byrd/ (accessed 26 May 2016).

Cacho, Lydia. *Slavery Inc.: The Untold Story of International Sex Trafficking*. London: Portobello Books, 2012.

Câmara, Hélder. *The Spiral of Violence*. Denville, NJ: Dimension Books, 1971.

Canadian Association of Petroleum Producers. 'What Are Oil Sands' (2016), at http://www.capp.ca/canadian-oil-and-natural-gas/oil-sands/what-are-oil-sands (accessed 21 June 2016).

Canadian Voice of Women for Peace—*La Voix des Femmes Canadiennes pour La Paix. VOW Peace* (2015), at http://vowpeace.org/ (accessed 13 November 2015).

Carson, Rachel. 'The Real World around Us'. In *Environment: An Interdisciplinary Anthology*, ed. Glenn Adelson, James Engell, Brent Rancali, and K. P. van Anglen, 557-59. New Haven, CT: Yale University Press, 2008.

Carter, John Ross, and Mahinda Palihawadana (trans.). *The Dhammapada: The Saying of the Buddha*. Oxford: Oxford University Press, 2000.

Cavoukian, Raffi (comp.). 'Resisto Dancing' (2006), at http://raffinews.com (accessed 1 January 2012).

—'Baby Beluga'. *Baby Beluga*. CD. Homeland Publishing, 1980.

—'A Covenant for Honouring Children'. Speech. Harvard University, 1992.

Cavoukian, Raffi, and Bailey Rattray (comp.). 'Whatever You Choose'. *Raffi Radio* CD. Homeland Publishing, 1995.

Cavoukian, Raffi, and Michael Creber (comp.). 'Turn This World Around'. CD. Homeland Publishing, 2001.

Cavoukian, Raffi, and Sharna Olfman (eds.). *Child Honouring: How to Turn This World Around*. Fergus, ON, CA: Homeland Press, [2006] 2010.

Cenovus. 'Cenovus is a Canadian Oil Company' (n.d.), at https://www.cenovus.com/about/ (accessed 21 June 2016).

Center for Gender Sanity. 'Home Page' (2001–2011), at http://www.gendersanity.com (accessed 15 July 2015).

Centre for Applied Nonviolent Action and Strategies. 'Homepage' (2016), at http://canvasopedia.org/ (accessed 10 February 2016).

Centre for Nonviolence and Social Justice. 'Homepage' (2014), at http://www.nonviolenceandsocialjustice.org/ (accessed 15 December 2015).

Chadwick, Douglas H. *The Fate of the Elephant*. San Francisco, CA: Sierra Club Books, 1992.

Chan, Wing-Tsit. *A Source Book in Chinese Philosophy*, trans. W. T. Chan. Princeton, NJ: Princeton University Press, 1963.

Chandrasekaran, B. 'The Forgotten Liberal Ideas of M. K. Gandhi'. *The Cobden Centre* (2011), at http://www.cobdencentre.org/2011/07/liberal-gandhi/.

Chapple, Christopher K. *Nonviolence to Animals, Earth, and Self in Asian Traditions*. Albany, NY: State University of New York Press, 1993.

—(ed.) *Jainism and Ecology: Nonviolence in the Web of Life*. Cambridge, MA: Center for the Study of World Religions, 2002.

Chen, Martha, and Joann Vanek. 'Progress of the World's Women: Women, Work and Poverty'. *UNIFEM* (2005), at http://www.unifem.org/attachment/products/POW W2055 (accessed 30 May 2010).

Chenoweth, Erica, and Maria J. Stephan. *Why Civil Resistance Works: The Strategic Logic of Nonviolent Conflict*. New York: Columbia University Press, 2011.

Chernus, Ira. *American Nonviolence: The History of an Idea*. Maryknoll, NY: Orbis Books, 2004.

Chernyak, Elena, and Betty Barrett. 'A Chicken is Not a Bird, Is a Woman a Human Being? Intimate Partner Violence and the Russian Orthodox Church'. *Currents: Scholarship in the Human Services* 10 (2011): 1-24.

Chiasson, Thomas, LeBel, and Benoît Coutu. 'La Petite Histoire du *Carré Rouge*'. *Relations* 760 (2012): 34-35.

Chief Luther Standing Bear. 'Indian Wisdom'. In *The Great New Wilderness Debate*, ed. J. Baird Callicott and Michael P. Nelson, 201-06. Athens, GA: University of Georgia Press, 1998.

Choquette, Hélène (dir.). *Avenue Zero*. Film. National Film Board (2009), at http://www.nfb.ca/playlists/global-issues/viewing/avenue_zero (accessed 26 July 2015).

Chouinard, Marie-Andrée. 'Grève Étudiante—Carton d'Invitation'. *Le Devoir* (17 April 2012), at http://www.ledevoir.com/societe/education/347550/greve-etudiante-carton-d-invitation.

Christopher, Paul. *The Ethics of War and Peace: An Introduction to Legal and Moral Issues*. Upper Saddle River, NJ: Prentice-Hall, 1994.

CLASSE. 'La Lutte Continue' (2011), at http://www.bloquonslahausse.com/laclasse/a-propos/ (accessed 4 September 2013).

Cohn, Carol. 'Women and Wars: Toward a Conceptual Framework'. In *Women and Wars*, ed. Carol Cohn, 1-35. Cambridge, UK: Polity Press, 2013.

Colborn, Theo, Dianne Dumanoski, and John Peterson Myers. *Our Stolen Future*. New York: Penguin, 1996.

Collins, Patricia Hill. *Black Feminist Thought: Knowledge, Consciousness, and the Politics of Empowerment*. New York: Routledge, 2000.

Comacchio, Cynthia. 'Challenging Strathcona: The Cadet Training Controversy in English Canada, 1920–1950'. In *Worth Fighting for: Canada's Tradition of War Resistance from 1812 to the War on Terror*, ed. Lara Campbell, Michael Dawson, and Catherine Gidney, 79-91. Toronto, ON, CA: Between the Lines, 2015.

Confortini, Catia C. 'Galtung, Violence, and Gender: The Case for a Peace Studies/Feminism Alliance'. *Peace & Change* 31 (2006): 333-67.

Connacher. 'Connacher Oil' (n.d.), at http://www.pageinsider.com/connacheroil.com (accessed 21 June 2016).

ConocoPhilips. 'Who We Are' (n.d.), at http://www.conocophillips.ca/who-we-are/Pages/default.aspx (accessed 21 June 2016).

Conway, Janet. 'Civil Resistance and the "Diversity of Tactics" in the Anti-Globalization Movement: Problems of Violence, Silence, and Solidarity in Activist Politics'. *Osgood Hall Law Journal* 41.2/3 (2003): 505-30.

Constant, Benjamin. 'The Liberty of the Ancients Compared with that of the Moderns' (2015), at http://www.earlymoderntexts.com/assets/pdfs/constant1819.pdf (accessed 18 May 2016).

Cooper, Levi. 'The Assimilation of *Tikkun Olam*'. *Jewish Political Studies Review* 25 (2013): 10-42.

Cortright, David. *Peace: A History of Movements and Ideas*. Cambridge, UK: Cambridge University Press, 2008.

—*Gandhi and Beyond: Nonviolence for a New Political Age*, 2nd edn. Boulder, CO: Paradigm Press, 2009.

Couper, Scott. *Albert Luthuli: Bound by Faith*. Scottsville, ZA: UKZN Press, 2010.

Cox, Harvey. *The Silencing of Leonardo Boff: The Vatican and the Future of World Christianity*. Oak Park, IL: Meyer Stone Books, 1988.

Crenshaw, Kimberlé Williams. 'Beyond Racism and Misogyny: Black Feminism and 2 Live Crew'. In *Feminist Social Thought: A Reader*, ed. Diana Tietjens Meyers, 245-64. New York: Routledge, 1997.

Cronon, William (ed.). *Uncommon Ground: Rethinking the Human in Nature*. New York: W. W. Norton, 1996.

Culhane, Claire. *Why is Canada in Vietnam? The Truth about our Foreign Aid*. Toronto, ON, CA: NC Press, 1972.

Dalton, Russel J. 'Citizenship Norms and the Expansion of Political Participation'. *Political Studies* 56 (2008): 76-98.

Dawkins, Richard. *Unweaving the Rainbow: Science, Delusion and the Appetite for Wonder*. Boston, MA: Houghton Mifflin, 1998.

de Beauvoir, Simone. *The Second Sex*. New York: Knopf, 1953.

de Nicolás, Antonio T. *Meditations through the Ṛg Veda: Four-Dimensional Man*. Boulder, CO: Shambhala, 1978.

De Roo, Remi. 'A New Pentecost: Vatican II Revisited'. Public lecture presented at Cathedral of the Holy Family, Saskatoon, ON, CA, October 2012.

Deane-Drummond, Celia. *Wonder and Wisdom: Conversations in Science, Spirituality and Theology*. London: Darton, Longman and Todd, 2006.

—'The Good, the Bad and the Ugly: Wonder, Awe, and Paying Attention to Nature'. In *Aesth/Ethics in Environmental Change: Hiking through the Arts, Ecology, Religion and Ethics of the Environment*, ed. Sigurd Bergmann, Irmgard Blindow, and Konrad Ott, 71-84. Berlin: LIT Verlag, 2013.

Dear, John. *The God of Peace: Toward a Theology of Nonviolence*. Eugene, OR: Wipf and Stock, 2005.

Deep Green Resistance. 'Decisive Ecological Warfare' (n.d.), at http://www.deepgree resistance.org/en/deep-green-resistance-strategy/decisive-ecological-warfare (accessed 15 April 2014).

Dekeseredy, Walter. *Violence against Women: Myths, Facts, Controversies*. Toronto, ON, CA: University of Toronto Press, 2011.

DeLuca, Anthony. *Gandhi, Mao, Mandela, And Gorbachev: Studies in Power, Personality, and Politics*. Westport, CT: Praeger, 2000.

Dennett, Daniel. 'Animal Consciousness: What Matters and Why'. *Social Research* 62.3 (1995): 691-710.

Densmore, Frances. 'Teton Sioux Music'. *Bureau of American Ethnology Bulletin*. Washington, DC: Smithsonian Institution, 1918.

Desai, Sabra, and Zehra Haffajee. 'Breaking the Silence: Reclaiming Qur'anic Interpretations as a Tool for Empowerment and Liberatory Praxis for Dealing with Domestic Violence in Canadian Muslim Communities'. *Canadian Woman Studies* 29.1/2 (2011): 127-34.

Descartes, René. *Discourse on the Method of Rightly Conducting One's Reason and of Seeking Truth in the Sciences*. Oxford, UK: Oxford University Press, 2006.

Desmond, William, *The Intimate Strangeness of Being: Metaphysics After Dialectic*. Washington, DC: Catholic University of America Press, 2012.

DeViney, E., Jeffrey Dickert, and Randall Lockwood. 'The Care of Pets within Child Abusing Families'. In *Child Abuse, Domestic Violence, and Animal Abuse: Linking the Circles of Compassion for Prevention and Intervention*, ed. Frank R. Ascione and Phil Arkow, 305-13. West Lafayette, IN: Purdue University Press, 1999.

Devon. 'About Us' (n.d.), at http://www.devonenergy.com/about-us (accessed 21 June 2016).

Diamond, Jared M. *Collapse: How Societies Choose to Fail or Succeed*. New York: Viking Books, 2005.

Donaldson, Sue, and Will Kymlicka. *Zoopolis—A Political Theory of Animal Rights*. Oxford: Oxford University Press, 2011.

Doniger, Wendy. *The Hindus: An Alternative History*. New York: Penguin Press, 2009.

Donovan, Josephine, and Carol J. Adams (eds.). *The Feminist Care Tradition in Animal Ethics*. New York: Columbia University Press, 2007.

Douglas, Peter. 'Men=Violence: A Pro-Feminist Perspective on Dismantling the Masculine Equation'. Paper presented at the Second Annual Conference on Violence, Australian Institute of Criminology, Canberra, AU (June 1993), at http://www.aic. gov.au/media_library/conferences/ncv2/douglas.pdf (accessed 28 July 2015).

Du Preez, Max. 'Foreword'. In *From Biko to Basson: Wendy Orr's Search for the Soul of South Africa as a Commissioner of the TRC*. Saxonwold, ZA: Contra Press, 2000.

Duchaine, Gabrielle. 'Le Conflit Étudiant a Fait des Centaines d'Éclopés'. *La Presse* (8 May 2012), at http://www.lapresse.ca/actualites/dossiers/conflit-etudiant/20 1205/08/01-4523017-le-conflit-etudiant-a-fait-des-centaines-declopes.php (accessed 4 September 2013).

Dumézil, Georges. *The Destiny of a King*. Chicago, IL: University of Chicago Press, 1973.

Dumont, Albert. *Broad Winged Hawk: A Book of Poetry and Short Stories*. Mishawaka, IN: Better World Books, 2007. Also at http://albertdumont.com (accessed 26 May 2016).

Dunn, Kevin C. 'The Clash of Civilization'. In *Resounding International Relations: On Music, Culture, and Politics*, ed. M. I. Franklin, 263-83. New York, NY: Palgrave MacMillan, 2005.

Earth Charter Commission. 'The Earth Charter' (2000), at http://www.earthcharterin-action.org/invent/images/uploads/echarter_english.pdf (accessed 1 June 2015.

Eaton, Heather. 'The Spirit of Climate Change'. Paper presented at the 11th Conference of the International Environment Forum Responding to Climate Change, Volunteer Place, Ottawa, ON, CA (October 2007), at http://tyne.ca/ief2007/uploads/Heather_Eaton.doc (accessed 13 June 2013).

—'Forces of Nature: Aesthetics and Ethics'. In *Aesth/Ethics in Environmental Change: Hiking through the Arts, Ecology, Religion and Ethics of the Environment*, ed. Sigurd Bergmann, Irmgard Blindow, and Konrad Ott, 109-26. Berlin: LIT Verlag, 2013.

Ekta Parishad. *Ekta Parishad* (n.d.), at http://www.ektaparishad.com/ (accessed 18 November 2015).

Ellul, Jacques. *The Technological Society*, trans. John Wilkinson. New York: Alfred A. Knopf, 1966.

Encana. 'About Us', at https://www.encana.com/about/ (accessed 21 June 2016).

Endicott, Stephen. *James G. Endicott: Rebel out of China*. Toronto, ON, CA: University of Toronto Press, 1980.

Esquivel, Aldofo Pérez. *Christ in a Poncho: Testimonials of the Nonviolent Struggles in Latin America*. Maryknoll, NY: Orbis Books, 1983.

Eyerman, Ron, and Andrew Jamieson. *Music and Social Movements: Mobilizing Traditions in the Twentieth Century*. Cambridge, UK: Cambridge University Press, 1998.

Fanon, Frantz. *Les Damnés de la Terre* (The Wretched of the Earth). Paris: Gallimard, 1991.

Farmer, Paul, *Pedagogies of Power*. Berkeley, CA: University of California Press, 2005.

Farmer, Paul, Margaret Connors, and Janie Simmons (eds.). *Women, Poverty and AIDS: Sex, Drugs and Structural Violence*. Monroe, ME: Common Courage Press, 1996.

FECQ. 'La FECQ Dénonce les Gestes de Violence tant du Côté des Forces Policières que des Étudiants' (18 April 2012), at http://www.fecq.org/nouvelles/la-fecq-denonce-les-gestes-de-violence-tant-du-cote-des-forces-policieres-que-des-etudiants/ (accessed 3 October 2013).

Fenrich, Keith K., and P. Ken Rose. 'Axons with Highly Branched Terminal Regions Successfully Regenerate across Spinal Midline Transections in the Adult Cat'. *Journal of Comparative Neurology* 519 (2011): 3240-58.

Fernandez, James W. F. 'Meditations on Animals—Figuring Out Humans'. In *Animals in African Art*, ed. Allen Roberts, 1-9. New York: The Museum for African Art, 1995.

Fiddles, Paul S. *Past Event and Present Salvation*. London: Darton, Longman and Todd, 1989.

Fischlin, Daniel, Ajay Heble, and George Lipsitz. *The Fierce Urgency of Now: Improvisation, Rights, and the Ethics of Cocreation*. Durham, NC: Duke University Press, 2013.

Fitzgerald, Mary. 'Rwanda's Example for Women'. *The Guardian Weekly* 40.1 (2010), at https://www.theguardian.com/commentisfree/2010/jun/20/positive-discrimination-rwanda (accessed 21 June 2016).

Fong, Josephine. 'Explaining the Abuse of Women: An Examination of Conventional and Dominant Theoretical Perspectives'. In *Out of the Shadows: Woman Abuse in Ethnic, Immigrant and Aboriginal Communities*, ed. Josephine Fong, 8-28. Toronto, ON, CA: Women's Press, 2010.

Foreman, Dave. 'Strategic Monkeywrenching'. In *Ecodefense: A Field Guide to Monkey-wrenching*, 3rd edn., ed. Dave Foreman and Billy Haywood, 9-11. Chico, CA: Abbzug, 1993.

Fortin, Andrée. 'La Longue Marche des *Carrés Rouges'*. *Recherches Sociographiques* 54.3 (2013): 513-29.

Fouts, Roger. *Next of Kin: What Chimpanzees Have Taught Me about Who We Are*. New York: William Morrow, 1997.

Fox, Everett. *The Five Books of Moses: A New English Translation with Commentary and Notes: The Schocken Bible*. Vol. 1. New York: Schocken Books, 1995.

Francione, Gary L. 'Animals—Property or Persons?' In *Animal Rights*, ed. Cass R. Sunstein and Martha C. Nussbaum, 108-42. Oxford: Oxford University Press, 2004.

Frankl, Victor E. *Man's Search for Meaning*. New York: Simon & Schuster, 1984.

—*Man's Search for Meaning: An Introduction to Logotherapy*, 4th edn. Boston, MA: Beacon Press, 1992.

Franklin, Ursula. *The Ursula Franklin Reader: Pacifism as a Map*. Toronto, ON, CA: Between the Lines, 2006.

Freeman, Harrop A. 'The Right of Protest and Civil Disobedience'. *Indiana Law Journal* 41.2 (1992): 228-54.

Friedman, Hershey H., and Yehuda L. Klein. 'Respect for God's World: The Biblical and Rabbinic Foundations of Environmentalism'. *International Journal of Business and Globalisation* 4 (2010): 192-200.

Friedman, Thomas L. 'Without Water, Revolution'. *New York Times* (2013), at http://www.nytimes.com/2013/05/19/opinion/sunday/friedman-without-water-rev-olution.html (accessed 12 November 2013).

Frost, J. William. 'Quakers (Religious Society of Friends)'. In *Protest, Power and Change: An Encyclopedia of Nonviolent Action from ACT-UP to Women's Suffrage*, ed. Roger S. Powers and William B. Vogele, 419-23. New York: Garland Publishing, 1997.

Frowe, Helen. *The Ethics of War and Peace: An Introduction*. London: Routledge, 2011.

Fuller, Robert C. *Wonder: From Emotion to Spirituality*. Chapel Hill, NC: University of North Carolina Press, 2006.

Gaffney, James. 'The Relevance of Animal Experimentation to Roman Catholic Ethical Methodology'. In *Animal Sacrifices: Religious Perspectives on the Use of Animals in Science*, ed. Tom Regan, 149-70. Philadelphia, PA: Temple University Press, 1986.

Gallagher, Sally. *Evangelical Identity and Gendered Family Life*. New Brunswick, NJ: Rutgers University Press, 2003.

Galtung, Johan. 'Theories of Peace: A Synthetic Approach to Peace Thinking', International Peace Research Institute, Oslo, NO (1967), at http://www.transcend.org/files/Galtung_Book_unpub_Theories_of_Peace_-_A_Synthetic_Approach_to_Peace_Thinking_1967.pdf (accessed 2 August 2015).

—'Violence, Peace, and Peace Research'. *Journal of Peace Research* 6.3 (1969): 167-91.

—'Structural and Direct Violence: Note on Operationalization'. *Peace: Research, Education, Action*, Essays in Peace Research 1. Copenhagen, DE: Christian Ejlers, 1975.

—'Cultural Violence'. *Journal of Peace Research* 27 (1990): 291-305.

—*Human Rights in Another Key*. Cambridge, MA: Polity Press, 1994.

—*Peace by Peaceful Means: Peace and Conflict, Development and Civilization*. Oslo, NO: International Peace Research Institute, 1996.

—'Violence: Direct, Structural and Cultural'. In *Johan Galtung: Pioneer of Peace Research*, ed. Johan Galtung and Dietrich Fischer, 35-40. New York: Springer, 2013.

Galtung, Johan, and Dietrich Fischer. 'Johan Galtung, the Father of Peace Studies'. In *Johan Galtung: Pioneer of Peace Research*, ed. Johan Galtung and Dietrich Fischer, 3-23. New York: Springer, 2013.

Gandhi Heritage Portal. 'Homepage' (2016), at https://www.gandhiheritageportal.org/ (accessed 15 December 2016).

Gandhi, Mohandas K. *Non-violence in Peace and War*. Vol. 1. Ahmedabad, IN: Navajivan Publishing House, 1948.

—*The Collected Works of Mahatma Gandhi*. 98 vols. New Delhi, IN: Publications Division Government of India, [1884-1948] 1999.

—*Non-violent Resistance*. New York: Schocken Books, 1958.

—*All Men Are Brothers*. Ahmedabad, IN: Navajivan Publishing House, 1960a.

—*Discourses on the Gita*. Ahmedabad, IN: Navajivan Publishing House, 1960b.

—*Village Swaraj*. Ahmedabad, IN: Navajivan Publishing House, 1963.

—*Non-Violence in Peace and War 1942-1949*. New York: Garland Publishing, 1972.

—'Ahimsa, or the Way of Nonviolence'. In *A Peace Reader: Essential Readings on War, Justice, Non-Violence and World Order*, ed. Joseph J. Fahley and Richard Armstrong, 171-75. New York: Paulist Press, 1992.

—*Hind Swaraj*, ed. Anthony J. Parel. Cambridge, UK: Cambridge University Press, 1997.

—*An Autobiography: or the Story of my Experiments with Truth*, trans. M. Desai. London: Penguin, 2001.

—*The Collected Works of Mahatma Gandhi*. 100 vols. New Delhi, IN: Sage, 2009.

Gandhi Research Foundation. 'Homepage' (2015), at http://www.gandhifoundation. net/about%20grf.htm (accessed 15 December 2015).

Gandhi, Sonia. 'Rediscovering the Mahatma's Way'. In *Gandhian Way: Peace, Nonviolence and Empowerment*, ed. A. Sharma, 23-28. New Delhi, IN: Academic Foundation, 2007.

GandhiMedia: Bringing Mahatma Gandhi to Life! 'Homepage' (2011–2015), at http:// www.gandhimedia.org/ (accessed 15 December 2015).

GandhiServe Foundation: Mahatma Gandhi Research and Media Service. 'Homepage' (2008–2015), at http://www.gandhiserve.org/e/ (accessed 15 December 2015).

Garcia, Maria Elisa Pinto. 'Music and Reconciliation in Columbia: Opportunities of Songs Composed by Victims'. *Music and Arts in Action* 4.2 (2014): 24-51. Also at http://www.musicandartsinaction.net/index.php/maia/article/view/music reconciliationcolombia/97 (accessed 24 August 2014).

Gat, Azar. *War in Human Civilization*. Oxford: Oxford University Press, 2006.

Gebara, Ivone. 'Ecofeminism: A Latin American Perspective'. *Cross Currents* 53.1 (2003): 93-103.

—'What do we Mean by Change: Conflict Arising from a Feminist Ethical Perspective'. Paper presented at the Catholic Network for Women's Equality Conference, Saint Paul University, Ottawa, ON, CA, June 2009.

Gender Spectrum. 'Gender Spectrum: Understanding Gender' (n.d.), at http://www. genderspectrum.org (accessed 15 July 2015).

Gerhardt, Elizabeth. *The Cross and Gendercide: A Theological Response to Global Violence against Women and Girls*. Downers Grove, IL: InterVarsity Press, 2014.

Ghosh, Sagarika. Arundhati Roy Interview. CNN-IBN (2013), at http://www.firstpost. com/india/maoist-attacks-are-a-counter-violence-of-resistance-against-the-state-arundhati-roy-820173.html (accessed 8 August 2015).

Gilgoff, Dan and Eric Marrapodi. 'Reversing JFK: Santorum's Bid to Marry Faith and Politics'. *CNN Belief Blog* (2012), at http://religion.blogs.cnn.com/2012/01/07/seeking-to-reverse-jfk-santorum-marries-catholicism-and-politics/ (accessed 12 June 2015).

Gill, Carmen. 'Understanding Theories and Their Links to Intervention Strategies'. In *Intimate Partner Violence: Reflections on Experience, Theory and Policy*, ed. Mary Rucklos Hampton and Nikki Gerrard, 47-66. Toronto: Cormorant Books, 2006.

Gingerich, Owen. *God's Planet*. Cambridge, MA: Harvard University Press, 2014.

Glendon, M. A. *A World Made New: Eleanor Roosevelt and the Universal Declaration of Human Rights*. New York: Random House, 2001.

Global Gender Gap (2015), at http://www.agenda.weforum.org/2015/03/gender-gap-calculator-2015/ (accessed 21 July 2015).

Godse, Nathuram. 'Trial Speech'. In *Sources of Indian Tradition: Modern India, Pakistan, and Bangladesh*, ed. Rachel Fell McDermott et al., 440-42. New York: Columbia University Press, 2014.

Goldhagen, Daniel Jonah. *Worse than War: Genocide, Eliminationism, and the Ongoing Assault on Humanity*. New York: Public Affairs, 2009.

Goldman, Danielle. 'Bodies on the Line: Contact Improvisation and Techniques of Nonviolent Protest'. *Dance Research Journal* 39.1 (2007): 60-74.

Gordon, Ann D. (ed.). *Selected Papers of Elizabeth Cady Stanton and Susan B. Anthony*, vol. 5. Piscataway, NJ: Rutgers University Press, 2009.

Gould, Carol C. *Gender: Key Concepts in Critical Theory*. Atlantic Heights, NJ: Humanities Press, 1997.

Govier, Trudy. 'Violence, Nonviolence and Definitions'. *Peace Research: The Canadian Journal of Peace and Conflict Studies* 40.2 (2008): 61-83.

Grandin, Temple, and Catherine Johnson. *Animals Make Us Human: Creating the Best Life for Animals*. Boston, MA: Houghton Mifflin Harcourt, 2009.

Greenspan, Stanley, and Stuart Shanker. 'Council of Human Development' (n.d.), at http://www.councilhd.ca (accessed 1 January 2012).

Griffin, Donald R. *Animal Minds: Beyond Cognition to Consciousness*. Chicago, IL: University of Chicago Press, 2001.

Grotius, Hugo. *On the Law of War and Peace*, ed. Stephen Neff. Cambridge, UK: Cambridge University Press, 2012.

Grove Dictionary Online. 'Rebetika'. Oxford Music Online (n.d.), at http://www.oxfordmusiconline.com.proxy.bib.uottawa.ca/subscriber/article/grove/music/51102 (accessed 13 March 2012).

Guindon, Hubert. 'Quebec's "Quiet Revolution" and the Push for Sovereignty'. *The Public Perspective* (1996: 26-28), at http://www.ropercenter.uconn.edu/public-perspective/ppscan/71/71026.pdf (accessed 5 October 2013).

Gustafson, James. *Theology and Ethics*. Chicago, IL: University of Chicago Press, 1981.

Gutierrez, Gustavo. *Las Casas: In Search of the Poor of Jesus Christ*. Eugene, OR: Wipf and Stock, 2003.

Gutkin, Harry, and Mildred Gutkin. *Profiles in Dissent: The Shaping of Radical Thought in the Canadian West*. Edmonton, AB, CA: NeWest Publishers, 1997.

Hammond-Callaghan, Marie. 'Bridging and Breaching Cold Divides: Transnational Peace Building, State Surveillance, and the Voice of Women'. In *Worth Fighting For: Canada's Tradition of War Resistance from 1812 to the War on Terror*, ed. Lara Campbell, Michael Dawson, and Catherine Gidney, 135-45. Toronto, ON, CA: Between the Lines, 2015.

Hallward, Maia Carter, and Julie M. Norman. *Understanding Nonviolence: Contours and Contexts*. Malden, MA: Polity, 2015.

Harder, Cilja. 'Gender Relations, Violence and Conflict Transformation'. (2011), at http://www.berghof-foundation.org/fileadmin/redaktion/Publications/Hand book/Articles/harders_handbook.pdf (accessed 19 July 2015).

Harris, Ian. 'Peace Education Theory'. *Journal of Peace Education* 1 (2004): 5-20.

Harrison, Beverly Wildung. *Justice in the Making: Feminist Social Ethics*. Louisville, KY: Westminster John Knox Press, 2004.

Harrison, Peter. *The Territories of Science and Religion*. Chicago, IL: University of Chicago Press, 2015.

Hart, John. *Cosmic Commons: Spirit, Science, & Space*. Eugene, OR: Wipf and Stock, 2013.

Hedges, Christopher. *War is a Force that Gives Us Meaning*. Rockland, NY: Anchor Press, 2003.

—*Wages of Rebellion: The Moral Imperative of Revolt*. New York: Nation Books, 2015.

Hegel, Georg Wilhelm Friedrich. *The Phenomenology of Spirit*. Oxford: Oxford University Press, 1977.

Helwig, Maggie. 'Low-Level Flight Testing: Innu Women Fight Back'. *Canadian Women's Studies* 13.3 (1993): 52-53.

Hepburn, Ronald W. *'Wonder' and Other Essays: Eight Studies in Aesthetics and Neighbouring Fields*. Edinburgh, UK: Edinburgh University Press, 1984.

Hernandez-Truyol, Berta Esperanza. 'The Gender Bend: Culture, Sex, and Sexuality—A LatCritical Human Rights Map of Latina/o Border Crossings'. *Indiana Law Journal* 83 (2008): 1283-1331.

Heschel, Abraham Joshua, and Susannah Heschel. *Abraham Joshua Heschel: Essential Writings*. Maryknoll, NY: Orbis, 2011.

Higgs, Eric S. 'A Quantity of Engaging Work to be Done: Ecological Restoration and Morality in a Technological Culture'. *Restoration & Management Notes* 9 (1991): 97-104.

Ho, Kathleen. 'Structural Violence as a Human Rights Violation'. *Essex Human Rights Review* 4.2 (2007): 1-17.

Holmes, Richard. *The Age of Wonder: How the Romantic Generation Discovered the Beauty and Terror of Science*. London: Harper Press, 2008.

Holtmann, Catherine. 'From the Top: What Does It Mean When Catholic Bishops Speak out on Issues of Family Violence?' In *Strengthening Families and Ending Abuse: Churches and Their Leaders Look to the Future*, ed. Nancy Nason-Clark, Barbara Fisher-Townsend, and Victoria Fahlberg, 139-59. Eugene, OR: Wipf & Stock, 2013a.

—'Risks and Strengths Among Religious Immigrant Women: An Analysis of the Maritimes'. Paper presented at the Canadian Domestic Violence Conference 3, Toronto, ON, CA, February 2013b.

Homer-Dixon, Thomas F. *Environmental Scarcity and Global Security*. New York: Foreign Policy Association, 1993.

hooks, bell. *Feminism is for Everybody: Passionate Politics*. Cambridge, MA: South End Press, 2000.

—*The Will to Change: Men, Masculinity and Love*. New York: Atria Books, 2004.

—*Understanding Patriarchy* (n.d.), at http://imaginenoborders.org/pdf/zines/Under standingPatriarchy.pdf. (accessed 15 September 2015).

Hooper, John. 'Pope Francis and the Vatican Played Key Roles in US-Cuba Thaw, Leaders Reveal: Pope Sent Letters to Obama and Castro Calling on Pair to "Resolve Humanitarian Questions of Common Interest" While Vatican Helped Broker

Talks'. *The Guardian* (2014), at http://www.theguardian.com/world/2014/dec/17/us-cuba-pope-franicis-key-roles (accessed 12 June 2015).

Horsburgh, H. J. N. *Non-violence and Aggression: A Study of Gandhi's Moral Equivalent of War*. London: Oxford University Press, 1968.

Howard, Michael. 1999. "When Are Wars Decisive?" *Survival* 41 (1): 126-35.

Howard, Veena R. *Gandhi's Ascetic Activism: Renunciation and Social Action*. Albany, NY: State University of New York Press, 2013.

Hreljac, Ryan. 'Ryan's Well' (n.d.), at https://www.ryanswell.ca/ (accessed 1 January 2012).

Hrynkow, Christopher. 'Christian Peacemaker Teams, Solidarist Nonviolent Activism and the Politics of Peace: Peace Witness that Challenges Militarism and Destructive Violence'. *Journal of Peace Research: The Canadian Journal of Peace and Conflict Studies* 40.1 (2009): 111-34.

Hrynkow, Christopher, and Dennis Patrick O'Hara. 'Catholic Social Teaching and Climate Justice from a Peace Studies Perspective: Current Practice, Tensions, and Promise'. *New Theology Review* 26.2 (2014): 23-32.

Hudson, Valerie M., and Andrea M. den Boer. *Bare Branches: The Security Implications of Asia's Surplus Male Population*. Cambridge, MA: MIT Press, 2004.

Hunnicutt, Gwen. 'Varieties of Patriarchy and Violence against Women: Resurrecting "Patriarchy" as a Theoretical Tool'. *Violence against Women* 15 (2009): 553-73.

Hunter, Mary Ann. 'Cultivating the Art of Safe Space'. *Research in Drama Education* 13.1 (2008): 5-21.

Hutchinson, Braden. 'Fighting the War at Home: Voice of Women and War Toy Activism in Postwar Canada'. In *Worth Fighting For: Canada's Tradition of War Resistance from 1812 to the War on Terror*, ed. Lara Campbell, Michael Dawson, Catherine Gidney, 147-58. Toronto, ON, CA: Between the Lines, 2015.

Ici Radio Canada. 'Grève Étudiante: Charest et Beauchamp Haussent le Ton' (11 April 2012), at http://ici.radio-canada.ca/nouvelles/societe/2012/04/11/003-beauchamp-boycottage-etudiant.shtml (accessed 5 October 2013).

—'La FEUQ et la FECQ Condamnent la Violence, la CLASSE ne Bouge pas' (18 April 2012), at http://ici.radio-canada.ca/nouvelles/societe/2012/04/18/002-etudiants-conflit-mercredi.shtml (accessed 26 September 2013).

—'La CLASSE Condamne la Violence Délibérée dans les Manifestations' (23 April 2012), at http://ici.radio-canada.ca/nouvelles/societe/2012/04/22/002-fecq-utlimatum-classe.shtml (accessed 12 September 2013).

—'Grève Étudiante: Charest Intransigeant' (26 April 2012), at http://ici.radio-canada.ca/nouvelles/societe/2012/04/26/001-conflit-etudiant-jeudi.shtml (accessed 24 September 2013).

—'SPVM: Matricule 728 au Cœur d'une Nouvelle Controverse' (11 October 2012), at http://www.radio-canada.ca/regions/montreal/2012/10/10/004-matricule-728-spvm-arrestation.shtml (accessed 25 September 2013).

ICRC. *Addressing the Needs of Women Affected by Armed Conflict*. Geneva, SZ: ICRC, 2004.

Idle No More. *Idle No More* (2007), at http://www.idlenomore.ca/vision (accessed 26 May 2016).

IMA World Health. 'Broken Silence: A Call for Churches to Speak Out'. Sojourners and IMA World Health (2014), at http://www.imaworldhealth.org/images/stories/technical-publications/PastorsSurveyReport_final.pdf (accessed 25 May 2016).

International Center on Nonviolent Conflict. 'Homepage' (2016), at https://www.nonviolent-conflict.org/ (accessed 10 February 2016).

International Peace Research Association Foundation. 'Homepage' (2015), at http:// iprafoundation.org/ (accessed 10 February 2016).

Jacob, Jeffrey. *New Pioneers: The Back-To-The-Land Movement and the Search for a Sustainable Future*. University Park, PA: Pennsylvania State University Press, 1997.

Jahanbegloo, Ramin. 'Can Politics Be Spiritualized'. *Journal of Democratic Theory* (1963): 325-32.

—*Introduction to Nonviolence*. New York: Palgrave MacMillan, 2014.

Jain Vegans. *Why Vegan?* (n.d.), at http://www.jainvegans.org/why-vegan (accessed 20 October 2015).

James, William. 'The Moral Equivalent of War'. *Popular Science Monthly* 77 (1910).

—*Varieties of Religious Experience*. New York: Crowell-Collier, 1961.

Jensen, Derrick. *Endgame* (2006), at http://www.derrickjensen.org/work/endgame/ endgame-premises-english/ (accessed 18 May 2015).

Johnson, Holly, and Myrna Dawson. *Violence against Women in Canada: Research and Policy Perspectives*. Don Mills, ON, CA: Oxford University Press, 2011.

Jonas, Hans. *The Imperative of Responsibility: In Search of an Ethics for the Technological Age*. Chicago, IL: University of Chicago Press, 1984.

Jones, Eileen Kerwin. 'Femmes Pacificatrices: l'Action d'une ONG Face au Problème Global de l'Esclavage Contemporain et du Trafic d'Êtres Humains'. In *Femmes Artisans de Paix: Des Profils à Découvrir*, ed. Pierrette Daviau, 101-43. Montreal, QC, CA: Mediaspaul, 2013.

Jones, Rufus M. (ed.). *The Journal of George Fox*. New York: Capricorn Books, [1694] 1963.

Juckes, Tim J. *Opposition in South Africa: The Leadership of Z.K. Matthews, Nelson Mandela, and Stephen Biko*. Westport, CT: Praeger, 1995.

Juergensmeyer, Mark. *Gandhi's Way: A Handbook of Conflict Resolution*. Berkeley: University of California Press, 2005.

Journet, Paul. '*Carré Rouge*, Fred Pellerin et Violence: la Ministre St-Pierre Refuse de s'Excuser, *La Presse*' (12 June 2012), at http://www.lapresse.ca/actualites/polit ique/politique-quebecoise/201206/13/01-4534514-christine-st-pierre-sexcuse- pour-ses-propos-sur-le-carre-rouge.php?utm_categorieinterne=trafficdrivers &utm_contenuinterne=cyberpresse_vous_suggere_4534228_article_POS1 (accessed 29 September 2013).

Kaiser, Robert Blair. 'Stories of Vatican II: The Human Side of the Council', Tablet Lecture, October 5 2012. Heythrop College, London. Video at http://www.thetablet. co.uk/page/ lecture Tablet2012. (accessed 9 May 2013).

Kant, Immanuel. *Lectures on Ethics*, trans. Louis Infeld. New York: Harper Torchbooks, 1963.

Karuna Centre for Peace-building. 'Program and Services' (n.d.), at http://www.karu nacenter.org/our-services.html (accessed 10 February 2016).

Kastenholz, Hans G., and Karl-Heinz Erdmann. 'Education for Responsibility within the Framework of UNESCO'. *Journal of Environmental Education* 25 (1994): 15-21.

Kattau, Colleen. 'The Power of Song for Nonviolent Transformative Action'. In *Positive Peace: Reflections on Peace Education, Nonviolence, and Social Change*, ed. Andrew Fitz-Gibbon, 107-18. Amsterdam, NL: Rodopi, 2010.

Kaufman, Debra. *Rachel's Daughters: Newly Orthodox Jewish Women*. New Brunswick, NJ: Rutgers University Press, 1991.

Kazemipur, Abdolmohammad. *The Muslim Question in Canada: A Story of Segmented Integration*. Vancouver, BC, CA: UBC Press, 2014.

Keith, Lierre, Aric McBay, and Derrick Jensen. *Deep Green Resistance: Strategy to Save the Planet*. New York: Seven Stories Press, 2011.

Kelsey, Elin, and Carly Armstrong. 'Finding Hope in a World of Environmental Catastrophe'. In *Learning for Sustainability in Times of Accelerating Change*, ed. A. E. J. Wals and P. B. Corcoran, 187-200. Wageningen, NL: Wageningen Academic Publishers, 2012.

Kerans, Marion Douglas. *Muriel Duckworth: A Very Active Pacifist*. Halifax, NS, CA: Fernwood Publishing, 1996.

Keter Publishing House. *Encyclopedia Judaica*. Jerusalem, IS: Keter Publishing House, 1971.

Khanam, Farida (ed.). *The Quran*. New Delhi, IN: Goodward Books, 2014.

Khilnani, Sunil. *The Idea of India*. New York: Ferrar, Strauss and Giroux, 1997.

King Jr, Martin Luther. *Stride Toward Freedom: The Montgomery Story*. New York: Harper and Row, 1958.

—'A Letter from Birmingham Jail'. *Ebony* (1963): 23-32.

—'Conscience for Change'. Seventh Annual Massey Lectures, CBC Ideas (1967a), at http://www.cbc.ca/radio/ideas/the-1967-cbc-massey-lectures-conscience-for-change-1.2946809 (accessed 25 October 2015). Orig. pub. as *Conscience for Change*, Toronto, ON, CA: CBC Publications/Maracle Press, 1967. Rep. as *The Trumpet of Conscience*, Foreword Coretta Scott King, New York: Harper & Row, 1968.

—*Where Do We Go from Here: Chaos or Community?* New York: Harper and Row, 1967b.

—*Why We Can't Wait*. New York: Harper and Row, 1967c.

—*Stride Toward Freedom: The Montgomery Story*. Boston, MA: Beacon Press, [1958] 2010.

Kino-nda-niimi Collective (ed.). *The Winter We Danced: Voices from the Past, the Future, and the Idle No More Movement*. Winnipeg, MB, CA: ARP Books, 2014.

Kirchgaessner, Stephanie. 'Pope Francis tells Putin: "Sincere" Peace Efforts Needed for Ukraine'. *The Guardian* (2015), at http://www.theguardian.com/world/2015/jun/10/pope-francis-putin-sincere-peace-effort-ukraine-russia-vatican (accessed 3 July 2015).

Kojève, Alexandre. *Introduction à la Lecture de Hegel*. Paris: Gallimard, 1947.

Kool, Richard. 'Hope and Deeds and Environmental Education'. *Interactions* 22 (2010): 24-26.

Korteweg, Anna. 'Understanding Honour Killing and Honour-Related Violence in the Immigration Context: Implications for the Legal Profession and Beyond'. *Canadian Criminal Law Review* 16 (2012): 135-60.

Korteweg, Anna, and Jennifer Selby (eds.). *Debating Sharia: Islam, Gender Politics, and Family Law Arbitration*. Toronto, ON, CA: University of Toronto Press, 2012.

Krane, Julia, Jacqueline Oxman-Martinez, and Kimberley Ducey. 'Violence against Women and Ethnoracial Minority Women: Examining Assumptions about Ethnicity and Race'. *Canadian Ethnic Studies* 32 (2000): 1-18.

Kroeger, Catherine Clark. 'Let us Grow Up unto Him in all Things'. In *Responding to Abuse in Christian Homes: A Challenge to Churches and their Leaders*, ed. Nancy Nason-Clark, Catherine Clark Kroeger, and Barbara Fisher-Townsend, 3-11. Eugene, OR: Wipf & Stock, 2011.

Krug, E. G. et al. (eds.). 'World Report on Violence and Health' (2002), at http://www.who.int/violence_injury_prevention/violence/world_report/en/ (accessed 26 May 2016).

Krutch, Joseph W. *The Twelve Seasons: A Perpetual Calendar for the Country*. New York: W. Sloane Associates, 1949.

Kulwicki, Anahid, Barbara Aswad, Talita Carmona, and Suha Ballout. 'Barriers to the Utilization of Domestic Violence Services among Arab Immigrant Women: Perceptions of Professionals, Service Providers and Community Leaders'. *Journal of Family Violence* 25 (2010): 727-35.

Kumar, Satish. *No Destination: An Autobiography*. Foxhole, UK: Green Books, 1992.

—*Path Without Destination: The Long Walk of a Gentle Hero*. New York: William Morrow, 1999.

Kurlansky, Mark. *Non-Violence: The History of a Dangerous Idea*. New York: Random House, 2007.

La Presse. 'Droits de Scolarité: "l'Avenir n'est pas dans le Gel" dit Charest' (1 April 2012), at http://www.lapresse.ca/actualites/education/201204/01/01-4511427-droits-de-scolarite-lavenir-nest-pas-dans-le-gel-dit-charest.php (accessed 4 October 2013).

Lacroix, C. A. 'Another Weapon for Combating Family Violence'. In *Child Abuse, Domestic Violence, and Animal Abuse: Linking the Circles of Compassion for Prevention and Intervention*, ed. Frank R. Ascione and Phil Arkow, 62-80. West Lafayette, IN: Purdue University Press, 1999.

Lagacé, Patrick and Gary Mason. 'Quebec Students: Legitimate Strikers or Self-absorbed Brats?'. *The Globe and Mail* (4 May 2012), at http://www.theglobeandmail.com/news/politics/quebec-students-legitimate-strikers-or-self-absorbed-brats/article4104939/ (accessed 4 October 2013).

Langille, David. 'The Long March of the Canadian Peace Movement'. *Canadian Dimension* 42.3 (2008): 27-32.

Latin American Bishops at Medellin, Columbia. 'Peace' (6 September 1968), at http://personal.stthomas.edu/gwschlabach/docs/medellin.htm#peace (accessed 22 April 2013).

Le Devoir News Staff. 'Fred Pellerin Refuse l'Ordre National du Québec'. *Le Devoir* (8 June 2012), at http://www.ledevoir.com/politique/quebec/352008/fred-pellerin-refuse-l-ordre-national-du-quebec (accessed 29 September 2013).

Le Quéré, C. et al. 'Global Carbon Budget 2014'. *Earth System Science Data* 7 (2015): 47-85.

Lederach, John Paul. 'Civil Society and Reconciliation'. In *Turbulent Peace: The Challenges of Managing International Conflict*, ed. Chester A. Crocker, Fen Osler Hampson, and Pamela Aall, 841-54. Washington, DC: United States Institute of Peace, 2001.

—*The Moral Imagination: The Art and Soul of Building Peace*. Oxford: Oxford University Press, 2005.

Lee, Carol E., and Heidi Vogt. 'President Barack Obama Condemns Kenya on Gay Rights'. *Wall Street Journal* (25 July 2015), at http://www.wsj.com/articles/president-obama-praises-africa-in-kenya-summit-speech-1437820696 (accessed 25 July 2015).

Leff, Gordon. *Heresy in the Later Middle Ages: The Relation of Heterodoxy to Dissent c.1250-c.1450*. New York: Barnes and Noble, 1967.

Leopold, Aldo. *A Sand County Almanac, with Essays on Conservation from Round River*. New York: Ballantine, [1948] 1991.

Lerner, Gerda. *The Creation of Patriarchy*. New York: Oxford University Press, 1986.

—*The Creation of Feminist Consciousness: From the Middle Ages to Eighteen Seventy*. New York: Oxford University Press, 1994.

Lertzman, Renee. 'The Myth of Apathy'. *The Ecologist* 38 (2008): 16.

LeVasseur, Todd. 'Decisive Ecological Warfare: Triggering Industrial Collapse via Deep

Green Resistance'. *Journal for the Study of Religion, Nature, and Culture*. Forthcoming.

Levin, Kelly, Benjamin Cashore, Steven Bernstein, and Graeme Auld. 'Overcoming the Tragedy of Super Wicked Problems: Constraining Our Future Selves to Ameliorate Global Climate Change'. *Policy Sciences* 45 (2012): 123-52.

Levy, Jack S., and William R. Thompson. *Causes of War*. Chichester, UK: Wiley-Blackwell, 2010.

—*The Arc of War: Origins, Escalations and Transformations*. Chicago, IL: University of Chicago Press, 2011.

LGBT Community Centre of New Orleans (2014), at http://www.lgbtccneworleans.org. (accessed 22 October 2015).

Liedloff, Jean. *The Continuum Concept*. Reading, MA: Addison-Wesley, [1977] 1985.

Linden, Eugene. *The Ragged Edge of the World: Encounters at the Frontier where Modernity, Wildlands, and Indigenous Peoples Meet*. New York: Viking, 2011.

Lindley, Mark. 'Gandhi on Corresponding Duties/ Rights'. *Anasati Darshan* (2006), at https://www.academia.edu/371221/Gandhi_on_corresponding_duties_rights (accessed 21 June 2016).

Lisée, Jean-François. 'Un Conflit Créatif'. *Le Blogue de Jean-François Lisée* (2012), at http://jflisee.org/category/mouvement-etudiant/printemps-erable-2/un-conflit-creatif/ (accessed 13 September 2013).

Lisieux, Therese of. *Soeur Therese of Lisieux, the Little Flower of Jesus: A New and Complete Translation of l'Histoire d'une Ame, with an Account of Some Favours Attributed to the Intersession of Soeur Therese*, ed. T. N. Taylor. London: Burns, Oates & Washbourne, 1912.

Llewellyn, Othman Abd Ar-Rahman. 'Islamic Jurisprudence and Environmental Planning'. *Journal of Research in Islamic Economics* 1 (1984): 27-46.

Loney, James. *Captivity: 118 Days in Iraq and the Struggle for a World Without War*. Toronto, ON, CA: Alfred A. Knopf Canada, 2011.

Los Angeles Times. 'Peace Activist Slain in Iraq is Mourned around US, World' (2006), at http://articles.latimes.com/2006/mar/12/nation/na-fox12 (accessed 5 May 2016).

Louv, Richard. *Last Child in the Woods: Saving Our Children from Nature-Deficit Disorder*. Chapel Hill, NC: Algonquin, 2005.

Loye, David. *Darwin's Lost Theory of Love*. New York: iUniverse, 1998.

Lucas, Arthur M. 'Environment and Environmental Education: Conceptual Issues and Curriculum Implications'. PhD Dissertation, Ohio State University, Columbus, OH, 1972.

Luthuli, Albert. *Let My People Go*. London: Collins, 1962.

Lynskey, Dorian. *33 Revolutions per Minute: A History of Protest Songs*. London: Faber and Faber, 2010.

Lyons, Oren. 'The Politics of Human Beings against Mother Earth: The Nature of Global Warming'. Sol Kanee Lecture on Peace and Justice presented at the University of Manitoba, Winnipeg, MB, CA (8 November 2007), at https://www.youtube.com/watch?v=HiA4_e4YwZE (accessed 27 June 2015).

MacDonald, Linda and Jeanne Sarson. 'Nova Scotia Voice of Women: A Walk Down Memory Lane. An Interview with Muriel Duckworth and Betty Peterson'. Nova Scotia Voice of Women for Peace (2008), at http://www.nsvow.org/wp-content/uploads/2015/04/A-Walk-Down-Memory-Lane.pdf (accessed 25 October 2015).

Macpherson, Kay. 'The Voice of Women'. In *Up and Doing: Canadian Women and Peace*, ed.

Janice Williamson and Deborah Gorham, 204-210. Toronto, ON, CA: The Women's Press, 1989.

Macpherson, Kay, and Sara Good. 'Canadian Voice of Women for Peace'. *Peace Magazine* (Oct-Nov 1987): 26-27.

Mahmood, Saba. 'Agency, Performativity, and the Feminist Subject'. In *Bodily Citations: Religion and Judith Butler*, ed. Ellen Armour and Susan St Ville, 177-221. New York: Columbia University Press, 2006.

Mahony, William K. *The Artful Universe: An Introduction to the Vedic Religious Imagination.* Albany: State University of New York Press, 1998.

Mamdani, Mahmood. *Citizen and Subject: Contemporary Africa and the Legacy of Late Colonialism.* Princeton, NJ: Princeton University Press, 1996.

Mandel, Robert. *The Meaning of Military Victory.* Boulder, CO: Lynne Rienner, 2006.

—'Reassessing Victory in Warfare'. *Armed Forces & Society* 33.4 (2007): 461-95.

Mandela, Nelson. *Nelson Mandela Speaks: Forging a Democratic Nonracial South Africa*, ed. Steve Clark. New York: Pathfinder Press, 1993.

—Address given to the Parliament of the World's Religions, Capetown, ZA (1999), at https://parliamentofreligions.org/content/nelson-mandelas-speech-1999-parliament-still-soars-full-text (accessed 17 May 2016).

—'The Sacred Warrior'. *Time* 4.27 (31 December 1999): 124-25. Also in *Gandhian Way: Peace, Nonviolence and Empowerment*, ed. Arvind Sharma, 19-20. New Delhi, IN: Academic Foundation, 2007.

Mangcu, Xolela. *Biko: A Life.* London: I. B. Taurus, 2014.

Martel, William. *Victory in War: Foundations of Modern Strategy.* Cambridge, UK: Cambridge University Press, 2011.

Martin, Eric, and Simon Tremblay-Pépin. *Faut-il Vraiment Augmenter les Frais de Scolarité: Huit Arguments Trompeurs sur la Hausse.* Montréal, QC, CA: IRIS, 2012.

Mascaro, Juan (trans.) *The Dhammapada.* London: Penguin Books, 1973.

Mazurana, Dyan, and Keith Proctor. 'Gender, Conflict and Peace', *World Peace Foundation* (15 October 2013), at http://www.fletcher.tufts.edu/~/media/Fletcher/Microsites/World%20Peace%20Foundation/Gender%20Conflict%20and%20Peace.pdf (accessed 18 July 2015).

McBeth, Mark K., Donna L. Lybecker, and Kacee A. Garner. 'The Story of Good Citizenship: Framing Public Policy in the Context of Duty-Based versus Engaged Citizenship'. *Politics & Policy* 38 (2010): 1-23.

McCarthy, Ronald M., Gene Sharp, and Brad Bennett. *Nonviolent Action: A Research Guide.* London: Routledge, 1997.

McEvoy, Joanne. *Politics of Northern Ireland.* Edinburgh, UK: Edinburgh University Press, 2008.

McFague, Sallie. 'An Ecological Christology: Does Christianity Have It?' In *Christianity and Ecology*, ed. Dieter T. Hessel and Rosemary Radford Ruether, 29-45. Cambridge, MA: Harvard University Press, 2000.

McKay, Ian, and Jamie Swift. *Warrior Nation: Rebranding Canada in the Age of Anxiety.* Toronto, ON, CA: Between the Lines, 2012.

McKay, Stan. 'An Aboriginal Perspective on the Integrity of Creation'. In *Liberating Faith: Religious Voices for Justice, Peace and Ecological Wisdom*, ed. Roger S. Gottlieb, 519-22. Lanham, MA: Rowan & Littlefield, 2003.

McKibben, Bill. *The End of Nature.* New York: Random House, 1989.

McMahan, Jeff. 2009. *Killing in War.* Oxford: Oxford University Press.

McQuaid, John. 'Mining the Mountains'. *Smithsonian Magazine* (January 2009), at http://

www.smithsonianmag.com/ecocenter-energy/mining-the-mountains-13045 4620/?all.. (accessed 13 November 2014).

Melchin, Kenneth R., and Cheryl A. Picard. *Transforming Conflict Through Insight*. Toronto, ON, CA: University of Toronto Press, 2008.

Mellon, Christian, and Jacques Semelin. *La Non-violence*. Paris: Presses Universitaires de France, 1994.

Melucci, Alberto. *Challenging Codes: Collective Action in the Information Age*. Cambridge, UK: Cambridge University Press, 1996.

Mendoza, Diana. 'Poverty Still has a Woman's Face'. *Development-Asia Inter Press Service* (February 2010), at http://www.ipsnews.net/2010/02/development-asia-lsquo poverty-still-has-a-womanrsquos-facersquo/ (accessed 2 August 2015).

Merchant, Carolyn. *The Death of Nature: Women, Ecology and the Scientific Revolution*. New York: Harper Open Library, 1983.

Metta Centre for Nonviolence. 'Homepage' (n.d.), at http://mettacenter.org/ (accessed 10 February 2016).

Midgley, Mary. 'The Concept of Beastliness: Philosophy, Ethics and Animal Behavior'. *Philosophy* 48 (1973): 111-35.

Miller, Jerome. *In the Throe of Wonder: Intimations of the Sacred in a Postmodernist World*. Albany, NY: State University of New York Press, 1992.

Miller, Webb. *I Found No Peace*. New York: Simon and Schuster, 1936.

Mills, Allen. *Fool for Christ: The Political Thought of J. S. Woodsworth*. Toronto, ON, CA: University of Toronto Press, 1991.

Mojab, Shahrzad. 'The Politics of Culture, Racism and Nationalism in Honour Killing'. *Canadian Criminal Law Review* 16 (2012): 115-34.

Monier-Williams, Monier. *A Sanskrit-English Dictionary*. Oxford: Clarendon Press, 1899.

Monk, Ray. *Ludwig Wittgenstein: The Duty of Genius*. New York: The Free Press, 1990.

Moore, Basil (ed.). *Black Theology: The South African Voice*. London: C. Hurst, 1973.

Mowat, Farley. *Woman in the Mists: The Story of Dian Fossey and the Mountain Gorillas of Africa*. New York: Warner, 1987.

Munck, Johannes. *Paul and the Salvation of Mankind*, trans. F. Clarke. London: SCM. 1959.

Murphy-O'Connor, Jerome. *The Theology of the Second letter to the Corinthians*. Cambridge, UK: Cambridge University Press, 1991.

Nagler, Michael N. *The Search for a Nonviolent Future: A Promise of Peace for Ourselves, Our Families, and our World*. Maui, HI: Inner Ocean, 2004.

—*The Nonviolence Handbook: A Guide for Practical Action*. San Francisco, CA: Berrett-Koehler, 2014.

Nason-Clark, Nancy. *The Battered Wife: How Christian Families Confront Family Violence*. Louisville, KY: Westminster John Knox Press, 1997.

Nason-Clark, Nancy, and Catherine Clark Kroeger. *No Place for Abuse: Biblical and Practical Resources to Counteract Domestic Violence*, 2nd edn. Downers Grove, IL: Inter-Varsity Press, 2010.

Nason-Clark, Nancy, and Catherine Holtmann. 'Thinking about Cooperation and Collaboration between Diverse Religious and Secular Community Responses to Domestic Violence'. In *Varieties of Religious Establishments*, ed. Lori G. Beaman and Winnifred Sullivan, 187-200. Farnham, UK: Ashgate Press, 2013.

Nason-Clark, Nancy, Barbara Fisher-Townsend, and Victoria Fahlberg (eds.). *Strengthening Families and Ending Abuse: Churches and their Leaders Look to the Future*. Eugene, OR: Wipf & Stock, 2013.

Natural News Staff. 'Supporting World Population at U.S. Consumption Rates Would

Require Five Earths' (2008), at http://www.naturalnews.com/022890.html (accessed 26 July 2015).

Nayyar, Pyarelal. *Mahatma Gandhi: The Last Phase*. Ahmedabad, IN: Navajivan Publishing House, 1958.

Needleman, H. L., and P. J. Landrigan. *Raising Children Toxic Free*. New York: Farrar, Straus, and Giroux, 1994.

Nehru, Jawaharlal. *Towards Freedom: The Autobiography of Jawaharlal Nehru*. New York: John Day, 1941.

Nelson, Sharon L. 'The Connection between Animal Abuse and Family Violence: A Selected Annotated Bibliography'. *Animal Law* 17.2 (2011): 369-414.

Nepstad, Sharon Erickson. *Nonviolent Revolutions: Civil Resistance in the Late 20th Century*. Oxford: Oxford University Press, 2011.

—*Nonviolent Struggle: Theories, Strategies and Dynamics*. Oxford: Oxford University Press, 2015.

Nepstad, Sharon Erickson, and Lester R. Kurtz. *Nonviolent Conflict and Civil Resistance*. Bingley: Emerald Group, 2012.

Neveu, Érik. *Sociologie des Mouvements Sociaux*. Paris: La Découverte, 1996.

New English Bible: With the Apocrypha. New York: Oxford University Press, 1970.

Newman, Lenore, and Ann Dale. 'The Role of Agency in Sustainable Local Community Development'. *Local Environment* 10.5 (2005): 477-86.

Nir, David. 'A Critical Examination of the Jewish Environmental Law of *Bal Tashchit*: "Do Not Destroy"'. *Georgetown International Environmental Law Review* 18 (2006): 335-54.

Nocella II, Anthony J., John Sorenson, Kim Socha, and Atsuko Matsuoka. 'Introduction: The Emergence of Critical Animal Studies'. In *Defining Critical Animal Studies*, ed. Anthony J. Nocella II, John Sorenson, Kim Socha, and Atsuko Matsuoka, xix-xxxv. New York: Peter Lang, 2014.

Nonviolence International. 'Homepage' (n.d.), at http://nonviolenceinternational.net/ (accessed 15 December 2015).

Nonviolent Peaceforce. 'Homepage' (2015), at http://www.nonviolentpeaceforce.org/ (accessed 15 December 2015).

Nonviolence Project Foundation. 'Homepage' (n.d.), at http://www.nonviolence.com/ (accessed 15 December 2015).

Nussbaum, Martha C. *Sex and Social Justice*. Oxford: Oxford University Press, 1999.

—*Women and Human Development: The Capabilities Approach*. Cambridge, UK: Cambridge University Press, 2000.

—'Women's Bodies: Violence, Security, Capabilities'. *Journal of Human Development* 6.2 (2005): 167-83.

—*Creating Capabilities: The Human Development Approach*. Cambridge, MA: Harvard University Press, 2011.

Nussbaum, Martha C. and Amartya Sen. 'Gendercide: What Happened to 100 Million Baby Girls?'. *The Economist* (2010): 12-13, 77-80. Also at http://www.economist.com/node/15636231 (accessed 25 July 2015).

O'Connell, Robert. *Of Arms and Men: A History of War, Weapons, and Aggression*. Oxford: Oxford University Press, 1989.

Ojala, Maria. 'Confronting Macrosocial Worries: Worry About Environmental Problems and Proactive Coping among a Group of Young Volunteers'. *Futures* 39 (2007): 729-45.

—'How Do Children Cope with Global Climate Change? Coping Strategies, Engagement, and Well-Being'. *Journal of Environmental Psychology* 32 (2012): 225-33.

Olfman, Sharna (ed.). *Childhood Lost.* Westport, CT: Praeger, 2005.

O'Malley, John W. *What Happened at Vatican II?* Cambridge, MA: Belknap Press of Harvard University Press, 2008.

Orr, David. *Hope is an Imperative: The Essential David Orr.* Washington, DC: Island Press, 2010.

Orr, Wendy (ed.). *From Biko to Basson: Wendy Orr's search for the soul of South Africa as a Commissioner of the TRC.* Saxonwold, ZA: Contra Press, 2000.

Otto, Rudolph. *The Idea of the Holy: An Inquiry into the Non-rational Factor in the Idea of the Divine and Its Relationship to the Rational.* London: Oxford University Press, 1958.

Oxford University Press (OUP). *The New English Bible: With the Apocrypha.* New York: Oxford University Press, 1970.

Pace e Bene. 'Campaign Nonviolence' (n.d.), at http://www.paceebene.org/programs/campaign-nonviolence/ (accessed 15 December 2015).

PACT-Ottawa. 'Guiding Principles: Organizational Stance on the Relationship between Human Trafficking and Sex Work' (2012), at http://www.pact-ottawa.org (accessed 14 July 2015).

Palestinian Centre for the Study of Nonviolence (Nonviolence International). 'Palestine' (2015), at http://nonviolenceinternational.net/ (accessed 10 February 2016).

Parekh, Bhikhu. *Gandhi's Political Philosophy.* London: MacMillan Press, 1989.

Parel, Anthony J. *Gandhi's Philosophy and the Quest for Harmony.* Cambridge, UK: Cambridge University Press, 2006.

Parent, Alphonse-Marie. *Rapport Parent, Première Partie: Les Structures Supérieures du Système Scolaire de la Province de Québec.* Quebec, QC, CA: Ronalds-Federated Limited for the Quebec Government, 1965.

Paterson, Stephanie. 'ReConstructing Women's Resistance to Woman Abuse: Resources, Strategy Choice and Implications of and for Public Policy in Canada'. *Critical Social Policy* 29.1 (2009): 121-45.

PBS. '2015: The Year of Mass Shootings' (2015), at http://www.pbs.org/newshour/rundown/2015-the-year-of-mass-shootings/ (accessed 16 February 2016).

Peace Appeal. 'The Appeal of the Nobel Peace Laureates for Pease and Non-violence' (n.d.), at http://www.peaceappeal.org/the-appeal-of-the-nobel-peace-laureates-for-peace-and-non-violence.html (accessed 20 December 2015).

Peace and Conflict Studies. 'International Area Studies and Academic Program, University of California, Berkeley: Peace and Conflict Studies' (2006–2011), at http://iastp.berkeley.edu/pacs (accessed 14 December 2015).

Penner, Carol. *Healing Waters: Churches Working to End Violence against Women.* Toronto, ON, CA: Women's Inter-Church Council of Canada, 2000.

Pennington, Doris. *Agnes Macphail: Reformer.* Toronto, ON, CA: Simon & Pierre, 1989.

Perrin, Benjamin. *Invisible Chains: Canada's Underground World of Human Trafficking.* Toronto, ON, CA: Viking Canada, 2011.

Philo. 'De Praemiis et Poenis', trans. F. H. Colson. London: Heinemann, 1968.

Phull, Hardeep. *Story Behind the Protest Song: A Reference Guide to the 50 Songs that Changed the 20th Century.* Westport, CT: Greenwood Press, 2008.

Pinker, Steven. *The Better Angels of Our Nature: Why Violence Has Declined.* New York: Penguin Books, 2011.

Pirkei Avot. *Sayings of the Jewish Fathers* (2003), at http://aren.org/prison/documents/religion/Misc/Pirke Avot, Traditional Text (1).pdf (accessed 19 June 2016).

Pityana, Barney, Mamphela Ramphele, Malusi Mpumlwana, and Lindy Wilson (eds.).

Bounds of Possibility: The Legacy of Steve Biko and Black Consciousness. Cape Town, ZA: David Philip, 1991.

Plato. 'Theaetetus', *Plato* 12, trans. Harold N. Fowler. Cambridge, MA: Harvard University Press (1921), at http://www.perseus.tufts.edu/hopper/text?doc=plat.+the aet.+155 (accessed 12 May 2014).

Pollan, Michael. *The Omnivore's Dilemma: A Natural History of Four Meals*. New York: Penguin Press, 2006.

Pontecorvo, Gillo (dir.). *The Battle of Algiers*. Film. Rizzoli and Rialto Pictures, 1966.

Pope Benedict XVI. 'Message of his Holiness Pope Benedict XVI for the Celebration of the World Day of Peace 1 January 2010: If You Want to Cultivate Peace, Protect Creation' (2009), at http://www.vatican.va/holy_father/benedict_xvi/messages/ peace/documents/hf_ben-xvi_mes_20091208_xliii-world-day-peace_en.html (accessed 7 May 2013).

Pope Francis. 'Angelus'. St. Peter's Square address (2013a), at http://w2.vatican.va/ content/francesco/en/angelus/2013/documents/papa-francesco_angelus_20 130901.html. (accessed 11 June 2015).

—'*Evangelii Gaudium*: Apostolic Exhortation of the Holy Father to the Bishops, Clergy, Consecrated Persons and the Lay Faithfull on the Proclamation of the Gospel in Today's World' (2013b), at http://w2.vatican.va/content/dam/francesco/pdf/ apost_exhortations/documents/papa-francesco_esortazione-ap_20131124_ evangelii-gaudium_en.pdf (accessed 27 May 2015).

—'Invocation for Peace' (2014a), at http://w2.vatican.va/content/francesco/en/spe eches/2014/june/documents/papa-francesco_20140608_invocazione-pace. html#Distinguished_Presidents (accessed 14 June 2015).

—'Pope Francis tells Presidents Only God can bring peace to Holy Land: Israeli and Palestinian Presidents Embrace in Vatican Gardens During Historic "Invocation for Peace"' (2014b), at http://www.catholicherald.co.uk/news/2014/06/ 08/pope-francis-tells-presidents-only-god-can-bring-peace-to-holy-land/ (accessed 3 July 2015).

—'Encyclical Letter *Laudato Si'* of the Holy Father Francis on Care for our Common Home' (2015a), at http://w2.vatican.va/content/dam/francesco/pdf/encyclicals/ documents/papa-francesco_20150524_enciclica-laudato-si_en.pdf (accessed 18 June 2015).

—'Comments after the Recitation of the Angelus', trans. Junno Arocho Esteves. *Zenit* (2015b), at http://www.zenit.org/en/articles/angelus-on-the-parable-of-the-seed (accessed 14 June 2015).

—'Holy Mass Homily of His Holiness Pope Francis: Plaza de la Revolución, Havana' (2015c), at http://w2.vatican.va/content/francesco/en/homilies/2015/docum ents/papa-francesco_20150920_cuba-omelia-la-habana.html (accessed 6 October 2015).

Pope John XXIII. '*Pacem in Terris*: Encyclical of Pope John XXIII on Establishing Universal Peace in Truth, Justice, Charity and Liberty' (1963), at https://w2.vatican.va/con tent/john-xxiii/en/encyclicals/documents/hf_j-xxiii_enc_11041963_pacem.html (accessed 12 June 2015).

Pope Paul VI. 'Address to the UN General Assembly' (1964), at http://unyearbook. un.org/1965YUN/1965_P1_SEC1_CH16.pdf (accessed 23 April 2013).

Porter, Bruce. *War and the Rise of the State: The Military Foundations of Modern Politics*. New York: The Free Press, 1994.

Proffit, Norma Jean. *Women Survivors, Psychological Trauma, and the Politics of Resistance.* New York: The Haworth Press, 2000.

Pruitt, Lesley J. *Youth Peacebuilding: Music, Gender, and Change.* Albany: State University of New York Press, 2013.

Pullella, Philip. 'Raul Castro Meets Pope, Says Might Return to the Church'. *Reuters* (2015), at http://uk.reuters.com/article/2015/05/10/uk-pope-cuba-castro-idUK KBN0NV0AP20150510 (accessed 12 June 2015).

Pullella, Philip and Jamie Hamre. 'Pope's Trip Ties Cuba to U.S. with Message of Reconciliation' (2015b), at http://www.reuters.com/article/2015/09/22/us-pope-cuba-idUSKCN0RK07X20150922 (accessed 6 October 2015).

Quebec (Canada) Court of Appeal. *R. v. Menard* (1978), 43 Canadian Citation Committee, (2d) 458.

Rajagopal P. V. 'Rajagopal P. V.' (2015), at https://en.wikipedia.org/wiki/Rajagopal_P._V (accessed 10 September 2015).

Ratey, John, and Richard Manning. *Go Wild: Free Your Body and Mind from the Afflictions of Civilization.* New York: Little, Brown, 2014.

Rawls, John. 1999. *A Theory of Justice.* Cambridge, MA: Belknap.

Razack, Sherene H. *Casting Out - The Eviction of Muslims from Western Law and Politics.* Toronto, ON, CA: University of Toronto Press, 2008.

RCMP. 'Frequently Asked Questions on Human Trafficking' (13 March 2014), at http://www.rcmp-grc.gc.ca/ht-tp/q-a-trafficking-traite-eng.htm#q3 (accessed 23 July 2015).

Regan, Tom. *The Case for Animal Rights.* Oakland, CA: University of California Press, 1983.

Regehr, Ernie. *Disarming Conflict: Why Peace Cannot be Won on the Battlefield.* London: Zed Books, 2015.

Richardson, Boyce (ed.). *Drumbeat: Anger and Renewal in Indian Country.* Ottawa, ON, CA: Summerhill Press and The Assembly of First Nations, 1989.

Richer, Jocelyne. 'Que Chacun Paye sa Juste Part'. *La Presse* (11 March 2012), at http://www.lapresse.ca/le-soleil/affaires/actualite-economique/201203/11/01-4504478-que-chacun-paye-sa-juste-part-plaide-bachand.php (accessed 7 October 2013).

Ricoeur, Paul. *Temps et Récit.* Paris: Seuil, 1983.

Rittel, Horst W. J., and Melvin M. Webber. 'Dilemmas in a General Theory of Planning'. *Policy Sciences* 4 (1973): 155-69.

Roberts, Dan. 'Green Light for Gay Marriage across US'. *The Guardian Weekly* 193.4 (3 July 2015), at http://www.pressreader.com/uk/the-guardian-weekly/20150703/281616714023807 (accessed 23 June 2016).

Rockström, Johan, et al. 'Planetary Boundaries: Exploring the Safe Operating Space for Humanity'. *Ecology and Society* 14.2 (2009): 1-32.

Roesch-Marsh, Edward. 'Sobering up with Levinas: Trauma, *Etonnement*, and the Anarchy of Philosophy'. *The Heythrop Journal* 44.3 (2003): 305-27.

Rose, Deborah Bird. *Dingo Makes Us Human: Life and Land in an Aboriginal Australian Culture.* Cambridge, UK: Cambridge University Press, 1992.

Rosenthal, Gilbert S. '*Tikkun ha-Olam*: The Metamorphosis of a Concept'. *Journal of Religion* 85 (2005): 214-40.

Rosenthal, Rob, and Richard Flacks. *Playing for Change: Music and Musicians in the Service of Social Movements.* Boulder, CO: Paradigm Publishers, 2011.

RT News Staff. 'Putin and Pope Francis's First Meeting Focuses on Christians' Plight in

Mideast' (2013), at http://rt.com/news/putin-pope-christians-east-274/ (accessed 3 July 2015).

Rubenstein, Mary-Jane. *Strange Wonder: The Closure of Metaphysics and the Opening of Awe*. New York: Columbia University Press, 2008.

Ruether, Rosemary Radford. *Sexism and God-talk: Toward a Feminist Theology*. Boston, MA: Beacon Press, 1983.

—*Gaia and God: An Ecofeminist Theology of Earth Healing*. San Francisco, CA: Harper San Francisco, 1992.

—'On the Front Lines of Faith'. *Sojourners* 28.6 (1999): 22.

Runciman, Steven. *The Medieval Manichee: A Study of the Christian Dualist Heresy*. Cambridge, UK: Cambridge University Press, 1982.

Rupra, Angie. 'Experiences of Front-line Shelter Workers in Providing Services to Immigrant Women Impacted by Family Violence'. In *Out of the Shadows: Woman Abuse in Ethnic, Immigrant and Aboriginal Communities*, ed. Josephine Fong, 134-46. Toronto, ON, CA: Women's Press, 2010.

Russell, Jeffrey B. *Dissent and Reform in the Early Middle Ages*. Berkeley, CA: University of California Press, 1965.

Sagan, Carl, and Ann Druyan. *Shadows of Forgotten Ancestors: A Search for Who We Are*. New York: Random House, 1992.

Santorum, Rick. 'Interview with Dom Giordano'. *Talk Radio 1210 WPHT Philadelphia* (2015), at http://tinyurl.com/pope-francis-letter (accessed 12 June 2015).

Sarbanes, Janet. 'Musicking and Communitas: The Aesthetic Mode of Sociality in Rebetika Subculture'. *Popular Music and Society* 29.1 (2006): 11-35.

Saul, John Ralston. *Louis-Hippolyte LaFontaine and Robert Baldwin*. Toronto, ON, CA: Penguin Group, 2010.

Savage, Tim B. *Power Through Weakness: Paul's Understanding of the Christian Ministry in 2 Corinthians*. Cambridge, UK: Cambridge University Press, 1996.

Scharper, Stephen Bede. *For Earth's Sake: Toward a Compassionate Ecology*, ed. Simon Appolloni. Toronto, ON, CA: Novalis Press, 2013.

Scheid, Daniel P. 'Thomas Aquinas, the Cosmic Common Good, and Climate Change'. In *Confronting the Climate Crisis: Catholic Theological Perspectives*, ed. by Jame Schaefer, 125-44. Milwaukee, WI: Marquette University Press, 2011.

Schock, Kurt. *Civil Resistance Today*. Cambridge, UK: Polity, 2015.

—(ed.). *Civil Resistance: Comparative Perspectives on Nonviolent Struggle*. Minneapolis, MN: University of Minnesota Press, 2015.

Schnelle, Udo. *Apostle Paul: His Life and Theology*, trans. M.E. Boring. Grand Rapids, MI: Baker Publishing Group, 2003.

Schoenfeld, Clay (ed.). *Outlines of Environmental Education*. Madison, WI: Dembar Educational Research Services, 1971.

Science Channel. *Question Everything* (n.d.), at http://www.sciencechannel.com/tv-shows/science-channel-presents/videos/science-promos-question-everything/ (accessed 26 May 2016).

Scully, Matthew. *Dominion: The Power of Man, the Suffering of Animals, and the Call to Mercy*. New York: St Martin's Press, 2002.

Second Vatican Council 'Dogmatic Constitution on Divine Revelation—*Dei Verbum*' (1965), at http://www.vatican.va/archive/hist_councils/ii_vatican_council/documents/vat-ii_const_19651118_dei-verbum_en.html (accessed 24 April 2013).

Sedwick, Eve Kosofsky. *Epistemology of the Closet*. Berkeley, CA: University of California Press, 1990.

Segundo, Juan-Luis. *The Humanist Christology of Paul*. Maryknoll, NY: Orbis Books, 1986.

Shantz, Jeff. *Protest and Punishment: The Repression of Resistance in the Era of Neoliberal Globalization*. Durham, NC: Carolina Academic Press, 2012.

SHARK (Show Animals Respect and Kindness). 'Cowardly Canned Hunt' (2014), at http://www.sharkonline.org/ (accessed 26 September 2014).

Sharma, Arvind. *Classical Hindu Thought: An Introduction*. New Delhi, IN: Oxford University Press, 2000.

Sharon Temple National Historic Site. 'History', (n.d.), at http://www.sharontemple.ca/index.php?option=com_content&view=section&id=6&Itemid=3 (accessed 25 October 2015).

Sharp, Gene. *The Politics of Nonviolent Action*. Boston, MA: Extending Horizons Books, 1973.

—*Waging Nonviolent Struggle: 20th Century Practice and 21st Century Potential*. Boston, MA: Porter Sargent, [1995] 2005.

—*La Force sans la Violence*. Paris: l'Harmattan, 2009.

Shepard, Paul. *Thinking Animals: Animals and the Development of Human Intelligence*. New York, NY: Viking, 1978.

Shiva, Vandana. *Soil Not Oil: Environmental Justice in an Age of Climate Crisis*. Brooklyn, NY: South End Press, 2008.

Sibley, C. G., and J. E. Ahlquist. 'The Phylogeny of the Hominoid Primates, as Indicated by DNA-DNA Hybridization'. *Journal of Molecular Evolution* 20 (1984): 2-15.

Simpson, Leanne Betasamosake, and Kiera Ladner (eds.). *This is an Honour Song: Twenty Years Since the Blockades*. Winnipeg, AB, CA: Arbeiter Ring Press, 2012.

Singer, Peter. 1975. *Animal Liberation*. New York, NY: Harper Collin.

Small, Christopher. *Musicking: The Meanings of Performance and Listening*. Middletown, CT: Wesleyan University Press, 1998.

—'Prologue: Misunderstanding and Reunderstanding'. In *Music and Solidarity: Questions of Universality, Consciousness, and Connection*, ed. Felicity Laurence and Olivier Urbain, vii-xviii. New Brunswick, NJ: Transaction, 2011.

Smith, Graeme. *The Dogs are Eating Them Now: Our War in Afghanistan*. Berkeley, CA: Counterpoint, 2013.

Social Affairs Committee of the Assembly of Quebec Bishops (SACAQB). *A Heritage of Violence: A Pastoral Reflection on Conjugal Violence*. Montreal, QC, CA: SACAQB, 1989.

Socknat, Thomas P. *Witness Against War: Pacifism in Canada 1900-1945*. Toronto, ON, CA: University of Toronto Press, 1987.

—'Conscientious Objectors in the Context of Canadian Peace Movements'. *Journal of Mennonite Studies* 25 (2007): 61-74.

—'Canada, Peace Movements in'. In *The Oxford International Encyclopedia of Peace*, vol. 1, ed. Nigel J. Young, 236-39. New York: Oxford University Press, 2010.

—'A Very Major Wheel That Helped Grind Down the War: The Canadian Anti-Draft Movement, 1966–1973'. In *Worth Fighting For: Canada's Tradition of War Resistance from 1812 to the War on Terror*, ed. Lara Campbell, Michael Dawson, and Catherine Gidney, 173-84. Toronto, ON, CA: Between the Lines, 2015.

Squires, Jessica. *Building Sanctuary: The Movements to Support Vietnam War Resisters in Canada*. Vancouver, BC, CA: UBC Press, 2013.

Stanton, Elizabeth C. *The Woman's Bible: Part I*. Salem, NH: Ayer, 1895.

The Star News Staff. 'Abuse of Veal Calves Unveiled by Hidden Camera' (2014), at http://www.thestar.com/news/investigations/2014/04/19/abuse_of_veal_calves_unveiled_by_hidden_camera.html (accessed 21 September 2014).

Statistics Canada. *Family Violence in Canada: A Statistical Profile*. Ottawa, ON, CA: Canadian Centre for Justice Statistics, 2005.

—'Immigration in Canada: A Portrait of the Foreign-born Population, 2006 Census' (2007), at http://www.statcan.ca (accessed 18 January 2013).

—'Towards the Development of a National Data Collection Framework to Measure Trafficking in Persons' (June 2010), at http://www.statcan.gc.ca/pub/85-561-m/ 2010021/appendix-appendice3-eng.htm (accessed 21 October 2015).

—*Family Violence in Canada: A Statistical Profile 2009*. Ottawa, ON, CA: Canadian Centre for Justice Statistics, 2011.

Stedman, Thomas Lathrop (ed.). *Stedman's Medical Dictionary for Health Professions and Nursing*, 5th edn. Philadelphia, PA: Lippincott Williams and Wilkins, 2005.

Steffen, Will, Paul J. Crutzen, and John R. NcNeill. 'The Anthropocene: Are Humans Now Overwhelming the Great Forces of Nature?'. *Ambio* 36.8 (2007): 614-21.

Steger, B. Manfred. *Gandhi's Dilemma*. New York: St Martin's Press, 2000.

Stokes, Emanuel et al. 'Thailand's Fishing Shame'. *The Guardian Weekly* 193.8 (2015): 32-33.

Stryker, Susan. *Transgender History*. Berkeley, CA: Seal, 2008.

Sumney, Jerry L. *Identifying Paul's Opponents: The Question of Method in 2 Corinthians*. Sheffield, UK: Sheffield Academic Press, 1990.

Suncor Energy. 'Suncor Energy'. *Wikipedia* (n.d.), at https://en.wikipedia.org/wiki/Sun cor_Energy (accessed 21 June 2016).

Swimme, Brian Thomas, and Mary Evelyn Tucker. *Journey of the Universe*. New Haven, CT: Yale University Press, 2011.

Swimme, Brian Thomas, and Thomas Berry. *The Universe Story: From the Primordial Flaring Forth to the Ecozoic Era: A Celebration of the Unfolding of the Cosmos*. New York: HarperSanFrancisco, 1992.

Syrian Nonviolence Movement. 'Homepage' (n.d.), at http://www.alharak.org/ (accessed 10 February 2016).

Taehtinen, Unto. *Ahimsa—Non-violence in Indian Tradition*. London: Rider, 1976.

Taylor, Bron. 'Earth First!'. In *Encyclopedia of Religion*, 2nd edn., ed. Lindsay Jones, 2561-66. New York: MacMillan Reference, 2005.

—'Earth First! and the Earth Liberation Front'. In *Encyclopedia of Religion and Nature*, ed. Bron Taylor, 518-24. New York: Continuum, 2005.

Tervita. 'About us' (n.d.), at http://www.tervita.com/about-us/overview (accessed 21 June 2016).

Thomas, Keith. *Man and the Natural World: Changing Attitudes in England 1500-1800*. New York: Pantheon, 1983.

Thoreau, Henry David. *Walden and Civil Disobedience: Authoritative Texts, Background, Reviews, and Essays in Criticism*, ed. Owen Thomas. New York: W. W. Norton, 1966.

Toronto Star News Staff. 'Act or Face Threat of Violence, Native Leader Warns Ottawa'. *Toronto Star* (1 June 1988): A1.

Tough, David. 'A Better Truth: The Democratic Legacy of Resistance to Conscription, 1917–1921'. In *Worth Fighting For: Canada's Tradition of War Resistance from 1812 to the War on Terror*, ed. Lara Campbell, Michael Dawson, and Catherine Gidney, 518-24. Toronto, ON, CA: Between the Lines, 2015.

Touraine, Alain. *Lutte Étudiante*. Paris: Seuil, 1978.

Townson, Monica. 'Canadian Women On Their Own Are Poorest of the Poor'. *Canadian Centre for Policy Alternatives* (8 September 2009), at http://www.policyalter

natives.ca/publications/commentary/canadian-women-their-own-are-poorest-poor (accessed 20 September 2015).

Transition Network. 'About Transition Network' (2016), at https://www.transitionnet work.org (accessed 21 June 2016).

Truthdig. 'Homepage' (2016), at http://www.truthdig.com (accessed 10 February 2016).

Tuan, Yi-Fu. 'Discrepancies between Environmental Attitude and Behavior: Examples from Europe and China'. *Canadian Geographic* 12 (1968): 176-91.

Tuan, Ti-Fu, and Yi-Fu Tuan. 'Views: Our Treatment of the Environment in Ideal and Actuality: A Geographer Observes Man's Effect on Nature in China and in the Pagan and Christian West'. *American Scientist* 58 (1970): 244-49.

Tucker, Mary Evelyn. *Worldly Wonder: Religions Enter Their Ecological Phase*. Chicago, IL: Open Court Printing, 2003.

Tusty, James, and Maureen Tusty (dirs.). *The Singing Revolution*. 2008. DVD. US, Sky Films.

Tutty, Leslie M. *Effective Practices in Sheltering Women: Leaving Violence in Intimate Relationships*. Toronto, ON, CA: YWCA Canada, 2006.

Tutu, Desmond. 'The Spirit of Togetherness'. In *Gandhian Way: Peace, Nonviolence and Empowerment*, ed. Arvind Sharma, 43-47. New Delhi, IN: Academic Foundation, 2007.

Tyler, Patrick E. 'A New Power in the Streets'. *New York Times* (February 17, 2013): A1 (N), A1 (L).

UNESCO and UNEP. 'Final Report of the Intergovernmental Conference on Environmental Education'. Tbilisi, USSR, 1977.

TVA Nouvelles avec Agence QMI. 'Grève Étudiante: La CLASSE Condamne la Violence' (22 April 2012), at http://tvanouvelles.ca/lcn/infos/national/archives/2012/04/2012 0422-113731.html (accessed 8 September 2013).

UKPGA. '2006 Animal Welfare Act' (2006), at http://www.legislation.gov.uk/ukpga/20 06/45/contents (accessed 10 September 2014).

UN Department of Public Information. 'Violence Against Women: The Situation' (2011), at http://www.endviolence.un.org (accessed 3 January 2014).

Union of Concerned Scientists. 'Warning to Humanity' (1992), at http://www.action-bioscience.org/environment/worldscientists.html (accessed 1 May 2010).

United Nations. *Livestock's Long Shadow: Environmental Issues and Options*. Rome: Food and Agriculture Organization, 2006.

—'UNite to End Violence against Women' (2008), at http://endviolence.un.org/ (accessed 9 March 2011).

United Nations Environment Programme. 'GEO 2000 Report' (2000), at http://www. unep.org/geo2000/ov-e/index.htm (accessed 1 May 2010).

United Nations General Assembly. 'Declaration on the Elimination of Violence Against Women'. A/RES/48/104 (1993), at http://www.un.org/documents/ga/res/48/a4 8r104.htm (accessed 9 March 2011).

United Nations Global Initiative to Fight Human Trafficking (UN.GIFT). 'Human Trafficking: The Facts' (2007), at http://www.unglobalcompact.org/docs/issues (accessed 20 December 2011).

United Nations Office on Drugs and Crime (UNODC). 'Prevention' (2012), at http://www. unodc.org/unodc/en/human-trafficking/prevention.html (accessed 13 January 2012).

University of British Columbia. 'Animals Research at UBC' (2014), at http://www.anim alresearch.ubc.ca/research-process-3-more.html (accessed 24 September 2014).

University of Victoria (UVic). World We Want Global Arts Project (n.d.), at http://www.digitaltao.ca/testarea/latwww2/index.html (accessed 1 May 2010).

UTexas. 'LGBT Vocabulary 101'. Gender and Sexuality Center (2008), at http://www.utexas.edu/student/housing/pdfs/staff/LGBTQ_Vocab.pdf (accessed 27 July 2015).

Vagianos, Alanna. '30 Shocking Domestic Violence Statistics that Remind Us It's an Epidemic'. *The Huffington Post* (13 February 2015), at http://www.huffingtonpost.com/2014/10/23/domestic-violence-statistics_n_5959776.html (accessed 25 July 2015).

Valen, Gary. 'Agribusiness: Farming without Culture'. In *A Communion of Subjects: Animals in Religion, Science, and Ethics*, ed. Paul Waldau and Kimberly Patton, 568-84. New York: Columbia University Press, 2006.

van Wieren, Gretel. 'Ecological Restoration as Public Spiritual Practice'. *Worldviews: Environment, Culture, Religion* 12.2/3 (2008): 237-54.

—*Restored to Earth: Christianity, Environmental Ethics, and Ecological Restoration*. Washington, DC: Georgetown University Press, 2013.

Varner, Gary E. *Personhood, Ethics, and Animal Cognition*. Oxford: Oxford University Press, 2012.

Varyrynen, Raimo (ed.). *The Waning of Major War: Theories and Debates*. New York: Routledge, 2006.

Villa, Dana. *Arendt and Heidegger. The Fate of the Political*. Princeton, NJ: Princeton University Press, 1996.

Verodagg. 'Lipdub ROUGE' (2012), at http://www.youtube.com/watch?v=9YVprVrnfZ0 (accessed 29 September 2013).

Waging Nonviolence: People Powered News and Analysis. 'Homepage' (n.d.), at http://wagingnonviolence.org/ (accessed 15 December 2015).

Walby, Sylvia. *Globalization and Inequalities: Complexity and Contested Modernities*. London: SAGE, 2009.

Waldau, Paul. *The Specter of Speciesism: Buddhist and Christian Views of Animals*. New York: Oxford University Press, 2001.

—*Animal Rights*. New York: Oxford University Press, 2011.

—*Animal Studies—An Introduction*. New York: Oxford University Press, 2013a.

—'Venturing Beyond the Tyranny of Small Differences: The Animal Protection Movement, Conservation and Environmental Education'. In *Ignoring Nature No More: The Case for Compassionate Conservation*, ed. Marc Bekoff, 27-44. Chicago, IL: University of Chicago Press, 2013b.

Walzer, Michael. *Just and Unjust Wars: A Moral Argument with Historical Illustrations*. New York: Basic Books, 2006.

Ward, Keith. *Christianity*. Oxford: Oneworld, 2008.

Warren, Karen J. 'The Power and Promise of Ecological Feminism'. *Environmental Ethics* 12.2 (Summer 1990): 125-46.

Weber, Max. *Max Weber: Essays in Sociology*, trans. Hans W. Gerth and C. Wright Mills. New York: Oxford University Press, 1958.

Weil, Eric. *Philosophie Morale*. Paris: J. Vrin, 1981.

Wesangula, Daniel. 'Homophobia in Kenya: Is a Change Going to Come?' *The Guardian* (29 June 2015), at http://www.theguardian.com/global-development-professionals-network/2015/jun/29/homophobia-in-kenya-nairobi-prejudice-acceptance (accessed 26 July 2015).

White Jr, Lynn. 'The Historical Roots of Our Ecological Crisis'. *Science* 155.3767 (1967): 1203-07.

White, Thomas I. *In Defense of Dolphins: The New Moral Frontier*. Malden, MA: Blackwell, 2007.

Whitehead, Alfred North. *The Aims of Education*. New York: Mentor Books, [1929] 1949.

Wierzbicki, Alfred M. *The Ethics of Struggle for Liberation: Towards a Personalistic Interpretation of the Principle of Non-violence*. Frankfurt: Peter Lang, 1992.

Williamson, Janice. 'A Power We Have Been Taught to Bury'. In *Up and Doing: Canadian Women and Peace*, ed. Janice Williamson and Deborah Gorham, 175-86. Toronto, ON, CA: Women's Press, 1989.

Williamson, Janice, and Deborah Gorham. 'Introduction'. In *Up and Doing: Canadian Women and Peace*, ed. Janice Williamson and Deborah Gorham, 12-26. Toronto, ON, CA: Women's Press, 1989.

Wilson, E. O. *Biophilia*. Cambridge, MA: Harvard University Press, 1984.

—*The Future of Life*. New York: Alfred A. Knopf, 2002.

Wink, Walter. *Engaging the Powers: Discernment and Resistance in A World of Domination*. Minneapolis, MN: Fortress Press, 1992.

—*The Powers That Be: A Theology for The New Millennium*. New York: Galilee Doubleday, 1999.

—*Jesus and Nonviolence: A Third Way*. Minneapolis, MN: Augsburg Fortress, 2003.

Winter, Miriam Therese, Adair Lumis, and Allison Stokes. *Defecting in Place: Women Claiming Responsibility for Their Own Spiritual Lives*. New York: Crossroads, 1995.

Wohlbold, Elise, Katie Lemay, Christina Harrison Baird. 'Project imPACT, The Local Safety Audit Report: Towards the Prevention of Trafficking in Persons and Related Exploitation in the Ottawa Area'. PACT-Ottawa (2014), at http://www.pact-ottawa.org (accessed 23 June 2016).

Wolff, Keith A. '*Bal Tashchit*: The Jewish Prohibition against Needless Destruction' (2009), at https://openaccess.leidenuniv.nl/bitstream/handle/1887/14448/complete.final4.pdf?sequence=1 (accessed 1 May 2015).

World Health Organization. 'Global and Regional Estimates of Violence against Women: Prevalence and Health Effects of Intimate Partner Violence and Non-partner Sexual Violence' (2013), at http://www.who.int/iris/.../9789241564625_eng.pd (accessed 15 December 2015).

—'Maternal Mortality: Factsheet #348' (May 2014a), at http://www.who.int/mediacentre/factsheets/fs348/en/ (accessed 19 July 2015).

—'Health Topics/Violence' (2014b), at http://www.who.int/topics/violence/en/ (accessed 15 January 2015).

—'Violence Prevention' (2016), at http://www.who.int/violenceprevention/approach/definition/en/ (accessed 26 May 2016).

Wrangham, Richard W., W. C. McGrew, Frans B. M. de Waal, and Paul Heltne. *Chimpanzee Cultures*. Cambridge, MA: Harvard University Press, 1994.

Wright, Ronald. *A Short History of Progress*. Toronto, ON, CA: Anansi, 2004.

Wyatt, Rachel. *Agnes Macphail: Champion of the Underdog*. Montreal, QC, CA: XYZ, 2000.

Zine, Jasmine (ed.). *Islam in the Hinterlands: Muslim Cultural Politics in Canada*. Vancouver, BC, CA: UBC Press, 2012.

Index